Advances in Dynamical Systems and Control

Advances in Dynamical Systems and Control

Guest Editors

**Nohe R. Cazarez-Castro
Selene L. Cardenas-Maciel
Jorge A. Lopez-Renteria**

Basel • Beijing • Wuhan • Barcelona • Belgrade • Novi Sad • Cluj • Manchester

Guest Editors

Nohe R. Cazarez-Castro
Instituto Tecnológico de
Tijuana
Tecnológico Nacional de
México
Tijuana
Mexico

Selene L. Cardenas-Maciel
Instituto Tecnológico de
Tijuana
Tecnológico Nacional de
México
Tijuana
Mexico

Jorge A. Lopez-Renteria
Secretaría de Ciencia,
Humanidades, Tecnología e
Innovación (SECIHTI)
Instituto Tecnológico de
Tijuana, Tecnológico Nacional
de México
Tijuana
Mexico

Editorial Office
MDPI AG
Grosspeteranlage 5
4052 Basel, Switzerland

This is a reprint of the Special Issue, published open access by the journal *Axioms* (ISSN 2075-1680), freely accessible at: https://www.mdpi.com/journal/axioms/special_issues/K67J84531Y.

For citation purposes, cite each article independently as indicated on the article page online and as indicated below:

Lastname, A.A.; Lastname, B.B. Article Title. *Journal Name* **Year**, *Volume Number*, Page Range.

ISBN 978-3-7258-4183-7 (Hbk)
ISBN 978-3-7258-4184-4 (PDF)
https://doi.org/10.3390/books978-3-7258-4184-4

© 2025 by the authors. Articles in this book are Open Access and distributed under the Creative Commons Attribution (CC BY) license. The book as a whole is distributed by MDPI under the terms and conditions of the Creative Commons Attribution-NonCommercial-NoDerivs (CC BY-NC-ND) license (https://creativecommons.org/licenses/by-nc-nd/4.0/).

Contents

About the Editors vii

Selene Lilette Cardenas-Maciel, Jorge Antonio Lopez-Renteria and Nohe Ramon Cazarez-Castro
Advances in Dynamical Systems and Control
Reprinted from: *Axioms* 2025, *14*, 326, https://doi.org/10.3390/axioms14050326 1

Jiri Petrzela
Chaotic Steady States of the Reinartz Oscillator: Mathematical Evidence and Experimental Confirmation
Reprinted from: *Axioms* 2023, *12*, 1101, https://doi.org/10.3390/axioms12121101 4

Ali Akgül and J. Alberto Conejero
Fractal Fractional Derivative Models for Simulating Chemical Degradation in a Bioreactor
Reprinted from: *Axioms* 2024, *13*, 151, https://doi.org/10.3390/axioms13030151 20

Benito Chen-Charpentier
On Population Models with Delays and Dependence on Past Values
Reprinted from: *Axioms* 2024, *13*, 206, https://doi.org/10.3390/axioms13030206 36

Juan Antonio Rojas-Quintero, François Dubois and José Guadalupe Cabrera-Díaz
Simpson's Variational Integrator for Systems with Quadratic Lagrangians
Reprinted from: *Axioms* 2024, *13*, 255, https://doi.org/10.3390/axioms13040255 58

Mirela Garić-Demirović, Mustafa R.S. Kulenović, Mehmed Nurkanović, and Zehra Nurkanović
The Existence of Li–Yorke Chaos in a Discrete-Time Glycolytic Oscillator Model
Reprinted from: *Axioms* 2024, *13*, 280, https://doi.org/10.3390/axioms13040280 81

Huina Zhang, Jianguo Sun, Peng Yu and Daqing Jiang
Dynamical Behaviors of Stochastic SIS Epidemic Model with Ornstein–Uhlenbeck Process
Reprinted from: *Axioms* 2024, *13*, 353, https://doi.org/10.3390/axioms13060353 98

Chih-Peng Huang
Robust State Feedback Control with D-Admissible Assurance for Uncertain Discrete Singular Systems
Reprinted from: *Axioms* 2024, *13*, 634, https://doi.org/10.3390/axioms13090634 113

Yuney Gorrin-Ortega, Selene Lilette Cardenas-Maciel, Jorge Antonio Lopez-Renteria and Nohe Ramon Cazarez-Castro
Parameters Determination via Fuzzy Inference Systems for the Logistic Populations Growth Model
Reprinted from: *Axioms* 2025, *14*, 36, https://doi.org/10.3390/axioms14010036 127

Moustafa El-Shahed and Mahmoud Moustafa
Dynamics of a Fractional-Order Eco-Epidemiological Model with Two Disease Strains in a Predator Population Incorporating Harvesting
Reprinted from: *Axioms* 2025, *14*, 53, https://doi.org/10.3390/axioms14010053 147

Mohammad Akil, Genni Fragnelli, Amine Sbai
Exponential Stability for a Degenerate/Singular Beam-Type Equation in Non-Divergence Form
Reprinted from: *Axioms* 2025, *14*, 159, https://doi.org/10.3390/axioms14030159 163

About the Editors

Nohe R. Cazarez-Castro

Nohe R. Cazarez-Castro holds a degree in Computer Systems Engineering and an MSc in Computer Sciences degrees from the Tijuana Institute of Technology (Instituto Tecnológico de Tijuana), earned in 2002 and 2005, respectively. He obtained his Doctor of Science degree from Baja California's Autonomous University (Universidad Autónoma de Baja California) in 2010 and is a Mathematician from the Mexican Open and Distance University (Universidad Abierta y a Distancia de México) in 2014. He is currently a full professor at the Tijuana Institute of Technology, part of the National Technological Institute of Mexico (Tecnológico Nacional de México), where he heads the Centre for Computational and Mathematical Modelling, Analysis and Applications. His research interests lie in mathematical and computational modeling and its applications. He is a Level 2 National Researcher of the National System of Researchers in Mexico and is an IEEE Senior Member.

Selene L. Cardenas-Maciel

Selene L. Cardenas-Maciel holds the degrees of Computer Systems Engineer and the MSc in Computer Sciences from the Tijuana Institute of Technology (Instituto Tecnológico de Tijuana) in 2002 and 2005, respectively; the Doctor of Science degree from the Baja California's Autonomous University (Universidad Autónoma de Baja California) in 2015; and is Mathematician from the Mexican Open and Distance University (Universidad Abierta y a Distancia de México) in 2015. She is a professor at the Tijuana Institute of Technology, part of the National Technological Institute of Mexico (Tecnológico Nacional de México). Her research interests are in mathematical and computational modeling and its applications. She is a Level 1 National Researcher of the National System of Researchers in Mexico.

Jorge A. Lopez-Renteria

Dr. Jorge Antonio López Rentería studied for a BSc and MSc in Mathematics at the Mathematics Department of the University of Sonora, Mexico, and obtained his Doctorate in Mathematical Sciences at the Mathematics Department of the Metropolitan Autonomous University, Iztapalapa, Mexico. He completed two postdoctoral positions at the Department of Physics and Mathematics of Iberoamerican University. Currently, Dr. Rentería is a Research Professor at the Ministry of Science, Humanities, Technology, and Innovation (SECIHTI, in Spanish) of Mexico, assigned to the National Technological of Mexico, Campus Tijuana Technological Institute. Dr. Jorge is a founding member of the Mexican Association of Dynamical Systems and Complexity (AMESDYC, in Spanish). He has been recognized as a Level 1 researcher by the National System of Researchers in Mexico. He has led Basic Science Projects in Fractional Dynamical Systems. His research interests include Mathematical Control Theory, Fractional Calculus and Systems, Stability and Stabilization, Chaos and Bifurcations, and Algebraic and Topological Methods in Applied Mathematics.

Editorial

Advances in Dynamical Systems and Control

Selene Lilette Cardenas-Maciel [1,*], Jorge Antonio Lopez-Renteria [2,*] and Nohe Ramon Cazarez-Castro [1,3,*]

1. Instituto Tecnologico de Tijuana, Tecnologico Nacional de Mexico, Tijuana 22414, Mexico
2. SECIHTI—Tecnológico Nacional de México, Instituto Tecnológico de Tijuana, Tijuana 22414, Mexico
3. Facultad de Ingenieria Quimica, Universidad Michoacana de San Nicolas de Hidalgo, Morelia 58030, Mexico
* Correspondence: lilettecardenas@ieee.org (S.L.C.-M.); jorge.lopez@tectijuana.edu.mx (J.A.L.-R.); nohe@ieee.org (N.R.C.-C.)

1. Introduction

In this Editorial, we present "Advances in Dynamical Systems and Control", a Special Issue of *Axioms*. This Special Issue comprises 10 articles contributing frontier research in the areas of dynamical systems and control, both in theoretical and application advances. The study of dynamical systems and control is crucial for advancing engineering. It encompasses a wide range of topics, including chaos and bifurcations, complex systems, fractional difference and differential equations, fuzzy control and systems, linear and nonlinear control systems, mathematical education in science and engineering, matrix and spectral analysis, modeling, stability and robust stability, as well as the stability of pseudo-polynomials and quasi-polynomials. Therefore, this Special Issue aims to address issues pertaining to the above fields through articles concerned with a variety of related topics.

2. Overview of the Published Papers

In contribution 1, entitled "Chaotic Steady States of the Reinartz Oscillator: Mathematical Evidence and Experimental Confirmation", the Reinartz sinusoidal oscillator is analyzed to study its chaotic steady states and solve the chaos and hyperchaos localization. The oscillator is considered in its conventional topology. The results show that a pair of positive Lyapunov exponents are sufficient to verify that physically reasonable circuit values yield robust dynamical behavior. All the necessary fingerprints of structural stable chaos are proven via the numerical results, and the dynamics are compared with the strange attractor captured as oscilloscope screenshots.

In contribution 2, entitled "Fractal Fractional Derivative Models for Simulating Chemical Degradation in a Bioreactor", a three-equation differential mathematical model is presented to describe the degradation of a phenol and p-cresol combination in a continually agitated bioreactor. The authors conducted a stability analysis of the model's equilibrium points and used three alternative kernels to analyze the model with fractal–fractional derivatives, exploring the effects of the fractal size and fractional order. They developed highly efficient numerical techniques for the concentration of biomass, phenol, and p-cresol. To complete the study, numerical simulations were used to illustrate the accuracy of the suggested method.

In contribution 3, entitled "On Population Models with Delays and Dependence on Past Values", the authors present a study on methods for adding dependence onto past values in population dynamics models. The studied methods include the following: (i) populations at earlier time units, (ii) the use of non-local operators in the model descriptions, and (iii) the introduction of exposed population groups. The authors conclude that modeling assumptions should be clearly stated when using fractional derivatives.

In contribution 4, entitled "Simpson's Variational Integrator for Systems with Quadratic Lagrangians", the authors proposed a variational symplectic integrator, which is then compared with the Newmark's variational integrator. The proposed scheme is implicit, symplectic, and conditionally stable. The precision and convergence of the proposed integrator are illustrated via simulations.

In contribution 5, entitled "The Existence of Li–Yorke Chaos in a Discrete-Time Glycolytic Oscillator Model", the existence of chaos is proven by finding a snap-back repeller, using Marotto's theorem. The study was performed for an autonomous discrete-time glycolytic oscillator model, which exhibits chaos in the Li-Yorke sense.

In contribution 6, entitled "Dynamical Behaviors of Stochastic SIS Epidemic Model with Ornstein–Uhlenbeck Process", for an incomplete inoculation stochastic SIS epidemic model perturbed by the Ornstein–Uhlenbeck and Brownian motion, the existence of a unique global solution is established and control conditions for extinction are derived. The authors established sufficient conditions for the existence of stationary distribution via two Lyapunov functions and the ergodicity of the Ornstein–Uhlenbeck process.

Contribution 7, entitled "Robust State Feedback Control with D-Admissible Assurance for Uncertain Discrete Singular Systems", addresses the state feedback control associated with D-admissible assurance for discrete singular systems subjected to parameter uncertainties in both the difference term and system matrices. A refined analysis criterion of D-admissible assurance is reported, where the distinct form embraces multiple slack matrices and reduces linear matrix inequality (LMI) constraints, which may be beneficial for reducing conservatism in admissibility analysis.

In contribution 8, entitled "Parameters Determination via Fuzzy Inference Systems for the Logistic Populations Growth Model", the problem of determining parameters for the logistic population growth model is addressed. Unlike traditional schemes, the proposed approach incorporates ecosystem variables as inputs into a fuzzy inference system designed to capture the inherent uncertainties of population dynamics. As the resulting model uses fuzzy numbers as coefficients, it is represented by a fuzzy differential equation.

In contribution 9, entitled "Dynamics of a Fractional-Order Eco-Epidemiological Model with Two Disease Strains in a Predator Population Incorporating Harvesting", the authors formulated and analyzed a fractional-order eco-epidemical model, which considers two disease strains in a predator population. They examined the positivity, boundedness, existence, and uniqueness of the solutions. In the model's formulation, the population is considered to comprise three groups: susceptible predators infected by the first disease, predators infected by the second disease, and a prey population.

Contribution 10, entitled "Exponential Stability for a Degenerate/Singular Beam-Type Equation in Non-Divergence Form", presents a stability analysis for a degenerate/singular beam equation in non-divergence form. The authors employed energy methods to derive stability conditions for the problem under consideration.

Funding: This research was funded by Tecnologico Nacional de Mexico grants number 21808.25-P and 22705.25-P. Nohe R. Cazarez-Castro, specially thanks to Universidad Michoacana de San Nicolas de Hidalgo for the facilities granted to carry out a postdoctoral stay. The APC was funded by MDPI-Axioms.

Conflicts of Interest: The authors declare no conflicts of interest.

List of Contributions

1. Petrzela, J. Chaotic Steady States of the Reinartz Oscillator: Mathematical Evidence and Experimental Confirmation. *Axioms* **2023**, *12*, 1101. https://doi.org/10.3390/axioms12121101.
2. Akgül, A.; Conejero, J.A. Fractal Fractional Derivative Models for Simulating Chemical Degradation in a Bioreactor. *Axioms* **2024**, *13*, 151. https://doi.org/10.3390/axioms13030151.
3. Chen-Charpentier, B. On Population Models with Delays and Dependence on Past Values. *Axioms* **2024**, *13*, 206. https://doi.org/10.3390/axioms13030206.
4. Rojas-Quintero, J.A.; Dubois, F.; Cabrera-Díaz, J.G. Simpson's Variational Integrator for Systems with Quadratic Lagrangians. *Axioms* **2024**, *13*, 255. https://doi.org/10.3390/axioms13040255.
5. Garić-Demirović, M.; Kulenović, M.R.S.; Nurkanović, M.; Nurkanović, Z. The Existence of Li–Yorke Chaos in a Discrete-Time Glycolytic Oscillator Model. *Axioms* **2024**, *13*, 280. https://doi.org/10.3390/axioms13040280.
6. Zhang, H.; Sun, J.; Yu, P.; Jiang, D. Dynamical Behaviors of Stochastic SIS Epidemic Model with Ornstein–Uhlenbeck Process. *Axioms* **2024**, *13*, 353. https://doi.org/10.3390/axioms13060353.
7. Huang, C.-P. Robust State Feedback Control with D-Admissible Assurance for Uncertain Discrete Singular Systems. *Axioms* **2024**, *13*, 634. https://doi.org/10.3390/axioms13090634.
8. Gorrin-Ortega, Y.; Cardenas-Maciel, S.L.; Lopez-Renteria, J.A.; Cazarez-Castro, N.R. Parameters Determination via Fuzzy Inference Systems for the Logistic Populations Growth Model. *Axioms* **2025**, *14*, 36. https://doi.org/10.3390/axioms14010036.
9. El-Shahed, M.; Moustafa, M. Dynamics of a Fractional-Order Eco-Epidemiological Model with Two Disease Strains in a Predator Population Incorporating Harvesting. *Axioms* **2025**, *14*, 53. https://doi.org/10.3390/axioms14010053.
10. Akil, M.; Fragnelli, G.; Sbai, A. Exponential Stability for a Degenerate/Singular Beam-Type Equation in Non-Divergence Form. *Axioms* **2025**, *14*, 159. https://doi.org/10.3390/axioms14030159.

Disclaimer/Publisher's Note: The statements, opinions and data contained in all publications are solely those of the individual author(s) and contributor(s) and not of MDPI and/or the editor(s). MDPI and/or the editor(s) disclaim responsibility for any injury to people or property resulting from any ideas, methods, instructions or products referred to in the content.

Article

Chaotic Steady States of the Reinartz Oscillator: Mathematical Evidence and Experimental Confirmation

Jiri Petrzela

Department of Radio Electronics, Faculty of Electrical Engineering and Communications, Brno University of Technology, Technicka 12, 616 00 Brno, Czech Republic; petrzela@vut.cz; Tel.: +420-541146561

Abstract: This paper contributes to the problem of chaos and hyperchaos localization in the fundamental structure of analog building blocks dedicated to single-tone harmonic signal generation. This time, the known Reinartz sinusoidal oscillator is addressed, considering its conventional topology, both via numerical analysis and experiments using a flow-equivalent lumped electronic circuit. It is shown that physically reasonable values of circuit parameters can result in robust dynamical behavior characterized by a pair of positive Lyapunov exponents. Mandatory numerical results prove that discovered strange attractors exhibit all necessary fingerprints of structurally stable chaos. The new "chaotic" parameters are closely related to the standard operation of the investigated analog functional block. A few interestingly shaped, strange attractors have been captured as oscilloscope screenshots.

Keywords: Reinartz oscillator; generalized transistor; two-port admittance parameters; numerical analysis; hyperchaos; chaos; strange attractors

MSC: 37M05

1. Introduction

Irregular behavior associated with analog electronic systems is caused by serious problems that have been intensively studied by engineers and researchers in the last three decades. From the viewpoint of typical properties, long-term unpredictability, broad-band frequency spectrum, and dense strange attractors are the fundamental fingerprints of chaos. Once upon a time, this kind of repeatable dynamical motion was misinterpreted as phase noise, because similar apparent properties are observed in the time and frequency domains. From the application point of view, chaotic tangles have been reported during the analysis of seemingly linear analog and digital [1] frequency filters, phase-locked loops [2], amplifiers working under different operational regimes [3], power converters [4], switched capacitor circuits [5], modulators and demodulators, mixers, very simple multi-state static memory cells [6], logic gates [7], random number generators [8], and many others. This very short and surely incomplete list implies that both autonomous and driven dynamical systems are subject to chaotic behavior; only the presence of at least one nonlinearity is mandatory.

Since the practical designs of sinusoidal oscillators require a mechanism for amplitude stabilization, these common building blocks should be treated as nonlinear. Therefore, the existence of chaos within circuit models as well as practical realizations is not a surprise. The chaotic motion is often excited by the unstable fixed points, i.e., generated strange orbits, which are members of the so-called self-exited attractors. Because of the simultaneous acting exponential divergency of state space neighboring orbits and the attractor boundedness within a finite state space volume, the minimum number of working accumulation elements is three, regardless of the combination of circuit elements. The famous Colpitts oscillator probably represents the oldest topology where chaos has been confirmed, both numerically and experimentally [9]. This kind of circuit modified to operate in the higher frequency band is addressed in paper [10]. It is shown that the parasitic base-emitter capacitance of a bipolar transistor should be a working accumulation element as well. The basic circuit structure of Hartley oscillators and chaos evolution are discussed in the framework of papers [11,12]. For nonlinear sinusoidal oscillators that have four accumulation elements, both chaos and hyperchaos represent a possible time-domain solution, as mentioned in work [13]. Also, RC feedback oscillators have been studied with respect to the generation of robust chaotic waveforms. The existence of such steady states has been observed in Wien bridge-based feedback [14], phase shift type of feedback loop [15], and atypical but very simple feedback, as suggested in paper [16]. Interesting lumped chaotic oscillators having one or two transistors and packs of surrounding passive components can be found in research paper [17]. There, authors use a heuristic approach to develop many canonical circuits with experimentally measurable, structurally stable, chaotic self-oscillations. It is shown that the natural nonlinear features of used transistors can perform folding and stretching of vector field quite easily.

This paper is organized as follows: The next section describes a path leading to a mathematical model dedicated to numerical analysis, which is the content of the third paper section. The fourth part brings experimental verification, i.e., the construction of a flow-equivalent dynamical system based on the following two different but universal methods. Commercially available active devices are used for the realization of both the linear and nonlinear parts of the vector field. Captured oscilloscope screenshots prove that the observed chaotic behavior is neither a numerical artifact nor a long transient.

2. Mathematical Model of Reinartz Oscillator

Figure 1a illustrates a circuit topology that is ready for harmonic signal generation, namely, the well-known Reinartz oscillator. This circuit typically produces low-distortion sinusoidal waveforms within a frequency band of about hundreds of kHz, typically up to units of MHz. Of course, the topology can differ slightly for specific applications.

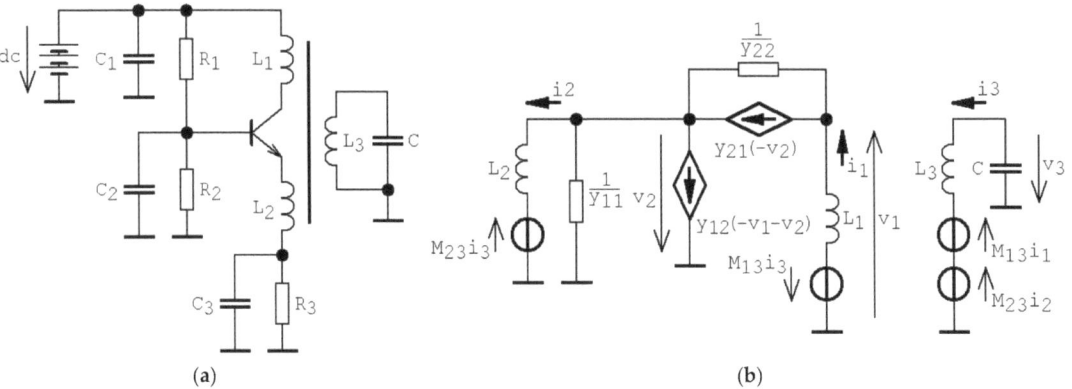

Figure 1. Reinartz sinusoidal oscillator: (**a**) practical configuration, and (**b**) simplified calculation schematic. Numerical values of passive elements are not provided.

In fact, all resistors are used to set up a bias point of a bipolar transistor, while capacitors C_1, C_2, and C_3 serve for filtering, DC blocking, and temperature drift stabilization of a bias point. Thus, an equivalent circuit for analysis in an operational frequency band can be obtained by shorting the capacitors mentioned above, causing the removal of all resistors. The hypothetical bias point of a generic bipolar transistor will be represented by a conventional two-port network described using four frequency-independent admittance parameters. The input and output admittances will be exclusively positive real numbers. Moreover, we will consider odd-symmetrical cubic polynomial forward transconductance and zero backward transconductance. Investigated autonomous lumped electronic system exploits inductively coupled emitter and collector windings to the main tank circuit formed by passive components L_3 and C. However, to avoid unwanted parasitic oscillations, inductors L_1 and L_2 are not coupled to each other.

Of course, small signal models of bipolar transistors allow us to perform a linear analysis, leading to symbolic formulas for oscillation frequency in the case that the electronic system works just on the boundary of stability. Generally, the characteristic equation will be a fourth-order polynomial with relatively complicated nonzero coefficients. However, a straightforward analysis for a complex frequency $j\omega$ combined with a few justified simplifications leads to the formula for oscillation frequency $f_{osc} = \left(2\pi\sqrt{L_3 C}\right)^{-1}$.

In linear dynamical systems, chaotic behavior is out of the question. Nevertheless, a bipolar transistor is a nonlinear active element if a large signal must be processed. The dynamical behavior of the circuit given in Figure 1b is uniquely determined by following the set of first-order ordinary differential equations (ODEs)

$$\frac{d}{dt}v_3 = -\frac{i_3}{C},\ \frac{d}{dt}i_1 = \frac{1}{L_1}\left[M_{13}\cdot i_3 - \frac{i_1}{y_{22}} - \frac{i_1-i_2}{y_{11}} + \frac{1}{y_{22}}y_{21}\left(\frac{i_1-i_2}{y_{11}}\right)\right], \\ \frac{d}{dt}i_2 = \frac{1}{L_2}\left[\frac{i_1-i_2}{y_{11}} + M_{23}\cdot i_3\right],\ \frac{d}{dt}i_3 = \frac{1}{L_3}(v_3 + M_{13}\cdot i_1 + M_{23}\cdot i_2), \quad (1)$$

where four-dimensional state space is formed by the vector of state variables $\mathbf{x} = (v_3, i_1, i_2, i_3)^T$.

Note that voltage-controlled current-source $y_{12}(v) = 0$ S and forward trans-conductance $y_{21}(v)$ will be a scalar nonlinear function of the form

$$y_{21}(v) = \alpha \cdot v^3 + \beta \cdot v, \quad (2)$$

and symbols M_{13} and M_{23} represent the mutual inductances of three-wind loss-less transformers described by three linear differential equations $\mathbf{Z}\cdot\mathbf{I} = \mathbf{V}$ (symmetry of impedance matrix $\mathbf{Z}$ along main diagonal indicates that the transformer is a reciprocal element)

$$\begin{pmatrix} L_1\frac{d}{dt} & 0 & -M_{13}\frac{d}{dt} \\ 0 & L_2\frac{d}{dt} & -M_{23}\frac{d}{dt} \\ -M_{13}\frac{d}{dt} & -M_{23}\frac{d}{dt} & L_3\frac{d}{dt} \end{pmatrix} \cdot \begin{pmatrix} i_1 \\ i_2 \\ i_3 \end{pmatrix} = \begin{pmatrix} v_1 \\ v_2 \\ v_3 \end{pmatrix}. \quad (3)$$

The shape of the cubic function (2) reflects the fact that the linear part of i_C vs. v_{BE} transfer characteristic is limited on one side by the region where the transistor is closed, and the other side is smoothly trimmed by the region of maximal output current.

The localization of fixed points associated with the dynamical system (1) in conjunction with (2) is very important. Regardless of the values of the system parameters, the origin of state space is always the only equilibrium. The search-for-chaos algorithm that allows us to find chaos within the Reinartz oscillator is focused on the self-excited strange attractors. In this case, the close neighborhood of origin will be unstable (saddle-spiral local geometry $\Re^2 \oplus \Re^2$ is preferred) for all combinations of parameters. An absence of offset and quadratic terms in formula (2) leads to the symmetry of a vector field with respect to the origin. Also, forward trans-conductance $y_{21}(v)$ is of saturation type, meaning that $\alpha < 0 \wedge \beta > 0$. This kind of output–input characteristic of the active element de facto represents the linear transformation of coordinates between a circuit-oriented model and a mathematical model. In other words, the bias point of a bipolar transistor is initially centered within the linear part of the $i_C = f(v_{BE})$ curve. Then, this point is shifted toward the origin of state space. The dynamical system (1) together with (2) is invariant under full linear change of the coordinates $v_3 \to -v_3$, $i_1 \to -i_1$, $i_2 \to -i_2$, and $i_3 \to -i_3$. Simultaneously, both M_{13} and M_{23} are the subject of physical realization constraints and will not be larger than the value of 0.6 H.

Several recent papers, for example, [18–22], utilize a multi-objective fitness function to find a robust chaotic motion within the lower-order deterministic dynamical systems. The proposed methods are often general, such that both autonomous and driven systems can be investigated. In our case, the same approach as proposed in [18] has been adopted, i.e., a three-step calculation toward weighted cost function. The first step covers a simple check of the stability of the fixed point located at the origin. In this stage, all sets of parameters leading to unwanted local geometry near the state space origin can be omitted early, significantly saving time demands for optimization. The second test is a calculation of attractor boundedness and dissipation of the flow. If passed, the full spectrum of Lyapunov exponents (LE) is established, and the Kaplan–Yorke dimension of the state space attractor is calculated. For chaos, the first LE needs to be positive, and the sum of all LEs must be negative. For hyperchaos, there is a pair of two significantly positive Les, while the sum of all LEs stands negative. Within each optimization step, the numerical values of all system parameters (defined up to two decimal places) are known. Thus, corresponding eigenvalues associated with a fixed point at the origin can be easily obtained, and an optimal time step size for numerical calculations can be determined and updated accordingly; check paper [23] for more details. Note that the calculations of individual cost functions are independent; the sets of system parameters are exclusive input variables. Therefore, a search-for-chaos routine is a good candidate for multi-core parallel processing.

Thanks to impedance and time scaling, working accumulation elements can be kept in unity, i.e., $L_3 = 1$ H and $C = 1$ F, such that the fundamental frequency component equals 159 mHz. The common operational regime deals with the ratio $L_1/L_2 \to 10$. In an upcoming analysis, we suppose unity inductances $L_1 = L_2 = 1$ H to unify the time constants associated with individual differential equations. From the viewpoint of watched dynamical system properties, the existence of long-term structurally stable strange attractors is conditioned by the flow dissipation, that is

$$\mathbf{x} \in \boldsymbol{\phi}(t) : \mathrm{div}(\mathbf{F}) = \frac{\partial}{\partial v_3}\mathbf{F}_1 + \frac{\partial}{\partial i_1}\mathbf{F}_2 + \frac{\partial}{\partial i_2}\mathbf{F}_3 + \frac{\partial}{\partial i_3}\mathbf{F}_4 = \frac{1}{L_1 \cdot y_{11}^3 \cdot y_{22}}\left[3\cdot\alpha\cdot(i_1^2+i_2^2) - 6\cdot\alpha\cdot i_1\cdot i_2 + y_{11}^2(\beta - y_{22} - y_{11})\right] - \frac{1}{L_2 \cdot y_{11}}, \quad (4)$$

where $\boldsymbol{\phi}(t)$ represents a state orbit, $\mathbf{F}$ means a four-dimensional vector field, and $\mathbf{F}_k$ is the right-hand side of k-th ODE. In both cases of investigated chaotic systems (will be revealed below), this function stands negative (in average) for complete ranges of state variables i_1 and i_2 of a fully evolved strange attractor. Another key property of the final dynamical system is the existence of an unstable fixed point located at the origin. This requirement means that the characteristic polynomial

$$\lambda^4 + \frac{2\cdot y_{11}+y_{22}-\beta}{y_{11}\cdot y_{22}}\lambda^3 + \frac{y_{11}^2\cdot y_{22}^2(1-M_{13}^2-M_{23}^2)+y_{11}(y_{22}-\beta)-y_{22}(y_{22}-\beta)}{y_{11}^2\cdot y_{22}^2}\lambda^2 + \frac{y_{11}(2-M_{13}^2-M_{23}^2)-\beta+y_{22}+M_{23}^2(\beta+y_{22})-M_{13}\cdot M_{23}(2\cdot y_{22}-\beta)}{y_{11}^2\cdot y_{22}}\lambda + \frac{y_{11}^2+y_{11}\cdot y_{22}-y_{22}^2+\beta(y_{22}-y_{11})}{y_{11}^2\cdot y_{22}^2} = 0, \quad (5)$$

has at least one root with positive real parts. Assume a limited case of zero coupling between windings, i.e., $M_{13} = 0$ H and $M_{23} = 0$ H. Solving for the roots of polynomial (5) gives us information about the oscillating solution of isolated L_3C tanks and the stability of the rest of the circuit, namely

$$\lambda_{1,2} = \pm j, \lambda_{3,4} = \pm \frac{\sqrt{(\beta-y_{22})\cdot(\beta-5\cdot y_{22})}}{2\cdot y_{11}\cdot y_{22}} - \frac{2\cdot y_{11}^2\cdot y_{22}+y_{11}\cdot y_{22}^2-\beta\cdot y_{11}\cdot y_{22}}{2\cdot y_{11}^2\cdot y_{22}^2}. \quad (6)$$

The eigenvalues $\lambda_{3,4}$ can be of any conceivable configuration depending on the relations between y_{11}, y_{22}, and β. This includes eigenvalues that are both real and negative, real with opposite signs, real eigenvalues with positive parts, and complex conjugated numbers with either positive or negative real parts. Obviously, both the input and output admittance of transistors cannot be zero. Important bifurcation planes are given by $\beta = y_{22}$ and $\beta = 5\cdot y_{22}$ since the third and fourth eigenvalues form a complex conjugated pair between these lines. It is worth mentioning that each change in the vector field geometry near the state space origin is followed by a dramatic change in the global system dynamics. During intensive numerical analysis (especially using the searching for chaos routine), it finally turns out that at least one stable manifold associated with state space origin is needed for chaos and/or hyperchaos evolution. Of course, the existence of unpredictable behavior in the case of full repelor at the origin of state space is not definitely excluded, and it can be considered a possible topic for future investigations.

In the upcoming section of this paper, the results originating from the application of such a brute-force numerical search algorithm applied on basic AC-ready circuit topology of a Reinartz oscillator are provided. Proposed optimization/search routine was implemented in Matlab and can be adopted (with small adaptation changes) for any type of finite-order dynamical system, including those with fractional-order derivations of some state variable. However, the huge number of required numerical operations makes it usable only if appropriate computing power is available. In the case of this work, a workstation composed of i9-10900K (3.7 GHz) and 128 GB RAM was utilized.

3. Numerical Analysis and Results

A mathematical model dedicated to numerical analysis and optimization will be considered dimensionless and expressed in the form of system (1) with nonlinear features of transistor (2), and with $\{M_{13}, M_{23}, y_{11}, y_{22}, \alpha, \beta\}$ being a group of unknowns. Within the optimization procedure, the value of each unknown is encoded into a binary expression; the sought parameters can take non-extreme, physically reasonable discrete values only. Two decimal places represent a smooth-enough resolution.

Two distinct sets of parameters that lead to the topologically similar, robust, and chaotic behavior were discovered. Concretely, the first set (case I) is

$$M_{13} = 0.6H, M_{23} = 0.1H, y_{11} = 1S, y_{22} = 1S, \alpha = -8A \cdot V^{-3}, \beta = 10S. \tag{7}$$

while the second set (case II) is

$$M_{13} = 0.52H, M_{23} = 0.22H, y_{11} = 2S, y_{22} = 4S, \alpha = -8A \cdot V^{-3}, \beta = 18S. \tag{8}$$

Figure 2 shows both the geometrical shape of a chaotic attractor and the sensitivity dependance on the tiny changes in the initial conditions. For each case mentioned above, a group of 10^4 initial conditions was generated randomly around the state space origin with a normal distribution and standard deviation 10^{-2} (red dots). Then, the final states after short-term (t_{max} = 10 s, purple points), average-term (t_{max} = 50 s, green points), and long-term (t_{max} = 100 s, blue points) evolution are stored and visualized. For all simulations, the fourth-order Runge–Kutta integration method was utilized with a fixed time step of 100 µs.

Figure 3 contains interesting numerical results concerning the Reinartz oscillator, case I. Firstly, plots showing the divergency of the vector field along a chaotic orbit can be found there. A typical strange attractor (for β = 10 S and β = 11 S) is located within the state space volume with very small positive values and a negative value close to zero. Figure 3 also provides the distribution of dynamic energy along the trajectory associated with parameter set (7). Note that all mutual inductances M_{13} and M_{23} for dynamical system case I and II represent tight coupling between primary and secondary windings. For both cases of chaotic systems, the origin is an unstable equilibrium point, as monitored frequently during the search-for-chaos optimization procedure. For parameter set (7), zero equilibrium exhibits a stable two-dimensional manifold, and the corresponding eigenvalues are

$$\lambda_1 = 6.904, \lambda_2 = 0.149, \lambda_{3,4} = -0.026 \pm j0.985. \tag{9}$$

In comparison with these results, parameter set (8) leads to the following eigenvalues:

$$\lambda_{1,2} = -0.089 \pm j0.915, \lambda_{3,4} = 0.714 \pm j0.285. \tag{10}$$

Because of different vector field geometry near the 4D state space origin, self-excited chaotic attractors discovered by searching routine can be marked as distinct types.

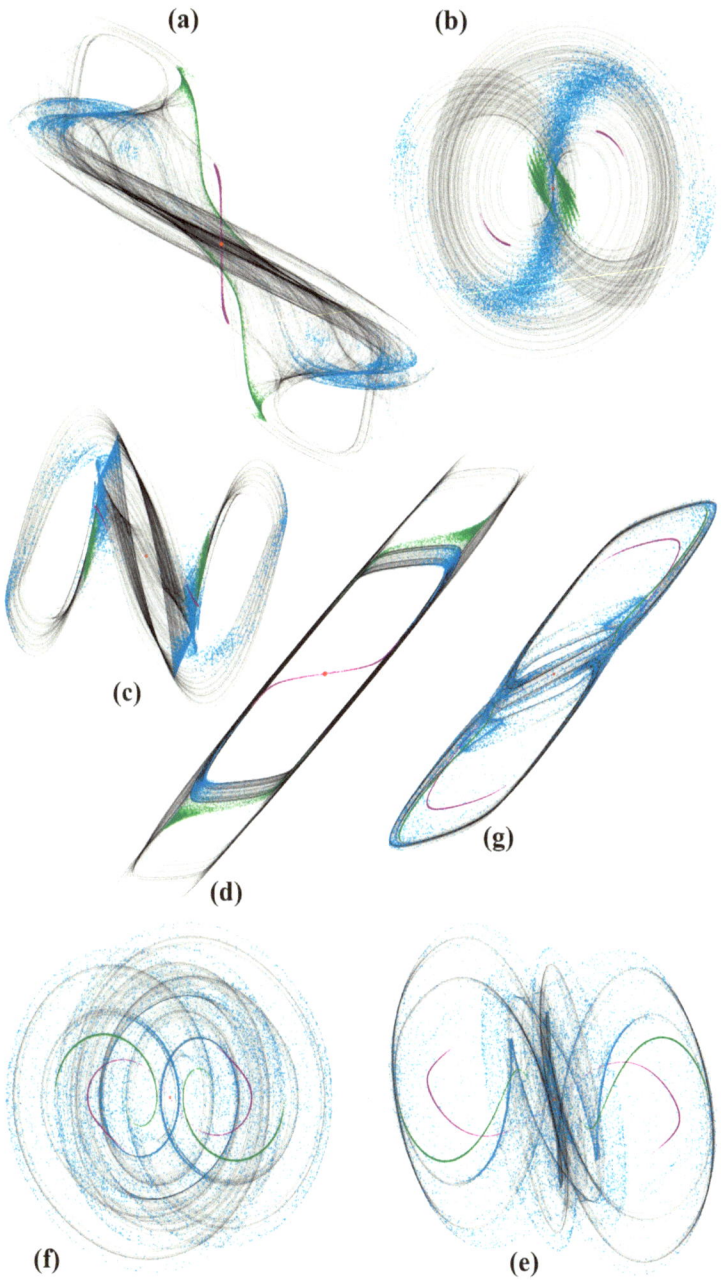

Figure 2. Sensitivity analysis of chaotified Reinartz oscillator plotted in different state space plane projections, case I: (**a**) v_3 vs. i_1, (**b**) v_3 vs. i_3, (**c**) i_2 vs. i_3, (**d**) i_1 vs. i_2, and (**e**) v_3 vs. i_2. For parameter set case II: (**f**) v_3 vs. i_3 and (**g**) i_1 vs. i_2. Color representation of time evolution: initial states (red dots), short-term (red), medium-term (purple), and long-term (blue).

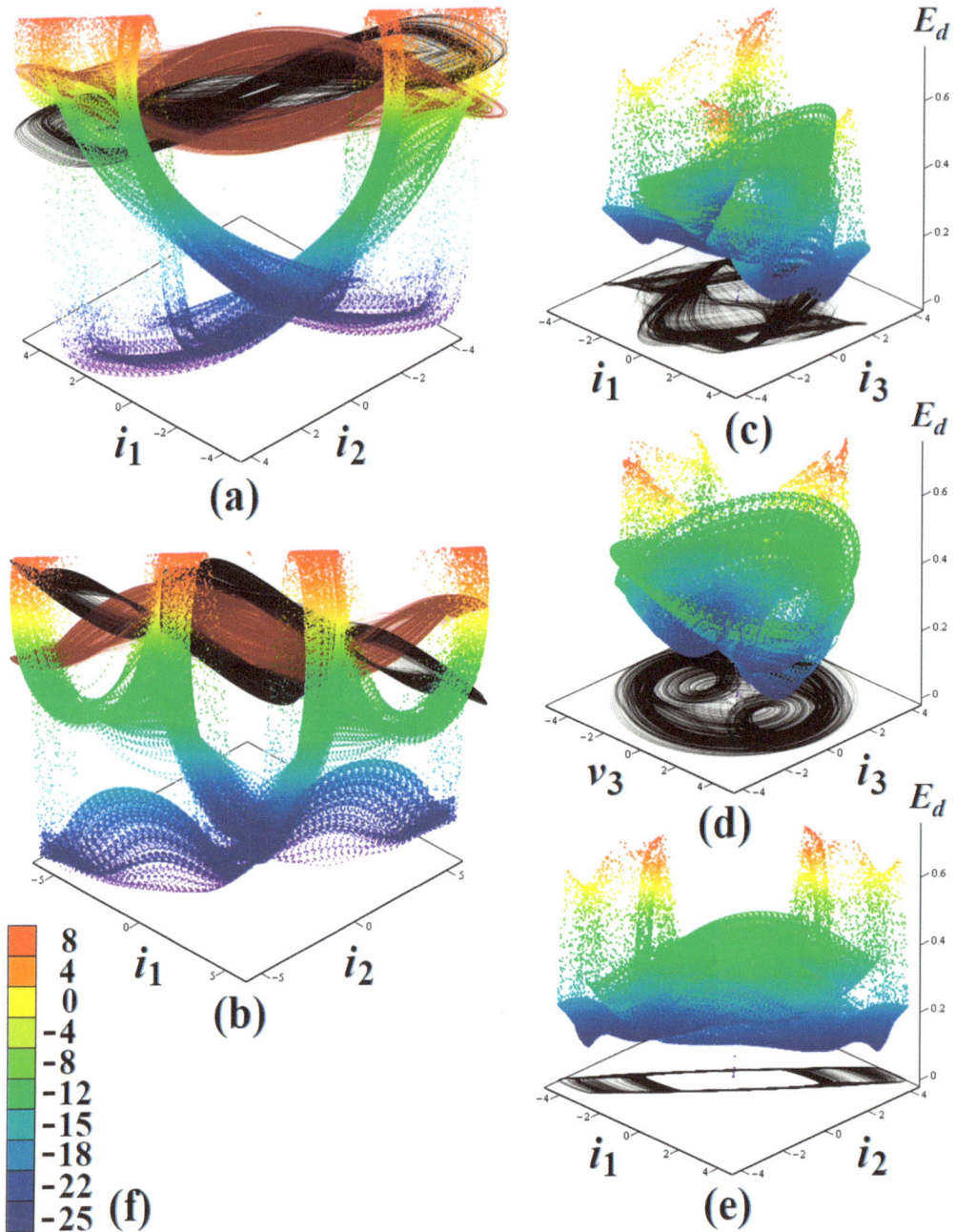

Figure 3. Snippets of numerical analysis of dynamical system case I. Divergence of the vector field including color legend for the following: (**a**) $\beta = 10$ S and, (**b**) $\beta = 11$ S. Plane projections showing dynamic energy distribution E_d over the state space plane fragments: (**c**) i_1 vs. i_3, (**d**) v_3 vs. i_3, and (**e**) i_1 vs. i_2. Color legend: (**f**) numerical values for energy plots.

Figure 4 provides a closer insight into how regions of chaos (of course, only a small fragment is addressed) within a hyperspace of system parameters look. These are high-resolution plots with a total number of calculated values of 50 × 50 = 2500 in each square. Transitions between chaotic and hyperchaotic behavior do not follow conventional rules such as changes in eigenvalues or the stability index of zero equilibrium; see paper [24] for more details. Little can be known about these routes, only that they are rare and cannot be described by a closed-form mathematical formula.

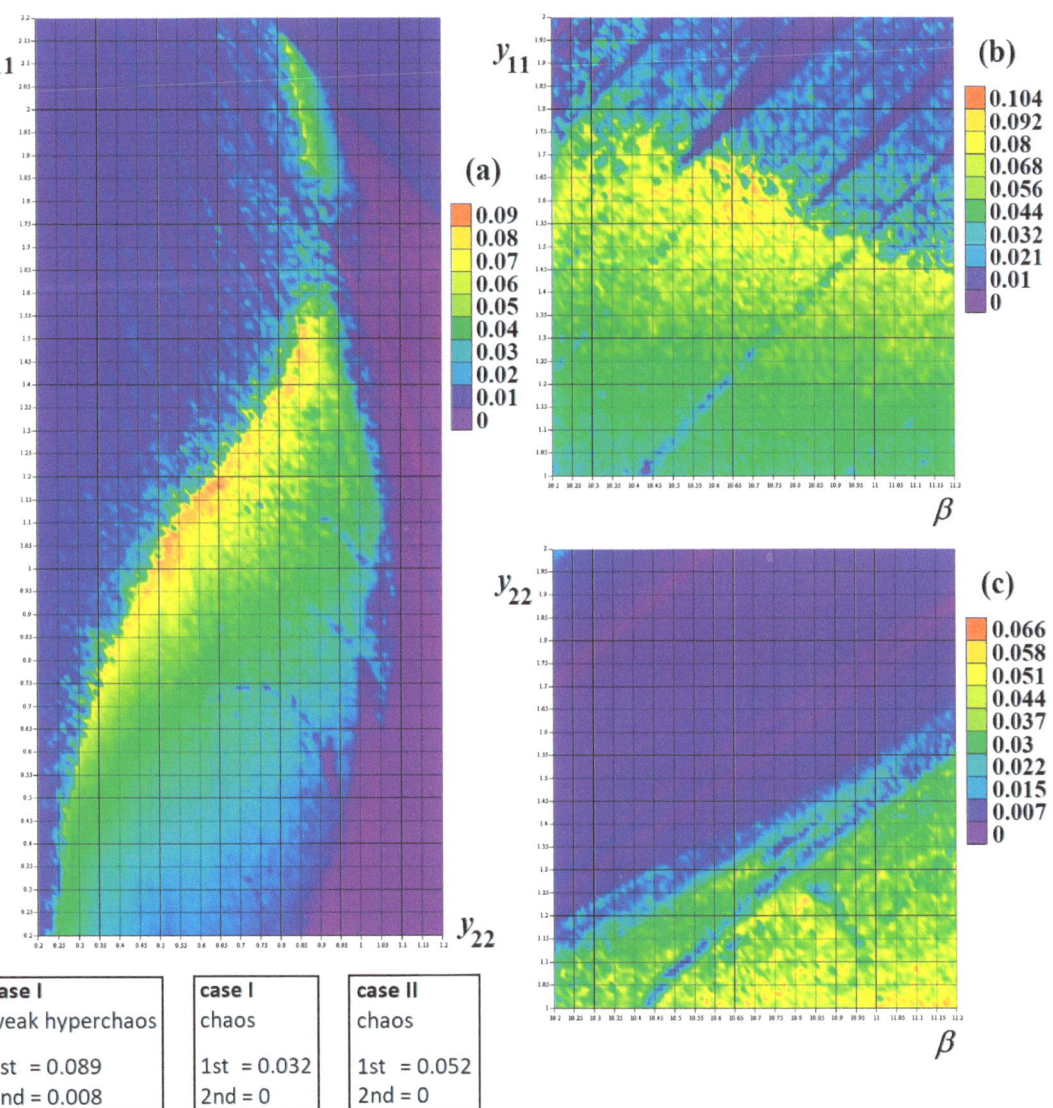

case I	case I	case II
weak hyperchaos	chaos	chaos
1st = 0.089	1st = 0.032	1st = 0.052
2nd = 0.008	2nd = 0	2nd = 0

Figure 4. Fragments of rainbow-scaled contour plot of the largest LE as a two-dimensional function of biasing point of bipolar transistor: (**a**) input vs. output admittance, (**b**) input admittance vs. linear part of forward trans-admittance, (**c**) output admittance vs. linear part of forward trans-admittance. Used resolution deals with uniform parameter step 10^{-3} for each plot.

Figure 5 provides a continuation of numerical results, showing time-domain analysis results for the Reinartz oscillator (1) coupled with a parameter set (7). The bifurcation diagram reveals a sudden transition from periodic to chaotic motion and several narrow periodic windows for continuous change in the parameter β from 9.5 S up to 10.9 S. This bifurcation sequence ends up with an unbounded solution. For all numerical integrations, the initial conditions were chosen as small disturbances (100 mV) of capacitor voltage.

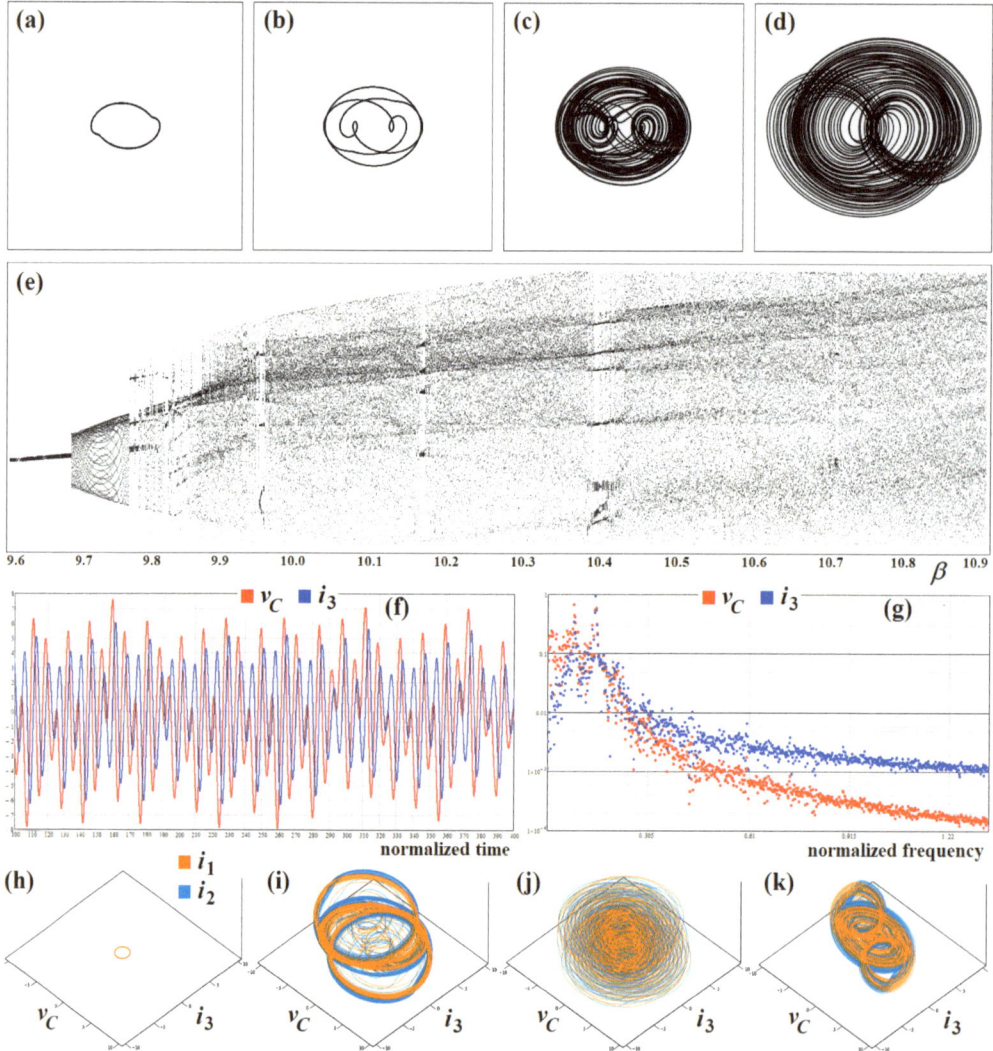

Figure 5. Plane projections reflecting the state changes of parallel resonant tank v_C vs. i_3: (**a**) $\beta = 9.5$ S, (**b**) $\beta = 9.7$ S, (**c**) $\beta = 10$ S, and (**d**) $\beta = 10.9$ S. Each plot has horizontal axis range $v_C \in (-8, 8)$ V and vertical scale $i_3 \in (-8, 8)$ A. Subplot (**e**) provides half-return map calculated for plane $v_C = 0$ V, captured for state variable i_3 and in range $\beta \in (9.6, 10.9)$ S with step 1 mS. Subplot (**f**) represents visualization of v_C and i_3 in time domain; subplot (**g**) shows corresponding frequency spectrum. Three-dimensional projections showing changes of attractors for magnetic coupling: (**h**) $M_{13} = 0$ H and $M_{23} = 0$ H, (**i**) $M_{13} = 0.3$ H and $M_{23} = 0$ H, (**j**) $M_{13} = 0.1$ H and $M_{23} = 0.1$ H, (**k**) $M_{13} = 0.5$ H and $M_{23} = 0.1$ H.

4. Design of Chaotic Oscillators and Experiments

Since fully analog circuit-aided solutions of ODE sets are free of numerical errors, a truly chaotic steady state can be distinguished from a long chaotic transient or numerical artifact. For further reading about the credibility aspects of research focused on chaotic dynamical systems, papers [25,26] are recommended.

Modeling nonlinear dynamics using analog circuits is a well-established task, with multiple correct solutions achieved by the following different approaches. The main goal is to reach one-to-one correspondence between the behavior of the mathematical and circuit models of the dynamical system. The complete framework on how to proceed is outlined in the comprehensive review paper [27] for voltage-mode networks and in paper [28] for current-mode operation regimes.

In the upcoming subsections, two universal methods dedicated to nonlinear circuit synthesis of flow-equivalent, case I, chaotic Reinartz oscillator are given, including the numerical values of all passive components. By considering the dynamical system (1) with nonlinearity (2) and the discovered parameters (7), the normalized (with respect to time and impedance) set of the ODE becomes

$$\frac{d}{dt}v_1 = -v_4, \frac{d}{dt}v_2 = 0.6 \cdot v_4 - 2 \cdot v_2 + v_3 - 8 \cdot (v_2 - v_3) + 10 \cdot (v_2 - v_3)^3, \frac{d}{dt}v_3 = v_2 - v_3 + 0.1 \cdot v_4,$$
$$\frac{d}{dt}v_4 = v_1 + 0.6 \cdot v_2 + 0.1 \cdot v_3, \qquad (11)$$

where $\mathbf{x} = (v_1, v_2, v_3, v_4)^T$ is a new state vector composed of node voltages only. Parameters α and β need to be separated because they will be considered the variables. The circuit design of system case II is completely analogical; no changes in the circuit element's interconnections are necessary. It is worth nothing that the Orcad Pspice circuit simulations lead to the same results as real experimental observations captured by an oscilloscope. Hence, these results are not provided.

4.1. Analog Multiplier-Based Design

For the generation of any type of attractors, continuous offset voltage applied to the inputs of operational amplifier-based ideal integrators can be problematic simply because of the output saturation. This event can also be caused by the intrinsic nonideal offset voltage of an operational amplifier. In such cases, the classical approach, where the right-hand side of each equation of system (1) represents a sum of the currents flowing through a grounded capacitor, will probably be the better design approach. To minimize the final number of active elements, the linear part of the vector field should be decomposed: in part $\mathbf{Y}_{passive}$, which contains grounded and passive resistors and in part $\mathbf{Y}_{active}$ where individual entries are implemented using active transadmittance cells. Then, the final matrix equations will be

$$\frac{d}{dt}(C_1 \quad C_2 \quad C_3 \quad C_4)^T = (\mathbf{Y}_{passive} + \mathbf{Y}_{active}) \cdot \mathbf{V} + \mathbf{f}(\mathbf{V}), \qquad (12)$$

where $\mathbf{V}$ is a vector of the main node voltages and $\mathbf{f}$ comprises nonlinear functions. For the dynamical system (11), the matrices and vectors mentioned above can be of the form

$$\mathbf{Y}_{passive} = \begin{pmatrix} 0 & 0 & 0 & 0 \\ 0 & -9.6 & 1 & 0.6 \\ 0 & 1 & -1.1 & 0.1 \\ 0 & 0.6 & 0.1 & -0.7 \end{pmatrix}, \mathbf{Y}_{active} = \begin{pmatrix} 0 & 0 & 0 & -1 \\ 0 & 7.6 & 0 & 0 \\ 0 & 0 & 0.1 & 0 \\ 1 & 0 & 0 & 0.7 \end{pmatrix}, \mathbf{f} = \begin{pmatrix} 0 \\ -8 \cdot (v_2 - v_3) + 10 \cdot (v_2 - v_3)^3 \\ 0 \\ 0 \end{pmatrix}. \qquad (13)$$

A corresponding chaotic oscillator is provided in Figure 6. There, resistors and capacitors have fixed values derived from the basic time constants of integrators chosen quite large, namely $\tau = R_{nom} \cdot C = 10^4 \cdot 10^{-8} = 100$ µs. The corresponding sets of ODEs are

$$C_1\frac{d}{dt}v_1 = -\frac{K_2}{R_2}v_4, C_2\frac{d}{dt}v_2 = \left(\frac{K_8}{R_{12}} - \frac{1}{R_3} - \frac{1}{R_5} - \frac{1}{R_8}\right)v_2 + \frac{1}{R_3}v_3 + \frac{1}{R_5}v_4 + \frac{1}{R_8}(v_2 - v_3) - \frac{K_7}{R_{11}}(v_2 - v_3)^3,$$
$$C_3\frac{d}{dt}v_3 = \frac{1}{R_3}v_2 + \left(\frac{K_4}{R_7} - \frac{1}{R_3} - \frac{1}{R_4}\right)v_3 + \frac{1}{R_4}v_4, C_4\frac{d}{dt}v_4 = \frac{K_1}{R_1}v_1 + \frac{1}{R_5}v_2 + \frac{1}{R_4}v_3 + \left(\frac{K_3}{R_6} - \frac{1}{R_4} - \frac{1}{R_5}\right)v_4. \qquad (14)$$

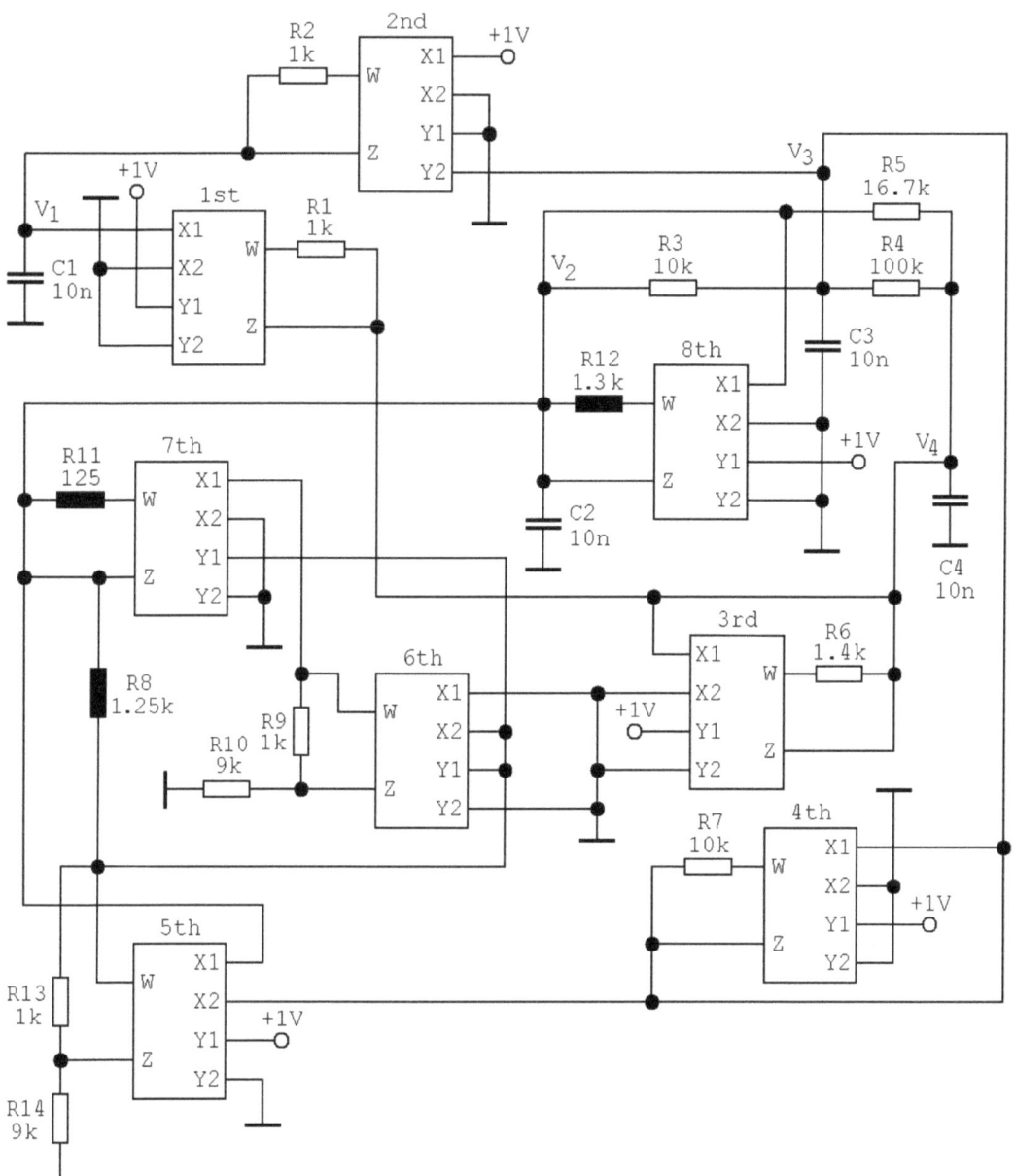

Figure 6. Fully analog circuit realization of equivalent chaotic Reinartz oscillator, system case I; only four-quadrant analog multipliers AD633 are used.

For derivation of these ODEs, an ideal transfer function of analog multipliers has been used, i.e., $V_W = K \cdot (V_{X1} - V_{X2}) \cdot (V_{Y1} - V_{Y2}) + V_Z$, where $K = 0.1$ is an internally trimmed constant. Obviously, entries of the admittance matrix $\mathbf{Y}_{active}$ can be changed via external DC voltage; in our design case, we chose default 1 V for simplicity. The chaotic system working in a lower frequency band is well suited for a breadboard realization. Resistors R_9 and R_{10} do not appear in (14) since these serve only to compensate for constant K_6.

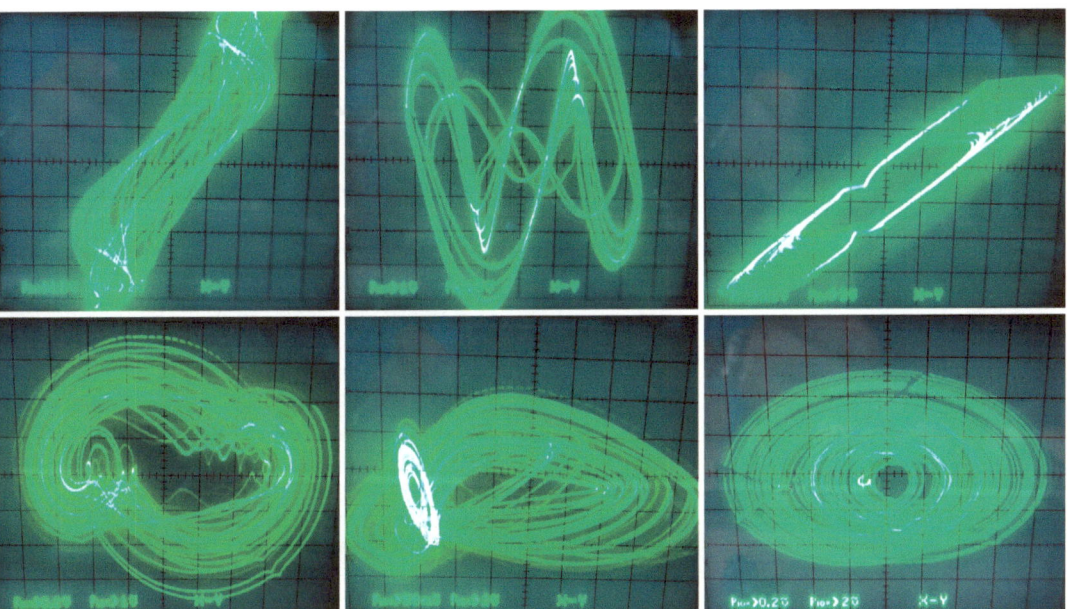

Figure 9. The chaotic Reinartz oscillator, system case I, integrator block schematic design method, with few measurement outputs.

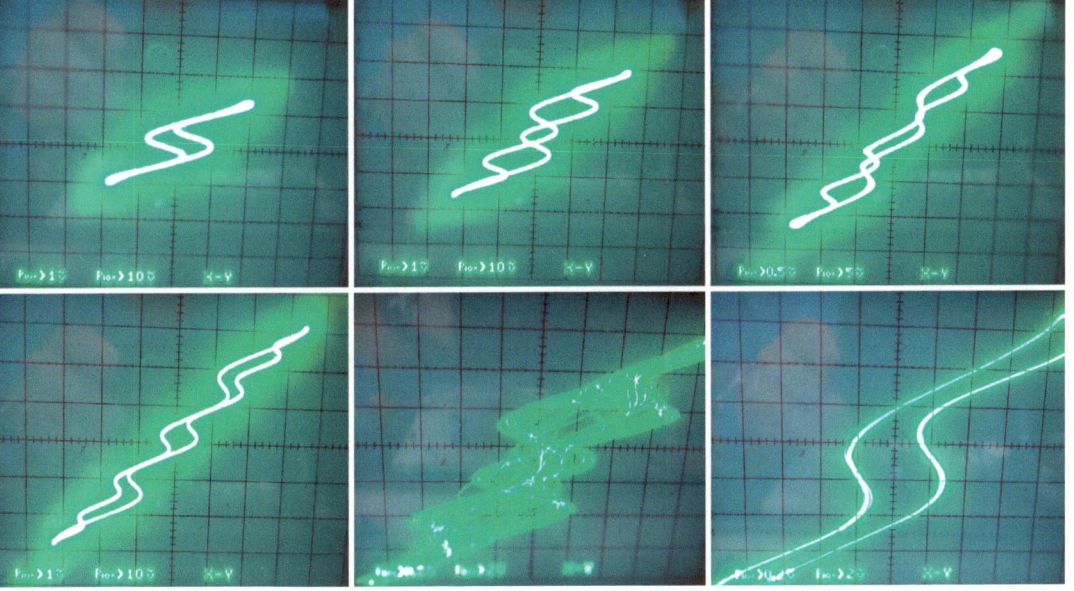

Figure 10. The chaotic Reinartz oscillator, dynamical system case I, integrator block-based schematic design method, and different limit cycles with captured intermittent chaos.

5. Discussion

The main aim and importance of this work is to demonstrate the existence of robust, non-predictable waveforms coming from a significantly simplified mathematical model of a conventional LC oscillator. The investigated mathematical model includes only a single scalar nonlinear function intrinsic to the bipolar transistor instead of dealing with an enormously complicated large-signal global model of this three-terminal device. The presented results can motivate other design engineers and mathematicians to follow this research and extend it by including the following:

1. Findings from the area of non-integer order dynamics associated with individual accumulation elements [29,30].
2. Discoveries from higher-order dynamics that originate in considering parasitic properties of transistors [31].
3. A description of circuit behavior under nonlinear magnetic coupling that is closer to practical reality [32].

6. Conclusions

The simplified topology of the well-known Reinartz circuit can produce either chaotic or weakly hyperchaotic self-oscillations, even under conditions of linear magnetic coupling coefficients. Proof is demonstrated within this study on both a numerical and an experimental basis. A bipolar transistor is modeled by two-port admittance parameters with the assumption of neutralized backward signal transmission. The bias point of the transistor is derived from a class A amplifier. Although biasing is hypothetical, parameter sets that result in observed chaotic steady states represent physically reasonable quantities (after suitable time and impedance rescaling) not far away from common numerical values. In accordance with explicit model vs. circuit parameter comparison and visual observation, very good agreement between measurement results and theoretical assumptions has been achieved.

Funding: This research was funded by BRNO UNIVERSITY OF TECHNOLOGY, grant number FEKT-S-23-8191.

Data Availability Statement: There are no data associated with research described in this paper.

Conflicts of Interest: The author declares no conflict of interest.

References

1. Jiang, T.; Wang, B.; Bi, M.; Chen, X.; Cheng, S.; Wang, F. Digital filter based on chaos theory used for removing narrow-frequency band noise in PD signals. *J. Eng.* **2020**, *13*, 357–360. [CrossRef]
2. Endo, T.; Chua, L.O. Chaos from phase-locked loops. *IEEE Trans. Circuits Syst.* **1988**, *35*, 987–1003. [CrossRef]
3. Petrzela, J. Generalized single stage class C amplifier: Analysis from the viewpoint of chaotic behavior. *Appl. Sci.* **2020**, *10*, 50. [CrossRef]
4. Hamill, D.C.; Jeffries, D.J. Subharmonics and chaos in a controlled switched-mode power converter. *IEEE Trans. Circuits Syst.* **1988**, *35*, 1059–1061. [CrossRef]
5. Rodriguez-Vazquez, A.; Huertas, J.; Chua, L.O. Chaos in switched-capacitor circuit. *IEEE Trans. Circuits Syst.* **1985**, *32*, 1083–10. [CrossRef]
6. Petrzela, J. Strange attractors generated by multiple-valued static memory cell with polynomial approximation of resonant tunneling diodes. *Entropy* **2018**, *20*, 697. [CrossRef]
7. Behnia, S.; Pazhotan, Z.; Ezzati, N.; Akhshani, A. Reconfigurable chaotic logic gates based on novel chaotic circuit. *Chaos Solitons Fractals* **2014**, *69*, 74–80. [CrossRef]
8. Drutarovsky, M.; Galajda, P. A robust chaos-based true random number generator embedded in reconfigurable switched-capacitor hardware. *Radioengineering* **2007**, *16*, 120–127.
9. Kennedy, M.P. Chaos in the Colpitts oscillator. *IEEE Trans. Circuits Syst. I Fund. Theory Appl.* **1994**, *41*, 771–774. [CrossRef]
10. Wafo Tekam, R.B.; Kengne, J.; Kenmoe, G.D. High frequency Colpitts oscillator: A simple configuration for chaos generation. *Chaos Solitons Fractals* **2019**, *126*, 351–360. [CrossRef]
11. Kvarda, P. Chaos in Hartley's oscillator. *Int. J. Bifurc. Chaos* **2002**, *12*, 2229–2232.
12. Tchitnga, R.; Fotsin, H.B.; Nana, B.; Louodop Fotso, P.H.; Woafo, P. Hartley's oscillator: The simplest chaotic two-component circuit. *Chaos Solitons Fractals* **2019**, *126*, 351–360. [CrossRef]

Petrzela, J. Chaotic and hyperchaotic dynamics of a Clapp oscillator. *Mathematics* **2022**, *10*, 1868. [CrossRef]

Morgul, O. Wien bridge based RC chaos generator. *Electron. Lett.* **1995**, *31*, 2058–2059. [CrossRef]

Hosokawa, Y.; Nishio, Y.; Ushida, A. Analysis of chaotic phenomena in two RC phase oscillators coupled by a diode. *IEICE Trans. Fundam. Electron. Comm. Comput. Sci.* **2001**, *84*, 2288–2295.

Bernat, P.; Balaz, I. RC autonomous circuits with chaotic behavior. *Radioengineering* **2002**, *11*, 1–5.

Minati, L.; Frasca, M.; Oswiecimka, P.; Faes, L.; Drozdz, S. Atypical transistor-based chaotic oscillators: Design, realization, and diversity. *Chaos Interdiscip. J. Nonlinear Sci.* **2017**, *27*, 073113. [CrossRef]

Petrzela, J. Chaotic states of transistor-based tuned-collector oscillator. *Mathematics* **2023**, *11*, 2213. [CrossRef]

Jafari, S.; Sprott, J.C.; Pham, V.-T.; Mohammad Reza Hashemi Golpayegani, S.; Jafari, A.H. A new cost function for parameter estimation of chaotic systems using return maps as fingerprints. *Int. J. Bifurc. Chaos* **2014**, *24*, 1450134. [CrossRef]

Petrzela, J. New chaotic dynamical system with a conic-shaped equilibrium located on the plane structure. *Appl. Sci.* **2017**, *7*, 976. [CrossRef]

Adeyemi, V.-A.; Tlelo-Cuautle, E.; Perez-Pinal, F.-J.; Nunez-Perez, J.-C. Optimizing the maximum Lyapunov exponent of fractional order chaotic spherical system by evolutionary algorithms. *Fractal Fract.* **2022**, *6*, 448. [CrossRef]

Nunez-Perez, J.-C.; Adeyemi, V.-A.; Sandoval-Ibarra, Y.; Perez-Pinal, F.-J.; Tlelo-Cuautle, E. Maximizing the chaotic behavior of fractional order Chen system by evolutionary algorithm. *Mathematics* **2021**, *9*, 1194. [CrossRef]

Valencia-Ponce, M.A.; Tlelo-Cuautle, E.; de la Fraga, L.G. Estimating the highest time-step in numerical methods to enhance the optimization of chaotic oscillators. *Mathematics* **2021**, *9*, 1938. [CrossRef]

Nikolov, S.; Clodong, S. Hyperchaos-chaos-hyperchaos transition in modified Rossler system. *Chaos Solitons Fractals* **2006**, *28*, 252–263. [CrossRef]

Sprott, J.C. A proposed standard for the publication of new chaotic systems. *Int. J. Bifurc. Chaos* **2011**, *21*, 2391–2394. [CrossRef]

Munoz-Pacheco, J.M.; Tlelo-Cuautle, E.; Toxqui-Toxqui, I.; Sanchez-Lopez, C.; Trejo-Guerra, R. Frequency limitations in generating multi-scroll chaotic attractors using CFOAs. *Int. J. Electron.* **2014**, *101*, 1559–1569. [CrossRef]

Itoh, M. Synthesis of electronic circuits for simulating nonlinear dynamics. *Int. J. Bifurc. Chaos* **2001**, *11*, 605–653. [CrossRef]

Petrzela, J.; Gotthans, T.; Guzan, M. Current-mode network structures dedicated for simulation of dynamical systems with plane continuum of equilibrium. *J. Circuits Syst. Comput.* **2018**, *27*, 1830004. [CrossRef]

Rajagopal, K.; Li, C.; Nazarimehr, F.; Karthikeyan, F.; Duraisamy, P.; Jafari, S. Chaotic dynamics of modified Wien bridge oscillator with fractional order memristor. *Radioengineering* **2019**, *28*, 165–174. [CrossRef]

Kartci, A.; Herencsar, N.; Machado, J.T.; Brancik, L. History and progress of fractional-order element passive emulators: A review. *Radioengineering* **2020**, *29*, 296–304. [CrossRef]

Hu, G. Hyperchaos of higher order and its circuit implementation. *Int. J. Circuit Theory Appl.* **2011**, *39*, 79–89. [CrossRef]

Mayergoyz, I.D.; Lawson, W. *Basic Electric Circuit Theory*; Elsevier: Amsterdam, The Netherlands, 1996; 450p, ISBN 978-0-08-057228-4.

Disclaimer/Publisher's Note: The statements, opinions and data contained in all publications are solely those of the individual author(s) and contributor(s) and not of MDPI and/or the editor(s). MDPI and/or the editor(s) disclaim responsibility for any injury to people or property resulting from any ideas, methods, instructions or products referred to in the content.

Article

Fractal Fractional Derivative Models for Simulating Chemical Degradation in a Bioreactor

Ali Akgül [1,2,3] and J. Alberto Conejero [4,*]

[1] Department of Mathematics, Art and Science Faculty, Siirt University, 56100 Siirt, Turkey; aliakgul00727@gmail.com
[2] Department of Computer Science and Mathematics, Lebanese American University, Beirut P.O. Box 13-5053, Lebanon
[3] Department of Mathematics, Mathematics Research Center, Near East University, Near East Boulevard, 99138 Mersin, Turkey
[4] Instituto Universitario de Matemática Pura y Aplicada, Universitat Politècnica de València, 46022 València, Spain
* Correspondence: aconejero@upv.es

Abstract: A three-differential-equation mathematical model is presented for the degradation of phenol and p-cresol combination in a bioreactor that is continually agitated. The stability analysis of the model's equilibrium points, as established by the study, is covered. Additionally, we used three alternative kernels to analyze the model with the fractal–fractional derivatives, and we looked into the effects of the fractal size and fractional order. We have developed highly efficient numerical techniques for the concentration of biomass, phenol, and p-cresol. Lastly, numerical simulations are used to illustrate the accuracy of the suggested method.

Keywords: bioreactor model; numerical methods; fractal–fractional derivatives; numerical simulations

MSC: 26A33; 34A08; 35R11.

1. Introduction

In a bioreactor, chemical degradation is the process by which certain chemicals or compounds are broken down or changed by living things in the bioreactor's controlled environment. Bioreactors are widely used to support biological processes, including fermentation, enzyme manufacturing, and wastewater treatment in various industries, including pharmaceuticals, biotechnology, wastewater treatment, and food production.

Many scientific papers have presented the isolation and work of microbial species with higher-degradation action and abilities to degrade chemical compounds [1]. Many isolated bacteria have been investigated in [2]. The biodegradation of one or all chemical parts hinges on the composition of the specific mixture and the utilized microorganisms [3–6]. Fractional calculus is an influential extension of the classical derivatives. Fractional differential equations (FDEs) have recently been implemented in different fields. Many authors have worked on these equations, such as the KdV equation [7], advection-dispersion equation [8], telegraph equation [9], Schrodinger equation [10], heat equation [11], convection-diffusion equation [12], Fokker Planck equation [13], and Lambert–Beer equation [14,15]. Some of the FDEs do not have exact solutions. Therefore, it is required to work on numerical methods to solve the mentioned equations, such as solving nonlinear fractional diffusion wave equations with the homotopy analysis technique [16], solving PDEs of fractal order by Adomian decomposition method [17]. In [1], the authors have given a bioreactor model but do not consider the bacteria's death rate and general configuration of the reactor. We have provided the bioreactor model with the fractal–fractional operators. The model with fractal–fractional derivatives has never been analyzed so far. Our model includes the death rate of bacteria, which is important in the process's environment. We also consider the general configuration of the reactor, where our model includes a membrane and continuous reactor. Additionally, we fractionalize the model and apply a novel numerical technique to achieve the numerical simulations. In these simulations, we use different fractal dimensions and fractional orders. For more details, see [18–30].

We organize our manuscript as follows. Problem formulation is performed in Section 2. In Section 3, we discuss the model's analysis in the classical case and present the equilibrium and stability analysis. Next, we explore the analysis of the model with three different kernels viz. the power-law kernel (Section 4), the exponential-decay kernel (Section 5), and the Mittag–Leffler function (Section 6). Finally, in Section 7, we illustrate the numerical simulations of the proposed models.

2. Preliminaries

The following definitions of fractional differentiation operator and fractal–fractional integral operator with three different kernels are taken from [21] .

Definition 1. *The fractional differentiation operator with the power-law-type kernel is described as:*

$$\prescript{FFP}{c}{D}_t^{\alpha,\eta} f(t) = \frac{1}{1-\alpha} \frac{d}{du^\eta} \int_c^t f(s)(t-s)^{-\alpha} ds, \ 0 < \alpha, \eta \leq 1, \quad (1)$$

where,

$$\frac{df(s)}{ds^\eta} = \lim_{t \to s} \frac{f(t)-f(s)}{t^\eta - s^\eta} \quad (2)$$

Definition 2. *The fractional differentiation operator with the exponential-decay-type kernel is described as:*

$$\prescript{FFE}{c}{D}_t^{\alpha,\eta} f(t) = \frac{M_1(\alpha)}{1-\alpha} \frac{d}{dt^\eta} \int_c^t f(s) \exp\left(\frac{-\alpha}{1-\alpha}(t-s)\right) ds, \ 0 < \alpha, \eta \leq 1. \quad (3)$$

Definition 3. *The fractional differentiation operator with the Mittag–Leffler-type kernel is described as:*

$$\prescript{FFM}{c}{D}_t^{\alpha,\eta} f(t) = \frac{AB(\alpha)}{1-\alpha} \frac{d}{dt^\eta} \int_c^t f(s) E_\alpha\left(\frac{-\alpha}{1-\alpha}(t-s)^\alpha\right) ds, \ 0 < \alpha, \eta \leq 1, \quad (4)$$

where $AB(\alpha) = 1 - \alpha + \frac{\alpha}{\Gamma(\alpha)}$.

Definition 4. *The fractional integration operator with the power-law-type kernel is described as:*

$$\prescript{FFP}{0}{I}_t^{\alpha,\eta} f(t) = \frac{\eta}{\Gamma(\alpha)} \int_0^t (t-s)^{\alpha-1} s^{\tau-1} \phi(s) ds. \quad (5)$$

Definition 5. *The fractional integration operator with the exponential-decay-type kernel is described as:*

$$\prescript{FFE}{0}{I}_t^{\alpha,\eta} f(t) = \frac{\alpha \eta}{M_1(\alpha)} \int_0^t s^{\alpha-1} f(s) ds + \frac{\tau(1-\alpha)t^{\tau-1}}{M_1(\alpha)} \phi(t). \quad (6)$$

Definition 6. *The fractional integration operator with the Mittag–Leffler-type kernel is described as:*

$$\prescript{FFM}{0}{I}_t^{\alpha,\eta} f(t) = \frac{\alpha \eta}{AB(\alpha)} \int_0^t s^{\alpha-1} f(s)(t-s)^{\alpha-1} ds + \frac{\tau(1-\alpha)t^{\tau-1}}{AB(\alpha)} f(t). \quad (7)$$

Here, we present the model to be investigated in this research. We present the model as:

$$\frac{dS_{ph}}{dt} = D\left(S_{ph0} - S_{ph}\right) - k_{ph} \cdot \mu\left(S_{ph}, S_{cr}\right) \cdot X, \qquad (8)$$

$$\frac{dS_{cr}}{dt} = D(S_{cr0} - S_{cr}) - k_{cr} \cdot \mu\left(S_{ph}, S_{cr}\right) \cdot X, \qquad (9)$$

$$\frac{dX}{dt} = -D\beta X + \mu\left(S_{ph}, S_{cr}\right) X, \qquad (10)$$

$$\mu\left(S_{ph}, S_{cr}\right) = \frac{\mu_{max(ph)} S_{ph}}{K_{s(ph)} + S_{ph} + \frac{S_{ph}^2}{k_{i(ph)}} + I_{cr/ph} S_{cr}} + \frac{\mu_{max(cr)} S_{cr}}{K_{s(cr)} + S_{cr} + \frac{S_{cr}^2}{k_{i(cr)}} + I_{ph/cr} S_{ph}}, \qquad (11)$$

The model parameters and variables are detailed in [1]. The parameter β is presented in the general configuration. When $\beta = 1$, we have continued the reactor. When $\beta = 0$, we have a membrane reactor.

3. Analysis of the Model in Classical Sense

Now, we begin with analyzing the properties of the model in classical sense.

We consider the number of equilibrium solutions of the model ((8)–(10)). It is obvious that the model has a branch of the washout given by

$$E_0 = (S_{ph}, S_{cr}, X) = \left(S_{ph0}, S_{cr0}, 0\right). \qquad (12)$$

We obtain the steady state solution of ((8)–(10)) by setting to zero the right side. From the model ((8)–(10)), we have:

$$S_{cr} = \frac{S_{cr0} k_{ph} + k_{cr}(S_{ph} - S_{ph0})}{k_{ph}},$$

$$X = \frac{D\left(S_{ph0} - S_{ph}\right)}{k_{ph}(\beta D)}. \qquad (13)$$

$$f = \begin{pmatrix} -k_{cr}\mu(S_{ph}, S_{cr})X \\ \mu(S_{ph}, S_{cr})X \end{pmatrix} \rightarrow F = \begin{bmatrix} \frac{\partial \mu(S_{ph}, S_{cr})(-k_{cr})X}{\partial (S_{ph}, S_{cr})X} & -k_{cr}\mu(S_{ph}, S_{cr}) \\ \frac{\partial \mu(S_{ph}, S_{cr})X}{\partial (S_{ph}, S_{cr})X} & \mu(S_{ph}, S_{cr})k_{cr}(S_{ph}, S_{cr}) \end{bmatrix}$$

$$V = \begin{pmatrix} -D(S_{cr0} - S_{cr}) \\ D\beta X \end{pmatrix} \rightarrow V = \begin{bmatrix} D & 0 \\ 0 & D\beta \end{bmatrix}, V^{-1} = \begin{bmatrix} D\beta & 0 \\ 0 & D \end{bmatrix}$$

$$FV^{-1} = \begin{bmatrix} 0 & -k_{cr}\mu(S_{ph}, S_{cr}) \\ 0 & \mu(S_{ph}, S_{cr}) \end{bmatrix} \begin{bmatrix} D & 0 \\ 0 & D\beta \end{bmatrix} = \begin{bmatrix} 0 & -\beta D k_{cr}\mu(S_{ph}, S_{cr}) \\ 0 & \beta D \mu(S_{ph}, S_{cr}) \end{bmatrix}$$

$$\det[FV^{-1} - \lambda I_2] = 0, \quad \begin{vmatrix} -\lambda & -\beta D k_{cr}\mu(S_{ph}, S_{cr}) \\ 0 & \beta D \mu(S_{ph}, S_{cr}) - \lambda \end{vmatrix} = 0$$

Thus, we obtain $\lambda_1 = 0$, $\lambda_2 = \beta D \mu(S_{ph}, S_{cr}) = R_0$.

Lemma 1. *The steady state solution E_0 is locally asymptotically stable when $D > D_{cr}$ and is unstable when $D < D_{cr}$, where*

$$D_{cr} = \frac{k_{icr} k_{ph} (S_{cr0} k_{ph} - S_{ph0} k_{cr})^{-} max_{cr}}{\left[k_{icr} k_{ph} (K_{scr} k_{ph} + S_{cr0} k_{ph} - S_{ph0} k_{cr}) + (S_{cr} k_{ph} - S_{ph0} k_{cr})^2\right] \beta}.$$

Proof. We have
$$E_0 = (s_{ph}, s_{cr}, x) = (s_{ph0}, s_{cr0}, 0)$$

$$J(E_0) = \begin{bmatrix} -D - \frac{\partial \mu(s_{ph}, s_{cr})}{\partial s_{ph}} k_{ph} x & -\frac{\partial \mu(s_{ph}, s_{cr})}{\partial s_{ph}} k_{ph} x & -\mu(s_{ph}, s_{cr}) k_{ph} \\ -k_{cr} \frac{\partial \mu(s_{ph}, s_{cr})}{\partial s_{ph}} x & -D - \frac{\partial \mu(s_{ph}, s_{cr})}{\partial s_{ph}} k_{cr} x & -\mu(s_{ph}, s_{cr}) k_{cr} \\ \frac{\partial \mu(s_{ph}, s_{cr})}{\partial s_{ph}} x & -\frac{\partial \mu(s_{ph}, s_{cr})}{\partial s_{ph}} x & -D\beta + \mu(s_{ph}, s_{cr}) \end{bmatrix}$$

$$J(E_0) = \begin{bmatrix} -D & 0 & -\mu(s_{ph0}, s_{cr0}) k_{ph} \\ 0 & -D & -\mu(s_{ph0}, s_{cr0}) k_{cr} \\ 0 & 0 & -D\beta + \mu(s_{ph0}, s_{cr0}) \end{bmatrix}$$

where

$$\mu(s_{ph}, s_{cr}) = \frac{\mu_{max(ph)} s_{ph}}{K_{s(ph)} + s_{ph} + \frac{s_{ph}^2}{K_{i(ph)}} + I_{cr/ph} s_{cr}} + \frac{\mu_{max(cr)} s_{ph}}{K_{s(cr)} + s_{cr} + \frac{s_{cr}^2}{K_{i(cr)}} + I_{ph/cr} s_{ph}}$$

$$\det[J(E_0) - \lambda I_3] = \begin{vmatrix} -D - \lambda & 0 & -\mu(s_{ph}, s_{cr}) k_{ph} \\ 0 & -D - \lambda & -\mu(s_{ph}, s_{cr}) k_{cr} \\ 0 & 0 & \mu(s_{ph}, s_{cr}) - D\beta - \lambda \end{vmatrix} = 0$$

$$= (-D - \lambda)(-D - \lambda)(\mu(s_{ph}, s_{cr}) - D\beta - \lambda) = 0$$

$$\lambda_1 = -D, \quad \lambda_2 = -D, \quad \lambda_3 = -\beta D + \mu(s_{ph}, s_{cr})$$

and

$$\mu(s_{ph}, s_{cr}) = \bar{\max}_{ph} s_{ph0} \left(k_{sph} + s_{ph0} + \frac{s_{ph0}^2}{K_{i(ph)}} + I_{cr/ph} s_{cr0} \right)^{-1}$$
$$+ \bar{\max}_{cr} s_{cr0} \left(k_{scr} + s_{cr0} + \frac{s_{cr0}^2}{K_{i(ph)}} + I_{ph/cr} s_{ph0} \right)^{-1}$$

$$D_{cr} = \frac{k_{icr} k_{ph} (s_{cr0} k_{ph} - s_{ph0} k_{cr})^- \max_{cr}}{\left[k_{icr} k_{ph} (K_{scr} k_{ph} + s_{cr0} k_{ph} - s_{ph0} k_{cr}) + (s_{cr} k_{ph} - s_{ph0} k_{cr})^2 \right] \beta}$$

If $D > D_{cr}$, then $\lambda_3 < 0$. Thus, all eigenvalues are negative. This shows that the steady state solution E_0 is locally asymptotically stable. □

4. Analysis of the Model with the Power-Law Kernel

Here, we analyze the model with fractional differentiation operator using the power-law kernel as:

$$^{FFP}_0 D_t^{\alpha, \eta} S_{ph} = D(S_{ph0} - S_{ph}) - k_{ph} \cdot \mu(S_{ph}, S_{cr}) \cdot X. \tag{14}$$

$$^{FFP}_0 D_t^{\alpha, \eta} S_{cr} = D(S_{cr0} - S_{cr}) - k_{cr} \cdot \mu(S_{ph}, S_{cr}) \cdot X. \tag{15}$$

$$^{FFP}_0 D_t^{\alpha, \eta} X = -D\beta X + \mu(S_{ph}, S_{cr}) X. \tag{16}$$

We have the following relation between the classical and fractal derivative [21]:

$$D^\eta f(t) = \frac{f'(t)}{\eta t^{\eta-1}}. \tag{17}$$

A relation between the classical derivative and the fractal derivative gives

$$^{RL}_0 D^\alpha_t S_{ph} = \eta t^{\eta-1}\left(D\left(S_{ph0} - S_{ph}\right) - k_{ph} \cdot \mu\left(S_{ph}, S_{cr}\right) \cdot X\right). \tag{18}$$

$$^{RL}_0 D^\alpha_t S_{cr} = \eta t^{\eta-1}\left(D(S_{cr0} - S_{cr}) - k_{cr} \cdot \mu\left(S_{ph}, S_{cr}\right) \cdot X\right). \tag{19}$$

$$^{RL}_0 D^\alpha_t X = \eta t^{\eta-1}\left(-D\beta X + \mu\left(S_{ph}, S_{cr}\right) X\right). \tag{20}$$

For simplicity, we define

$$A(t, S_{ph}, S_{cr}, X) = \eta t^{\eta-1}\left(D\left(S_{ph0} - S_{ph}\right) - k_{ph} \cdot \mu\left(S_{ph}, S_{cr}\right) \cdot X\right). \tag{21}$$

$$B(t, S_{ph}, S_{cr}, X) = \eta t^{\eta-1}\left(D(S_{cr0} - S_{cr}) - k_{cr} \cdot \mu\left(S_{ph}, S_{cr}\right) \cdot X\right). \tag{22}$$

$$C(t, S_{ph}, S_{cr}, X) = \eta t^{\eta-1}\left(-D\beta X + \mu\left(S_{ph}, S_{cr}\right) X\right). \tag{23}$$

Then, we obtain

$$^{RL}_0 D^\alpha_t S_{ph} = A(t, S_{ph}, S_{cr}, X). \tag{24}$$

$$^{RL}_0 D^\alpha_t S_{cr} = B(t, S_{ph}, S_{cr}, X). \tag{25}$$

$$^{RL}_0 D^\alpha_t X = C(t, S_{ph}, S_{cr}, X). \tag{26}$$

Applying the Riemann–Liouville integral yields:

$$S_{ph}(t) - S_{ph}(0) = \frac{1}{\Gamma(\alpha)} \int_0^t A(\tau, S_{ph}, S_{cr}, X)(t-\tau)^{\alpha-1} d\tau. \tag{27}$$

$$S_{cr}(t) - S_{cr}(0) = \frac{1}{\Gamma(\alpha)} \int_0^t B(\tau, S_{ph}, S_{cr}, X)(t-\tau)^{\alpha-1} d\tau. \tag{28}$$

$$X(t) - X(0) = \frac{1}{\Gamma(\alpha)} \int_0^t C(\tau, S_{ph}, S_{cr}, X)(t-\tau)^{\alpha-1} d\tau. \tag{29}$$

Discretizing the above equations at t_{n+1}, we receive:

$$S_{ph}(t_{n+1}) - S_{ph}(0) = \frac{1}{\Gamma(\alpha)} \int_0^{t_{n+1}} A(\tau, S_{ph}, S_{cr}, X)(t_{n+1}-\tau)^{\alpha-1} d\tau. \tag{30}$$

$$S_{cr}(t_{n+1}) - S_{cr}(0) = \frac{1}{\Gamma(\alpha)} \int_0^{t_{n+1}} B(\tau, S_{ph}, S_{cr}, X)(t_{n+1}-\tau)^{\alpha-1} d\tau. \tag{31}$$

$$X(t_{n+1}) - X(0) = \frac{1}{\Gamma(\alpha)} \int_0^{t_{n+1}} C(\tau, S_{ph}, S_{cr}, X)(t_{n+1}-\tau)^{\alpha-1} d\tau. \tag{32}$$

$$S_{ph}(t_{n+1}) - S_{ph}(0) = \frac{1}{\Gamma(\alpha)} \sum_{j=0}^n \int_{t_j}^{t_{j+1}} A(\tau, S_{ph}, S_{cr}, X)(t_{n+1}-\tau)^{\alpha-1} d\tau. \tag{33}$$

$$S_{cr}(t_{n+1}) - S_{cr}(0) = \frac{1}{\Gamma(\alpha)} \sum_{j=0}^n \int_{t_j}^{t_{j+1}} B(\tau, S_{ph}, S_{cr}, X)(t_{n+1}-\tau)^{\alpha-1} d\tau. \tag{34}$$

$$X(t_{n+1}) - X(0) = \frac{1}{\Gamma(\alpha)} \sum_{j=0}^n \int_{t_j}^{t_{j+1}} C(\tau, S_{ph}, S_{cr}, X)(t_{n+1}-\tau)^{\alpha-1} d\tau. \tag{35}$$

We use two-step Lagrange polynomial as:

$$p_j(\tau, S_{ph}, S_{cr}, X) = \frac{\tau - t_{j-1}}{t_j - t_{j-1}} A(t_j, S_{ph}, S_{cr}, X) - \frac{\tau - t_j}{t_j - t_{j-1}} A(t_{j-1}, S_{ph}, S_{cr}, X). \tag{36}$$

$$q_j(\tau, S_{ph}, S_{cr}, X) = \frac{\tau - t_{j-1}}{t_j - t_{j-1}} B(t_j, S_{ph}, S_{cr}, X) - \frac{\tau - t_j}{t_j - t_{j-1}} B(t_{j-1}, S_{ph}, S_{cr}, X). \tag{37}$$

$$s_j(\tau, S_{ph}, S_{cr}, X) = \frac{\tau - t_{j-1}}{t_j - t_{j-1}} C(t_j, S_{ph}, S_{cr}, X) - \frac{\tau - t_j}{t_j - t_{j-1}} C(t_{j-1}, S_{ph}, S_{cr}, X). \tag{38}$$

Then, we obtain

$$\begin{aligned}
S_{ph}(t_{n+1}) - S_{ph}(0) &= \frac{1}{\Gamma(\alpha)} \sum_{j=0}^{n} \int_{t_j}^{t_{j+1}} p(\tau, S_{ph}, S_{cr}, X)(t_{n+1} - \tau)^{\alpha-1} d\tau \\
&= \sum_{j=0}^{n} \left[\frac{h^\alpha A(t_j, S_{ph}, S_{cr}, X)}{\Gamma(\alpha+2)} ((n+1-j)^\alpha (n-j+2+\alpha) \right. \\
&\quad \left. - (n-j)^\alpha (n-j+2+2\alpha)) \right] \\
&\quad - \sum_{j=0}^{n} \left[\frac{h^\alpha A(t_{j-1}, S_{ph}, S_{cr}, X)}{\Gamma(\alpha+2)} \left((n+1-j)^{\alpha+1} \right. \right. \\
&\quad \left. \left. - (n-j)^\alpha (n-j+1+\alpha) \right) \right]
\end{aligned}$$

$$\begin{aligned}
S_{cr}(t_{n+1}) - S_{cr}(0) &= \frac{1}{\Gamma(\alpha)} \sum_{j=0}^{n} \int_{t_j}^{t_{j+1}} q(\tau, S_{ph}, S_{cr}, X)(t_{n+1} - \tau)^{\alpha-1} d\tau \\
&= \sum_{j=0}^{n} \left[\frac{h^\alpha B(t_j, S_{ph}, S_{cr}, X)}{\Gamma(\alpha+2)} ((n+1-j)^\alpha (n-j+2+\alpha) \right. \\
&\quad \left. - (n-j)^\alpha (n-j+2+2\alpha)) \right] \\
&\quad - \sum_{j=0}^{n} \left[\frac{h^\alpha B(t_{j-1}, S_{ph}, S_{cr}, X)}{\Gamma(\alpha+2)} \left((n+1-j)^{\alpha+1} \right. \right. \\
&\quad \left. \left. - (n-j)^\alpha (n-j+1+\alpha) \right) \right]
\end{aligned}$$

$$\begin{aligned}
X(t_{n+1}) - X(0) &= \frac{1}{\Gamma(\alpha)} \sum_{j=0}^{n} \int_{t_j}^{t_{j+1}} s(\tau, S_{ph}, S_{cr}, X)(t_{n+1} - \tau)^{\alpha-1} d\tau \\
&= \sum_{j=0}^{n} \left[\frac{h^\alpha C(t_j, S_{ph}, S_{cr}, X)}{\Gamma(\alpha+2)} ((n+1-j)^\alpha (n-j+2+\alpha) \right. \\
&\quad \left. - (n-j)^\alpha (n-j+2+2\alpha)) \right] \\
&\quad - \sum_{j=0}^{n} \left[\frac{h^\alpha C(t_{j-1}, S_{ph}, S_{cr}, X)}{\Gamma(\alpha+2)} \left((n+1-j)^{\alpha+1} \right. \right. \\
&\quad \left. \left. - (n-j)^\alpha (n-j+1+\alpha) \right) \right]
\end{aligned}$$

Thus, the numerical scheme for the model with power law kernel has been obtained. We used this scheme and obtained Figures 1–4.

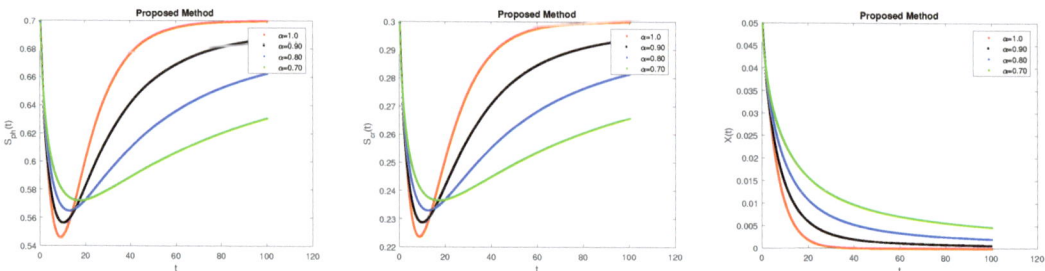

Figure 1. Solutions of (14)–(16) for $\beta = 1$, fractal dimension 1, and $\alpha = 1, 0.9, 0.8, 0.7$ with the power-law kernel.

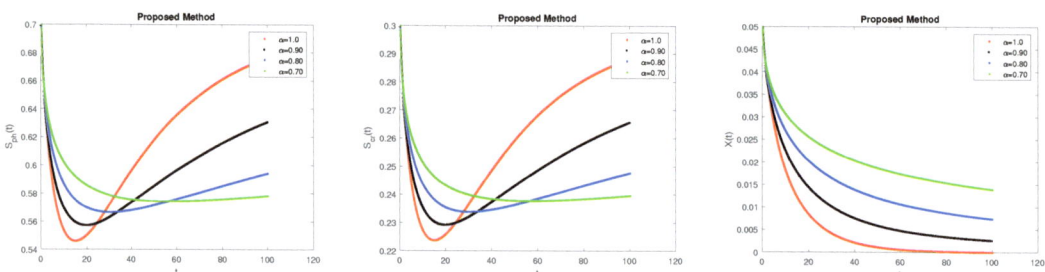

Figure 2. Solutions of (14)–(16) for $\beta = 1$, fractal dimension 0.8, and $\alpha = 1, 0.9, 0.8, 0.7$ with the power-law kernel.

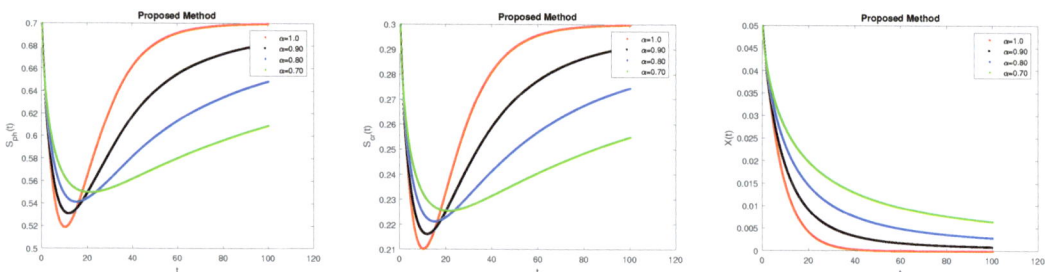

Figure 3. Solutions of (14)–(16) for $\beta = 0.5$, fractal dimension 1, and $\alpha = 1, 0.9, 0.8, 0.7$ with the power-law kernel.

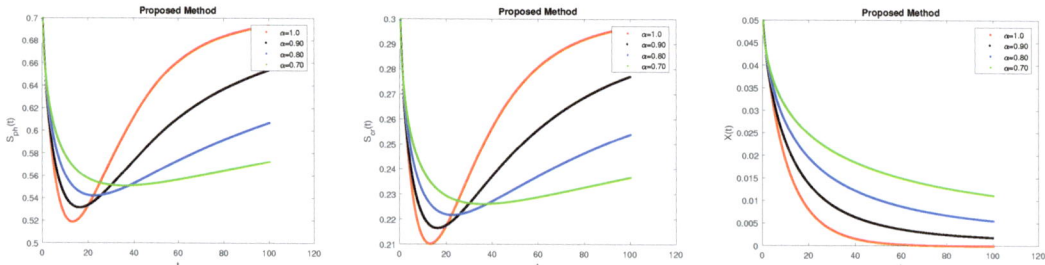

Figure 4. Solutions of (14)–(16) for $\beta = 0.5$, fractal dimension 0.9, and $\alpha = 1, 0.9, 0.8, 0.7$ with the power-law kernel.

5. Analysis of the Model with the Exponential-Decay Kernel

Next we analyze the model with using the exponential-decay kernel as:

$$^{FFE}_0D_t^{\alpha,\eta}S_{ph} = D\left(S_{ph0} - S_{ph}\right) - k_{ph} \cdot \mu\left(S_{ph}, S_{cr}\right) \cdot X. \tag{39}$$

$$^{FFE}_0D_t^{\alpha,\eta}S_{cr} = D(S_{cr0} - S_{cr}) - k_{cr} \cdot \mu\left(S_{ph}, S_{cr}\right) \cdot X. \tag{40}$$

$$^{FFE}_0D_t^{\alpha,\eta}X = -D\beta X + \mu\left(S_{ph}, S_{cr}\right)X. \tag{41}$$

Using the relation between the classical derivative and the fractal derivative yields

$$^{CF}_0D_t^{\alpha}S_{ph} = \eta t^{\eta-1}\left(D\left(S_{ph0} - S_{ph}\right) - k_{ph} \cdot \mu\left(S_{ph}, S_{cr}\right) \cdot X\right). \tag{42}$$

$$^{CF}_0D_t^{\alpha}S_{cr} = \eta t^{\eta-1}\left(D(S_{cr0} - S_{cr}) - k_{cr} \cdot \mu\left(S_{ph}, S_{cr}\right) \cdot X\right). \tag{43}$$

$$^{CF}_0D_t^{\alpha}X = \eta t^{\eta-1}\left(-D\beta X + \mu\left(S_{ph}, S_{cr}\right)X\right). \tag{44}$$

For simplicity, we define

$$K(t, S_{ph}, S_{cr}, X) = \eta t^{\eta-1}\left(D\left(S_{ph0} - S_{ph}\right) - k_{ph} \cdot \mu\left(S_{ph}, S_{cr}\right) \cdot X\right). \tag{45}$$

$$L(t, S_{ph}, S_{cr}, X) = \eta t^{\eta-1}\left(D(S_{cr0} - S_{cr}) - k_{cr} \cdot \mu\left(S_{ph}, S_{cr}\right) \cdot X\right). \tag{46}$$

$$M(t, S_{ph}, S_{cr}, X) = \eta t^{\eta-1}\left(-D\beta X + \mu\left(S_{ph}, S_{cr}\right)X\right). \tag{47}$$

Then, we obtain

$$^{CF}_0D_t^{\alpha}S_{ph} = K(t, S_{ph}, S_{cr}, X). \tag{48}$$

$$^{CF}_0D_t^{\alpha}S_{cr} = L(t, S_{ph}, S_{cr}, X). \tag{49}$$

$$^{CF}_0D_t^{\alpha}X = M(t, S_{ph}, S_{cr}, X). \tag{50}$$

Applying the CF integral yields [22]:

$$S_{ph}(t) - S_{ph}(0) = \frac{1-\alpha}{M(\alpha)}K(t, S_{ph}, S_{cr}, X) + \frac{\alpha}{M(\alpha)}\int_0^t K(\tau, S_{ph}, S_{cr}, X)d\tau.$$

$$S_{cr}(t) - S_{cr}(0) = \frac{1-\alpha}{M(\alpha)}L(t, S_{ph}, S_{cr}, X) + \frac{\alpha}{M(\alpha)}\int_0^t L(\tau, S_{ph}, S_{cr}, X)d\tau.$$

$$X(t) - X(0) = \frac{1-\alpha}{M(\alpha)}M(t, S_{ph}, S_{cr}, X) + \frac{\alpha}{M(\alpha)}\int_0^t M(\tau, S_{ph}, S_{cr}, X)d\tau.$$

Discretizing the above equations at t_{n+1} and t_n, we receive:

$$S_{ph}^{n+1} = S_{ph}^0 + \frac{1-\alpha}{M(\alpha)}K(t_n, S_{ph}^n, S_{cr}^n, X^n)$$
$$+ \frac{\alpha}{M(\alpha)}\int_0^{t_{n+1}} K(\tau, S_{ph}, S_{cr}, X)d\tau$$

$$S_{cr}^{n+1} = S_{cr}^0 + \frac{1-\alpha}{M(\alpha)}L(t_n, S_{ph}^n, S_{cr}^n, X^n)$$
$$+ \frac{\alpha}{M(\alpha)}\int_0^{t_{n+1}} L(\tau, S_{ph}, S_{cr}, X)d\tau$$

$$X^{n+1} = X^0 + \frac{1-\alpha}{M(\alpha)}M(t_n, S_{ph}^n, S_{cr}^n, X^n)$$
$$+ \frac{\alpha}{M(\alpha)}\int_0^{t_{n+1}} M(\tau, S_{ph}, S_{cr}, X)d\tau$$

and

$$S_{ph}^n = S_{ph}^0 + \frac{1-\alpha}{M(\alpha)} K(t_{n-1}, S_{ph}^{n-1}, S_{cr}^{n-1}, X^{n-1})$$
$$+ \frac{\alpha}{M(\alpha)} \int_0^{t_n} K(\tau, S_{ph}, S_{cr}, X) d\tau$$
$$S_{cr}^n = S_{cr}^0 + \frac{1-\alpha}{M(\alpha)} L(t_{n-1}, S_{ph}^{n-1}, S_{cr}^{n-1}, X^{n-1})$$
$$+ \frac{\alpha}{M(\alpha)} \int_0^{t_n} L(\tau, S_{ph}, S_{cr}, X) d\tau$$
$$X^n = X^0 + \frac{1-\alpha}{M(\alpha)} M(t_{n-1}, S_{ph}^{n-1}, S_{cr}^{n-1}, X^{n-1})$$
$$+ \frac{\alpha}{M(\alpha)} \int_0^{t_n} M(\tau, S_{ph}, S_{cr}, X) d\tau$$

Thus, we reach

$$S_{ph}^{n+1} = S_{ph}^n + \frac{1-\alpha}{M(\alpha)} \left(K(t_n, S_{ph}^n, S_{cr}^n, X^n) - K(t_{n-1}, S_{ph}^{n-1}, S_{cr}^{n-1}, X^{n-1}) \right)$$
$$+ \frac{\alpha}{M(\alpha)} \int_{t_n}^{t_{n+1}} K(\tau, S_{ph}, S_{cr}, X) d\tau$$
$$S_{cr}^{n+1} = S_{cr}^n + \frac{1-\alpha}{M(\alpha)} \left(L(t_n, S_{ph}^n, S_{cr}^n, X^n) - L(t_{n-1}, S_{ph}^{n-1}, S_{cr}^{n-1}, X^{n-1}) \right)$$
$$+ \frac{\alpha}{M(\alpha)} \int_{t_n}^{t_{n+1}} L(\tau, S_{ph}, S_{cr}, X) d\tau$$
$$X^{n+1} = X^n + \frac{1-\alpha}{M(\alpha)} \left(M(t_n, S_{ph}^n, S_{cr}^n, X^n) - M(t_{n-1}, S_{ph}^{n-1}, S_{cr}^{n-1}, X^{n-1}) \right)$$
$$+ \frac{\alpha}{M(\alpha)} \int_{t_n}^{t_{n+1}} M(\tau, S_{ph}, S_{cr}, X) d\tau$$

Using the two-step Lagrange polynomial yields, we receive:

$$S_{ph}^{n+1} = S_{ph}^n + \frac{1-\alpha}{M(\alpha)} \left(K(t_n, S_{ph}^n, S_{cr}^n, X^n) - K(t_{n-1}, S_{ph}^{n-1}, S_{cr}^{n-1}, X^{n-1}) \right)$$
$$+ \frac{\alpha}{M(\alpha)} \left(\frac{3h}{2} K(t_n, S_{ph}^n, S_{cr}^n, X^n) - \frac{h}{2} K(t_{n-1}, S_{ph}^{n-1}, S_{cr}^{n-1}, X^{n-1}) \right)$$
$$S_{cr}^{n+1} = S_{cr}^n + \frac{1-\alpha}{M(\alpha)} \left(L(t_n, S_{ph}^n, S_{cr}^n, X^n) - L(t_{n-1}, S_{ph}^{n-1}, S_{cr}^{n-1}, X^{n-1}) \right)$$
$$+ \frac{\alpha}{M(\alpha)} \left(\frac{3h}{2} L(t_n, S_{ph}^n, S_{cr}^n, X^n) - \frac{h}{2} L(t_{n-1}, S_{ph}^{n-1}, S_{cr}^{n-1}, X^{n-1}) \right)$$
$$X^{n+1} = X^n + \frac{1-\alpha}{M(\alpha)} \left(M(t_n, S_{ph}^n, S_{cr}^n, X^n) - M(t_{n-1}, S_{ph}^{n-1}, S_{cr}^{n-1}, X^{n-1}) \right)$$
$$+ \frac{\alpha}{M(\alpha)} \left(\frac{3h}{2} M(t_n, S_{ph}^n, S_{cr}^n, X^n) - \frac{h}{2} M(t_{n-1}, S_{ph}^{n-1}, S_{cr}^{n-1}, X^{n-1}) \right)$$

Thus, the numerical scheme for the model with exponential decay kernel has been obtained. We used this scheme and obtained Figures 5–8.

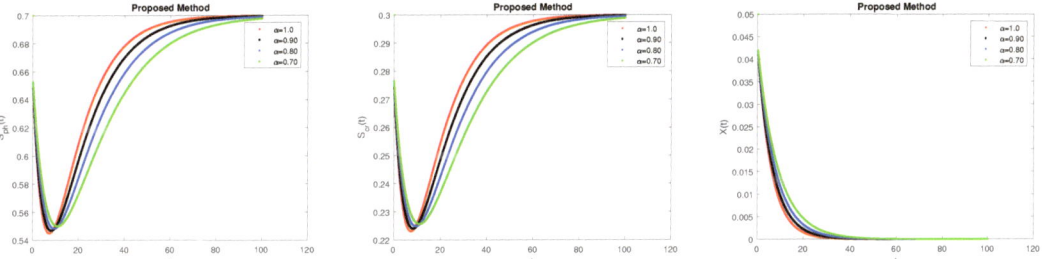

Figure 5. Solutions of (39)–(41) for $\beta = 1$, fractal dimension 1, and $\alpha = 1, 0.9, 0.8$, and 0.7 with exponential decay kernel.

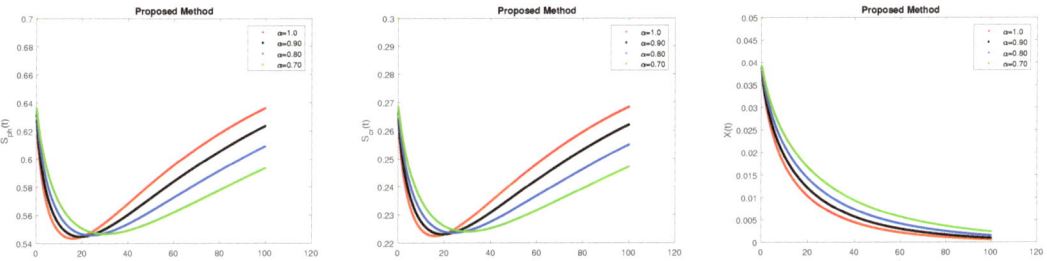

Figure 6. Solutions of (39)–(41) for $\beta = 1$, fractal dimension 0.7, and $\alpha = 1, 0.9, 0.8$, and 0.7 with exponential decay kernel.

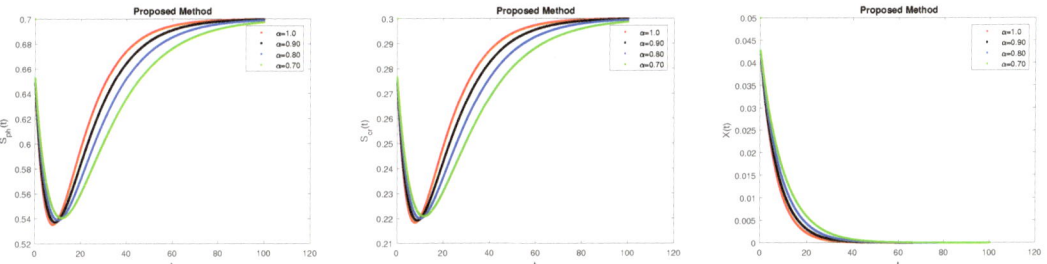

Figure 7. Solutions of (39)–(41) for $\beta = 0.8$, fractal dimension 1, and $\alpha = 1, 0.9, 0.8$, and 0.7 with exponential decay kernel.

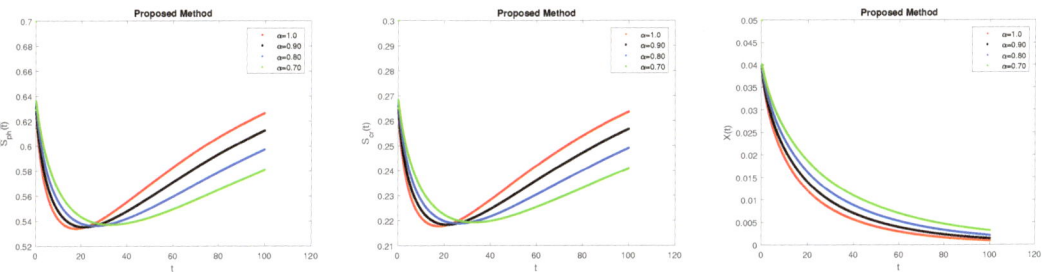

Figure 8. Solutions of (39)–(41) for $\beta = 0.8$, fractal dimension 0.7, and $\alpha = 1, 0.9, 0.8$, and 0.7 with exponential decay kernel.

6. Analysis of the Model with the Mittag–Leffler Kernel

Now, we analyze the model with fractional differentiation operator using the Mittag–Leffler kernel as:

$${}_0^{FFM}D_t^{\alpha,\eta}S_{ph} = D(S_{ph0} - S_{ph}) - k_{ph}\cdot\mu(S_{ph}, S_{cr})\cdot X. \quad (51)$$

$${}_0^{FFM}D_t^{\alpha,\eta}S_{cr} = D(S_{cr0} - S_{cr}) - k_{cr}\cdot\mu(S_{ph}, S_{cr})\cdot X. \quad (52)$$

$${}_0^{FFM}D_t^{\alpha,\eta}X = -D\beta X + \mu(S_{ph}, S_{cr})X. \quad (53)$$

Then, we obtain

$${}_0^{AB}D_t^{\alpha}S_{ph} = \eta t^{\eta-1}\left(D(S_{ph0} - S_{ph}) - k_{ph}\cdot\mu(S_{ph}, S_{cr})\cdot X\right). \quad (54)$$

$${}_0^{AB}D_t^{\alpha}S_{cr} = \eta t^{\eta-1}\left(D(S_{cr0} - S_{cr}) - k_{cr}\cdot\mu(S_{ph}, S_{cr})\cdot X\right). \quad (55)$$

$${}_0^{AB}D_t^{\alpha}X = \eta t^{\eta-1}\left(-D\beta X + \mu(S_{ph}, S_{cr})X\right). \quad (56)$$

For simplicity, we define

$$Y(t, S_{ph}, S_{cr}, X) = \eta t^{\eta-1}\left(D(S_{ph0} - S_{ph}) - k_{ph}\cdot\mu(S_{ph}, S_{cr})\cdot X\right). \quad (57)$$

$$Z(t, S_{ph}, S_{cr}, X) = \eta t^{\eta-1}\left(D(S_{cr0} - S_{cr}) - k_{cr}\cdot\mu(S_{ph}, S_{cr})\cdot X\right). \quad (58)$$

$$T(t, S_{ph}, S_{cr}, X) = \eta t^{\eta-1}\left(-D\beta X + \mu(S_{ph}, S_{cr})X\right). \quad (59)$$

Then, we receive

$$ {}_0^{AB}D_t^{\alpha}S_{ph} = Y(t, S_{ph}, S_{cr}, X). \quad (60)$$

$$ {}_0^{AB}D_t^{\alpha}S_{cr} = Z(t, S_{ph}, S_{cr}, X). \quad (61)$$

$$ {}_0^{AB}D_t^{\alpha}X = T(t, S_{ph}, S_{cr}, X). \quad (62)$$

Applying the AB integral gives:

$$S_{ph}(t) - S_{ph}(0) = \frac{1-\alpha}{AB(\alpha)}Y(t, S_{ph}, S_{cr}, X) + \frac{\alpha}{AB(\alpha)\Gamma(\alpha)}\int_0^t (t-p)^{\alpha-1}Y(p, S_{ph}, S_{cr}, X)dp.$$

$$S_{cr}(t) - S_{cr}(0) = \frac{1-\alpha}{AB(\alpha)}Z(t, S_{ph}, S_{cr}, X) + \frac{\alpha}{AB(\alpha)\Gamma(\alpha)}\int_0^t (t-p)^{\alpha-1}Z(p, S_{ph}, S_{cr}, X)dp.$$

$$X(t) - X(0) = \frac{1-\alpha}{AB(\alpha)}T(t, S_{ph}, S_{cr}, X) + \frac{\alpha}{AB(\alpha)\Gamma(\alpha)}\int_0^t (t-p)^{\alpha-1}T(p, S_{ph}, S_{cr}, X)dp.$$

Discretizing the above equations at t_{n+1}, we receive:

$$S_{ph}^{n+1} = S_{ph}^0 + \frac{1-\alpha}{AB(\alpha)} Y(t_{n+1}, S_{ph}^n, S_{cr}^n, X^n)$$
$$+ \frac{\alpha}{AB(\alpha)\Gamma(\alpha)} \int_0^{t_{n+1}} (t_{n+1}-p)^{\alpha-1} Y(p, S_{ph}, S_{cr}, X) dp$$
$$S_{cr}^{n+1} = S_{cr}^0 + \frac{1-\alpha}{AB(\alpha)} Z(t_{n+1}, S_{ph}^n, S_{cr}^n, X^n)$$
$$+ \frac{\alpha}{AB(\alpha)\Gamma(\alpha)} \int_0^{t_{n+1}} (t_{n+1}-p)^{\alpha-1} Z(p, S_{ph}, S_{cr}, X) dp$$
$$X^{n+1} = X^0 + \frac{1-\alpha}{AB(\alpha)} T(t_{n+1}, S_{ph}^n, S_{cr}^n, X^n)$$
$$+ \frac{\alpha}{AB(\alpha)\Gamma(\alpha)} \int_0^{t_{n+1}} (t_{n+1}-p)^{\alpha-1} T(p, S_{ph}, S_{cr}, X) dp$$

Then, we obtain

$$S_{ph}^{n+1} = S_{ph}^0 + \frac{1-\alpha}{AB(\alpha)} Y(t_{n+1}, S_{ph}^n, S_{cr}^n, X^n)$$
$$+ \frac{\alpha}{AB(\alpha)} \sum_{i=0}^n \left[\frac{h^\alpha Y(t_i, S_{ph}^n, S_{cr}^n, X^n)}{\Gamma(\alpha+2)} ((n+1-i)^\alpha (n-i+2+\alpha) \right.$$
$$\left. - (n-i)^\alpha (n-i+2+2\alpha)) \right]$$
$$- \frac{\alpha}{AB(\alpha)} \sum_{i=0}^n \left[\frac{h^\alpha Y(t_{i-1}, S_{ph}^{n-1}, S_{cr}^{n-1}, X^{n-1})}{\Gamma(\alpha+2)} ((n+1-i)^{\alpha+1} \right.$$
$$\left. - (n-i)^\alpha (n-i+1+\alpha)) \right]$$

$$S_{cr}^{n+1} = S_{cr}^0 + \frac{1-\alpha}{AB(\alpha)} Z(t_{n+1}, S_{ph}^n, S_{cr}^n, X^n)$$
$$+ \frac{\alpha}{AB(\alpha)} \sum_{i=0}^n \left[\frac{h^\alpha Z(t_i, S_{ph}^n, S_{cr}^n, X^n)}{\Gamma(\alpha+2)} ((n+1-i)^\alpha (n-i+2+\alpha) \right.$$
$$\left. - (n-i)^\alpha (n-i+2+2\alpha)) \right]$$
$$- \frac{\alpha}{AB(\alpha)} \sum_{i=0}^n \left[\frac{h^\alpha Z(t_{i-1}, S_{ph}^{n-1}, S_{cr}^{n-1}, X^{n-1})}{\Gamma(\alpha+2)} ((n+1-i)^{\alpha+1} \right.$$
$$\left. - (n-i)^\alpha (n-i+1+\alpha)) \right]$$

$$X^{n+1} = X^0 + \frac{1-\alpha}{AB(\alpha)} T(t_{n+1}, S_{ph}^n, S_{cr}^n, X^n)$$
$$+ \frac{\alpha}{AB(\alpha)} \sum_{i=0}^n \left[\frac{h^\alpha T(t_i, S_{ph}^n, S_{cr}^n, X^n)}{\Gamma(\alpha+2)} ((n+1-i)^\alpha (n-i+2+\alpha) \right.$$
$$\left. - (n-i)^\alpha (n-i+2+2\alpha)) \right]$$
$$- \frac{\alpha}{AB(\alpha)} \sum_{i=0}^n \left[\frac{h^\alpha T(t_{i-1}, S_{ph}^{n-1}, S_{cr}^{n-1}, X^{n-1})}{\Gamma(\alpha+2)} ((n+1-i)^{\alpha+1} \right.$$
$$\left. - (n-i)^\alpha (n-i+1+\alpha)) \right].$$

Thus, the numerical scheme for the model with Mittag–Leffler kernel has been obtained. We used this scheme and obtained Figures 9–12.

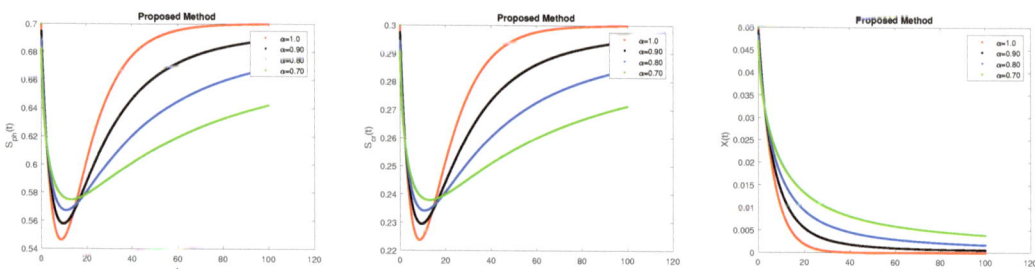

Figure 9. Solutions of (54)–(56) for $\beta = 1$, fractal dimension 1, and $\alpha = 1, 0.9, 0.8,$ and 0.7 with Mittag–Leffler kernel.

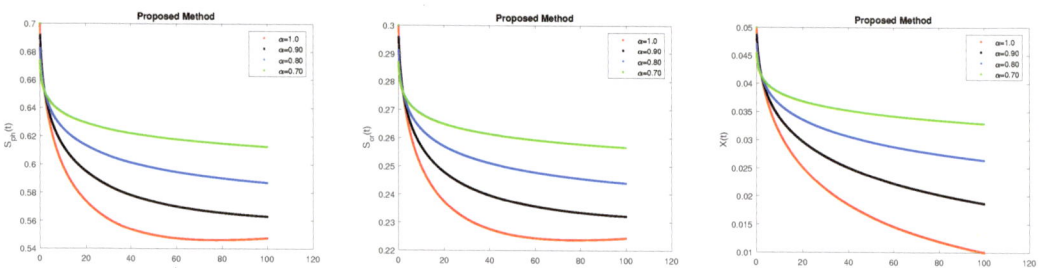

Figure 10. Solutions of (39)–(41) for $\beta = 1$, fractal dimension 0.5, and $\alpha = 1, 0.9, 0.8,$ and 0.7 with Mittag–Leffler kernel.

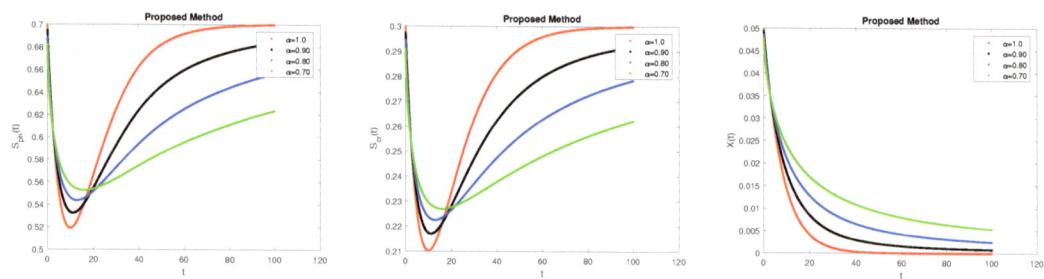

Figure 11. Solutions of (39)–(41) for $\beta = 0.5$, fractal dimension 1, and $\alpha = 1, 0.9, 0.8,$ and 0.7 with Mittag–Leffler kernel.

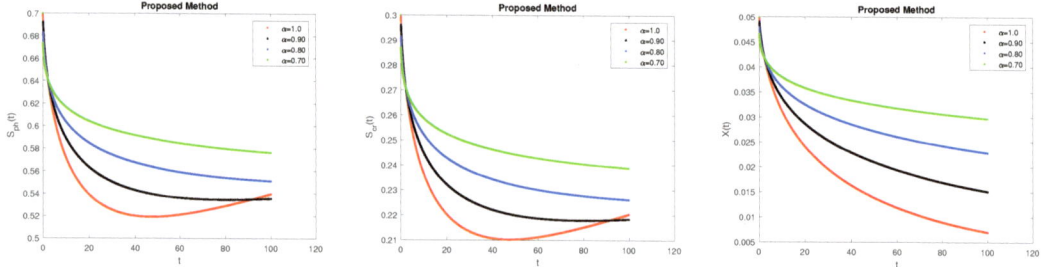

Figure 12. Solutions of (39)–(41) for $\beta = 0.5$, fractal dimension 0.6, and $\alpha = 1, 0.9, 0.8,$ and 0.7 with Mittag–Leffler kernel.

Remark 1. *A valuable and huge benefit of fractional differentiation operator is that we can formulate models better defining the systems with memory effects. It is known that the use of integro-*

differential kernels of a certain type in integro-differential equations leads us to the fractional derivative operator [31]. The kernels with degree functions in integro-differential equations of the Voltaire type [32], allow us to describe this memory effect [33,34].

Fractal–fractional operators with different memories are related to the non-local dynamical systems' different types of relaxation processes. Thus, models with fractional differentiation operators are more effective and valuable.

7. Results and Discussions

In this section, we present numerical simulations for different fractional order and fractal dimension values. We also add the classical derivative with the integer fractal dimension equal to 1.

We chose fractal dimension as the integer and noninteger in the figures. We discuss the results with the three kernels described in Sections 5–7. The figures α, β, and η are between zero and one. In these simulations, β is the parameter given on the model, η is the fractal dimension, and α is the fractional order. We see the effect of the fractional order α under different kernels and values of the parameter β and the fractal dimension η. Figures 1 and 2 show the numerical simulations for $\beta = 1$, the fractal dimensions $\eta = 1$ and $\eta = 0.8$, and for different fractional order α values with the power-law kernel. We also show how this kernel behaves for $\beta = 0.5$ and the fractal dimension $\eta = 1$ and $\eta = 0.9$ in Figures 3 and 4. We see that the convergence is faster for the case $\beta = 1$ than to the case $\beta = 0.5$, as long as the fractal dimension is close to 1. The concentrations $S_{ph}(t)$ and $S_{cr}(t)$ decrease as long as α decreases. In all the cases, the concentration $X(t)$ decreases to 0.

The results for the exponential-decay kernel are shown for $\beta = 1$ in Figure 5 (with fractal dimension $\eta = 1$) and Figure 6 (with fractal dimension $\eta = 0.7$). We demonstrate the results for $\beta = 0.8$ and $\eta = 1$ (Figure 7) and $\eta = 0.7$ (Figure 8). Despite varying the parameters β, α, and the fractal dimension, there are fewer differences in the concentrations with respect to the results shown by the power-law kernel.

Finally, in Figures 9–12, we show the results for the Mittag–Leffler kernel. The numerical simulations for $\beta = 1$ are shown in Figure 9 ($\eta = 1$) and Figure 10 ($\eta = 0.5$). We also see the behavior of the solution for $\beta = 0.5, \eta = 1$ in Figure 11 and $\beta = 0.5, \eta = 0.6$ in Figure 12.

We have seen that the exponential-decay kernel is the one that converges faster to the equilibrium, with the smaller difference among concentrations of the substances.

8. Conclusions

This work provides a mathematical model for breaking down a phenol and p-cresol mixture in a bioreactor with continuous stirring. Three nonlinear ordinary differential equations served as the foundation for the model. The equilibrium points of the model were identified, and their stability was examined and shown. Additionally, we used the fractional differentiation operator to examine the model and three distinct kernels to examine the effects of the fractal dimension and fractional order. We developed very efficient numerical algorithms for biomass, phenol, and p-cresol concentrations. To demonstrate the accuracy of the suggested approach, we offered numerical simulations for different α and β values. The right choice of model parameters would require validation with experimental data.

Author Contributions: Conceptualization, A.A. and J.A.C.; methodology, A.A. and J.A.C.; software, A.A.; formal analysis, A.A. and J.A.C.; investigation, A.A. and J.A.C.; writing—original draft preparation, A.A.; writing—review and editing, A.A. and J.A.C. All authors have read and agreed to the published version of the manuscript.

Funding: JAC is supported by Generalitat Valenciana, Project PROMETEO CIPROM/2022/21.

Data Availability Statement: All data used in this work has been obtained from the mathematical formulas described in the paper.

Conflicts of Interest: The authors declare no conflicts of interest.

References

1. Dimitrova, N.; Zlateva, P. Global stability analysis of a bioreactor model for phenol and cresol mixture degradation. *Process* **2021**, *9*, 124. [CrossRef]
2. Seo, J.S.; Keum, Y.S.; Li, Q.X. Bacterial degradation of aromatic compounds. *Int. J. Environ. Res. Public Health* **2009**, *6*, 278–30. [CrossRef]
3. Sharma, N.K.; Philip, L.; Bhallamudi, S.M. Aerobic degradation of phenolics and aromatic hydrocarbons in presence of cyanic *Bioresour. Technol.* **2012**, *121*, 263–273. [CrossRef]
4. Tomei, M.C.; Annesini, M.C. Biodegradation of phenolic mixtures in a sequencing batch reactor: A kinetic study. *Environ. S Pollut. Res.* **2008**, *15*, 188–195. [CrossRef]
5. Yemendzhiev, H.; Zlateva, P.; Alexieva, Z. Comparison of the biodegradation capacity of two fungal strains toward a mixture phenol and cresol by mathematical modeling. *Biotechnol. Biotechnol. Equip.* **2012**, *26*, 3278–3281. [CrossRef]
6. Kietkwanboot, A.; Chaiprapat, S.; Müller, R.; Suttinun, O. Biodegradation of phenolic compounds present in palm oil mill efflue as single and mixed substrates by Trameteshirsuta AK04. *J. Environ. Sci. Health Part A Toxic/Hazard. Subst. Environ. Eng.* **2020**, 989–1002.
7. Momani, S. An explicit and numerical solutions of the fractional KdV equation. *Math. Comput. Simul.* **2005**, *70*, 110–1 [CrossRef]
8. Li, C.; Cao, J. A finite difference method for time-fractional telegraph equation. In Proceedings of the IEEE/ASME Internation Conference on Mechatronics and Embedded Systems and Applications (MESA), Suzhou, China, 8–10 July 2012; pp. 314–318.
9. Huang, F.; Liu, F. The fundamental solution of the space-time fractional advection-dispersion equation. *J. Appl. Math. Comp* **2005**, *18*, 21–36. [CrossRef]
10. Bhrawy, A.H.; Doha, E.H.; Ezz-Eldien, S.S.; Van Gorder, R.A. A new Jacobi spectral collocation method for solving $(1+1)$fraction Schrodinger equations and fractional coupled Schrodinger systems. *Eur. Phys. J. Plus* **2014**, *129*, 260. [CrossRef]
11. Karatay, T.; Bayramoglu, S.R.; Sahin, A. Implicit difference approximation for the time fractional heat equation with the nonloc condition. *Appl. Numer. Math.* **2011**, *61*, 1281–1288. [CrossRef]
12. Chen, Y.; Yi, M.; Chen, C.; Yu, C. Bernstein polynomials method for fractional convection-diffusion equation with variab coefficients. *Comput. Model. Eng. Sci.* **2012**, *83*, 639–653.
13. Liu, F.; Anh, V.; Turner, I. Numerical solution of space fractional FokkerPlanck equation. *J. Comp. Appl. Math.* **2004**, *166*, 209–2 [CrossRef]
14. Fuente, D.; Lizama, C.; Urchueguía, J.F.; Conejero, J.A. Estimation of the light field inside photosynthetic microorganism cultur through Mittag-Leffler functions at depleted light conditions. *J. Quant. Spectrosc. Radiat. Transf.* **2018**, *204*, 23–26. [CrossRef]
15. Lizama, C.; Murillo-Arcila, M.; Trujillo, M. Fractional Beer-Lambert law in laser heating of biological tissue. *AIMS Math.* **2022**, 14444–14459. [CrossRef]
16. Momani, S.; Odibat, Z. Comparison between the homotopy perturbation method and the variational iteration method for line fractional partial differential equations. *Comput. Math. Appl.* **2007**, *54*, 910–919. [CrossRef]
17. El-Sayed, A.M.A.; Gaber, M. The Adomian decomposition method for solving partial differential equations of fractal order finite domains. *Phys. Lett. A* **2006**, *359*, 175–182. [CrossRef]
18. Ahmad, H.; Khan, M.N.; Ahmad, I.; Omri, M.; Alotaibi, M.F. A meshless method for numerical solutions of linear and nonline time-fractional Black-Scholes models. *AIMS Math.* **2023**, *8*, 19677–19698. [CrossRef]
19. Khaliq, S.; Ahmad, S.; Ullah, A.; Ahmad, H.; Saifullah, S.; Nofal, T.A. New waves solutions of the $(2+1)$-dimensional generalize Hirota–Satsuma–Ito equation using a novel expansion method. *Res. Phys.* **2023**, *50*, 106450. [CrossRef]
20. Adel, M.; Khader, M.M.; Ahmad, H.; Assiri, T.A. Approximate analytical solutions for the blood ethanol concentration syste and predator-prey equations by using variational iteration method. *AIMS Math.* **2023**, *8*, 19083–19096. [CrossRef]
21. Atangana, A. Fractal-fractional differentiation and integration: Connecting fractal calculus and fractional calculus to pred complex, system. *Chaos Solitons Fractals* **2017**, *102*, 396–406. [CrossRef]
22. Toufik, M.; Atangana, A. New numerical approximation of fractional derivative with non-local and non-singular kern Application to chaotic models. *Eur. Phys. J. Plus* 132, **2017**, *10*, 444. [CrossRef]
23. Mohammadi, H.; Kumar, S.; Rezapour, S.; Etemad, S. A theoretical study of the Caputo-Fabrizio fractional modeling for hearing loss due to Mumps virus with optimal control. *Chaos Solitons Fractals* **2021**, *144*, 110668. [CrossRef]
24. Baleanu, D.; Jajarmi, A.; Mohammadi, H.; Rezapour, S. A new study on the mathematical modelling of human liver wi Caputo-Fabrizio fractional derivative. *Chaos Solitons Fractals* **2021**, *134*, 109705. [CrossRef]
25. Alzabut, J.; Selvam, A.; Dhineshbabu, R.; Tyagi, S.; Ghaderi, M.; Rezapour, S. A Caputo discrete fractional-order thermos model with one and two sensors fractional boundary conditions depending on positive parameters by using the Lipschitz-ty inequality. *J. Inequal. Appl.* **2022**, *2022*, 56. [CrossRef]
26. Heydarpour, Z.; Izadi, J.; George, R.; Ghaderi, M.; Rezapour, S. On a partial fractional hybrid version of generalized Sturr Liouville–Langevin equation. *Fractal Fract.* **2022**, *6*, 269. [CrossRef]
27. George, R.; Houas, M.; Ghaderi, M.; Rezapour, S.; Elagan, S.K. On a coupled system of pantograph problem with three sequent fractional derivatives by using positive contraction-type inequalities. *Results Phys.* **2022**, *39*, 105687. [CrossRef]
28. Matar, M.M.; Abbas, M.I.; Alzabut, J.; Kaabar, M.K.A.; Etemad, S.; Rezapour, S. Investigation of the p-Laplacian nonperiod nonlinear boundary value problem via generalized Caputo fractional derivatives. *Adv. Differ. Equ.* **2021**, *2021*, 68. [CrossRef]

compartments in the model, where the individuals spend an average time before moving out of the compartment. Introducing delays is a straightforward way of adding the dependence of the past to a biological process. Adding delays may change the dynamics of the process [1–3]. Some possible changes are the introduction of oscillations, the introduction of discontinuities in the time derivatives, the non-uniqueness of solutions, and different stability regions. There is a vast amount of literature spanning many years on epidemic or disease transmission models using delay differential equations (DDEs) (see, for example, [1,4–8]). For epidemic models at the population level, the time between a susceptible having contact with an infective and actually getting the disease (time of infection) is the most commonly considered delay. But there are also other delays like maturation times, the time it takes a vaccine to become effective, the time it takes an infected individual to recover after getting the disease, etc. For a within-host infection, delays include the time it takes the pathogen to replicate or reproduce and spread over the affected organ, the time it takes the immune system to react, and the time it takes cells to reproduce, among others. There are different types of delays. Discrete-constant delays are used when each delay has the same value for the entire population. Distributed or continuous delays are used when the delay varies according to a given distribution, such as normal or gamma, around the mean value. In this paper, we will only consider discrete delays. Fractional calculus started with a letter from L'Hôpital to Leibniz asking about derivatives in non-integer order. There are several different definitions for fractional derivatives and integrals, with the most common ones being the Riemann–Liouville and the Caputo versions. There are many good papers and books about differential equations using fractional derivatives (FDEs), such as [9–12]. In recent years, a vast number of papers have used fractional derivatives in epidemic models, including many for specific epidemics such as influenza, dengue, and COVID-19 [13–17]. The Caputo form is the most widely used fractional derivative. It has the advantages that its derivative of a constant is zero and for FDEs, the initial conditions are given in terms of the unknown and, if necessary, integer-order derivatives at the initial point. Exact solutions of FDEs are hard to find. There are several numerical methods [18–21]. Fractional derivatives are non-local operators that involve the solution from the initial time until the current time. So, the solution at the current time depends on the solution at all previous times, so FDEs incorporate memory. ODEs neglect such effects. In addition, when fitting data, fractional models have more degrees of freedom through the orders of the fractional derivatives compared to ODE models. In fact, many papers that use fractional derivative models for epidemics justify their use by demonstrating superior data fitting compared to ordinary differential equation models. This has been done for different epidemics such as dengue, Ebola, and COVID-19 [14,22,23]. Discrete-time fractional differential equations have also been used [24–26] but not as widely as continuous-time fractional differential equations. Possible reasons for this are that popular methods become more popular and the widespread availability of ready-to-use software for FDEs. A third way of introducing dependence on the past in a population mathematical model is to add more compartments. For models including birth processes, this can be achieved by adding an immature population, with individuals staying in this compartment for an average time equal to the maturation period. Examples involving insect populations can be found in [27,28]. In epidemic models, this can be achieved by adding an exposed population [29–31]. The dependence of solutions on past values is a topic of very high interest, especially in epidemics, with some recent references being [32–36]. The main objective of this paper is to study how to introduce dependence on past values into ordinary differential models of population growth and disease transmission. This is discussed in Section 2. In Section 3, results and numerical simulations are presented. Finally, in Section 4, a discussion of the results is presented.

2. Materials and Methods

In this section, we present the addition of dependence on the past using delays, fractional derivatives, and additional compartments to several compartmental models of population growth, epidemics, and within-host infection propagation.

We start with very simple models and continue to more complicated ones. For all examples, dependence on the past is added to the ODE model using three methods. The first method is to introduce discrete delays. While this can be done in several ways, not all of them make biological sense. The second method is to use non-local fractional derivatives instead of time derivatives. The third method is to add more population compartments, such as immature or exposed populations, and incorporate dependence on the past based on the time individuals spend in these compartments. For the simplest model considered, with one population and described by a linear differential equation, it is possible to calculate exact solutions for the original ODE and all models based on the three methods. For the delay differential equation models, the solution requires numerical approximation of the solution of a transcendental equation. For the logistic model, there is an exact solution only for the ODE, but stability can be found for all models. For the epidemic models, there are no exact solutions, and the local asymptotic stability of the disease-free equilibrium can be determined for all methods. But the expressions become more complicated with the complexity of the model.

The pyramid flowchart depicted in Figure 1 illustrates the sequence of models used in this paper. These models progress from linear, with one state given by the Malthus model, to non-linear, with one state given by the logistic model, and finally, to non-linear epidemic models with several states, each increasing in complexity. ODE refers to the corresponding ordinary differential equations model, DDE refers to the delay differential equations model, EXP refers to the model with immature or exposed populations, and FRAC refers to the fractional differential equations model. E indicates that the model has an exact solution, S indicates the local asymptotic stability of the steady states for the Malthus and logistic models, and of the disease-free equilibrium for the infection models. These results are shown later in this section. In Section 3, the simulations show that all methods that incorporate dependence on the past can produce similar results, except for the fractional derivative equations models, where this holds true only for specific values of the fractional order.

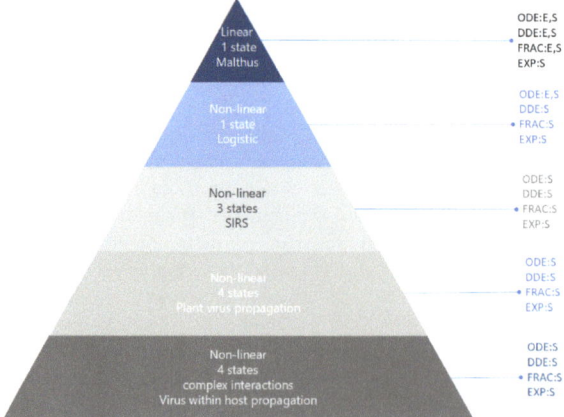

Figure 1. Flow diagram for the sequence of models used, from simplest to most complex. ODE is the ordinary differential equations model, DDE is the delay differential equations model, EXP is the model with immature or exposed populations, and FRAC is the fractional differential equations model. E indicates that the model has an exact solution, S indicates the local asymptotic stability of the steady states for the Malthus and logistic models, and of the disease-free equilibrium for the infection models.

2.1. Population Growth Models

Many mathematical population models can be derived by starting with a discrete-time population model [37,38]. All these models state that the current population is equal to the population at the previous time plus its change during the time step. For example, for a model considering only birth and death processes, the population at time $t + \Delta t$ can be given as the population at time t plus the new births minus the new deaths. The discrete-time model is

$$N(t + \Delta t) = N(t) + \Delta t b N(t) - \Delta t \mu N(t),$$

where $N(t)$ is the population at time t, $b > 0$ is the birth rate, and $\mu > 0$ is the death rate. By taking the limit as Δt tends to 0, we obtain the simplest continuous-time population model known as the Malthus model

$$\frac{dN}{dt} = (b - \mu)N(t). \tag{1}$$

For many populations, there is a delay $\tau > 0$ due to the maturation time in the birth process. But the number of deaths depends only on the current population. By adding a delay to the discrete-time model, we obtain

$$N(t + \Delta t) = N(t) + \Delta t b N(t - k\Delta t) - \Delta t \mu N(t),$$

where the delay is $\tau = k\Delta t$, with k being a positive integer. Again, taking the limit as Δt tends to 0 and keeping $k\Delta t$ constant, we obtain the delayed continuous-time model

$$\frac{dN}{dt} = bN(t - \tau) - \mu N(t) \tag{2}$$

that takes into consideration the maturation time. The Malthus model and the delayed Malthus model have only one equilibrium point, $N(t) = 0$. One issue with using the DDE model is that it requires initial values on the history interval $[t_0 - \tau, t_0]$, where t_0 is the initial time.

Instead of having a single value, the maturation time may take values in an interval $[k_i \Delta t, k_f \Delta t]$, where $0 \leq k_i \leq k_f$. The model is

$$N(t + \Delta t) = N(t) + \Delta t b \sum_{k=k_i}^{k_f} G(t - k\Delta t) N(t - k\Delta t) - \Delta t \mu N(t), \tag{3}$$

where $G(t - k\Delta t)$ is a weighting function with an average of one.

By taking the limit as Δt tends to 0 and keeping the terms $k\Delta t$ constant, $k = k_i, \ldots, k_f$, one obtains the distributed delay equation

$$\frac{dN}{dt} = \int_{-\infty}^{t} G(t - s) b N(t - s) \, ds - \mu N(t).$$

The function G is taken to have compact support and an average of 1. Usually, it has a very small support. For a discrete delay, it is taken as a Dirac delta function. The birth function bN can be replaced with another birth function or with a function F representing other processes happening in the past. Also, the death term μN can be substituted with a function H representing all the processes happening at the present time. A more general integro-differential equation for the growth of one population can be written as

$$\frac{dN}{dt} = \int_{-\infty}^{t} G(t - s) F(N(t - s)) \, ds - H(N(t)). \tag{4}$$

A discrete-time model that considers an immature population is

$$N(t + \Delta t) = N(t) + \Delta t \sigma Y(t) - \Delta t \mu N(t)$$
$$Y(t + \Delta t) = Y(t) + bN(t) - \Delta t \mu Y(t) - \Delta t \sigma Y(t),$$

where $Y(t)$ is the immature or young population, all new births are immature, and $\sigma = 1/\tau$ is the rate at which the immature population matures. Taking the limit as Δt tends to 0, we obtain the ODE model that consists of a system of equations for the two age groups, mature, N, and immature, Y [27,28],

$$\frac{dN}{dt} = \sigma Y - \mu N$$
$$\frac{dY}{dt} = bN - \sigma Y - \mu Y. \tag{5}$$

A modification of Malthus's continuous-time model using fractional derivatives is introduced later in this subsection.

A second population growth model that adds intra-species competition for resources is the logistic growth model given by

$$\frac{dN}{dt} = rN(t)\left(1 - \frac{N(t)}{K}\right), \tag{6}$$

where $N(t)$ is the population, $r = b - \mu$ is the growth rate, and K is the carrying capacity.

The maturation time delay can again be introduced into the birth term:

$$\frac{dN}{dt} = bN(t - \tau) - r\frac{N(t)^2}{K} - \mu N(t). \tag{7}$$

The competition and death terms depend on the current time t. One disadvantage of delay differential equations is that they require initial conditions given on the interval $[t_0 - \tau, t_0]$, where t_0 is the initial time. This interval is usually called the history interval.

Following the approach used in the Malthus model, an alternative way of adding dependence on the past is to introduce an immature population

$$\frac{dN}{t} = \sigma Y - rN^2/K - \mu N$$
$$\frac{dY}{dt} = bN - rY^2/K - \sigma Y - \mu Y, \tag{8}$$

where $r = b - \mu$ and σ is 1 over the maturation time. We assume that there is no competition between the adult and the immature populations, as is the case for insects, where the larvae feed on different food than the adults. But there are several other ways of introducing the immature population.

Before writing the model using FDEs, we introduce some definitions. The Caputo fractional derivative, which is now the most commonly used fractional operator in mathematical biology models, is obtained by modifying the definition of the Riemann–Liouville fractional derivative to regularize the initial conditions, so they are stated only in terms of ordinary derivatives [9,10]. In our definitions of Riemann–Liouville and Caputo fractional derivatives, we consider that the initial time is $t = 0$. The Riemann–Liouville fractional derivative is

$$^R_0D_t^\alpha y(t) = \frac{1}{\Gamma(m - \alpha)} \frac{d^m}{dt^m} \int_0^t (t - \tau)^{-\alpha - 1 + m} y(\tau) d\tau, \quad m - 1 < \alpha < m,$$

and the Caputo fractional derivative is

$$^C_0D_t^\alpha y(t) = \frac{1}{\Gamma(m - \alpha)} \int_0^t (t - \tau)^{-\alpha - 1 + m} \frac{d^m}{d\tau^m} y(\tau) d\tau, \quad m - 1 < \alpha < m, \tag{9}$$

where α is the order of the derivative. These two definitions are not equivalent to each other. Their difference is expressed by

$$_0^C D_t^\alpha y(t) = {_0^R} D_t^\alpha y(t) - \sum_{\nu=0}^{m-1} r_\nu^\alpha(t) y^{(\nu)}(0), \quad r_\nu^\alpha(t) = \frac{t^{\nu-\alpha}}{\Gamma(\nu+1-\alpha)}.$$

The Caputo operator $_0^C D_t^\alpha$ has the advantage for differential equations with initial values in that these initial values are given in terms of ordinary derivatives. The initial values for Caputo differential equations are given as

$$_0^C D_t^\alpha y(0) = b_\nu, \quad \nu = 1, 2, \ldots m,$$

with $m - 1 < \alpha \leq m$. In our examples, $m = 1$. From the definition of the Caputo derivative, $_0^C D_t^\alpha y(t)$, it can be seen that it is a non-local operator over the interval $(0, t)$ and that it does not depend on values for $t < 0$. From the kernel of the integral, it is clear that it is weighted toward the values of $y(t)$ at time t. The replacement of the integer-order derivative with a fractional-order one in population models is usually justified by stating that the population has memory, that is, it depends on the past. But it is not stated how it takes into account the actual dependence on the past and whether it is due to maturation or infection times, or to other processes.

Another definition of the fractional derivative $D_t^\alpha y(t)$, the Grünwald–Letnikov definition, is based on taking finite differences on equidistant time steps in $[0, t]$. Choose the grid

$$0 = t_0 < t_1 < \ldots < t = t_{n+1} = (n+1)\Delta t, \quad t_{n+1} - t_n = \Delta t,$$

and use the usual notation of finite differences,

$$\frac{1}{\Delta t^\alpha} \Delta_{\Delta t}^\alpha y(t) = \frac{1}{\Delta t^\alpha} \left(y(t_{n+1}) - \sum_{\nu=1}^{n+1} c_\nu^\alpha y(t_{n+1-\nu}) \right),$$

where

$$c_\nu^\alpha = (-1)^{\nu-1} \binom{\alpha}{\nu}.$$

Then, the Grünwald–Letnikov definition is [9,19]

$$D_t^\alpha y(t) = \lim_{\Delta t \to 0} \frac{1}{\Delta t^\alpha} \Delta_{\Delta t}^\alpha y(t).$$

Take the limit $\alpha \to 1$ to obtain the explicit or implicit Euler method. Compared with linear multistep methods for the approximation of the fractional derivative, the sum of divided differences becomes longer and longer [9,19], so it is not usually used in practice. But it is useful for comparing an approximation of a fractional differential equation to that of an ODE. We apply the Grünwald–Letnikov definition to the following fractional differential equation

$$_0^C D_t^\alpha N(t) = f(N(t)), \quad N(0) = N_0 \quad (0 < \alpha < 1),$$

and let $N(t)$ be the exact solution in the interval $[0, T]$. If N_k denotes the approximation of the true solution $N(t_k)$, then the explicit or implicit Grünwald–Letnikov method on a uniform grid is given by

$$N_{n+1} - \sum_{\nu=1}^{n+1} c_\nu^\alpha N_{n+1-\nu} - r_{n+1}^\alpha N_0 = \Delta t^\alpha f(N_n) \text{ or } \Delta t^\alpha f(N_{n+1}).$$

Here, $r^\alpha_{n+1} = \frac{(n+1)^{-\alpha}}{\Gamma(1-\alpha)}$, with Γ the Gamma function. Taking $n = 0$, the equation for the first step is
$$N_1 - c_1^\alpha N_0 - r_1^\alpha N_0 = \Delta t^\alpha f(N_0) \text{ or } \Delta t^\alpha f(N_1).$$
This equation does not agree with the first step of any standard finite approximation of Equation (3). The Caputo derivative incorporates past values of the solution starting at the initial time $t = 0$, but it also has terms that do not come from a standard discrete-time conservation equation. The population Malthus growth model in terms of Caputo fractional derivatives is
$${}^C_0D_t^\alpha N(t) = (b - \mu)N(t). \tag{10}$$

2.2. SIRS Models

A model commonly used for the propagation of many different diseases in a population is the SIRS model with no demographics [37]. It consists of three compartments: susceptibles ($S(t)$), infectives or infected ($I(t)$), and recovered ($R(t)$). A susceptible turns into an infective with a given probability after contact with an infective. An infective recovers with a rate γ. A recovered loses immunity at a rate ν and converts into a susceptible. The total population is assumed constant, $S(t) + I(t) + R(t) = N$, and the disease is assumed to be short enough so that births and deaths need not be considered. The infection coefficient is denoted by β/N. All parameters are positive. The system of ordinary differential equations (ODEs) describing the model is

$$\begin{aligned}\frac{dS}{dt} &= -\frac{\beta}{N}SI + \nu R \\ \frac{dI}{dt} &= \frac{\beta}{N}SI - \gamma I \\ \frac{dR}{dt} &= \gamma I - \nu R.\end{aligned} \tag{11}$$

Since the total population is constant, one equation can be eliminated using $R(t) = N - S(t) - I(t)$. The new system of equations is

$$\begin{aligned}\frac{dS}{dt} &= -\frac{\beta}{N}SI + \nu(N - S - I) \\ \frac{dI}{dt} &= \frac{\beta}{N}SI - \gamma I.\end{aligned}$$

This continuous-time model can also be derived from a discrete-time model [39,40].

There are several different methods of introducing delays in the infection into the model. The first one, which we call SIRS Model 1 [41–43], is given by

$$\begin{aligned}\frac{dS}{dt} &= -\frac{\beta}{N}S(t-\tau)I(t-\tau) + \nu(N - S(t) - I(t)) \\ \frac{dI}{dt} &= \frac{\beta}{N}S(t-\tau)I(t-\tau) - \gamma I(t),\end{aligned} \tag{12}$$

where the hypothesis is that an infective has contact with a susceptible and it takes time τ for this susceptible to turn infective. Until that time, it is counted as a susceptible. The second model is SIRS Model 2 [44], which is described by

$$\begin{aligned}\frac{dS}{dt} &= -\frac{\beta}{N}S(t)I(t-\tau) + \nu(N - S(t) - I(t)) \\ \frac{dI}{dt} &= \frac{\beta}{N}S(t)I(t-\tau) - \gamma I(t),\end{aligned} \tag{13}$$

where the assumption is that after contact between a susceptible and an infective, time τ has to pass before the susceptible turns into an infective and is able to infect another susceptible.

So, there is a new infective after contact between the susceptible and an individual infected a time ago equal to the delay.

The third model is SIRS Model 3, which is described by

$$\frac{dS}{dt} = -\frac{\beta}{N}S(t)I(t) + \nu(N - S(t) - I(t))$$
$$\frac{dI}{dt} = \frac{\beta}{N}S(t-\tau)I(t-\tau) - \gamma I(t),$$
(14)

where after contact with an infective, the susceptible leaves the susceptible population but takes time τ to be included in the infective population. It conserves the total population, and the infection contact is between individuals at the same time. These three models can all be derived from discrete-time models.

As shown in [45], temporary immunity can be included in the SIRS model. The authors used a distributed delay, but by introducing the delay after exposure τ_1, the delay due to the minimum duration of the disease τ_2, and the delay due to the minimum time with immunity τ_3, we obtain the model

$$\frac{dS}{dt} = -\frac{\beta}{N}S(t-\tau_1)I(t-\tau_1) + \nu R(t-\tau_3)$$
$$\frac{dI}{dt} = \frac{\beta}{N}S(t-\tau_1)I(t-\tau_1) - \gamma I(t-\tau_2)$$
$$\frac{dR}{dt} = \gamma I(t-\tau_2) - \nu R(t-\tau_3).$$

These are the equations for SIRS Model 1, but the equations for SIRS Models 2 and 3 are similar.

Models with delays introduced in different forms may have the same equilibrium solutions but the actual time-dependent solutions will be different. There is also the question of the influence of the initial conditions given in the history interval. For an epidemic, they can always be given as the equilibrium solutions with no disease. That is, the natural assumption that the epidemic starts at $t = 0$ can be used.

The SIRS fractional model is

$$^C_0D^\alpha_t S(t) = -\frac{\beta}{N}SI + \nu R$$
$$^C_0D^\alpha_t I(t) = \frac{\beta}{N}SI - \gamma I$$
(15)
$$^C_0D^\alpha_t R(t) = \gamma I - \nu R.$$

The same fractional order, α, was used for all three fractional derivatives. This is not necessary but is usually done for fractional epidemic models [13,14,46]. Two examples of papers using different orders are [22,47]. These fractional derivative models include dependence on all population values between the initial and the current times, but, again from looking at finite difference approximations, they do not arise from standard discrete-time models. But simulations may produce good agreement with real data due to the extra parameters, the fractional derivative orders.

A model that takes into account dependence on the past caused by the delay in transmission by including an exposed population, $E(t)$, is

$$\frac{dS}{dt} = -\frac{\beta}{N}SI + \nu R$$
$$\frac{dE}{dt} = \frac{\beta}{N}SI - \sigma E$$
$$\frac{dI}{dt} = \sigma E - \gamma I$$
(16)
$$\frac{dR}{dt} = \gamma I - \nu R.$$

The additional parameter is $\sigma = 1/\tau$. Models of this form are usually called SEIRS models, and the dependence on the past comes from the average time an individual spends in the exposed compartment.

2.3. Plant Virus with Vector Transmission Models

Humans, animals, and plants can all be affected by vector-transmitted viruses. The processes involved are the same. For simplicity, we consider a model for cultivated plants, for which it is reasonable to assume a constant plant population since farmers replace dead plants. Two examples of virus-causing diseases in plants are the cassava virus [48] and the cacao swollen shoot virus [49]. Again, we introduce the delay in different ways to see the differences in the solutions. We consider a simple model with two populations of plants: susceptible (healthy), $S(t)$, and infective (already infected), $I(t)$. Usually, plants do not recover so we do not consider a recovered class. There are also two populations of vectors: susceptible, $X(t)$, and infective, $Y(t)$. Vectors are only carriers and do not get the disease so they do not recover. A susceptible plant becomes infected when an infected vector feeds on it, and a susceptible vector becomes infected by feeding on an infected plant. This model is a simplified version of the models presented, for example, in [43,50].

The assumptions of the model are as follows: all new plants and vectors are susceptible; the total population of plants is a constant K; the infection terms between vectors and plants, and vice versa, are of mass-action type; the viruses only kill plants; and neither plants nor vectors recover from the disease.

The system of ODEs for the model is

$$\begin{aligned}
\frac{dS}{dt} &= \mu(K - S) + dI - \beta YS \\
\frac{dI}{dt} &= \beta YS - (d + \mu)I \\
\frac{dX}{dt} &= \Lambda - \beta_1 IX - mX \\
\frac{dY}{dt} &= \beta_1 IX - mY.
\end{aligned} \quad (17)$$

The parameters of the model are taken from [43,50] and are all positive: K is the total number of plants, β is the infection rate of plants due to infective vectors feeding on the plant and infecting it, β_1 is the infection rate of vectors due to feeding on an infected plant and becoming infected, μ is the natural death rate of plants, d is the additional death rate of plants due to the disease, m is the natural death rate of vectors, and Λ is the replenishing rate of vectors (due to birth and/or migration).

In this virus transmission via a vector model, there are two delays. The first one is the time it takes the virus to spread in the plant after infected contact. The second one is the time it takes the virus to spread in the vector after becoming infected through feeding. Since the virus usually stays around the feeding organs of the vector and does not replicate inside it, this second delay is much smaller than the first. For simplicity, we consider only the first delay.

Following the approach used in the SIRS model, we introduce the delay in the transmission in two different ways. The first one uses the assumption that after contact with an infective, a susceptible takes the delay time to become infective itself [42,43]. That is, a newly exposed susceptible remains a susceptible until a time equal to the delay elapses and only then does it become an infective. This is known as Model A1:

$$\begin{aligned}
\frac{dS}{dt} &= \mu(K - S(t)) + dI(t) - \beta Y(t-\tau)S(t-\tau) \\
\frac{dI}{dt} &= \beta Y(t-\tau)S(t-\tau) - (d+\mu)I(t) \\
\frac{dX}{dt} &= \Lambda - \beta_1 I(t)X(t) - mX(t) \\
\frac{dY}{dt} &= \beta_1 I(t)X(t) - mY(t).
\end{aligned} \qquad (18)$$

The second model with infection delay uses the assumption that after a contagion, the susceptible immediately stops being susceptible but it takes the delay time to become infective. It takes into account the probability of the newly infected plant dying before becoming infective using the term $\exp(-\mu\tau)$, which is the average survival percentage in the time period τ. This is known as Model A2:

$$\begin{aligned}
\frac{dS}{dt} &= \mu(K - S(t)) + dI(t) - \beta Y(t)S(t) \\
\frac{dI}{dt} &= \exp(-\mu\tau)\beta Y(t-\tau)S(t-\tau) - (d+\mu)I(t) \\
\frac{dX}{dt} &= \Lambda - \beta_1 I(t)X(t) - mX(t) \\
\frac{dY}{dt} &= \beta_1 I(t)X(t) - mY(t).
\end{aligned} \qquad (19)$$

Delay differential equations, while more realistic, have the drawback that it is necessary to specify initial conditions over an interval instead of just at a point, as with ordinary differential equations. These initial conditions may be unknown, and, if so, are usually assumed to be constant. What is more, they are usually assumed to represent disease-free values. A second drawback is that the analysis is much harder due to the infinite number of eigenvalues [1,51].

A common alternative is to use fractional derivatives, which have their own advantages and difficulties, as already mentioned for the population growth models and the SIRS models. The DFE model is

$$\begin{aligned}
{}_0^C D_t^\alpha S(t) &= \mu(K - S(t)) + dI(t) - \beta Y(t)S(t) \\
{}_0^C D_t^\alpha I(t) &= \beta Y(t)S(t) - (d+\mu)I(t) \\
{}_0^C D_t^\alpha X(t) &= \Lambda - \beta_1 I(t)X(t) - mX(t) \\
{}_0^C D_t^\alpha Y(t) &= \beta_1 I(t)X(t) - mY(t).
\end{aligned} \qquad (20)$$

A third alternative for accounting for dependence on the past is to introduce another compartment, the exposed population (E). After contact with an infective, a susceptible is converted into an exposed or latent, one that cannot yet infect. The exposed turns into an infective at a rate of $\epsilon = 1/\tau$. The model is

$$\begin{aligned}
\frac{dS}{dt} &= \mu(K - S(t)) + dI(t) - \beta Y(t)S(t) + \mu E \\
\frac{dE}{dt} &= \beta Y(t)S(t) - \mu E - \epsilon E \\
\frac{dI}{dt} &= \epsilon E - (d+\mu)I(t) \\
\frac{dX}{dt} &= \Lambda - \beta_1 I(t)X(t) - mX(t) \\
\frac{dY}{dt} &= \beta_1 I(t)X(t) - -mY(t).
\end{aligned} \qquad (21)$$

Epidemic models with an exposed class are very common (for plant virus propagation, see, for example, [30,52]). The advantages of using models with exposed populations are that they are based on ODEs, so they only require the initial condition at the initial time, and, as with all epidemic models based on ODEs, the local asymptotic stability at the beginning of the epidemic can be determined using the next-generation matrix method [53,54]. But, from a biological point of view, there is the complication that an individual only stays in the exposed state for a time equal to the delay, whereas some individuals may stay in this state for a much longer time.

2.4. Within-Host Virus Infection Models

A basic model of within-host virus infection considers three populations: susceptible cells, infected cells, and virus particles (virions). Susceptible cells are recruited and die naturally, and they can become infected through contact with a virus particle. Cells infected with a virus burst and release a certain number of virions. These free virions can infect healthy cells or die. More realistic models also include the elimination of infected cells and virions by the effector cells of the immune system, as well as cell-to-cell transmission. The equations for such models are [55–58]

$$\begin{aligned}
\frac{dx}{dt} &= \lambda - \mu_x x - \beta x v - \beta_{xy} x y \\
\frac{dy}{dt} &= \beta x v + \beta_{xy} x y - \beta_{ey} y e - \mu_y y \\
\frac{dv}{dt} &= B\mu_y y - \beta x v - \beta_{ev} v e - \mu_v v \\
\frac{de}{dt} &= s + \alpha_1 y - \beta_{ye} y e - \beta_{ve} v e - \mu_e e.
\end{aligned} \quad (22)$$

Here, x, y, v, and e are the concentrations of susceptible cells, infected cells, virions, and effector cells, respectively. λ is the recruitment rate of new susceptible cells, μ_x is their death rate, β is the infection rate, μ_y is the killing rate of infected cells by the virus, B is the number of virions produced per infected cell, and μ_v is the death rate of virions. Susceptible cells can be infected through direct contact with an infected cell at a rate β_{xy}; effector cells eliminate infected cells at a rate β_{ey}; free virus particles are introduced into susceptible cells at a rate β; and effector cells are recruited at a constant rate s and are also recruited depending on the number of infected cells y at a rate α_1. In addition, as effector cells eliminate infected cells and virus particles, they are also eliminated from the system with rates β_{ye} and β_{ve}, respectively. Finally, effector cells die naturally at a rate μ_e. All parameters are non-negative.

We add two delays to the model (22), τ_1, which is the time it takes the virus to replicate after invading a cell, and τ_2, which is the time it takes the immune system to recruit an effector cell after detecting an infected cell. The delay model is

$$\begin{aligned}
\frac{dx}{dt} &= \lambda - \mu_x x(t) - \beta x(t-\tau_1)v(t-\tau_1) - \beta_{xy} x(t-\tau_1)y(t-\tau_1) \\
\frac{dy}{dt} &= \beta x(t-\tau_1)v(t-\tau_1) + \beta_{xy} x(t-\tau_1)y(t-\tau_1) - \beta_{ey} y(t)e(t) - \mu_y y(t) \\
\frac{dv}{dt} &= B\mu_y y(t) - \beta x v - \beta_{ev} v(t)e(t) - \mu_v v(t) \\
\frac{de}{dt} &= s + \alpha_1 y(t-\tau_2) - \beta_{ye} y(t)e(t) - \beta_{ve} v(t)e(t) - \mu_e e(t).
\end{aligned} \quad (23)$$

The fractional derivative system is

$$\begin{aligned}
{}_0^C D_t^\alpha x(t) &= \lambda - \mu_x x(t) - \beta x(t)v(t) - \beta_{xy} x(t)y(t) \\
{}_0^C D_t^\alpha y(t) &= \beta x(t)v(t) + \beta_{xy} x(t)y(t) - \beta_{ey} y(t)e(t) - \mu_y y(t) \\
{}_0^C D_t^\alpha v(t) &= B\mu_y y(t) - \beta xv - \beta_{ev} v(t)e(t) - \mu_v v(t) \\
{}_0^C D_t^\alpha e(t) &= s + \alpha_1 y(t) - \beta_{ye} y(t)e(t) - \beta_{ve} v(t)e(t) - \mu_e e(t).
\end{aligned} \qquad (24)$$

And the model with an exposed cell population z is

$$\begin{aligned}
\frac{dx}{dt} &= \lambda - mu_x x(t) - \beta x(t)v(t) - \beta_{xy} x(t)y(t) \\
\frac{dz}{dt} &= \beta x(t)v(t) + \beta_{xy} x(t)y(t) - \mu_x z(t) - \sigma z(t) \\
\frac{dy}{dt} &= \sigma z(t) - \beta_{ey} y(t)e(t) - \mu_y y(t) \\
\frac{dv}{dt} &= B\mu_y y(t) - \beta x(t)v(t) - \beta_{ev} v(t)e(t) - \mu_v v(t) \\
\frac{de}{dt} &= s + \alpha_1 y(t) - \beta_{ye} y(t)e(t) - \beta_{ve} v(t)e(t) - \mu_e e(t),
\end{aligned} \qquad (25)$$

where $\sigma = 1/\tau_1$ is the rate at which exposed cells become infective cells.

We used 5 different models for population growth and infection propagation, each with its own set of hypotheses. Dependence on past values due to processes taking time was added to all of them using three different methods. For all three, their solutions approach the steady states at a slower rate than the one for the corresponding ODE model. While the fractional differential equations models incorporate dependence on the past in a different way, their simulations are similar if a value of α is chosen to make this happen. This value of α depends on the particular model and the value of the delay.

3. Results

This section presents the results for the models introduced in Section 2, including the numerical simulations. We show that the solutions using the different delay differential models are similar to each other and to the models with immature or exposed populations. We also show that even though the models given by FDEs do not have a dependence on the past based on common modeling assumptions, the additional parameters given by the order of the fractional derivatives enable the solutions to be similar to those obtained by DDEs or by introducing additional delaying populations.

3.1. Population Growth Models

We start with the Malthus ODE model (1). It is used to present the results in a simple form since it consists of only one population and one equation, and it is linear. The solution is $N(t) = N(0) \exp((b - \mu)t)$. It has no equilibrium points, but $N(t) = 0$ if $N(0) = 0$, and $N(t)$ is constant if $b = \mu$. The solution tends to 0 for $b - \mu < 0$ and to infinity for $b - \mu > 0$. The delayed Malthus model (2) has solutions of the form $N(t) = \exp(\lambda t)$, with λ a solution of the characteristic equation $\lambda = b \exp(-\lambda \tau) - \mu$. This transcendental equation has no exact solutions, but $\lambda > 0$ if $1 \geq \exp(-\lambda \tau) \geq \mu/b$. So, for $b > \mu$, the solution also tends to infinity as t tends to infinity and to 0 otherwise. Some delay differential equations can be solved analytically using the method of steps, as described in [1,59]. For example, for (2), taking $x(t) = x_0$ constant for $t \in [-\tau, 0]$ gives $x(t) = -b\frac{x_0}{m} + x_0(1 + \frac{b}{m})\exp(-mt)$ for $t \in [0, \tau]$, and so on. The solutions become complicated very fast. For the fractional derivative model (10), an exact solution can also be calculated using fractional tools such as Mathematica [60]. The solution is given by $N(t) = E_\alpha(rt^\alpha)$, where $E_\alpha(z) = \sum_{k=0}^\infty \frac{z^k}{\Gamma(\alpha k+1)}$ is the Mittag–Leffler function, Γ is the Gamma function, and $r = b - \mu$ is the growth rate. Exact solutions of fractional differential equations, except for linear problems, are very few. In this example, from the definition of the Caputo derivative (9), if $y(t)$ is of one sign, ${}_{0}^{C}D_{t}^{\alpha}y(t)$ has the same sign. So, if $b - \mu > 0$, the solution of the fractional equation increases as t tends to infinity.

The Malthus model with an immature population is given in (5). The exact solution is a long formula, but the eigenvalues are given by

$$ev_{1,2} = \frac{-\mu - \sigma \pm \sqrt{\sigma(4b + \sigma)}}{2}, \quad (26)$$

which implies that the solution will tend to infinity as t tends to infinity for $\sigma(4b + \sigma) > (2\mu + \sigma)^2$. It can also be seen that by adding the two equations, the equation for the total population is the same as the equation for the ODE Malthus model (1).

Numerical solutions were calculated for the four Malthus models. The ODEs and DDEs were solved using the *julia* package DifferentialEqns.jl [61,62], and the FDEs were solved using the package FdeSolver [63], which uses methods reviewed, for example, in [21]. The same software was used for all the other models. Figure 2 shows the simulation of the different Malthus models ((1), (2), (5), and (10)) for several values of the order α. The parameter values used are $b = 0.16$ (1/day), $\mu = 0.01$ (1/day), $\tau = 14$ (day), $N(0) = 0.5$, and $\sigma = 1/\tau$ (1/day), with $Y[0] = 0$ for (5). The values are not chosen for any specific population. The delay model and the model with an immature population have solutions that grow slower than the solution for the non-delay model. As can be seen, by changing the value of α, the fractional solution looks approximately like the delayed solution. As α decreases from 1, the solutions are more delayed. But there is no theoretical way to choose the α without comparing it to either empirical data or other calculated solutions. The fractional model involves memory (dependence on the past), but the memory does not come from modeling a population growth term in a common way (see (4)). So, the good agreement is due to the extra parameter in the FDE, α.

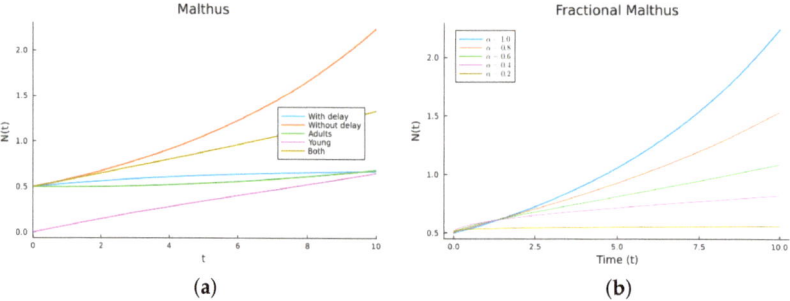

Figure 2. Malthus models. (a) ODE, DDE, and immature population models. The legend "Both" refers to the sum of the mature and immature populations for model (5). (b) Fractional models for several values of α.

Next, we studied the logistic model, which consists of one equation but is now nonlinear. The ODE logistic model (6) adds intra-species competition to the Malthus model. It has two steady solutions: $N^* = K$, which is stable, and $N^* = 0$, which is unstable, as can be seen by checking the sign of the derivative $\frac{dN}{dt}$. A delay can be added to the death term (7). It has the same steady states and stability as the ODE model. A fractional derivative model obtained by replacing the time derivative with a fractional Caputo derivative model also has the same steady states. It also has the same stability, as can be checked by looking at the sign on the right-hand side. The steady solutions and their stability conditions for the two-population logistic models (8) have long expressions. The numerical simulations show similar behavior. The parameters used are $b = 0.16$ (1/day), $r = 0.15$ (1/day), $\mu = 0.01$ (1/day), $K = 1$ (individual), $\tau = 14$ (day), $N(0) = 0.5$, and $\sigma = 1/\tau$ (1/day), with $Y(0) = 0$. The graphs are shown in Figure 3. Again, it can be seen that as α decreases from 1, the FDE solution is more delayed and can be made similar to the delayed solution. The α that gives the best agreement with the delay model depends on the value of the delay. For this example, $alpha$ is about 0.8. The model given by (6) is more realistic than the one given by (1) since the non-linear competition term keeps the solution bounded. Again, the fractional model produces similar solutions to the delay model provided that α is adequately chosen.

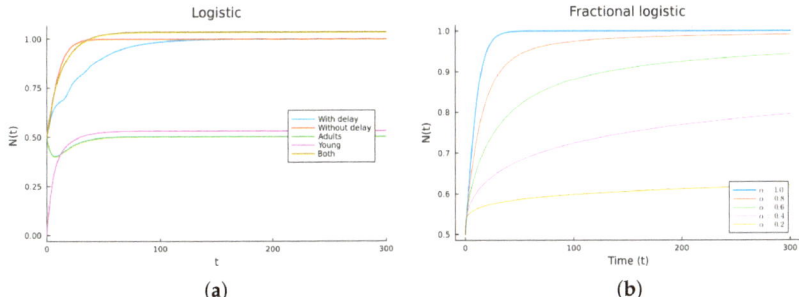

Figure 3. Logistic models. (**a**) ODE, DDE, and immature population models. The legend "Both" refers to the sum of the mature and the young or immature populations for model (8). (**b**) Fractional models for several values of α.

3.2. SIRS Models

The SIRS model is an epidemic model considering three populations: S(t), I(t), and R(t), satisfying three non-linear equations. The ODE model (11) has two equilibrium points: the disease-free equilibrium (DFE), $S^* = N, I^* = 0, R^* = 0$, with N the total constant population, and the endemic one, $S^* = N\gamma/\nu, I^* = (N - S^*)\nu/(\gamma + \nu)$, $R^* = \gamma I^*/\nu$ [38,64]. The local asymptotic stability of the DFE can be determined by finding the basic reproduction number R_0, which is usually calculated using the next-generation matrix method [53,54]. For $R_0 = \beta/\gamma < 1$, the DFE equilibrium is locally asymptotically stable. The three delay models, Equations (12)–(14), have the same equilibrium points with the same stability, as determined by linearizing about the DFE and analyzing the characteristic equation. The three models make biological sense. Their main difference is when the newly infected stops being counted as susceptible. For some epidemics, the first model may fit the data better than the others, but this may be due to factors not included in the models. For the FDE model, the equilibrium points are the same as for the ODE model. The stability can be analyzed by solving the linearized equation about the DFE, but the expressions for the solutions are not easy to analyze [11,65]. For the SEIRS model (16), the DFE is the same, but the endemic one is different due to the extra compartment, $E(t)$. The DFE is also locally asymptotically stable for $R_0 = \beta/\gamma < 1$, also calculated using the next-generation matrix method. Figures 4 and 5 show the simulations for SIRS models (11)–(14) and (16), as well as (15), using various values of α. All the solutions for the integer-order models tend to the same endemic equilibrium point, but the delay and exposed models take more time. The solutions of the fractional models also tend to the same equilibrium. Again, for the fractional model, it can be seen that decreasing α slows the solution and that there is a value of α that gives a good fit with the delay model solutions, but the fit is not good for small time values. The best value for α is between 0.7 and 0.8. The parameter values used are $N = 100$ (individual), $\beta = 1$ (1/day), $\gamma = 0.5$ (1/day), $\nu = 0.4$ (1/day), $\tau = 5$ (day), and $\sigma = 1/\tau$ (1/day). These parameters are not based on an actual infection. The initial conditions are $S(0) = 99, I(0) = 1$, which were also used as the history for the delay models, and $E(0) = 0$ is additionally used for the SEIRS model.

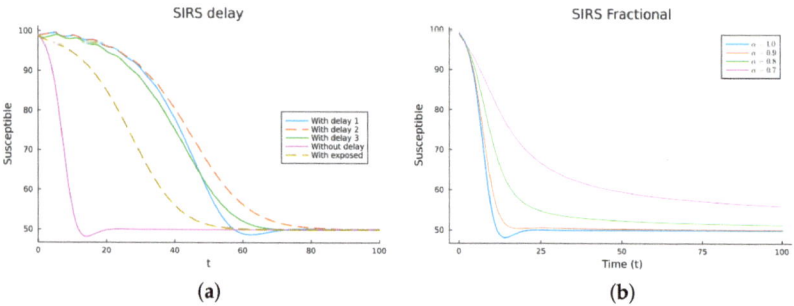

Figure 4. SIRS models, susceptibles. (**a**) ODE, DDE, and SEIRS models. (**b**) Fractional models for several values of α.

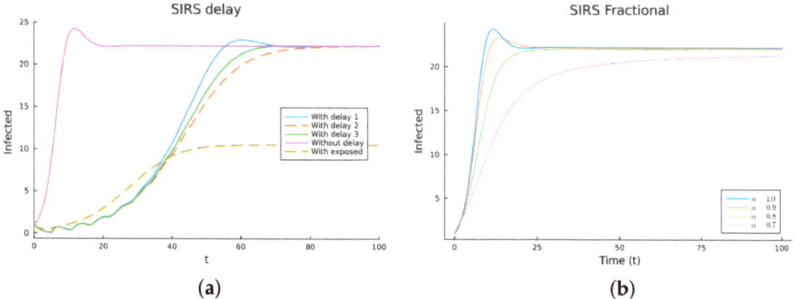

Figure 5. SIRS models, infectives. (**a**) ODE, DDE, and SEIRS models. (**b**) Fractional models for several values of α.

3.3. Plant Virus with Vector Transmission Models

The plant virus model introduces the transmission through a vector instead of through direct contact. Now, the infection of the plant depends on the past since it takes time for the virus to spread inside the plant. But the infection of the vector does not. It is a more complicated model, and the objective is to see if the fractional models can still approximate the results of a DDE model by varying the value of α. Two different ways of introducing the delay were presented, (18) and (19). Only model (18) conserves the total plant population. It can be argued that the way of introducing the delay in (19) is acceptable for a model with a total population that is not constant, but it is clearly not a good choice for a constant population model. This can also be seen in Figures 6–9. The plots on the left of the figures correspond to the simulations using the models given by (17)–(19) and (21). The plots on the right correspond to the simulation using (20) for different values of α. The parameters used in the simulations were taken from [43,50]: $K = 100$ (plant), $\beta = 0.01$ (1/(vector day)), $\beta_1 = 0.01$ (1/(plant day)), $\mu = 0.1$ (1/day), $d = 0.1$ (1/day), $m = 0.2$ (1/day), and $\Lambda = 10$ (vector/day). These values are for illustration purposes only. All the models, including the fractional ones, have solutions that tend to the same endemic equilibrium, except for the model given by (19), which does not conserve the total plant population. For the FDE models, as expected, the solutions change slower than for the ODE model, and as α decreases from 1, they keep slowing. Assuming that the only dependence on the past is due to the delay in the plant infection, the FDE models can produce similar time trajectories. The value of α that gives the best agreement with the solutions from the delay model is around 0.9.

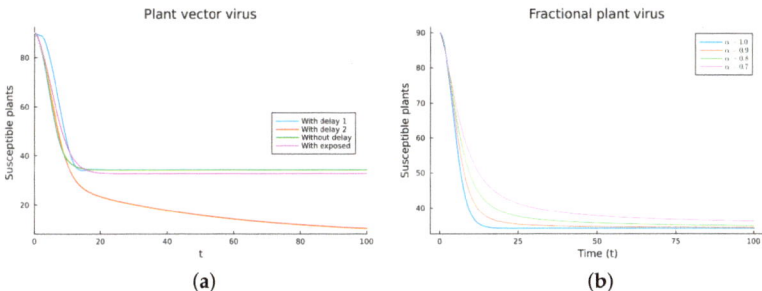

Figure 6. Plant vector virus models, susceptible plants. (**a**) ODE, DDE, and exposed population models. (**b**) Fractional models for several values of α.

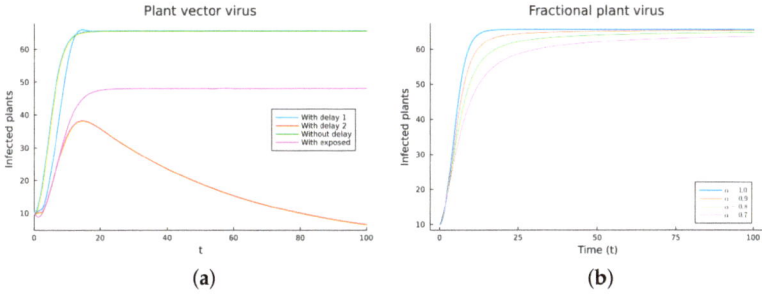

Figure 7. Plant vector virus models, infected plants. (**a**) ODE, DDE, and exposed population models. (**b**) Fractional models for several values of α.

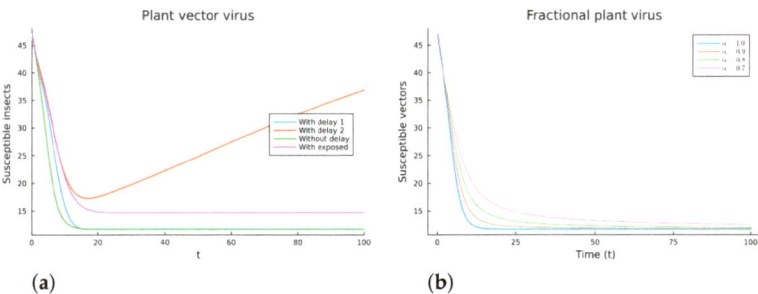

Figure 8. Plant vector virus models, susceptible vectors. (**a**) ODE, DDE, and exposed population models. (**b**) Fractional models for several values of α.

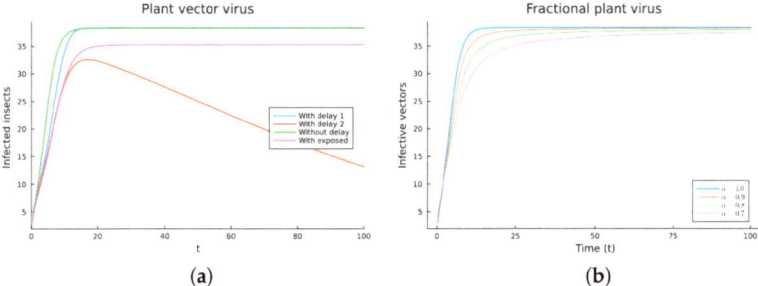

Figure 9. Plant vector virus models, infected vectors. (**a**) ODE, DDE, and exposed population models. (**b**) Fractional models for several values of α.

3.4. Within-Host Virus Propagation Models

Finally, we consider a more complicated model in which the populations can interact in several ways, and there are two terms of the equations for the susceptible and infected cells that have a delay. There is also a second delay. The values of the parameters used are $\Lambda = 5 \times 10^5$ (cells/mL), $\mu_x = 0.003$ (1/day), $\beta = 4 \times 10^{-10}$ (mL/(cells day)), $\mu_y = 0.043$ (1/day), $\mu_v = 0.7$ (1/day), $B = 5.58$, $\beta_{xy} = \beta/3$ (mL/(cells day)), $\mu_E = 0.5$ (1/day), $\alpha_1 = 2.2 \times 10^{-7}$ (1/day), $\beta_{Ey} = 0.6 \times 10^{-3}$ (mL/(cells day)), $\beta_{yE} = \beta_{Ey}$ (mL/(cells day)), $\beta_{Ev} = 4 \times 10^{-10}$ (mL/(cells day)), $\beta_{vE} = \beta_{Ev}$ (mL/(cells day)), $s = 30$ (cells/(mL day)), $\tau_1 = 1$ (day), and $\tau_2 = 24$ (day). These parameters are based on those in [55,56] for liver infection by the hepatitis B virus. The initial conditions are $x(0) = \Lambda/\mu_x, y(0) = 0, v(0) = 0.33$, and $E(0) = s/\mu_E$. Figures 10–13 show the simulations for the above-mentioned values of the parameters. The plots on the left of the figures correspond to the simulations using (22), (23), and (25). For the values of the parameters given above, the solutions tend to a chronic equilibrium state. The DFE is asymptotically unstable for the integer-order models, as was also shown in [66]. The plots on the right correspond to the simulations using (24) for different values of the order of the derivative α. As expected, for the number of infected cells, for the fractional model, the rate of increase of the solutions increases as α increases toward 1. The optimal value of α is between 0.9 and 1. Since the solutions increased very slowly, the plots were truncated to clearly show the differences for a short time. Another simulation was conducted with $\beta_{xy} = 0$, resulting in no transmission from cell to cell. In this case, the DFE is asymptotically stable, as illustrated in Figure 14.

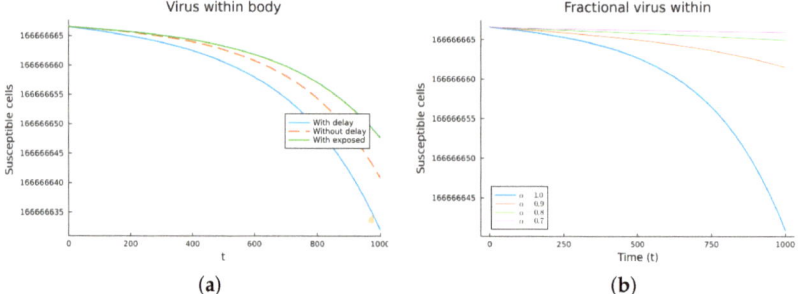

Figure 10. Virus within-host models, susceptible cells. (**a**) ODE, DDE, and exposed population models. (**b**) Fractional models for several values of α.

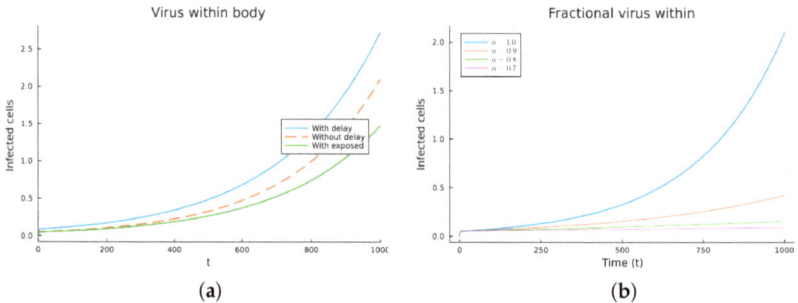

Figure 11. Virus within-host models, infected cells. (**a**) ODE, DDE, and exposed population models. (**b**) Fractional models for several values of α.

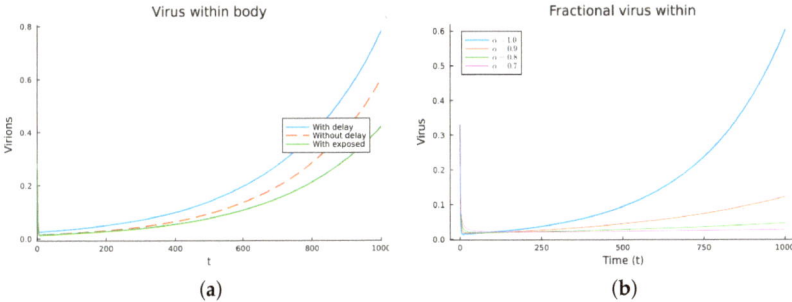

Figure 12. Virus within-host models, virus particles. (**a**) ODE, DDE, and exposed population models. (**b**) Fractional models for several values of α.

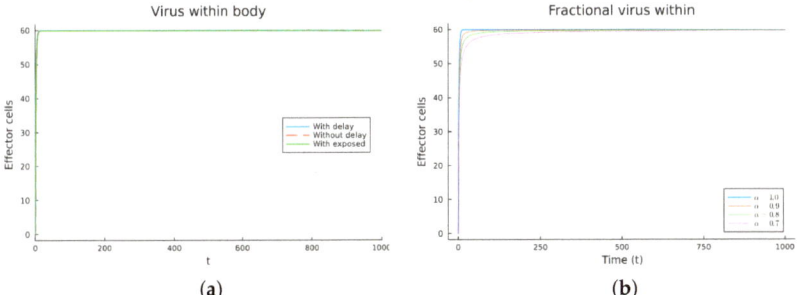

Figure 13. Virus within-host models, effector cells. (**a**) ODE, DDE, and exposed population models. (**b**) Fractional models for several values of α.

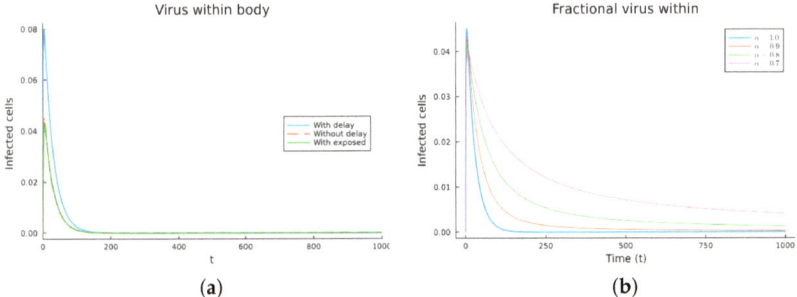

Figure 14. Virus within-host models, infected cells, for $\beta_{xy} = 0$. (**a**) ODE, DDE, and exposed population models. (**b**) Fractional models for several values of α.

4. Discussion

Many populations depend on their values in the past. The number of births depends on the population the maturation time ago. The number of newly infected depends on the number of contacts between an infected and a susceptible the infection time ago. Also, the immune system takes a certain time to react and start fighting an infection. Mathematical models for processes involving values in the past should incorporate this dependence and, therefore, produce solutions that are more realistic. Mathematical models are simplifications of reality. This can be due to keeping the model tractable or to the lack of information and data. ODE-based models assume that the population is homogeneously distributed and so avoid having spatial dependence. Usually, infection rates are assumed to be constant but they can vary with time, temperature, and the individual. There may be saturation effects not modeled by mass-action kinetics. Recovered individuals turning into susceptibles may retain some immunity and may infect others. Processes that take time should be modeled taking into account that time. As shown in Section 2, there are different ways of introducing delays into an ODE model, but they need to be introduced in a consistent manner. For example, model (19) does not conserve the total population and, therefore, should not be used. The maturation time is not a single time but has some variation. The same is true for the infection time. But usually, these variations are small, and using a single value is a good approximation. But if they are not, then a distributed delay model will be better. Also, there is the effect of population values on the history interval, $[t_0 - \tau, t_0]$, where t_0 is the initial time. But for epidemic or infection models, the values of the populations in those intervals can be assumed to correspond to the DFE, which is a reasonable assumption. There are many papers dealing with comparisons between a variety of epidemic models with delays and real data for diseases like dengue or COVID-19. A few examples can be found in [67–70]. Most show that the fit is good but do not compare their results with those of other methods. An exception is [70], where the results from a DDE model were compared with those from an ODE model.

A second way to introduce dependence on the past is to replace the time derivative with a fractional one. From the definition, for example, of the Caputo derivative at time t, it is a weighted average of the time derivatives at times from 0 to the current time t. As shown in Section 2, FDEs do not come from discrete-time conservation models by taking the limit as the time increment goes to zero. In models where the dependence on past times comes from the delay in a given process, the FDEs do not have a form similar to constant or distributed delay models. Furthermore, the effect of past times starts with the initial time of modeling, as opposed to models formulated using DDEs, where the influence extends over times $t \in [t_0 - \tau, t_0]$, with τ representing the delay. FDEs introduce memory, but there lacks a justification for the specific form of this memory. For epidemic models, it is true that susceptibles may remember previous infections, potentially leading to a different infection process. But this does not justify the form of the memory in the FDE. It is also true that many epidemic models based on FDEs fit data better than models based on ODEs, but this may be due to the additional parameter α. If there are susceptibles who previously had the infection and thus may react differently to a new infection due to their memory of the previous infection, an alternative is to add a new susceptible compartment. This can also be done for infectives and those who have recovered from previous infections. The main arguments for using FDEs in epidemic models are that they include memory and that they fit data better than models based on ODEs. This is true, but there is no justification that the memory that the FDEs provide has anything to do with any biological, physical, or chemical process with dependence on the past. Also, the value of the fractional order (or orders) is chosen to better fit the data. Mechanistic models should give a modeling reason or hypothesis on how to choose it. Statistical models, like linear regression, will find the values of the involved parameters to better fit a data set. But mechanistic models should do more than provide computational data that fit experimental data. Recently, there has been an awareness that fractional differential equations should also include delays to better model processes that have delays. This allows the fractional derivative to provide an additional memory effect. Some references supporting this notion are [71–73].

A third common way to introduce that processes take time, thus introducing dependence on the past, is to add new populations, immature populations for birth processes, or exposed populations or cells to epidemic or infection models. This approach has the advantage of being based on ODEs, and, for example, the next-generation matrix method can be used to determine if there will be an epidemic. Also, it does not require initial values for an interval prior to the initial value of t. But, just as a Malthus death model $\frac{dN}{dt} = -\mu N$ with $\mu > 0$ can have individuals living for very long times, some exposed individuals may stay in the compartment for a long time. Of course, this can happen with a very small probability.

All the example models used have a dependence on past values based on the assumption that the dependence is due to the time it takes processes like infection or maturation to happen. Delay models, as well as exposed or immature models, explicitly include this dependence. Fractional differential equation models have a dependence on past values, but this dependence has a different form that is independent of the actual value of the delay or delays. But fractional differential equation models offer the flexibility of more parameters, specifically the fractional orders of the derivatives. By choosing these orders adequately, these models can produce similar results to models that explicitly include the delays.

In conclusion, the terms added to an ODE model to take into account dependence on past values need justification. The justification should be more than just saying there is memory or achieving a better fit. The processes in mechanistic mathematical models need to be based on realistic assumptions. For processes depending on past values due to a delay, DDEs are good choices since there is flexibility in choosing the form of the delay, whether constant or distributed. But models based on adding more populations and still relying on ODEs are simpler to analyze. When using fractional derivatives, modeling assumptions should also be clearly stated.

Future work will include models with stochastic delays, models with partial immunity, and comparisons of the predicted results with real data.

Funding: This research received no external funding.

Informed Consent Statement: Not applicable.

Data Availability Statement: The code for the SIRS models presented can be accessed at https://drive.google.com/drive/folders/1qx7S4Wd1o3DaGloxmjD_wmr_NwGtjUhs?usp=sharing (accessed on 3 March 2024).

Conflicts of Interest: The authors declare no conflicts of interest.

Abbreviations

The following abbreviations are used in this manuscript:

ODE	ordinary differential equation
DDE	delay differential equation
FDE	fractional differential equation
DFE	disease-free equilibrium

References

Kuang, Y. *Delay Differential Equations: With Applications in Population Dynamics*; Academic Press: Cambridge, MA, USA, 1993.

Bellen, A.; Zennaro, M. *Numerical Methods for Delay Differential Equations*; Oxford University Press: Oxford, UK, 2013.

Wang, W. Modeling of Epidemics with Delays and Spatial Heterogeneity. In *Dynamical Modeling and Analysis of Epidemics*; World Scientific: Singapore, 2009; pp. 201–272.

Cooke, K.L. Stability analysis for a vector disease model. *Rocky Mt. J. Math.* **1979**, *9*, 31–42. [CrossRef]

Ruan, S. Delay differential equations in single species dynamics. In *Delay Differential Equations and Applications*; Springer: Dordrecht, The Netherlands, 2006; pp. 477–517.

McCluskey, C.C. Complete global stability for an SIR epidemic model with delay—Distributed or discrete. *Nonlinear Anal. Real World Appl.* **2010**, *11*, 55–59. [CrossRef]

Avila-Vales, E.; Pérez, Á.G. Dynamics of a time-delayed SIR epidemic model with logistic growth and saturated treatment. *Chaos Solitons Fractals* **2019**, *127*, 55–69. [CrossRef]

Kumar, A.; Goel, K.; Nilam. A deterministic time-delayed SIR epidemic model: Mathematical modeling and analysis. *Theory Biosci.* **2020**, *139*, 67–76. [CrossRef] [PubMed]

Podlubny, I. *Fractional Differential Equations: An Introduction to Fractional Derivatives, Fractional Differential Equations, to Methods of Their Solution and Some of Their Applications*; Elsevier: Amsterdam, The Netherlands, 1998.

Kilbas, A.A.; Srivastava, H.M.; Trujillo, J.J. *Theory and Applications of Fractional Differential Equations*; Elsevier: Amsterdam, The Netherlands, 2006; Volume 204.

Li, C.; Zhang, F. A survey on the stability of fractional differential equations: Dedicated to Prof. YS Chen on the Occasion of his 80th Birthday. *Eur. Phys. J. Spec. Top.* **2011**, *193*, 27–47. [CrossRef]

Jin, B. *Fractional Differential Equations*; Springer: Cham, Switzerland, 2021.

González-Parra, G.; Arenas, A.J.; Chen-Charpentier, B.M. A fractional order epidemic model for the simulation of outbreaks of influenza A (H1N1). *Math. Methods Appl. Sci.* **2014**, *37*, 2218–2226. [CrossRef]

14. Area, I.; Batarfi, H.; Losada, J.; Nieto, J.J.; Shammakh, W.; Torres, Á. On a fractional order Ebola epidemic model. *Adv. Differ. E.* **2015**, *2015*, 278. [CrossRef]
15. Hamdan, N.; Kilicman, A. A fractional order SIR epidemic model for dengue transmission. *Chaos Solitons Fractals* **2018**, *114*, 55–. [CrossRef]
16. Chatterjee, A.N.; Ahmad, B. A fractional-order differential equation model of COVID-19 infection of epithelial cells. *Cha Solitons Fractals* **2021**, *147*, 110952. [CrossRef]
17. Chen, Y.; Liu, F.; Yu, Q.; Li, T. Review of fractional epidemic models. *Appl. Math. Model.* **2021**, *97*, 281–307. [CrossRef]
18. Petrás, I. *Fractional Derivatives, Fractional Integrals, and Fractional Differential Equations in Matlab*; IntechOpen: London, UK, 20
19. Scherer, R.; Kalla, S.L.; Tang, Y.; Huang, J. The Grünwald–Letnikov method for fractional differential equations. *Comput. Ma Appl.* **2011**, *62*, 902–917. [CrossRef]
20. Li, Z.; Liu, L.; Dehghan, S.; Chen, Y.; Xue, D. A review and evaluation of numerical tools for fractional calculus and fractior order controls. *Int. J. Control* **2017**, *90*, 1165–1181. [CrossRef]
21. Garrappa, R. Numerical solution of fractional differential equations: A survey and a software tutorial. *Mathematics* **2018**, *6*, [CrossRef]
22. Li, T.; Wang, Y.; Liu, F.; Turner, I. Novel parameter estimation techniques for a multi-term fractional dynamical epidemic moc of dengue fever. *Numer. Algorithms* **2019**, *82*, 1467–1495. [CrossRef]
23. Das, M.; Samanta, G.; De la Sen, M. A Fractional Ordered COVID-19 Model Incorporating Comorbidity and Vaccinati *Mathematics* **2021**, *9*, 2806. [CrossRef]
24. Atici, F.; Eloe, P. Initial value problems in discrete fractional calculus. *Proc. Am. Math. Soc.* **2009**, *137*, 981–989. [CrossRef]
25. Cheng, J.F.; Chu, Y.M. Fractional difference equations with real variable. *Abstr. Appl. Anal.* **2012**, *2012*, 918529. [CrossRef]
26. Ferreira, R.A. *Discrete Fractional Calculus and Fractional Difference Equations*; Springer: Cham, Switzerland, 2022.
27. Esteva, L.; Yang, H.M. Mathematical model to assess the control of Aedes aegypti mosquitoes by the sterile insect techniq *Math. Biosci.* **2005**, *198*, 132–147. [CrossRef]
28. Anguelov, R.; Dumont, Y.; Lubuma, J. Mathematical modeling of sterile insect technology for control of anopheles mosqui *Comput. Math. Appl.* **2012**, *64*, 374–389. [CrossRef]
29. Li, M.Y.; Muldowney, J.S. Global stability for the SEIR model in epidemiology. *Math. Biosci.* **1995**, *125*, 155–164. [CrossRef]
30. Jeger, M.; Madden, L.; Van Den Bosch, F. Plant virus epidemiology: Applications and prospects for mathematical modeling a analysis to improve understanding and disease control. *Plant Dis.* **2018**, *102*, 837–854. [CrossRef]
31. He, S.; Peng, Y.; Sun, K. SEIR modeling of the COVID-19 and its dynamics. *Nonlinear Dyn.* **2020**, *101*, 1667–1680. [CrossRef]
32. Agaba, G.O.; Soomiyol, M.C. Analysing the spread of COVID-19 using delay epidemic model with awareness. *IOSR J. Ma* **2020**, *16*, 52–59.
33. Babasola, O.; Kayode, O.; Peter, O.J.; Onwuegbuche, F.C.; Oguntolu, F.A. Time-delayed modelling of the COVID-19 dynam with a convex incidence rate. *Inform. Med. Unlocked* **2022**, *35*, 101124. [CrossRef]
34. Sepulveda, G.; Arenas, A.J.; González-Parra, G. Mathematical Modeling of COVID-19 dynamics under two vaccination dos and delay effects. *Mathematics* **2023**, *11*, 369. [CrossRef]
35. Zhang, J. Pandemic Mathematical Models, Epidemiology, and Virus Origins. In *Optimization-Based Molecular Dynamics Studies SARS-CoV-2 Molecular Structures: Research on COVID-19*; Springer: Cham, Switzerland, 2023; pp. 897–908.
36. Dickson, S.; Padmasekaran, S.; Kumar, P. Fractional order mathematical model for B. 1.1. 529 SARS-Cov-2 Omicron variant w quarantine and vaccination. *Int. J. Dyn. Control* **2023**, *11*, 2215–2231. [CrossRef]
37. Allen, L. *An Introduction to Mathematical Biology*; Pearson-Prentice Hall: Hoboken, NJ, USA, 2007.
38. Edelstein-Keshet, L. *Mathematical Models in Biology*; SIAM: Philadelphia, PA, USA 2005.
39. Castillo-Chavez, C.; Yakubu, A.A. Discrete-time SIS models with simple and complex population dynamics. *IMA Vol. Math. Appl.* **2002**, *125*, 153–164.
40. Brauer, F.; Feng, Z.; Castillo-Chavez, C. Discrete epidemic models. *Math. Biosci. Eng.* **2009**, *7*, 1–15.
41. Cooke, K.L.; Yorke, J.A. Some equations modelling growth processes and gonorrhea epidemics. *Math. Biosci.* **1973**, *16*, 75–1 [CrossRef]
42. Khan, Q.J.A.; Krishnan, E.V. An Epidemic Model with a Time Delay in Transmission. *Appl. Math.* **2003**, *48*, 193–203. [CrossR
43. Jackson, M.; Chen-Charpentier, B.M. Modeling plant virus propagation with delays. *J. Comput. Appl. Math.* **2017**, *309*, 611–6 [CrossRef]
44. Liu, L. A delayed SIR model with general nonlinear incidence rate. *Adv. Differ. Equ.* **2015**, *2015*, 329. [CrossRef]
45. Hethcote, H.W. The Mathematics of Infectious Diseases. *SIAM Rev.* **2000**, *42*, 599–653. [CrossRef]
46. Al-Sulami, H.; El-Shahed, M.; Nieto, J.J.; Shammakh, W. On fractional order dengue epidemic model. *Math. Probl. Eng.* **20** *2014*, 456537. [CrossRef]
47. Sardar, T.; Rana, S.; Bhattacharya, S.; Al-Khaled, K.; Chattopadhyay, J. A generic model for a single strain mosquito-transmitt disease with memory on the host and the vector. *Math. Biosci.* **2015**, *263*, 18–36. [CrossRef]
48. Legg, J.P.; Kumar, P.L.; Makeshkumar, T.; Tripathi, L.; Ferguson, M.; Kanju, E.; Ntawuruhunga, P.; Cuellar, W. Cassava vir diseases: Biology, epidemiology, and management. In *Advances in Virus Research*; Elsevier: Amsterdam, The Netherlands, 20 Volume 91, pp. 85–142.

1. Gyamera, E.A.; Domfeh, O.; Ameyaw, G.A. Cacao Swollen Shoot Viruses in Ghana. *Plant Dis.* **2023**, *107*, 1261–1278. [CrossRef] [PubMed]
2. Shi, R.; Zhao, H.; Tang, S. Global dynamic analysis of a vector-borne plant disease model. *Adv. Differ. Equ.* **2014**, *2014*, 59. [CrossRef]
3. Erneux, T. *Applied Delay Differential Equations*; Springer Science & Business Media: New York, NY, USA, 2009; Volume 3.
4. Anwar, N.; Naz, S.; Shoaib, M. Reliable numerical treatment with Adams and BDF methods for plant virus propagation model by vector with impact of time lag and density. *Front. Appl. Math. Stat.* **2022**, *8*, 1001392. [CrossRef]
5. Diekmann, O.; Heesterbeek, J.; Roberts, M.G. The construction of next-generation matrices for compartmental epidemic models. *J. R. Soc. Interface* **2010**, *7*, 873–885. [CrossRef] [PubMed]
6. Van den Driessche, P. Reproduction numbers of infectious disease models. *Infect. Dis. Model.* **2017**, *2*, 288–303. [CrossRef] [PubMed]
7. Ciupe, S.M.; Ribeiro, R.M.; Nelson, P.W.; Dusheiko, G.; Perelson, A.S. The role of cells refractory to productive infection in acute hepatitis B viral dynamics. *Proc. Natl. Acad. Sci. USA* **2007**, *104*, 5050–5055. [CrossRef]
8. Kim, H.Y.; Kwon, H.D.; Jang, T.S.; Lim, J.; Lee, H.S. Mathematical modeling of triphasic viral dynamics in patients with HBeAg-positive chronic hepatitis B showing response to 24-week clevudine therapy. *PLoS ONE* **2012**, *7*, e50377. [CrossRef]
9. Pourbashash, H.; Pilyugin, S.S.; De Leenheer, P.; McCluskey, C. Global analysis of within host virus models with cell-to-cell viral transmission. *Discret. Contin. Dyn. Syst. Ser. B* **2014**, *19*, 3341–3357. [CrossRef]
10. Zhang, S.; Li, F.; Xu, X. Dynamics and control strategy for a delayed viral infection model. *J. Biol. Dyn.* **2022**, *16*, 44–63. [CrossRef]
11. Rihan, F.A. *Delay Differential Equations and Applications to Biology*; Springer: Singapore, 2021.
12. Wolfram Research, Inc. *Mathematica*; version 13.2; Wolfram: Champaign, IL, USA, 2022.
13. Rackauckas, C.; Nie, Q. DifferentialEquations.jl—A Performant and Feature-Rich Ecosystem for Solving Differential Equations in Julia. *J. Open Res. Softw.* **2017**, *5*, 15. Available online: https://app.dimensions.aion2019/05/05 (accessed on 3 March 2024). [CrossRef]
14. Widmann, D.; Rackauckas, C. DelayDiffEq: Generating Delay Differential Equation Solvers via Recursive Embedding of Ordinary Differential Equation Solvers. *arXiv* **2022**, arXiv:2208.12879.
15. Khalighi, M.; Benedetti, G.; Lahti, L. Fdesolver: A julia package for solving fractional differential equations. *arXiv* **2022**, arXiv:2212.12550.
16. Kermack, W.O.; McKendrick, A.G. Contributions to the mathematical theory of epidemics–I. 1927. *Bull. Math. Biol.* **1991**, *53*, 33–55. [PubMed]
17. Hattaf, K. On the Stability and Numerical Scheme of Fractional Differential Equations with Application to Biology. *Computation* **2022**, *10*, 97. [CrossRef]
18. Chen-Charpentier, B. A Model of Hepatitis B Viral Dynamics with Delays. *AppliedMath* **2024**, *4*, 182–196. [CrossRef]
19. Wu, C.; Wong, P.J. Dengue transmission: Mathematical model with discrete time delays and estimation of the reproduction number. *J. Biol. Dyn.* **2019**, *13*, 1–25. [CrossRef] [PubMed]
20. Dell'Anna, L. Solvable delay model for epidemic spreading: The case of Covid-19 in Italy. *Sci. Rep.* **2020**, *10*, 15763. [CrossRef] [PubMed]
21. Shayak, B.; Sharma, M.M.; Rand, R.H.; Singh, A.; Misra, A. A Delay differential equation model for the spread of COVID-19. *Int. J. Eng. Res. Appl.* **2020**, *10*, 1–13.
22. Saade, M.; Ghosh, S.; Banerjee, M.; Volpert, V. An epidemic model with time delays determined by the infectivity and disease durations. *Math. Biosci. Eng.* **2023**, *20*, 12864–12888. [CrossRef] [PubMed]
23. Rihan, F.; Al-Mdallal, Q.; AlSakaji, H.; Hashish, A. A fractional-order epidemic model with time-delay and nonlinear incidence rate. *Chaos Solitons Fractals* **2019**, *126*, 97–105. [CrossRef]
24. Singh, H. Numerical simulation for fractional delay differential equations. *Int. J. Dyn. Control* **2021**, *9*, 463–474. [CrossRef]
25. Sun, D.; Liu, J.; Su, X.; Pei, G. Fractional differential equation modeling of the HBV infection with time delay and logistic proliferation. *Front. Public Health* **2022**, *10*, 1036901. [CrossRef]

Disclaimer/Publisher's Note: The statements, opinions and data contained in all publications are solely those of the individual author(s) and contributor(s) and not of MDPI and/or the editor(s). MDPI and/or the editor(s) disclaim responsibility for any injury to people or property resulting from any ideas, methods, instructions or products referred to in the content.

Article

Simpson's Variational Integrator for Systems with Quadratic Lagrangians

Juan Antonio Rojas-Quintero [1,2,*], François Dubois [3,4] and José Guadalupe Cabrera-Díaz [5]

[1] CONAHCYT, Tecnológico Nacional de México, I. T. Ensenada, Ensenada 22780, B.C., Mexico
[2] IMT Atlantique, LS2N, UMR CNRS 6004, 44307 Nantes, France
[3] Université Paris-Saclay, Laboratoire de Mathématiques d'Orsay, 91400 Orsay, France
[4] Conservatoire National des Arts et Métiers, Structural Mechanics and Coupled Systems Laboratory, 75141 Paris, France
[5] Tecnológico Nacional de México, I. T. Ensenada, Ensenada 22780, B.C., Mexico
* Correspondence: jarojas@conahcyt.mx

Abstract: This contribution proposes a variational symplectic integrator aimed at linear systems issued from the least action principle. An internal quadratic finite-element interpolation of the state is performed at each time step. Then, the action is approximated by Simpson's quadrature formula. The implemented scheme is implicit, symplectic, and conditionally stable. It is applied to the time integration of systems with quadratic Lagrangians. The example of the linearized double pendulum is treated. Our method is compared with Newmark's variational integrator. The exact solution of the linearized double pendulum example is used for benchmarking. Simulation results illustrate the precision and convergence of the proposed integrator.

Keywords: ordinary differential equations; oscillator; numerical analysis; symplectic scheme

MSC: 34A30; 65L05; 65P10

1. Introduction

Simpson's quadrature is the name that is generally given to a numerical approximation of definite integrals that is exact for polynomials up to the third degree:

$$\int_0^1 \psi(\theta) \mathrm{d}\theta \simeq \frac{1}{6}\left(\psi(0) + 4\psi\left(\frac{1}{2}\right) + \psi(1)\right). \qquad (1)$$

It is well known that this rule was found by Bonaventura Cavalieri (1598–1647), known to James Gregory (1638–1675) [1], and even used by Johannes Kepler (1571–1630) to approximate the volume of barrels [2]. However, Thomas Simpson (1710–1761) is usually credited for this rule. As such, Formula (1) is also widely known as *Simpson's 1/3 rule*. It corresponds to a special case of Newton–Cotes's formula [1] and coincides with the classical fourth-order Runge–Kutta method [1,3].

Generally, numerical methods involving Simpson's quadrature estimate a definite integral by using quadratic polynomials to approximate the integrand on a sequence of intervals. This general idea is at the foundation of numerous methods that can be applied to solve engineering problems such as the low-thrust orbit transfer problem [4] or the gait optimization of a bipedal walking robot [5]. Recently, much attention has been brought to fractional calculus, for which solvers based on Simpson's quadrature (adapted to the fractional form) have been developed [6]. Some applications involve solving initial-value problems of fractional differential systems [7] or the solution of fractional equations affected by noisy signals [8]. Another recent application of Simpson's quadrature involves the solution of partial integro-differential equations [9].

Our contribution is aimed at solving differential equations characterizing the motions of mechanical systems. It is well known that the motions of a mechanical system are the extremals of the variational principle of least action [10]. This principle is one of the most general laws of theoretical physics and is foundational for characterizing a system's evolution in the form of differential equations. It is valid across disciplines such as classical and quantum mechanics, cosmology, electromagnetism, optics, and relativity [10–14]. As such, this variational principle is closely involved in the development of the finite-element method [15], which is used for the space and time integration of differential equations [16].

Numerical schemes for dynamical systems issued from the principle of least action are typically referred to as variational [17–20]. The general idea resides in performing a discretization at the least action principle level. As a result, the evolution equations deriving from this discretized principle characterize the system evolution, but are also a numerical scheme. It is well known that such numerical methods are endowed with interesting characteristics; one characteristic is the property of being symplectic [18–21]. One remarkable example of such methods is Newmark's integrator [17,19], which is very popular for solving problems in the dynamics of structures [22,23] and has recently been geometrized to solve the motion equations of sliding rods [24] and soft robots [25].

A symplectic scheme based on Simpson's rule has been proposed by the authors in [26], for the linear and scalar case of the harmonic oscillator. The scheme uses a quadratic finite-element interpolation. The method was adapted to the monodimensional non-linear pendulum system in [27]. In this work, Simpson's symplectic scheme is further studied as an alternative to Newmark's method. It is generalized to the case of multiple-degrees of freedom systems characterized by quadratic Lagrangians. The obtained results confirm the convergence rate previously observed in [26]. The new stability condition on the step size is revealed to be similar to the one previously obtained in [26]. A simplecticity analysis that applies to the multi-degree of freedom case, along with the expression of a related conserved quadratic form, is provided in this contribution.

We begin our study by detailing Newmark's classical scheme, deriving it from variational principles in Section 2. Then, Simpson's alternative scheme is detailed and derived from variational principles in Section 3. Section 4 analyzes the symplectic property of Simpson's scheme. A proof that applies to both Newmark's and Simpson's schemes is provided. To compare both methods in a case study, a two-degree of freedom system is presented. Therefore, the exact solution to the linearized double pendulum is provided in Section 5. This exact solution serves for benchmarking purposes in our comparisons. Section 6 presents and comments on the obtained numerical results. Simpson's scheme's convergence is revealed to be of the fourth order. The manuscript ends with a brief discussion and concluding remarks in Section 7.

2. Newmark's Scheme

2.1. Discrete Action

Let us derive the classical, symplectic variational integrator based on Newmark's scheme [17,19,22,23]. The continuous action is defined as

$$S_c = \int_0^T \mathcal{L}\left(\frac{d\mathbf{q}(t)}{dt}, \mathbf{q}(t)\right) dt \qquad (2)$$

where $\mathcal{L}$ is the system Lagrangian. We focus on dynamical systems for which the Lagrangian can be expressed quadratically as

$$\mathcal{L} = \frac{1}{2}\dot{\mathbf{q}}^T M \dot{\mathbf{q}} - \frac{1}{2}\mathbf{q}^T K \mathbf{q}, \qquad (3)$$

where M and K are symmetric, positive-definite n-dimensional matrices with constant coefficients; $\mathbf{q} \in \mathbb{R}^n$.

We can discretize Equation (2) by splitting the simulation interval $[0, T]$ into N elements using a time step $h = T/N$. An approximation q_j of $q(t_j)$ is calculated at each instance $t_j = jh$. The following action S_d represents the discrete version of Equation (2):

$$S_d = \sum_{j=1}^{N-1} L_d(\mathbf{q}_j, \mathbf{q}_{j+1}), \qquad (4)$$

where $L_d(\mathbf{q}_\ell, \mathbf{q}_r)$ is the discrete form of the Lagrangian (3). Subscripts ℓ and r stand for "left" and "right" values, respectively. Let us consider a centered finite-difference approximation:

$$\frac{d\mathbf{q}}{dt} \simeq \frac{\mathbf{q}_r - \mathbf{q}_\ell}{h},$$

and a midpoint quadrature:

$$\int_0^h \varphi(\mathbf{q}(t)) dt \simeq h \varphi\left(\frac{\mathbf{q}_\ell + \mathbf{q}_r}{2}\right).$$

The discrete Lagrangian becomes

$$L_d(\mathbf{q}_\ell, \mathbf{q}_r) = \frac{h}{2}\left[\left(\frac{\mathbf{q}_r - \mathbf{q}_\ell}{h}\right)^T M \left(\frac{\mathbf{q}_r - \mathbf{q}_\ell}{h}\right)\right] - \frac{h}{2}\left[\left(\frac{\mathbf{q}_\ell + \mathbf{q}_r}{2}\right)^T K \left(\frac{\mathbf{q}_\ell + \mathbf{q}_r}{2}\right)\right].$$

2.2. Discrete Euler–Lagrange Equations

The discrete action (4) being a sum, only two terms contain the variables $\mathbf{q}_j$:

$$S_d = \cdots + L_d(\mathbf{q}_{j-1}, \mathbf{q}_j) + L_d(\mathbf{q}_j, \mathbf{q}_{j+1}) + \cdots.$$

So, when the discrete action is stationary ($\delta S_d = 0$ for arbitrary variations $\delta \mathbf{q}_j$ of the states $\mathbf{q}_j$), only two terms remain. Necessarily,

$$\frac{\partial L_d}{\partial \mathbf{q}_r}(\mathbf{q}_{j-1}, \mathbf{q}_j) + \frac{\partial L_d}{\partial \mathbf{q}_\ell}(\mathbf{q}_j, \mathbf{q}_{j+1}) = 0. \qquad (5)$$

The generalized momenta $\mathbf{p}_j \in \mathbb{R}^n$ are defined, on the right, as

$$\mathbf{p}_j = \frac{\partial L_d}{\partial \mathbf{q}_r}(\mathbf{q}_\ell, \mathbf{q}_r). \qquad (6)$$

Therefore, the first term of Equation (5) is identified as $\mathbf{p}_j$, so applying Equation (6) in Equation (5) leads to

$$\mathbf{p}_j = -\frac{\partial L_d}{\partial \mathbf{q}_\ell}(\mathbf{q}_j, \mathbf{q}_{j+1}) = M\left(\frac{\mathbf{q}_{j+1} - \mathbf{q}_j}{h}\right) + \frac{h}{2} K\left(\frac{\mathbf{q}_j + \mathbf{q}_{j+1}}{2}\right). \qquad (7)$$

Then, $\mathbf{p}_{j+1}$ is constructed following Equation (6):

$$\mathbf{p}_{j+1} = M\left(\frac{\mathbf{q}_{j+1} - \mathbf{q}_j}{h}\right) - \frac{h}{2} K\left(\frac{\mathbf{q}_j + \mathbf{q}_{j+1}}{2}\right). \qquad (8)$$

Using Equations (7) and (8), it can be established that

$$\frac{\mathbf{p}_{j+1} - \mathbf{p}_j}{h} = -K\left(\frac{\mathbf{q}_j + \mathbf{q}_{j+1}}{2}\right); \quad \frac{\mathbf{p}_j + \mathbf{p}_{j+1}}{2} = M\left(\frac{\mathbf{q}_{j+1} - \mathbf{q}_j}{h}\right). \qquad (9)$$

Equations (9) are consistent with $\frac{d\mathbf{p}}{dt} = -K\mathbf{q}$ and $\mathbf{p} = M\frac{d\mathbf{q}}{dt}$, respectively.

2.3. Newmark's Scheme

System (9) can then be arranged in linear form as

$$A_n \eta_{j+1} = B_n \eta_j, \qquad (10)$$

where $\eta \in \mathbb{R}^{2n}, \eta = (\mathbf{p}, \mathbf{q})^T$ and

$$A_n = \begin{pmatrix} \mathbb{I}_n & -X_n \\ \mathbb{I}_n & Y_n \end{pmatrix}; \quad B_n = \begin{pmatrix} -\mathbb{I}_n & -X_n \\ \mathbb{I}_n & -Y_n \end{pmatrix}; \quad X_n = \frac{2}{h}M; \quad Y_n = \frac{h}{2}K; \qquad (11)$$

$\mathbb{I}_n$ is the n-dimensional identity matrix.

Newmark's symplectic scheme is obtained by matrix inversion of Equation (10). We can establish that

$$\eta_{j+1} = \Phi_n \eta_j, \quad \Phi_n = A_n^{-1} B, \qquad (12)$$

where matrices A and B are defined in Equation (11) above. It has been observed that this particular variant of Newmark's method is unconditionally stable and second-order convergent [19].

3. Simpson's Scheme

Newmark's scheme, presented in Section 2, uses a midpoint quadrature for the numerical integration of a regular function. This quadrature is exact only for polynomials up to the first degree. A better precision is obtained with Simpson's quadrature (1), which is exact for polynomials up to the third degree. Notice how Formula (1) introduces a midpoint. This midpoint will be regarded as an additional degree of freedom in our proposed integrator.

Let us now derive a symplectic scheme based on this integration rule. As with Newmark's scheme, the continuous action is defined by Equation (2) and the Lagrangian has the structure of Equation (3).

3.1. Quadratic Finite-Element Interpolation

An internal interpolation can be performed at each time step, for $t \in [0, h]$, using quadratic finite elements [16,28]. We use the following compact basis functions for $0 \leq \theta \leq 1$:

$$\varphi_0(\theta) = (1-\theta)(1-2\theta), \quad \varphi_{1/2}(\theta) = 4\theta(1-\theta), \quad \varphi_1(\theta) = \theta(2\theta - 1). \qquad (13)$$

At $t = h\theta$, the states $\mathbf{q}(t) \in P_2$ are approximated with the above basis functions as

$$\mathbf{q}(t) = \mathbf{q}_\ell \varphi_0(\theta) + \mathbf{q}_m \varphi_{1/2}(\theta) + \mathbf{q}_r \varphi_1(\theta). \qquad (14)$$

Note that $\mathbf{q}(0) = \mathbf{q}_\ell$, $\mathbf{q}\left(\frac{h}{2}\right) = \mathbf{q}_m$ and $\mathbf{q}(h) = \mathbf{q}_r$; here, subscript m stands for "middle".

This means that the finite-elements (13) are well adapted to the internal degree of freedom at $h/2$. Then, by time differentiation,

$$\begin{aligned}
\frac{d\mathbf{q}}{dt} &= \frac{1}{h}\left(\mathbf{q}_\ell \frac{d\varphi_0}{d\theta} + \mathbf{q}_m \frac{d\varphi_{1/2}}{d\theta} + \mathbf{q}_r \frac{d\varphi_1}{d\theta}\right) \\
&= \frac{1}{h}(\mathbf{q}_\ell(4\theta - 3) + 4\mathbf{q}_m(1 - 2\theta) + \mathbf{q}_r(4\theta - 1)) \\
&= \mathbf{g}_\ell(1-\theta) + \mathbf{g}_r \theta
\end{aligned}$$

where derivatives $\mathbf{g}_\ell, \mathbf{g}_r \in \mathbb{R}^n$ are given by Gear's scheme [29]. Gear's scheme is used as the differentiation approximation for $\mathbf{q}(t) \in P_2$ as

$$\mathbf{g}_\ell = \frac{d\mathbf{q}}{dt}(0) \quad -\frac{1}{h}(-3\mathbf{q}_\ell + 4\mathbf{q}_m - \mathbf{q}_r),$$
$$\mathbf{g}_m = \frac{d\mathbf{q}}{dt}\left(\frac{h}{2}\right) = \frac{\mathbf{g}_\ell + \mathbf{g}_r}{2} = \frac{\mathbf{q}_r - \mathbf{q}_\ell}{h}, \quad (15)$$
$$\mathbf{g}_r = \frac{d\mathbf{q}}{dt}(h) \quad = \frac{1}{h}(\mathbf{q}_\ell - 4\mathbf{q}_m + 3\mathbf{q}_r),$$

where $\mathbf{g}_m \in \mathbb{R}^n$. The above confirms that a first-order centered finite difference is recovered by $\mathbf{g}_m$, which is the derivative at the middle of the discretization interval.

The interpolation is used within an interval of length h by splitting the range $[0, T]$ into N pieces, giving a fixed step size of $h = T/N$. At each discrete time instance $t_j = jh$, we have

$$\mathbf{q}_j \simeq \mathbf{q}(t_j), \quad \forall\, 0 \leqslant j \leqslant N;$$
$$\mathbf{q}_{j+1/2} \simeq \mathbf{q}\left(t_j + \frac{h}{2}\right), \forall\, 0 \leqslant j \leqslant N-1.$$

Taking Equation (14), $\mathbf{q}(t)$ is a quadratic polynomial vector function within the interval $[t_j, t_{j+1}]$ with

$$t = t_j + \theta h, \quad \mathbf{q}_\ell = \mathbf{q}_j, \quad \mathbf{q}_m = \mathbf{q}_{j+1/2}, \quad \mathbf{q}_r = \mathbf{q}_{j+1}.$$

3.2. Discrete Lagrangian

Let us recall that the continuous action is defined by Equation (2) and that the Lagrangian is defined by Equation (3). In the present case, the discrete action sum Σ_d for a motion $t \mapsto \mathbf{q}(t)$ between the initial time and a given final time $T > 0$ is discretized with N regular intervals as

$$\Sigma_d = \sum_{j=1}^{N-1} L_h\left(\mathbf{q}_j, \mathbf{q}_{j+1/2}, \mathbf{q}_{j+1}\right), \quad (16)$$

where $L_h(\mathbf{q}_\ell, \mathbf{q}_m, \mathbf{q}_r)$ is the discrete form

$$L_h(\mathbf{q}_\ell, \mathbf{q}_m, \mathbf{q}_r) \simeq \int_0^h \mathcal{L}\, dt,$$

of the Lagrangian (3). Using Simpson's rule (1), the polynomial approximation (14) of the states, and derivatives (15), the discrete Lagrangian of a linear system is expressed as

$$L_h(\mathbf{q}_\ell, \mathbf{q}_m, \mathbf{q}_r) = \frac{h}{2}\left[\frac{1}{6}\mathbf{g}_\ell^T M \mathbf{g}_\ell + \frac{2}{3}\mathbf{g}_m^T M \mathbf{g}_m + \frac{1}{6}\mathbf{g}_r^T M \mathbf{g}_r\right]$$
$$- \frac{h}{2}\left[\frac{1}{6}\mathbf{q}_\ell^T K \mathbf{q}_\ell + \frac{2}{3}\mathbf{q}_m^T K \mathbf{q}_m + \frac{1}{6}\mathbf{q}_r^T K \mathbf{q}_r\right].$$

3.3. Discrete Euler–Lagrange Equations

Recall that Simpson's rule introduces an internal degree of freedom in the middle of the interpolation interval. The discrete action (16) is a sum where only two terms contain the variables $\mathbf{q}_j$ and $\mathbf{q}_{j+1/2}$:

$$\Sigma_d = \cdots + L_h\left(\mathbf{q}_{j-1}, \mathbf{q}_{j-1/2}, \mathbf{q}_j\right) + L_h\left(\mathbf{q}_j, \mathbf{q}_{j+1/2}, \mathbf{q}_{j+1}\right) + \cdots$$

Maupertuis's stationary action principle [10] implies that $\delta \Sigma_d = 0$ for an arbitrary variation of the internal degree of freedom $\delta \mathbf{q}_{j+1/2} \in [t_j, t_{j+1}]$. Considering Gear's scheme (15), we have

$$\frac{\partial g_\ell^i}{\partial q_m^k} = \frac{4}{h}, \frac{\partial g_m^i}{\partial q_m^k} = 0, \frac{\partial g_r^i}{\partial q_m^k} = -\frac{4}{h}, \forall i = k,\ 0 \text{ otherwise,}$$

where g^i is the i-th component of $\mathbf{g}$ and q^k is the k-th component of $\mathbf{q}$.

When $\delta\Sigma_d = 0$, $\frac{\partial L_h}{\partial \mathbf{q}_m}\left(\mathbf{q}_j, \mathbf{q}_{j+1/2}, \mathbf{q}_{j+1}\right) = 0$ by necessity. This conforms to the discrete Euler–Lagrange equations at the middle of the interpolation interval:

$$\frac{4}{3h}M\mathbf{g}_j - \frac{4}{3h}M\mathbf{g}_{j+1} - \frac{4}{3}K\mathbf{q}_{j+1/2} = 0. \quad (17)$$

However, $\mathbf{g}_j - \mathbf{g}_{j+1} = \frac{1}{h}\left(-4\mathbf{q}_j + 8\mathbf{q}_{j+1/2} - 4\mathbf{q}_{j+1}\right)$, so Equation (17) becomes

$$M\left(4\frac{\mathbf{q}_j - 2\mathbf{q}_{j+1/2} + \mathbf{q}_{j+1}}{h^2}\right) + K\mathbf{q}_{j+1/2} = 0. \quad (18)$$

This last equation is consistent with $M\frac{d^2\mathbf{q}}{dt^2} + K\mathbf{q} = 0$.

Additionally, for an arbitrary variation $\delta\mathbf{q}_j$, the Euler–Lagrange equations are given by the necessary condition that

$$\frac{\partial L_d}{\partial \mathbf{q}_r}\left(\mathbf{q}_{j-1}, \mathbf{q}_{j-1/2}, \mathbf{q}_j\right) + \frac{\partial L_d}{\partial \mathbf{q}_\ell}\left(\mathbf{q}_j, \mathbf{q}_{j+1/2}, \mathbf{q}_{j+1}\right) = 0. \quad (19)$$

The generalized momenta $\mathbf{p}_j$ are defined, on the right, as

$$\mathbf{p}_j = \frac{\partial L_d}{\partial \mathbf{q}_r}(\mathbf{q}_\ell, \mathbf{q}_m, \mathbf{q}_r). \quad (20)$$

Therefore, the first term of Equation (19) is identified as $\mathbf{p}_j$, and it can established that

$$\begin{aligned}\mathbf{p}_j &= -\frac{\partial L_d}{\partial \mathbf{q}_\ell}\left(\mathbf{q}_j, \mathbf{q}_{j+1/2}, \mathbf{q}_{j+1}\right) \\ &= -\frac{h}{2}\left[-\frac{3}{3h}M\mathbf{g}_j - \frac{4}{3h}M\mathbf{g}_{j+1/2} + \frac{1}{3h}M\mathbf{g}_{j+1}\right] + \frac{h}{6}K\mathbf{q}_j \\ &= -\frac{1}{6h}M\left(14\mathbf{q}_j - 16\mathbf{q}_{j+1/2} + 2\mathbf{q}_{j+1}\right) + \frac{h}{6}K\mathbf{q}_j,\end{aligned} \quad (21)$$

because $-3\mathbf{g}_j - 4\mathbf{g}_{j+1/2} + \mathbf{g}_{j+1} = \frac{1}{h}\left(14\mathbf{q}_j - 16\mathbf{q}_{j+1/2} + 2\mathbf{q}_{j+1}\right)$. Equation (18) is then multiplied by $h/3$, and the result is added to Equation (21). This eliminates $\mathbf{q}_{j+1/2}$ from the first term of the right-hand side:

$$\mathbf{p}_j = M\left(\frac{\mathbf{q}_{j+1} - \mathbf{q}_j}{h}\right) - \frac{h}{6}K\left(-2\mathbf{q}_{j+1/2} - \mathbf{q}_j\right). \quad (22)$$

Then, $\mathbf{p}_{j+1}$ is calculated according to Equation (20)

$$\begin{aligned}\mathbf{p}_{j+1} &= \frac{\partial L_d}{\partial \mathbf{q}_r}\left(\mathbf{q}_j, \mathbf{q}_{j+1/2}, \mathbf{q}_{j+1}\right) \\ &= \frac{h}{2}\left[-\frac{1}{3h}M\mathbf{g}_j + \frac{4}{3h}M\mathbf{g}_{j+1/2} + \frac{3}{3h}M\mathbf{g}_{j+1}\right] - \frac{h}{6}K\mathbf{q}_{j+1} \\ &= \frac{1}{6h}M\left(2\mathbf{q}_j - 16\mathbf{q}_{j+1/2} + 14\mathbf{q}_{j+1}\right) - \frac{h}{6}K\mathbf{q}_{j+1}\end{aligned} \quad (23)$$

because $-\mathbf{g}_j + 4\mathbf{g}_{j+1/2} + 3\mathbf{g}_{j+1} = \frac{1}{h}\left(2\mathbf{q}_j - 16\mathbf{q}_{j+1/2} + 14\mathbf{q}_{j+1}\right)$. Equation (18) is then multiplied by $-h/3$, and the result is added to Equation (23). This eliminates $\mathbf{q}_{j+1/2}$ from the first term of the right-hand side:

$$\mathbf{p}_{j+1} = M\left(\frac{\mathbf{q}_{j+1} - \mathbf{q}_j}{h}\right) - \frac{h}{6}K\left(2\mathbf{q}_{j+1/2} + \mathbf{q}_{j+1}\right). \quad (24)$$

Using Equations (22) and (24), we can establish that

$$\begin{cases} \dfrac{\mathbf{p}_{j+1} - \mathbf{p}_j}{h} = -K\left(\dfrac{1}{6}\mathbf{q}_j + \dfrac{2}{3}\mathbf{q}_{j+1/2} + \dfrac{1}{6}\mathbf{q}_{j+1}\right) \\ \dfrac{\mathbf{p}_j + \mathbf{p}_{j+1}}{2} = \left(M - \dfrac{h^2}{12}K\right)\left(\dfrac{\mathbf{q}_{j+1} - \mathbf{q}_j}{h}\right). \end{cases} \quad (25)$$

Equations (25) are consistent with $\frac{d\mathbf{p}}{dt} = -K\mathbf{q}$ and $\mathbf{p} = M\frac{d\mathbf{q}}{dt}$, respectively. Note that the term $\frac{h^2}{12}K$ in the second equation above vanishes as $h \to 0$.

3.4. First Variant of Simpson's Scheme

The system composed of Equations (18) and (25) can be rearranged as

$$\begin{cases} L\,\mathbf{q}_{j+1/2} - \dfrac{1}{2}\mathbf{q}_{j+1} = \dfrac{1}{2}\mathbf{q}_j \\ \mathbf{p}_{j+1} - \left(\dfrac{2}{h}M - \dfrac{h}{6}K\right)\mathbf{q}_{j+1} = -\mathbf{p}_j - \left(\dfrac{2}{h}M - \dfrac{h}{6}K\right)\mathbf{q}_j \\ \dfrac{2h}{3}K\mathbf{q}_{j+1/2} + \mathbf{p}_{j+1} + \dfrac{h}{6}K\mathbf{q}_{j+1} = \mathbf{p}_j - \dfrac{h}{6}K\mathbf{q}_j \end{cases} \quad (26)$$

where

$$L = \left(\mathbb{I}_n - \dfrac{h^2}{8}M^{-1}K\right).$$

System (26) can then be arranged in linear form:

$$A_\sigma \begin{pmatrix} \mathbf{q}_{j+1/2} \\ \eta_{j+1} \end{pmatrix} = B_\sigma\, \eta_{j+1}, \quad (27)$$

where $\eta \in \mathbb{R}^{2n}$, $\eta = (\mathbf{p}, \mathbf{q})^T$;

$$A = \begin{pmatrix} L & 0 & -\frac{1}{2}\mathbb{I}_n \\ 0 & \mathbb{I}_n & -\left(\frac{2}{h}M - \frac{h}{6}K\right) \\ \frac{2h}{3}K & \mathbb{I}_n & \frac{h}{6}K \end{pmatrix};\quad B = \begin{pmatrix} 0 & \frac{1}{2}\mathbb{I}_n \\ -\mathbb{I}_n & -\left(\frac{2}{h}M - \frac{h}{6}K\right) \\ \mathbb{I}_n & -\frac{h}{6}K \end{pmatrix}. \quad (28)$$

The first variant of Simpson's scheme is obtained by matrix inversion of Equation (27). We can establish that

$$\begin{pmatrix} \mathbf{q}_{j+1/2} \\ \eta_{j+1} \end{pmatrix} = A_\sigma^{-1} B_\sigma\, \eta_j, \quad (29)$$

where matrices A_σ and B_σ are defined in Equation (28) above.

3.5. Second Variant of Simpson's Scheme

Simpson's scheme's internal degree of freedom can be eliminated using the first equation of System (26):

$$\mathbf{q}_{j+1/2} = \dfrac{1}{2}L^{-1}\left(\mathbf{q}_{j+1} + \mathbf{q}_j\right).$$

This equation approximates the middle point when $h \to 0$, because then $L \to \mathbb{I}_n$. Substituting this value into the third equation of System (26) leads to

$$\mathbf{p}_{j+1} + \dfrac{h}{3}\left(KL^{-1} + \dfrac{1}{2}K\right)\mathbf{q}_{j+1} = \mathbf{p}_j - \dfrac{h}{3}\left(KL^{-1} + \dfrac{1}{2}K\right)\mathbf{q}_j,$$

and the second equation of System (26) remains unchanged. Therefore, the internal degree of freedom is successfully eliminated so that, now,

$$A_s \eta_{j+1} = B_s \eta_j \qquad (30)$$

where $\eta \in \mathbb{R}^{2n}$; $\eta = (\mathbf{p}, \mathbf{q})^T$;

$$A_s = \begin{pmatrix} \mathbb{I}_n & -X_s \\ \mathbb{I}_n & Y_s \end{pmatrix}; \quad B_s = \begin{pmatrix} -\mathbb{I}_n & -X_s \\ \mathbb{I}_n & -Y_s \end{pmatrix}; \quad X_s = \frac{2}{h}M - \frac{h}{6}K; \quad Y_s = \frac{h}{3}\left(KL^{-1} + \frac{1}{2}K\right). \qquad (31)$$

The second variant of Simpson's symplectic scheme is obtained by matrix inversion of Equation (30). We can establish that

$$\eta_{j+1} = \Phi_s \eta_j, \quad \Phi_s = A_s^{-1} B_s, \qquad (32)$$

where matrices A_s and B_s are defined in Equation (31) above. Note that schemes (29) and (32) are equivalent. However, this second variant eliminates the internal degree of freedom in the middle of the interval.

The symplecticity of Simpson's scheme (32) has not yet been proven. However, one can appreciate the similarity with Newmark's scheme by comparing Equation (11) and Equation (31). The symplectic property of both schemes is analyzed in Section 4.

4. Symplecticity of Newmark's and Simpson's Schemes

The symplectic property of both Newmark's scheme (12) and Simpson's scheme (32) is now analyzed.

4.1. Symplectic Property

A symplecticity proof is obtained by verifying that

$$\Phi^T \mathbb{J} \Phi = \mathbb{J}; \quad \mathbb{J} = \begin{pmatrix} 0 & -\mathbb{I}_n \\ \mathbb{I}_n & 0 \end{pmatrix}. \qquad (33)$$

Φ corresponds to the scheme transformation matrix and characterizes a discrete time evolution of the system. $\mathbb{J}$ is sometimes referred to as the canonical matrix for Hamiltonian systems [30] and has the property that $\mathbb{J}^{-1} = \mathbb{J}^T = -\mathbb{J}$. When Equation (33) holds, it means that Φ is an area-preserving transformation and that the scheme (12) is symplectic (see, e.g., [18–20,31] for more details on this demonstration).

Proposition 1. *An implicit scheme of the type*

$$\eta_{j+1} = A^{-1} B \eta_j; \quad \eta = (\mathbf{p}, \mathbf{q})^T,$$

is symplectic if

$$A = \begin{pmatrix} \mathbb{I}_n & -X \\ \mathbb{I}_n & Y \end{pmatrix}, \quad B = \begin{pmatrix} -\mathbb{I}_n & -X \\ \mathbb{I}_n & -Y \end{pmatrix}, \qquad (34)$$

are square, partitioned, invertible matrices and blocks X and Y are symmetric and positive-definite.

Proof of Proposition 1. Let us first make explicit the transformation A^{-1}. Since A is square and partitioned, its inversion is performed using auxiliary variables α and β. Let us establish that

$$A \begin{pmatrix} \mathbf{p} \\ \mathbf{q} \end{pmatrix} = \begin{pmatrix} \mathbf{p} - X\mathbf{q} \\ \mathbf{p} + Y\mathbf{q} \end{pmatrix} = \begin{pmatrix} \alpha \\ \beta \end{pmatrix} \qquad (35)$$

Subtracting both equations above gives

$$\mathbf{q} = Z^{-1}(\beta - \alpha); \quad Z = X + Y. \qquad (36)$$

Since Z is the sum of two symmetric, positive-definite matrices, it is invertible. Equation (36) is then substituted into the first equation of System (35):

$$\mathbf{p} = \left(\mathbb{I}_n - XZ^{-1}\right)\alpha + XZ^{-1}\beta. \tag{37}$$

Matrix A from Equation (34) is inverted in Equations (36) and (37) as:

$$A^{-1} = \begin{pmatrix} \mathbb{I}_n - XZ^{-1} & XZ^{-1} \\ -Z^{-1} & Z^{-1} \end{pmatrix}.$$

Then, it suffices to verify Equation (33) with $\Phi = A^{-1}B$. Thus,

$$\Phi^T \mathbb{J} \Phi = B^T A^{-T} \mathbb{J} A^{-1} B = B^T \begin{pmatrix} -Z^{-T} & -(\mathbb{I}_n - Z^{-T}X^T) \\ Z^{-T} & -Z^{-T}X^T \end{pmatrix} A^{-1} B$$

$$= B^T \begin{pmatrix} 0 & Z^{-1} \\ -Z^{-1} & 0 \end{pmatrix} B = \begin{pmatrix} Z^{-1} & Z^{-1} \\ -YZ^{-1} & XZ^{-1} \end{pmatrix} B$$

$$= \begin{pmatrix} -Z^{-1} + Z^{-1} & -Z^{-1}(X+Y) \\ (Y+X)Z^{-1} & YZ^{-1}X - XZ^{-1}Y \end{pmatrix}$$

$$= \begin{pmatrix} 0 & -\mathbb{I}_n \\ \mathbb{I}_n & (X^{-1}ZY^{-1})^{-1} - (Y^{-1}ZX^{-1})^{-1} \end{pmatrix} = \begin{pmatrix} 0 & -\mathbb{I}_n \\ \mathbb{I}_n & 0 \end{pmatrix} = \mathbb{J},$$

because $X = X^T$, $Y = Y^T$, so $Z^{-1} = Z^{-T}$. □

4.2. Symplectic Property of Newmark's Scheme

Proposition 2. *Newmark's scheme (12) is symplectic.*

Proof of Proposition 2. In Newmark's scheme's formulation (12), matrices A_n and B_n from Equation (11) are of the form of Equation (34), because X_n and Y_n (11) are symmetric and positive-definite. By Proposition 1, Newmark's scheme is symplectic. □

This confirms the classical result (e.g., [19]) on Newmark's scheme's symplecticity.

4.3. Symplectic Property of Simpson's Scheme

To prove that Simpson's scheme is symplectic, we first need to prove that A_s and B_s have the structure of Equation (34). For this, blocks X_s and Y_s are required to be symmetric and positive-definite.

Proposition 3. *Matrix Y_s (31) is symmetric.*

Proof of Proposition 3. Since M and K are symmetric, Y_s is symmetric if and only if its first term:

$$W = KL^{-1}$$

is symmetric as well. W is symmetric if W^{-1} is symmetric. As

$$W^{-1} = \left(\mathbb{I}_n - \frac{h^2}{8}M^{-1}K\right)K^{-1} = K^{-1} - \frac{h^2}{8}M^{-1},$$

is symmetric, Y_s is also symmetric. □

For Y_s to be positive-definite, the part KL^{-1} must be positive-definite. Since KL^{-1} is symmetric by Proposition 3, a condition on the step size h is required.

Let us introduce the smallest and largest eigenvalues of matrices M and K:

$$0 < \mu \|\varphi\|^2 \leqslant \varphi^T M \varphi \leqslant m \|\varphi\|^2$$
$$0 < \kappa \|\varphi\|^2 \leqslant \varphi^T K \varphi \leqslant k \|\varphi\|^2 \tag{38}$$

where (μ, κ) are the smallest and (m, k) are the largest eigenvalues of matrices M and K, respectively; $\varphi \neq \mathbf{0}$ is an eigenvector. Taking $M^{1/2}\varphi = \psi$ and then $K^{1/2}\varphi = \psi$, Equation (38) becomes

$$\frac{1}{m}\|\psi\|^2 \leqslant \psi^T M \psi \leqslant \frac{1}{\mu}\|\psi\|^2$$
$$\frac{1}{k}\|\psi\|^2 \leqslant \psi^T K \psi \leqslant \frac{1}{\kappa}\|\psi\|^2,$$

and so,

$$\psi^T \left(L K^{-1} \right) \psi \geqslant \left(\frac{1}{k} - \frac{h^2}{8} \frac{1}{\mu} \right) \|\psi\|^2. \tag{39}$$

The above expression is positive for

$$0 < \frac{k}{\mu} h^2 < 8. \tag{40}$$

This inequality is a sufficient stability condition for Simpson's scheme. Let us remark that k/μ corresponds to the maximum eigenvalue of the dynamical matrix inverse $M^{-1}K$ and is associated with the maximum characteristic eigenfrequency of the system (see [22]) by

$$\frac{k}{\mu} = \omega_{\max}{}^2.$$

The stability condition (40) can also be stated as

$$0 < \omega_{\max} h < 2\sqrt{2}.$$

This condition is similar to the stability condition characterizing the mono-dimensional case for Simpson's scheme [26].

Proposition 4. *Matrix Y_s from Equation (31) is positive-definite if $0 < \frac{k}{\mu} h^2 < 8$.*

Proof of Proposition 4. When the condition (40) is met, Equation (39) becomes

$$\psi^T \left(L K^{-1} \right) \psi > 0, \quad \forall \psi \neq \mathbf{0},$$

and LK^{-1} is positive-definite. Therefore, KL^{-1} is also positive-definite, and recalling Proposition 3, it is symmetric. Consequently,

$$\psi^T Y_s \psi > 0, \quad \forall \psi \neq \mathbf{0},$$

and Y_s is positive-definite. □

Now, only the positive-definiteness of block X_s from Equation (31) remains to be proven.

Proposition 5. *Matrix X_s from Equation (31) is positive-definite if $0 < \frac{k}{\mu} h^2 < 8$.*

Proof of Proposition 5. From inequality (38),

$$\varphi^T M \varphi - \frac{h^2}{12}\varphi^T K \varphi \geq \left(\mu - \frac{h^2}{12}k\right)\|\varphi\|^2,$$

and substituting the condition (40) for the first term of the right-hand side of the above inequality,

$$\varphi^T\left(M - \frac{h^2}{12}K\right)\varphi \geq \frac{\mu}{3}\|\varphi\|^2 > 0, \quad \forall \varphi \neq \mathbf{0}.$$

Therefore, matrix X_s is positive-definite. □

Proposition 6. *Simpson's scheme* (32) *is symplectic.*

Proof of Proposition 6. For the second variant of Simpson's scheme (32), matrices A_s and B_s from Equation (31) are of the form of Equation (34), because X_s is symmetric and positive-definite by Proposition 5 and Y_s is symmetric and positive-definite by Propositions 3 and 4. □

These results prove that the proposed Simpson's scheme is symplectic.

4.4. Conservation of a Discrete Quadratic Form

Symplectic integrators usually do not preserve the energy quantity. This has been summarized in [32] and outlined in [19]. The goal is to verify that Simpson's scheme preserves some quadratic form. It is required that some quadratic function $\phi(\mathbf{p}, \mathbf{q})$ verifies

$$\phi(\mathbf{p}_{j+1}, \mathbf{q}_{j+1}) = \phi(\mathbf{p}_j, \mathbf{q}_j),$$

where $(\mathbf{p}_{j+1}, \mathbf{q}_{j+1})$ and $(\mathbf{p}_j, \mathbf{q}_j)$ satisfy the dynamics of Simpson's scheme, Equations (31) and (32).

Proposition 7. *Given an implicit scheme of the type*

$$\eta_{j+1} = A^{-1} B \eta_j; \quad \eta = (\mathbf{p}, \mathbf{q})^T, \tag{41}$$

where

$$A = \begin{pmatrix} \mathbb{I}_n & -X \\ \mathbb{I}_n & Y \end{pmatrix}, \quad B = \begin{pmatrix} -\mathbb{I}_n & -X \\ \mathbb{I}_n & -Y \end{pmatrix},$$

are square, partitioned, invertible matrices and blocks X and Y are symmetric and positive-definite, there exists a quadratic form:

$$\phi(\mathbf{p}, \mathbf{q}) = \frac{1}{2}\mathbf{p}^T \xi \mathbf{p} + \frac{1}{2}\mathbf{q}^T \zeta \mathbf{q}, \tag{42}$$

which is conserved if

$$\xi = (X+Y)^{-1}; \quad \zeta = (X^{-1} + Y^{-1})^{-1}.$$

Proof of Proposition 7. Let us expand Equation (41):

$$\mathbf{p}_{j+1} - X\mathbf{q}_{j+1} = -\mathbf{p}_j - X\mathbf{q}_j,$$
$$\mathbf{p}_{j+1} + X\mathbf{q}_{j+1} = \mathbf{p}_j - Y\mathbf{q}_j.$$

The above can also be written as

$$\mathbf{p}_{j+1} + \mathbf{p}_j = X(\mathbf{q}_{j+1} - \mathbf{q}_j)$$
$$\mathbf{p}_{j+1} - \mathbf{p}_j = -Y(\mathbf{q}_{j+1} + \mathbf{q}_j).$$

Therefore, by multiplying ξ by the first equation above on the left and by the second equation above on the right,

$$(\mathbf{p}_{j+1}+\mathbf{p}_j)^T \xi (\mathbf{p}_{j+1}-\mathbf{p}_j) = (X(\mathbf{q}_{j+1}-\mathbf{q}_j))^T \xi(-Y)(\mathbf{q}_{j+1}+\mathbf{q}_j) \qquad (43)$$
$$= -(\mathbf{q}_{j+1}-\mathbf{q}_j)^T X\xi Y(\mathbf{q}_{j+1}+\mathbf{q}_j).$$

Since
$$(X\xi Y)^{-1} = Y^{-1}(X+Y)X^{-1} = X^{-1} + Y^{-1} = \zeta^{-1}$$
is symmetric and positive-definite, it is deduced that $\zeta = X\xi Y$ is symmetric and positive-definite. Following from Equation (43),
$$\mathbf{p}_{j+1}^T \xi \mathbf{p}_{j+1} + \mathbf{q}_{j+1}^T \zeta \mathbf{q}_{j+1} = \mathbf{p}_j^T \xi \mathbf{p}_j + \mathbf{q}_j^T \zeta \mathbf{q}_j,$$
and the property is proven since $\phi(\mathbf{p}_{j+1}, \mathbf{q}_{j+1}) = \phi(\mathbf{p}_j, \mathbf{q}_j)$. □

By Proposition 7 and Condition (40), Simpson's scheme is conditionally stable.

5. Linear Double Pendulum Model and Exact Solution

This section presents a case study for subsequent numerical experiments.

5.1. Lagrangian

Let us model the system depicted by Figure 1. It is a two-degree-of-freedom dynamical system composed of two masses (m_1, m_2) linked together by two massless thin rigid rods of respective fixed lengths (l_1, l_2). Each joint articulates the system with one rotational degree of freedom. The masses' coordinates are given by

$$(x_1, y_1) = (l_1 \sin q_1, -l_1 \cos q_1)$$
$$(x_2, y_2) = (l_1 \sin q_1 + l_2 \sin q_2, -l_1 \cos q_1 - l_2 \cos q_2),$$

and their velocities are obtained by time differentiation considering that $q_i = q_i(t)$. The system kinetic energy is then given by

$$T = \frac{1}{2} m_1 \left(\dot{x}_1^2 + \dot{y}_1^2 \right) + \frac{1}{2} m_2 \left(\dot{x}_2^2 + \dot{y}_2^2 \right),$$

where an overdot indicates time differentiation. Potential energy is calculated as

$$V = -m_1 g l_1 \cos q_1 - m_2 g (l_1 \cos q_1 + l_2 \cos q_2),$$

and finally, the system Lagrangian $\mathcal{L} = T - V$ can be explicated as

$$\mathcal{L} = \frac{1}{2}(m_1 + m_2) l_1^2 \dot{q}_1^2 + \frac{1}{2} m_2 l_2^2 \dot{q}_2^2 + m_2 l_1 l_2 \dot{q}_1 \dot{q}_2 \cos(q_1 - q_2) \qquad (44)$$
$$+ (m_1 + m_2) g l_1 \cos q_1 + m_2 g l_2 \cos q_2.$$

Small oscillations take place when $q_i(t)$ are small and around the stable equilibrium. This equilibrium corresponds to the system's resting position when it is aligned with the vertical axis pointing downwards. Such motions can be described by linear equations. In this situation, the Lagrangian (44) takes a simpler form provided that the following approximations take place:

$$\cos q_1 \approx 1 - \frac{q_1^2}{2};$$
$$\cos q_2 \approx 1 - \frac{q_2^2}{2}; \qquad (45)$$
$$\cos(q_1 - q_2) \approx 1 - \frac{(q_1 - q_2)^2}{2}.$$

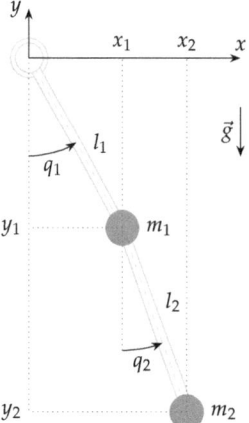

Figure 1. Double pendulum system subject to the gravity action. The system is composed of two masses (m_1, m_2) linked together by two massless thin rigid rods of respective fixed lengths (l_1, l_2). Each joint articulates the system with one rotational degree of freedom. Masses are located by the generalized coordinates $\mathbf{q} = (q_1, q_2)$.

Using Equation (45), the linear form L_L of Lagrangian (44) becomes

$$L_L = \frac{1}{2}(m_1 + m_2)l_1\left(l_1\dot{q}_1^2 + 2g - gq_1^2\right) + \frac{1}{2}m_2l_2\left(l_2\dot{q}_2^2 + 2l_1\dot{q}_1\dot{q}_2 + 2g - gq_2^2\right), \quad (46)$$

where the second term of the $\cos(q_1 - q_2)$ approximation in Equation (45) vanishes when multiplying the product $\dot{q}_1\dot{q}_2$. Generalized momenta are defined as

$$p_i = \frac{\partial L_L}{\partial \dot{q}_i}.$$

According to the Lagrangian (46), we have

$$p_1 = (m_1 + m_2)l_1^2\dot{q}_1 + m_2l_1l_2\dot{q}_2,$$
$$p_2 = m_2l_2(l_1\dot{q}_1 + l_2\dot{q}_2).$$

Motion equations are then obtained by applying Euler–Lagrange equations $\frac{d}{dt}\frac{\partial L_L}{\partial \dot{q}_i} - \frac{\partial L_L}{\partial q_i} = 0$:

$$\begin{aligned}(m_1 + m_2)l_1^2\ddot{q}_1 + m_2l_1l_2\ddot{q}_2 + (m_1 + m_2)gl_1q_1 &= 0, \\ m_2l_1l_2\ddot{q}_1 + m_2l_2^2\ddot{q}_2 + m_2gl_2q_2 &= 0.\end{aligned} \quad (47)$$

5.2. Exact Solution

Equation (47) can also be established as a linear system of the form

$$M\ddot{\mathbf{q}} + K\mathbf{q} = 0. \quad (48)$$

where

$$M = \begin{pmatrix} (m_1 + m_2)l_1^2 & m_2l_1l_2 \\ m_2l_1l_2 & m_2l_2^2 \end{pmatrix}; \quad \mathbf{q} = \begin{pmatrix} q_1 \\ q_2 \end{pmatrix}; \quad K = \begin{pmatrix} (m_1 + m_2)gl_1 & 0 \\ 0 & m_2gl_2 \end{pmatrix}.$$

The general solution of Equation (48) is of the form

$$\mathbf{q}(t) = \mathrm{Re}\left(\begin{bmatrix} \mathbf{x}_1 \\ \mathbf{x}_2 \end{bmatrix} \cdot e^{i\omega t} \right),$$

where $\mathbf{x}_1$ and $\mathbf{x}_2$ are eigenvectors and ω denotes the oscillation frequency. Two characteristic frequencies (ω_1, ω_2) are determined by the solution of the auxiliary equation $\det(K - \omega^2 M) = 0$:

$$(m_1 + m_2)g^2 - (m_1 + m_2)g(l_1 + l_2)\omega^2 + m_1 l_1 l_2 \omega^4 = 0.$$

Let us focus on the case where

$$l_1 = l_2 = l.$$

In this particular case, the oscillation frequencies are given by

$$\omega_{1,2} = \omega_0 \sqrt{\left(1 + \mu_r \pm \sqrt{\mu_r(1+\mu_r)}\right)}, \qquad (49)$$

with a mass ratio $\mu_r = m_2/m_1$ and frequency $\omega_0 = \sqrt{g/l}$.

Eigenvectors $\mathbf{x}_1$ and $\mathbf{x}_2$ are then obtained by solving $(K - \omega_i^2 M)\mathbf{x}_i = 0$ for $i = 1$ and $i = 2$:

$$m_1 l \begin{bmatrix} (1+\mu_r)(g - \omega_i^2 l) & -\omega_i^2 \mu_r l \\ -\omega_i^2 \mu_r l & \mu_r(g - \omega_i^2 \mu_r l) \end{bmatrix} \mathbf{x}_i = 0.$$

Solving the above system gives

$$\mathbf{x}_1 = \begin{bmatrix} 1 \\ -\sqrt{\frac{1+\mu_r}{\mu_r}} \end{bmatrix}, \quad \mathbf{x}_2 = \begin{bmatrix} 1 \\ \sqrt{\frac{1+\mu_r}{\mu_r}} \end{bmatrix}. \qquad (50)$$

Finally, using Equation (50), the general solution of Equation (48) (or Equation (47)) can be established as

$$\mathbf{q}(t) = c_1 \mathbf{x}_1 \cos(\omega_1 t + \varphi_1) + c_2 \mathbf{x}_2 \cos(\omega_2 t + \varphi_2), \qquad (51)$$

where constants $(c_1, c_2, \varphi_1, \varphi_2)$ are given by the chosen initial conditions on the positions and velocities.

6. Simulation Results

We will now assess the precision and convergence of our proposed integrator, previously described in Section 3. It will be compared with Newmark's symplectic scheme, described in Section 2. Some results obtained with Runge–Kutta's explicit fourth-order integrator, described in [3] and labeled as "RK4" throughout the rest of the document, are also given. Note that a thorough comparison with this classical integrator is beyond the scope of our contribution. The results are provided for reference since RK4 is among the most popular methods available. For benchmarking purposes, we applied these methods to the solution of the linear double pendulum (depicted by Figure 1), which has an exact solution described in the previous Section 5.

The results presented in this section are for a simulated motion of this linearized double pendulum. The computations were carried out using Wolfram's *Mathematica* software (version 12.3) [33]. The figure plots were then created using exported data with the *pgfplots* package from LATEX. Table 1 specifies the constants and initial conditions used for all of our simulations. Using these values and following Equation (51) with null initial phases (φ_1, φ_2), the exact solution that serves as the main reference in our comparisons is

$$\mathbf{q}_{\text{ex}}(t) = \frac{\pi}{12} \begin{pmatrix} \dfrac{-\cos(\omega_1 t) + \cos(\omega_2 t)}{\sqrt{2}} \\ \cos(\omega_1 t) + \cos(\omega_2 t) \end{pmatrix},$$

where ω_1 and ω_2 are given by Equation (49).

Table 1. Constants and initial conditions used for numerical simulations.

Constants	Initial Conditions
$\mu_r = 1$	$\mathbf{q}(0) = (0, \pi/6)^T$ rad
$\omega_0 = 2\pi\,\text{s}^{-1}$	$\mathbf{p}(0) = (0, 0)^T$ kg m^2 s^{-1}

Frequency ω_0 is used to show the results in terms of an oscillation period $\bar{t}$ such that

$$\bar{t} = \frac{1}{\omega_0}.$$

Therefore, both the total simulation duration T and step size h are given in terms of $\bar{t}$. It is to be noted that the presented results from Simpson's scheme were obtained using the second variant (see Section 3.5), hence the absence of the middle value at each interpolation interval. However, both variants provided lead to the same result at each node.

6.1. Configuration Parameters and Generalized Momenta

We begin by comparing the configuration parameter solutions $\mathbf{q}$ obtained with the proposed Simpson's rule-based variational integrator, against those given by Newmark's method. The proposed integrator uses quadratic finite elements for interpolation and Simpson's rule (see Section 3). It is expected to be more precise than Newmark's method, which uses a centered finite difference and the midpoint integration rule (see Section 2). Figure 2 shows the configuration parameters provided by each method, compared against the exact solution, during one period $\bar{t}$. Simpson's integrator is already more precise than Newmark's scheme. Runge–Kutta's solution is also close to the exact one, but not as much as Simpson's solution.

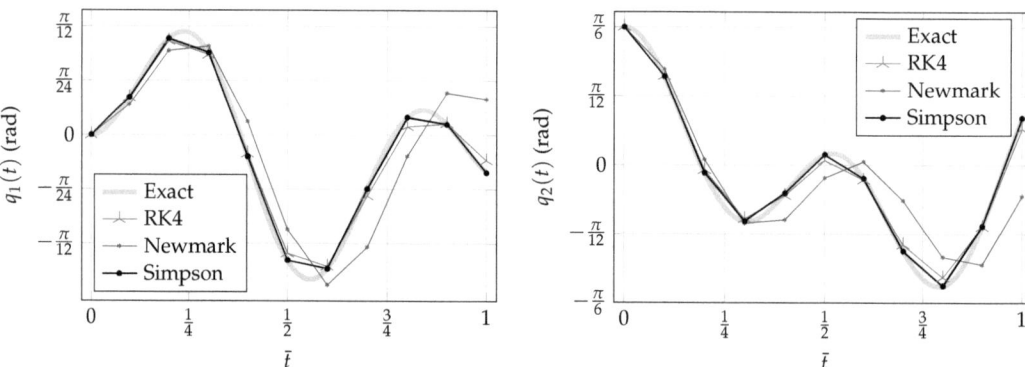

Figure 2. Configuration parameters', $\mathbf{q}$, evolution for the linear double pendulum. Initial conditions are specified in Table 1. The step size is fixed as $h = 0.1\,\bar{t}$. Simpson's integrator tracks the exact solution with more precision than Newmark's method and Runge–Kutta's integrator.

Figures 2 and 3 show that Simpson's integrator is more precise than both Newmark's and Runge–Kutta's integrators on a short simulation ($T = 1\,\bar{t}$). However, Simpson's solutions correctly follow the exact ones for longer simulations on both the configuration parameters and generalized momenta, as shown by Figure 4.

Newmark's integrator precision can be increased by refining the step size. With $h = 0.01\,\bar{t}$, the solutions improve, but still deviate from the exact solution after a couple of periods. Simpson's solutions correctly follow the exact solution for longer simulations.

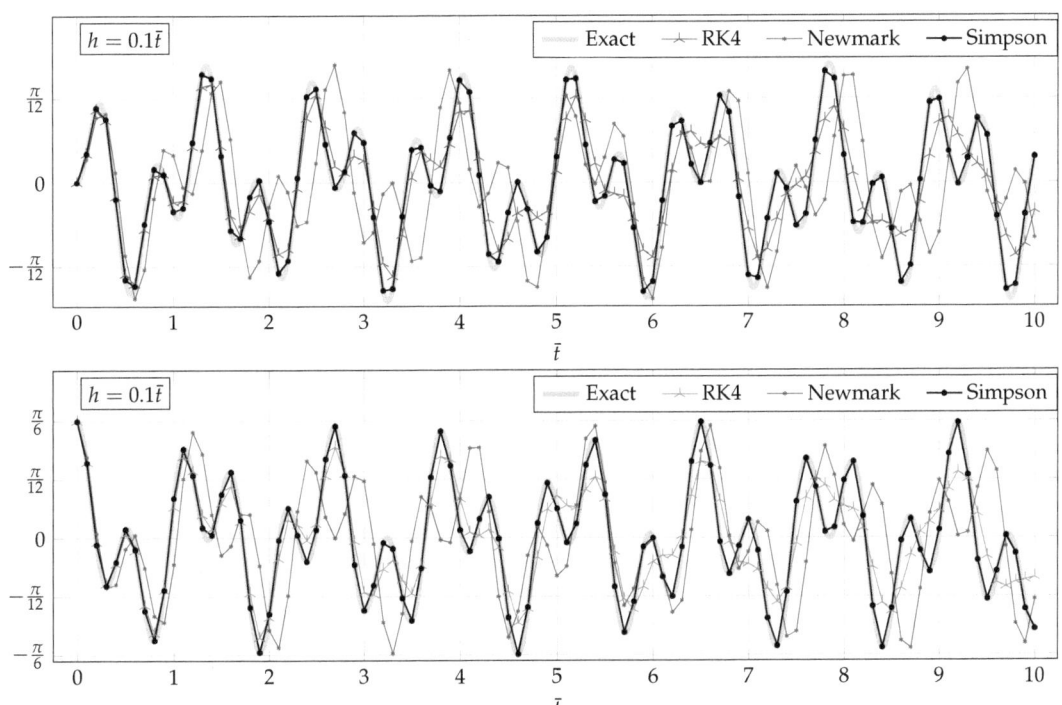

Figure 3. Configuration parameters', **q**, evolution for the linear double pendulum during ten periods. Initial conditions are specified in Table 1. The step size is fixed as $h = 0.1\,\bar{t}$. Simpson's solutions correctly follow the exact solution for longer simulations.

6.2. Phase Portraits

With a step size of $h = 0.1\,\bar{t}$, Newmark's solutions' deviations are particularly visible when tracing the motion phase portrait. Figure 5 shows the exact phase portraits topped by both Newmark's and Simpson's solutions. Notice how Simpson's phase portrait clearly follows the exact one throughout the motion. The total simulation time was limited to $T = 3\,\bar{t}$ for visualization purposes.

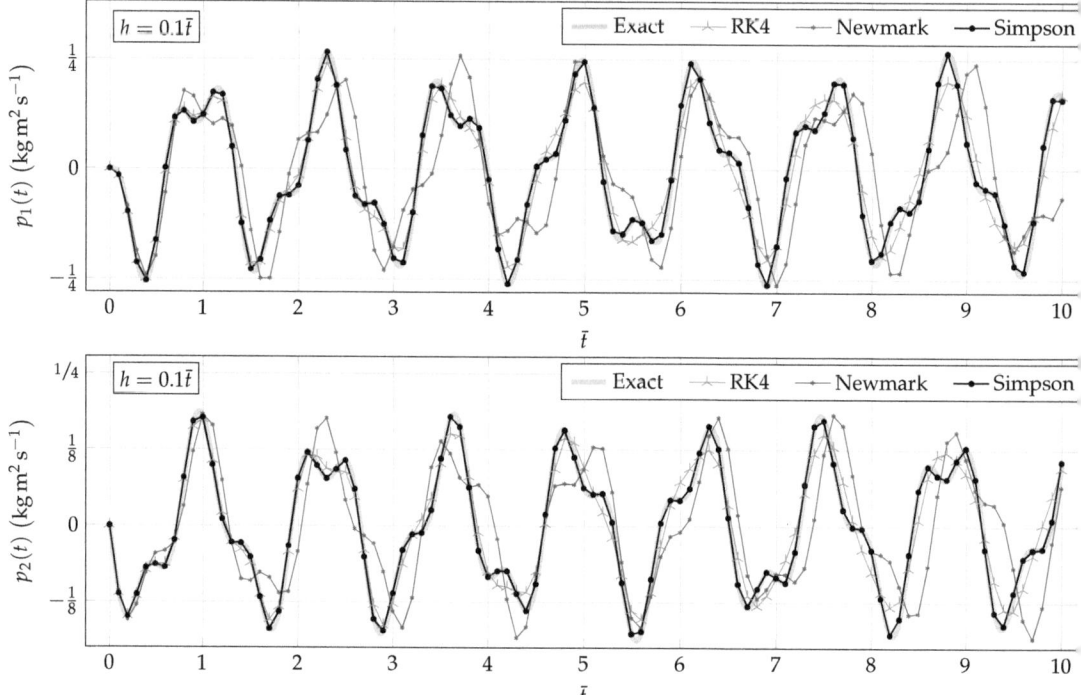

Figure 4. Generalized momenta's, **p**, evolution for the linear double pendulum during ten periods. Initial conditions are specified in Table 1. The step size is fixed as $h = 0.1\,\bar{t}$. Simpson's solutions correctly follow the exact solution for longer simulations.

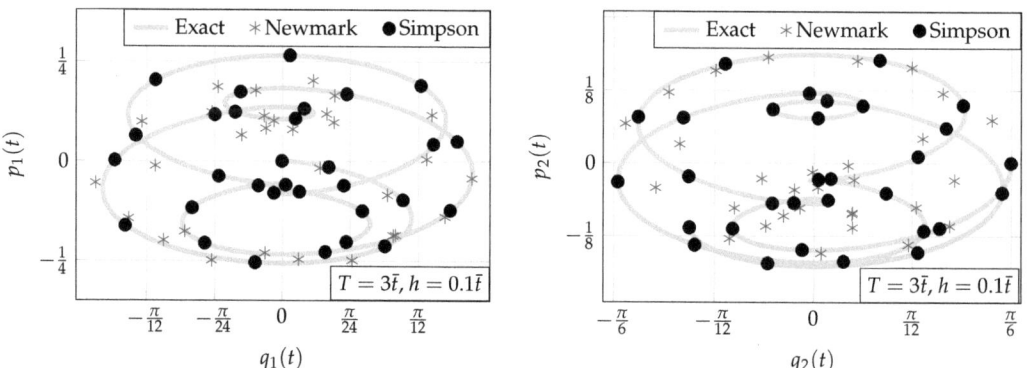

Figure 5. Phase portraits' evolution for the linear double pendulum. Initial conditions are specified in Table 1. The step size is fixed as $h = 0.1\,\bar{t}$, and three periods are shown ($T = 3\bar{t}$). Simpson's phase portrait clearly follows the exact one.

6.3. Energy Conservation

The following function gives the system energy:

$$H(\mathbf{p}, \mathbf{q}) = \frac{1}{2}\mathbf{p}^T M^{-1}\mathbf{p} + \frac{1}{2}\mathbf{q}^T K\mathbf{q}.$$

It has been previously observed (e.g., [19]) that Newmark's integrator exactly preserves the system energy. This is not the case for our proposed integrator based on Simpson's rule and is characteristic of most symplectic methods [19,32]. In the case of Simpson's scheme, the second equation of System (25) introduces the small and vanishing quantity $-\frac{h^2}{12}K\left(\frac{q_{j+1}-q_j}{h}\right)$ into the discrete momentum equation. Consequently, one could assume that the exact system energy may not be conserved, but a good energy behavior can be expected, as outlined in [32].

Figure 6 shows that Simpson's solutions lead to a non-conserved energy $H(\mathbf{p},\mathbf{q})$. Nevertheless, the maximum relative error with respect to the initial value is extremely small even for $h = 0.1\,\bar{t}$, as the evaluated values are in the order of 10^{-3}. Notice that the energy error from Simpson's solutions does not grow with time. Instead, it oscillates in a bounded fashion. Note that the error drops by four orders of magnitude when dividing the step size by ten (see Figure 6).

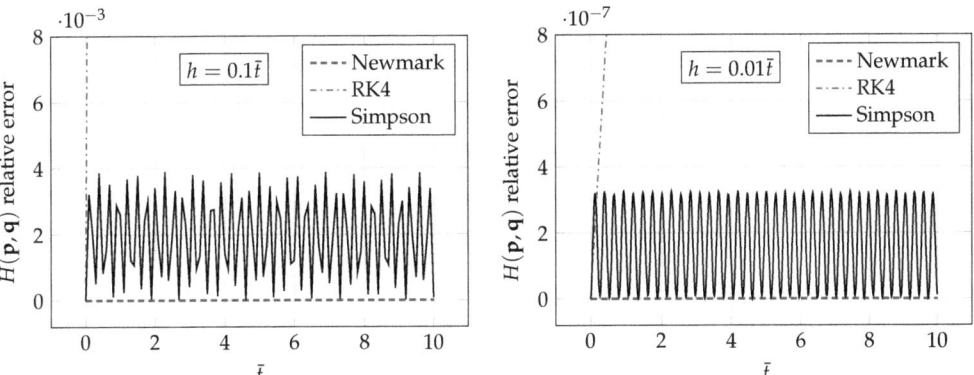

Figure 6. As expected, the classical RK4 integrator does not preserve the system energy. Relative error grows with simulation length. Newmark's integrator exactly preserves the system energy. Simpson's integrator does not, but the relative error is extremely small. Notice that such an error does not grow with time, but remains bounded. The relative error drops by four orders of magnitude when dividing the step size by ten, showcasing the quality of the proposed integrator and its good energy behavior.

Proposition 7 shows that Simpson's scheme preserves a quadratic form given by the function $\phi(\mathbf{p},\mathbf{q})$ of Equation (42). Matrices $\bar{\zeta}_s$ and ζ_s (where subscript s stands for Simpson) are according to Proposition 7 as

$$\bar{\zeta}_s = (X_s + Y_s)^{-1} = \left[\frac{2}{h}M + \frac{h}{3}KL^{-1}\right]^{-1};$$

$$\zeta_s = \left(X_s^{-1} + Y_s^{-1}\right)^{-1} = \left[\left(\frac{2}{h}M - \frac{h}{6}K\right)^{-1} + \frac{3}{h}\left(KL^{-1} + \frac{1}{2}K\right)^{-1}\right]^{-1}.$$

Figure 7 plots the absolute error on function $\phi(\mathbf{p},\mathbf{q})$ of Equation (42), by Simpson's scheme. The absolute error with respect to the initial value is minimal, in the order of 10^{-15}, and may come from accumulated rounding errors. Note that this absolute error magnitude changes very little when refining the step size.

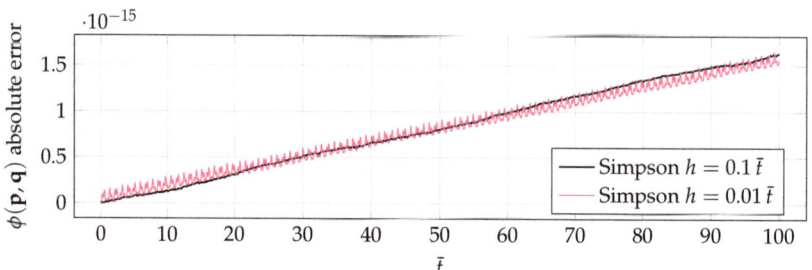

Figure 7. Simpson's scheme preserves the quadratic form $\phi(\mathbf{p},\mathbf{q})$ of Equation (42). The absolute errors are minimal and may come from accumulated rounding errors.

6.4. Convergence

The error $e(t) = \mathbf{q}(t) - \mathbf{q}_{ex}(t)$, and its convergence rate is measured following the prescriptions found in [16]. The schemes' precision was evaluated using an ℓ^∞ error norm $\|e\|_\infty = \|\mathbf{q} - \mathbf{q}_{ex}\|_\infty = \sup_n |\mathbf{q}_n - \mathbf{q}_{ex_n}|$. Several simulations were performed for decreasing values of h between $h = 0.1\,\bar{t}$ and $h = 0.001\,\bar{t}$. The $\|e\|_\infty$ norm was calculated for each case. These errors are plotted in Figure 8, on the logarithmic scale.

Convergence rates are expressed as the power of the step size. These rates correspond to the slope of the error logarithm, as a function of the logarithm of h (see Figure 8). These trials confirmed previous analyses on Newmark's method [17,19]: it is second-order convergent. Unsurprisingly, Runge–Kutta's integrator is fourth-order convergent. The results also confirm the analysis performed in [26] on the convergence rate of Simpson's scheme: it is fourth-order convergent. This rate is two degrees higher than the order of the chosen quadratic interpolation. This is known as superconvergence and is closely related to the mesh uniformity [16].

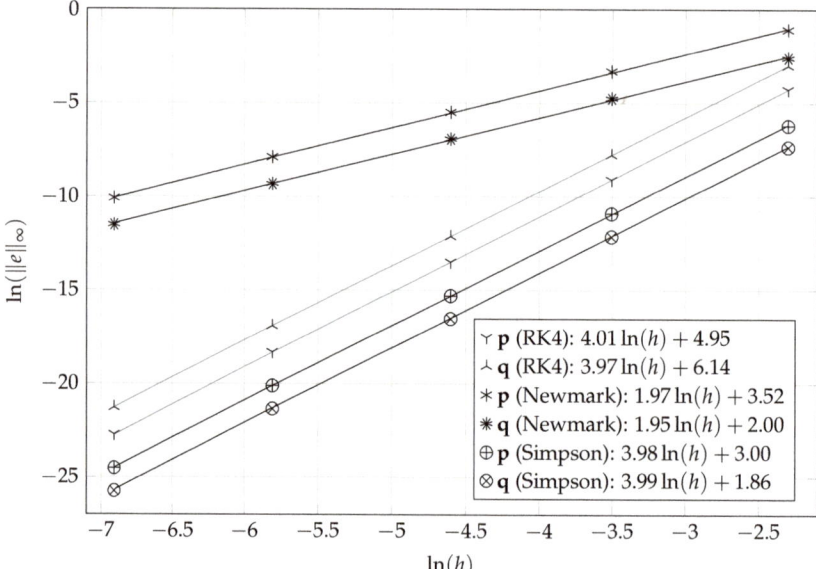

Figure 8. Integrators' convergence. The $\|e\|_\infty$ norm was calculated for several simulations. Each simulation used a fixed step size, which was decreased from $h = 0.1\,\bar{t}$ to $h = 0.001\,\bar{t}$. The convergence order corresponds to the slope of the error norm logarithm regression line. Runge–Kutta's classical integrator convergence is in h^4, as expected (fourth-order). Newmark's integrator convergence is in the order of h^2 (second-order). Simpson's integrator convergence is in the order of h^4 (fourth-order).

An important question is if convergence rates hold with growing simulation lengths T. Table 2 shows the convergence order evolution of Newmark's and Simpson's schemes with a growing simulation length, using a step size of $h = 0.1\,\bar{t}$. It can be observed that Newmark's scheme's convergence order decays to zero for a 1000-period simulation. RK4's convergence rate also degrades as the simulation duration increases, although not as much as Newmark's method. Simpson's scheme preserves its convergence order for higher simulation periods. Error norms $\|e\|_\infty$ are shown explicitly. Simpson's scheme loses precision according to one order of magnitude, each time the simulation length is multiplied by ten. Table 2 exposes a normal numerical behavior of the analyzed schemes since errors accumulate over long simulations.

Table 2. Convergence order with respect to simulation length for motion simulations performed for a linearized double pendulum (see Figure 1). The initial conditions are specified in Table 1. Error norms $\|e\|_\infty$ for momenta **p** and states **q** increase with simulation length T. Newmark's scheme's convergence decays to zero as T increases. RK4's convergence rate also decays with an increasing simulation length. Simpson's scheme preserves its convergence rate for higher simulation durations.

Simulation Length T	Number of Meshes		$\|e\|_\infty$ Error Norm Values			Convergence Order
			10	20	40	
$1\,\bar{t}$	Newmark	p	0.0751	0.0230	0.006 06	1.81
	RK4	p	0.0139	0.000 800	0.000 054 0	4.01
	Simpson	p	0.000 640	0.000 041 6	0.000 002 57	**3.98**
	Newmark	q	0.342	0.0961	0.0251	1.88
	RK4	q	0.0483	0.003 40	0.000 200	3.91
	Simpson	q	0.002 01	0.000 141	0.000 008 76	**3.92**
	Number of meshes		100	200	400	
$10\,\bar{t}$	Newmark	p	0.273	0.206	0.782	0.90
	RK4	p	0.0822	0.009 90	0.0137	1.29
	Simpson	p	0.007 20	0.000 433	0.000 026 8	**4.03**
	Newmark	q	0.694	0.657	0.244	0.75
	RK4	q	0.284	0.0329	0.0157	2.09
	Simpson	q	0.0235	0.001 41	0.000 090 6	**4.01**
	Number of meshes		1000	2000	4000	
$100\,\bar{t}$	Newmark	p	0.521	0.492	0.223	0.61
	RK4	p	0.108	0.0786	0.006 40	2.03
	Simpson	p	0.0705	0.004 39	0.000 272	**4.01**
	Newmark	q	1.02	0.964	0.665	0.31
	RK4	q	0.328	0.2650	0.0216	1.96
	Simpson	q	0.237	0.0147	0.000 914	**4.01**
	Number of meshes		10,000	20,000	40,000	
$1000\,\bar{t}$	Newmark	p	0.545	0.551	0.548	0.00
	RK4	p	0.326	0.119	0.0595	1.23
	Simpson	p	0.190	0.0438	0.002 74	**3.06**
	Newmark	q	1.02	1.03	1.03	0.01
	RK4	q	0.581	0.397	0.200	0.77
	Simpson	q	0.638	0.147	0.009 22	**3.06**

7. Concluding Remarks and Perspectives

In this contribution, Newmark's method has been recalled. It is a widely used integrator in certain fields of the engineering sciences, and it is symplectic. This method has been used for benchmarking purposes in our work, where an alternative variational integrator based on Simpson's integration rule has been proposed.

Simpson's numerical scheme presented applies to the case of multiple-degrees of freedom systems with quadratic Lagrangians. It has been formulated linearly with partitioned matrices. The method proves to be symplectic, as demonstrated with a proof that applies to both Newmark's and Simpson's scheme. A sufficient stability condition on the step size was given, and it was also proven that the proposed method preserves a certain quadratic form at each time step. Simpson's scheme is, therefore, conditionally stable.

Numerical trials on a linearized double pendulum have confirmed that the method is fourth-order accurate on both the states and generalized momenta. Numerical evaluations revealed that this convergence order is preserved for long simulations. The proposed method succeeds in predicting the evolution of dynamical systems characterized by quadratic Lagrangians.

An important extension of this work is the treatment of non-linear multi-degrees of freedom systems. In such a configuration, the middle value of the internal interpolation cannot be eliminated. This generalization should enable more applications of the proposed method, relating to Hamiltonian systems. Therefore, this is a natural objective for future developments and is currently under study. An important question relates to noise presence in matrices M and K. How would this affect the symplectic integrator? This question is relevant in the context of non-linear dynamical systems. It shall be the object of future developments as well.

A particular subject of interest relating to differential equations is the role of discrete symmetries. The analysis of discrete symmetries has many applications for finding solutions to differential equations. They can simplify a numerical scheme, as advocated in [34]. A description of finding discrete symmetries of differential equations has been given in [35]. A discrete symmetry analysis could lead to an improved symplectic integrator and is a future direction for our work.

An improved nonlinear Simpson's variational integrator could find its application in simulating complex non-linear mechanisms. Some application examples could involve a system of synchronized pendulums [36]; the discrete optimal control of robotic systems [37]; the modal analysis of dynamical systems [38]; the motion analysis of multibody systems evolving in fluid environments [39]; or the motion prediction of sliding rods [24] and soft robots [25].

Author Contributions: Conceptualization, formal analysis, funding acquisition, methodology, project administration, resources, and visualization by J.A.R.-Q. and F.D. Software and validation by J.A.R.-Q. and J.G.C.-D. Data curation, investigation, and writing—review and editing by J.A.R.-Q., F.D. and J.G.C.-D. Writing—original draft, J.A.R.-Q. Supervision, F.D. All authors have read and agreed to the published version of the manuscript.

Funding: This research received no external funding.

Data Availability Statement: The data underlying this article will be shared upon reasonable request to the corresponding author.

Acknowledgments: This research was conducted while the corresponding author held a one-year visiting position at the Laboratoire des Sciences du Numérique de Nantes (LS2N) of the Institut Mines-Télécom (IMT) Atlantique de Nantes, France, under the authorization of CONAHCYT. The corresponding author acknowledges the support received from IMT Atlantique and CONAHCYT. The authors would like to thank the anonymous reviewers. Their valuable comments and suggestions led to considerable improvement of this article.

Conflicts of Interest: The authors declare no conflicts of interest.

References

1. Goldstine, H.H. *A History of Numerical Analysis from the 16th through the 19th Century*; Studies in the History of Mathematics and Physical Sciences; Springer: New York, NY, USA, 1977. [CrossRef]
2. Albinus, H.J. The mathematical tourist. *Math. Intell.* **2002**, *24*, 50–58. [CrossRef]
3. Süli, E.; Mayers, D.F. *An Introduction to Numerical Analysis*; Cambridge University Press: Cambridge, UK, 2003.
4. Herman, A.L.; Conway, B.A. Direct optimization using collocation based on high-order Gauss-Lobatto quadrature rules. *J. Guid. Control. Dyn.* **1996**, *19*, 592–599. [CrossRef]

Kelly, M. An Introduction to Trajectory Optimization: How to Do Your Own Direct Collocation. *SIAM Rev.* **2017**, *59*, 849–904. [CrossRef]

Blaszczyk, T.; Siedlecki, J.; Ciesielski, M. Numerical algorithms for approximation of fractional integral operators based on quadratic interpolation. *Math. Methods Appl. Sci.* **2018**, *41*, 3345–3355. [CrossRef]

Sabir, A.; Ur Rehman, M. A numerical method based on quadrature rules for ψ-fractional differential equations. *J. Comput. Appl. Math.* **2023**, *419*, 114684. [CrossRef]

Mostaghim, Z.S.; Moghaddam, B.P.; Haghgozar, H.S. Numerical simulation of fractional-order dynamical systems in noisy environments. *Comput. Appl. Math.* **2018**, *37*, 6433–6447. [CrossRef]

Fakharany, M.; El-Borai, M.M.; Abu Ibrahim, M.A. Numerical analysis of finite difference schemes arising from time-memory partial integro-differential equations. *Front. Appl. Math. Stat.* **2022**, *8*, 1055071. [CrossRef]

Arnold, V.I. *Mathematical Methods of Classical Mechanics*, 2nd ed.; Springer: New York, NY, USA, 1989.

Feynman, R.P.; Hibbs, A.R. *Quantum Mechanics and Path Integrals*; International Series in Pure and Applied Physics; McGraw-Hill: New York, NY, USA, 1965.

Souriau, J.M. *Structure des Systèmes Dynamiques*; Maîtrises de Mathématiques, Dunod: Paris, France, 1970.

Nusser, A.; Branchini, E. On the least action principle in cosmology. *Mon. Not. R. Astron. Soc.* **2000**, *313*, 587–595. [CrossRef]

Rojo, A.; Bloch, A. *The Principle of Least Action: History and Physics*; Cambridge University Press: Cambridge, UK, 2018.

Courant, R. Variational methods for the solution of problems of equilibrium and vibrations. *Bull. Am. Math. Soc.* **1943**, *49*, 1–23. [CrossRef]

Allaire, G.; Craig, A. *Numerical Analysis and Optimization: An Introduction to Mathematical Modelling and Numerical Simulation*; Numerical Mathematics and Scientific Computation; Oxford University Press: Oxford, UK, 2007.

Newmark, N.M. A Method of Computation for Structural Dynamics. *J. Eng. Mech. Div.* **1959**, *85*, 67–94. [CrossRef]

Sanz-Serna, J.M. Symplectic integrators for Hamiltonian problems: An overview. *Acta Numer.* **1992**, *1*, 243–286. [CrossRef]

Kane, C.; Marsden, J.E.; Ortiz, M.; West, M. Variational integrators and the Newmark algorithm for conservative and dissipative mechanical systems. *Int. J. Numer. Methods Eng.* **2000**, *49*, 1295–1325. [CrossRef]

Hairer, E.; Wanner, G.; Lubich, C. *Geometric Numerical Integration*; Springer Series in Computational Mathematics; Springer: Berlin/Heidelberg, Germany, 2006. [CrossRef]

De Vogelaere, R. *Methods of Integration which Preserve the Contact Transformation Property of the Hamilton Equations*. Department of Mathematics, University of Notre Dame: Notre Dame, IN, USA, 1956. [CrossRef]

Géradin, M.; Rixen, D.J. *Mechanical Vibrations: Theory and Application to Structural Dynamics*; John Wiley & Sons: Chichester, UK, 2015.

Chopra, A.K. *Dynamics of Structures: Theory and Applications to Earthquake Engineering*, 5th ed.; Prentice-Hall International Series in Civil Engineering and Engineering Mechanics; Pearson Education Limited: Harlow, UK, 2020.

Boyer, F.; Lebastard, V.; Candelier, F.; Renda, F. Extended Hamilton's principle applied to geometrically exact Kirchhoff sliding rods. *J. Sound Vib.* **2022**, *516*, 116511. [CrossRef]

Boyer, F.; Gotelli, A.; Tempel, P.; Lebastard, V.; Renda, F.; Briot, S. Implicit Time-Integration Simulation of Robots With Rigid Bodies and Cosserat Rods Based on a Newton–Euler Recursive Algorithm. *IEEE Trans. Robot.* **2024**, *40*, 677–696. [CrossRef]

Dubois, F.; Rojas-Quintero, J.A. A Variational Symplectic Scheme Based on Simpson's Quadrature. In Proceedings of the Geometric Science of Information, St. Malo, France, 30 August–1 September 2023; Nielsen, F., Barbaresco, F., Eds.; Springer: Cham, Switzerland, 2023; pp. 22–31. [CrossRef]

Dubois, F.; Antonio Rojas-Quintero, J. Simpson's Quadrature for a Nonlinear Variational Symplectic Scheme. In Proceedings of the International Conference on Finite Volumes for Complex Applications, Strasbourg, France, 30 October–3 November 2023; Franck, E., Fuhrmann, J., Michel-Dansac, V., Navoret, L., Eds.; Springer: Cham, Switzerland, 2023; Volume 2, pp. 83–92. [CrossRef]

Raviart, P.A.; Thomas, J.M. *Introduction à l'Analyse Numérique des Équations aux Dérivées Partielles*; Collection Mathématiques Appliquées pour la Maîtrise; Masson: Paris, France, 1983.

Gear, C. Simultaneous Numerical Solution of Differential-Algebraic Equations. *IEEE Trans. Circuit Theory* **1971**, *18*, 89–95. [CrossRef]

Chyba, M.; Hairer, E.; Vilmart, G. The role of symplectic integrators in optimal control. *Optim. Control. Appl. Methods* **2009**, *30*, 367–382. [CrossRef]

Razafindralandy, D.; Salnikov, V.; Hamdouni, A.; Deeb, A. Some robust integrators for large time dynamics. *Adv. Model. Simul. Eng. Sci.* **2019**, *6*, 5. [CrossRef]

Zhong, G.; Marsden, J.E. Lie-Poisson Hamilton-Jacobi theory and Lie-Poisson integrators. *Phys. Lett. A* **1988**, *133*, 134–139. [CrossRef]

Wolfram Research, Inc. *Mathematica*, version 12.3; Wolfram Research, Inc.: Champaign, IL, USA, 2021.

Ibragimov, N.K. *Elementary Lie Group Analysis and Ordinary Differential Equations*; Wiley: Chichester, UK, 1999.

Hydon, P.E. *Symmetry Methods for Differential Equations: A Beginner's Guide*; Cambridge Texts in Applied Mathematics; Cambridge University Press: Cambridge, UK, 2000.

Gladkov, S.O.; Bogdanova, S.B. About the possibility of synchronization in dynamical systems. *J. Phys. Conf. Ser.* **2020**, *1479*, 012011. [CrossRef]

37. Rojas-Quintero, J.A.; Dubois, F.; Ramírez-de Ávila, H.C. Riemannian Formulation of Pontryagin's Maximum Principle for t Optimal Control of Robotic Manipulators. *Mathematics* **2022**, *10*, 1117. [CrossRef]
38. Shirafkan, N.; Gosselet, P.; Bamer, F.; Oueslati, A.; Markert, B.; de Saxcé, G. Constructing the Hamiltonian from the Behaviour o Dynamical System by Proper Symplectic Decomposition. In Proceedings of the Geometric Science of Information, Paris, Fran 21–23 July 2023; Nielsen, F., Barbaresco, F., Eds.; Springer : Cham, Switzerland , 2021; pp. 439–447. [CrossRef]
39. Terze, Z.; Pandža, V.; Andrić, M.; Zlatar, D. Lie group dynamics of reduced multibody-fluid systems. *Math. Mech. Complex S* **2021**, *9*, 167–177. [CrossRef]

Disclaimer/Publisher's Note: The statements, opinions and data contained in all publications are solely those of the individu author(s) and contributor(s) and not of MDPI and/or the editor(s). MDPI and/or the editor(s) disclaim responsibility for any injury people or property resulting from any ideas, methods, instructions or products referred to in the content.

The Existence of Li–Yorke Chaos in a Discrete-Time Glycolytic Oscillator Model

Mirela Garić-Demirović [1,†], Mustafa R. S. Kulenović [2,*,†], Mehmed Nurkanović [1,†] and Zehra Nurkanović [1,†]

1. Department of Mathematics, University of Tuzla, 75000 Tuzla, Bosnia and Herzegovina; mirela.garic@untz.ba (M.G.-D.); mehmed.nurkanovic@untz.ba (M.N.); zehra.nurkanovic@untz.ba (Z.N.)
2. Department of Mathematics, University of Rhode Island, Kingston, RI 02881, USA
* Correspondence: mkulenovic@uri.edu
† These authors contributed equally to this work.

Abstract: This paper investigates an autonomous discrete-time glycolytic oscillator model with a unique positive equilibrium point which exhibits chaos in the sense of Li–Yorke in a certain region of the parameters. We use Marotto's theorem to prove the existence of chaos by finding a snap-back repeller. The illustration of the results is presented by using numerical simulations.

Keywords: difference equations; snap-back repeller; Li–Yorke chaos; Marotto method

MSC: 39A10; 39A30; 39A33; 65P20

1. Introduction and Preliminaries

A first rigorous criterion for chaos in one-dimensional discrete dynamical systems, named *period three implies chaos*, was established by Li and Yorke in their seminal paper [1]. The definition of chaos given in that paper was the first rigorous description of chaos. A number of authors made attempts to extend this definition to multi-dimensional difference equations. One of the most used extensions of the definition of chaos to multi-dimensional cases was given by F. R. Marotto in [2–4], who observed that the crucial properties of chaos are the following: the existence of an infinite number of periodic solutions of various minimal periods; the existence of an uncountably infinite set of points which exhibit random behavior; and the presence of a high sensitivity to initial conditions. Marotto extended Li–Yorke's notion of chaos from one-dimensional to multi-dimensional by introducing the notion of a snap-back repeller in their famous theorem in 1978 [2]. Also, see [5]. However, the original result in [2] has an error, which was noticed by several mathematicians, including P. Kloeden and Li [6,7]. The error was corrected by F. Marotto in [8], where he redefined a snap-back repeller in 2005 [8]. In this paper's preliminary, we will give the corrected version of the definition for a snap-back repeller and then present Marotto's corrected theorem [3,8].

Here is Marotto's definition for "snap-back repeller" and then their theorem from [2,8].

Definition 1 ([4]). *Let $\Phi \in C^1$ in a neighborhood of a fixed point $\overline{\mathbf{w}}$ of Φ. We say that $\overline{\mathbf{w}}$ is a snap-back repeller if the following conditions are met:*
(i) *All the eigenvalues of $\det J_\Phi(\overline{\mathbf{w}})$ have a modulus greater than one ($\overline{\mathbf{w}}$ is a repeller);*
(ii) *There exists a finite sequence $\mathbf{w}_0, \mathbf{w}_1, \ldots, \mathbf{w}_M$ such that $\mathbf{w}_{k+1} = \Phi(\mathbf{w}_k)$, $\mathbf{w}_M = \overline{\mathbf{w}}$, and $\mathbf{w}_0 \neq \overline{\mathbf{w}}$, which belongs to a repelling neighborhood of $\overline{\mathbf{w}}$, and $|\det J_\Phi(\mathbf{w}_k)| \neq 0$ for $0 \leq k \leq M-1$.*

Remark 1. *It is clear that Definition 1 still implies that the sequence $\{\mathbf{w}_k\}_{k=-\infty}^M$, where $\mathbf{w}_{k+1} = \Phi(\mathbf{w}_k)$ for all $k < M$, satisfies $\mathbf{w}_M = \overline{\mathbf{w}}$ and $\mathbf{w}_k \to \overline{\mathbf{w}}$ as $k \to -\infty$, making this set of points a homoclinic orbit. Furthermore, since all $\mathbf{w}_k$ for $k \leq 0$ lie within the local unstable manifold of the* map Φ at the fixed point $\overline{\mathbf{w}}$, where Φ is $1-1$, and since $\det J_\Phi(\mathbf{w}_k) \neq 0$ for $1 \leq k \leq M$, then this homoclinic orbit is transversal in the sense that Φ is $1-1$ in a neighborhood of each $\mathbf{w}_k$ for all $k \leq M$. See [4].

Theorem 1 ([2]). *If a map Φ possesses a snap-back repeller, then Φ is chaotic in the sense of Li–Yorke. That is, the following exist:*
1. *A positive integer N, such that Φ has a point of period p, for each integer $p \geq N$;*
2. *A "scrambled set" of Φ, i.e., an uncountable set W containing no periodic points of Φ, such that*
   (a) *$\Phi(W) \subset W$;*
   (b) *$\limsup_{n\to\infty} \|\Phi^n(\mathbf{u}) - \Phi^n(\mathbf{v})\| > 0$ for all $\mathbf{u}, \mathbf{v} \in W$, with $\mathbf{u} \neq \mathbf{v}$;*
   (c) *$\limsup_{n\to\infty} \|\Phi^n(\mathbf{u}) - \Phi^n(\mathbf{v})\| > 0$ for all $\mathbf{u} \in W$, with $\mathbf{u} \neq \mathbf{v}$ and periodic point $\mathbf{v}$ of Φ;*
3. *An uncountable subset W_0 of W such that $\liminf_{n\to\infty} \|\Phi^n(\mathbf{u}) - \Phi^n(\mathbf{v})\| = 0$, for every $\mathbf{u}, \mathbf{v} \in W_0$.*

In this paper, we investigate the existence of Li–Yorke chaos for the following system of difference equations:

$$\left. \begin{array}{l} x_{n+1} = x_n + h(\alpha - \beta x_n - x_n y_n^2) \\ y_{n+1} = y_n + h(\beta x_n + x_n y_n^2 - y_n) \end{array} \right\}, \quad (1)$$

where the parameters α and β are positive; $0 < h < 1$ is the step size of the numerical method in the process of transferring a continuous model into a discrete counterpart. System (1) was obtained by the explicit Euler finite discretization of the following system of differential equations [9]:

$$\left. \begin{array}{l} x' = \alpha - \beta x - xy^2 \\ y' = \beta x + xy^2 - y \end{array} \right\}, \quad (2)$$

which was used as the model for glycolysis decomposition in [9]. In this model, glucose decomposes in the presence of various enzymes, including ten steps in which five are termed the preparatory phase, while the remaining five steps are called the pay-off phase.

In [9], the authors, using a non-standard finite discretization, obtained a different discrete analogon of the glycolytic oscillator model (2). They investigated the Neimark–Sacker bifurcation and hybrid control in their discrete model, but the local dynamics were not studied in detail. The reason is probably that the local dynamics were quite complicated and involved. See [10–12] for related results.

System (1) is a cubic polynomial system, which is well known to exhibit chaotic behavior. The global dynamics of such a system can be quite complicated, as we have shown in a series of papers [13,14]. An interesting problem is whether the local stability of System (1) implies the global stability of such a system and, in general, if System (1) is structurally stable. As we showed in [13,14] proving global stability requires different techniques and it might be more difficult to prove than a complicated, chaotic behavior. The case when the equilibrium of System (1) is a saddle point probably requires finding the stable and unstable manifolds or sets and using them to obtain the dynamics of that system (see [13]).

In this paper, we present the complete local dynamics of model (1) in Section 2. The local stability dynamics indicate the regions where Li–Yorke chaos is possible. Then, we prove the existence of Li–Yorke chaos in such a region by finding the snap-back repeller using a similar technique to that in [15]. One should mention that Li–Yorke chaos is common for many polynomial and rational systems of difference equations (see [16–18]), with the simplest and oldest being Hénon's map and system (see [4]). The techniques of rigorous proofs of chaos in dimensions higher than one are often based on Theorem 1. The other less rigorous techniques are based on calculations of Lyapunov exponents and the fractal dimension. See [19–22] for many examples of chaotic two-dimensional systems.

2. Local Stability Analysis

System (1) has a unique (positive) equilibrium point $\bar{z} = \left(\frac{\alpha}{\beta+\alpha^2}, \alpha\right)$. The investigation of the nature of the local stability of equilibrium point $\bar{z}$ is based on the well-known result of Theorem 2.12 in [19] or in [20–22].

The map T corresponding to System (1) is of the form

$$T\begin{pmatrix}x\\y\end{pmatrix} = \begin{pmatrix}x + h(\alpha - \beta x - xy^2)\\y + h(\beta x + xy^2 - y)\end{pmatrix},$$

and the Jacobian matrix of the map T is of the form

$$J_T(x,y) = \begin{pmatrix} -hy^2 - h\beta + 1 & -2hxy \\ h(y^2 + \beta) & 2hxy - h + 1 \end{pmatrix}, \qquad (3)$$

from which we obtain

$$\mathrm{tr}\, J_T(x,y) = -hy^2 + 2hxy - h\beta - h + 2,$$

and

$$\det J_T(x,y) = -h(1-h)y^2 + 2hxy + (1-h)(1-h\beta).$$

The corresponding characteristic equation has the form

$$\varphi(\lambda) = \lambda^2 + \left(hy^2 - 2hxy + h\beta + h - 2\right)\lambda - h(1-h)y^2 + 2hxy + (1-h)(1-h\beta) = 0, \quad (4)$$

which in the equilibrium $\bar{z} = \left(\frac{\alpha}{\beta+\alpha^2}, \alpha\right)$ becomes

$$\varphi(\lambda) = \lambda^2 + \frac{h\beta^2 + \beta(2h\alpha^2+h-2) - \alpha^2(h-h\alpha^2+2)}{\alpha^2+\beta}\lambda + \frac{-h\beta^2(1-h)-(1-h)(2h\alpha^2-1)\beta + \alpha^2(h\alpha^2(h-1)+h+1)}{\alpha^2+\beta} = 0.$$

Since $\varphi(1) = h^2(\alpha^2 + \beta) > 0$, by applying Theorem 2.12 in [19], we obtain the following result about the local dynamics of equilibrium point $\bar{z}$:

Let $0 < h < 1$ be fixed. Then,

$$\varphi(0) = 1 \iff \beta = \beta_0(\alpha) = \frac{-2\alpha^2(1-h) - 1 + \sqrt{1+8\alpha^2(1-h)}}{2(1-h)}$$

and

$$\varphi(-1) = 0 \iff \beta = \beta_{-1}(\alpha) = \frac{1}{h}\left(1 - \alpha^2 h + \sqrt{\frac{4\alpha^2 h^2 + 2 - h}{2-h}}\right),$$

where $\beta_0(\alpha)$ and $\beta_{-1}(\alpha)$ are continuous functions such that $\beta_0(\alpha) > 0$ for $0 < \alpha < \alpha_1 = \sqrt{\frac{1}{1-h}}$ and $\beta_{-1}(\alpha) > 0$ for $0 < \alpha < \alpha_2 = \sqrt{\frac{2(h+2)}{(2-h)h}}$. Note that α_1 and α_2 are the abscissas of the intersection points of curves $\beta = \beta_0(\alpha)$ and $\beta = \beta_{-1}(\alpha)$ with the $O\alpha$-axis, respectively, and $\beta_1 = 0$ and $\beta_2 = \frac{2}{h}$ are the abscissas of the intersection points of curves $\beta = \beta_0(\alpha)$ and $\beta = \beta_{-1}(\alpha)$ with the $O\beta$-axis, in the (α, β)-plane. Let $\mathcal{C}_0$ and $\mathcal{C}_{-1}$ be the graphs of the functions $\beta = \beta_0(\alpha)$ and $\beta = \beta_{-1}(\alpha)$ in the positive quadrant, respectively (excluding the points on the axes). It is easy to see that $\mathcal{C}_0 \cap \mathcal{C}_{-1} = \emptyset$ if $\alpha_1 \leq \alpha_2$ (i.e., $0 < h \leq 2(\sqrt{2}-1)$) and $\mathcal{C}_0 \cap \mathcal{C}_{-1} = \{\Gamma\}$ if $\alpha_1 > \alpha_2$ (i.e., $2(\sqrt{2}-1) < h < 1$), where $\Gamma = (\alpha_\Gamma, \beta_\Gamma) = \left(\frac{\sqrt{2}(2-h)}{h^2}, \frac{2(h^2+4h-4)}{h^4}\right)$.

Now, assume that $\varphi(0) = 1$, $\alpha < \alpha_1$, and $\beta = \beta_0(\alpha)$. Then, we have that $det J_T(\bar{z}) = 1$ and

$$(tr J_T(\bar{z}))^2 - 4 det J_T(\bar{z}) = \left(\frac{h\beta^2 + \beta(2h\alpha^2 + h - 2) - \alpha^2(h - h\alpha^2 + 2)}{\alpha^2 + \beta} \right)^2 - 4$$

$$= \frac{h^2 \left(4\alpha^2(1-h) + 1 - K\right) \left(4h^2\alpha^2(1-h) + (2-h)^2(1-K)\right)}{(1-h)^2(1-K)^2} < 0,$$

where $K = \sqrt{1 + 8\alpha^2(1-h)}$. Namely,

$$4\alpha^2(1-h) + 1 - K > 0 \iff \left(4\alpha^2(1-h) + 1\right)^2 > 1 + 8\alpha^2(1-h) \iff 16\alpha^4(h-1)^2 > 0,$$

which is true for every $h \in (0,1)$. On the other hand,

$$4h^2\alpha^2(1-h) + (2-h)^2(1-K) < 0 \iff 16\alpha^2(1-h)^2 \left(h^4\alpha^2 - 2(2-h)^2\right) < 0. \quad (5)$$

For $\alpha < \alpha_1$ and $h \leq 2(\sqrt{2} - 1)$, inequality (5) is true because

$$h^4\alpha^2 - 2(2-h)^2 < h^4 \left(\frac{1}{1-h}\right) - 2(2-h)^2 = \frac{(h^2 - 2h + 2)(h^2 + 4h - 4)}{1-h} \leq 0.$$

Also, for $2(\sqrt{2} - 1) < h < 1$ and $\alpha < \alpha_\Gamma$, (5) is true because

$$h^4\alpha^2 - 2(h-2)^2 < h^4 \left(\frac{2(2-h)^2}{h^4}\right) - 2(h-2)^2 = 0.$$

By using Theorem 2.12 in [19], we see that $\varphi(0) = 1$ and $(tr J_T(\bar{z})))^2 - 4 det J_T(\bar{z})) < 0$ if $\beta = \beta_0(\alpha)$ and

$$\left. \begin{array}{c} 0 < h \leq 2(\sqrt{2} - 1), \alpha < \alpha_1 \\ \text{or} \\ 2(\sqrt{2} - 1) < h < 1, \alpha < \alpha_\Gamma, \end{array} \right\}$$

which means that λ_1 and λ_2 are conjugate complex, and $|\lambda_1| = |\lambda_2| = 1$.

We will now prove that

$$tr J_T(\bar{z}) \neq 0 \text{ and } tr J_T(\bar{z}) \neq 2,$$

when $\varphi(-1) = 0$.

First, note that $tr J_T = 2$ if $2(\sqrt{2} - 1) < h < 1$, $\alpha = \alpha_\Gamma$, and $\beta = \beta_\Gamma$, where

$$\varphi(\lambda)|_\Gamma = (\lambda + 1)^2.$$

Also, if $\varphi(-1) = 0$, then $\beta = \beta_{-1}(\alpha)$. It implies that

$$tr J_T(\bar{z}) = 0 \iff \frac{h\beta^2 + \beta(2h\alpha^2 + h - 2) - \alpha^2(h - h\alpha^2 + 2)}{\alpha^2 + \beta} = 0$$

$$\iff \sqrt{\frac{4\alpha^2 h^2 + 2 - h}{2 - h}} = \frac{-2h^2\alpha^2 + h - 2}{2 - h} < 0,$$

which is impossible.

By Theorem 2.12 in [19], it means that $\lambda_1 = -1$ and $|\lambda_2| \neq 1$ if $\beta = \beta_{-1}(\alpha)$ and

$$0 < h < 2(\sqrt{2} - 1), 0 < \alpha < \alpha_2$$

or

$$2(\sqrt{2} - 1) < h < 1, \ \alpha \in (0, \alpha_2), \alpha \neq \alpha_\Gamma.$$

Also, note that it can be easily verified that $\varphi(0) > 1$ is valid at all points below the curve $\mathcal{C}_0$, and $\varphi(0) < 1$ is valid at all points above that curve. Likewise, in all points below the curve $\mathcal{C}_{-1}$, $\varphi(-1) > 0$ is valid, and in all points above that curve, $\varphi(-1) < 0$ is valid. See Figures 1–3.

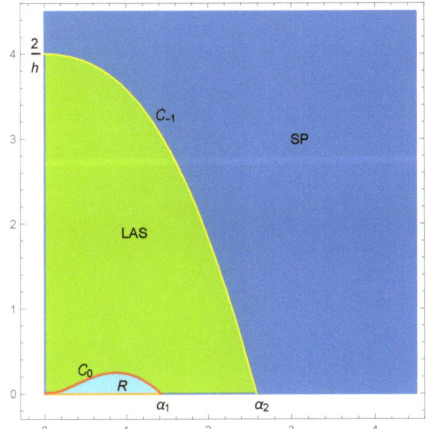

Figure 1. Parametric spaces of local dynamics in the (α, β)-plane for $h = 0.5 < 2(\sqrt{2} - 1)$, $\mathcal{C}_0 = \{(\alpha, \beta) : \varphi(0) = 1\}$, $\mathcal{C}_{-1} = \{(\alpha, \beta) : \varphi(-1) = 0\}$.

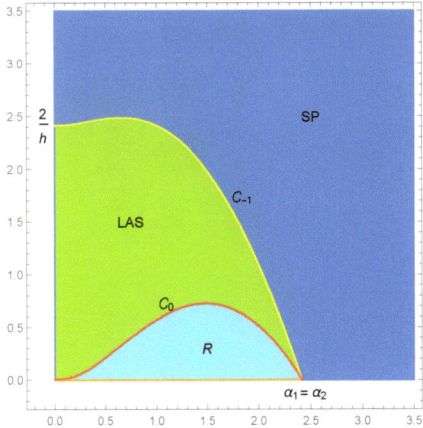

Figure 2. Parametric spaces of local dynamics in the (α, β)-plane for $h = 2(\sqrt{2} - 1)$, $\mathcal{C}_0 = \{(\alpha, \beta) : \varphi(0) = 1\}$, $\mathcal{C}_{-1} = \{(\alpha, \beta) : \varphi(-1) = 0\}$.

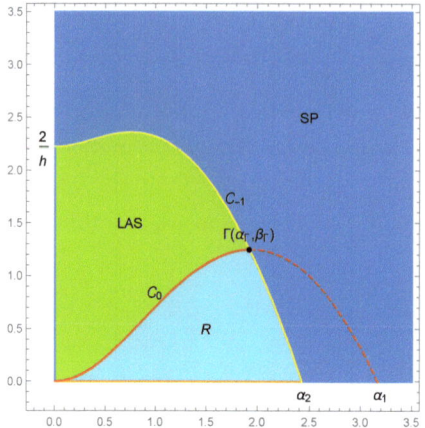

Figure 3. Parametric spaces of local dynamics in the (α, β)-plane for $h = 0.9 > 2(\sqrt{2} - 1)$, $C_0 = \{(\alpha, \beta) : \varphi(0) = 1\}$, $C_{-1} = \{(\alpha, \beta) : \varphi(-1) = 0\}$.

Denoting

$$\mathcal{L}_1 = \{(\alpha, \beta) : 0 < \alpha < \alpha_1, \beta_0(\alpha) < \beta < \beta_{-1}(\alpha)\},$$
$$\mathcal{L}_2 = \{(\alpha, \beta) : \alpha_1 \leq \alpha \leq \alpha_2, 0 < \beta < \beta_{-1}(\alpha)\},$$
$$\mathcal{L}_3 = \{(\alpha, \beta) : 0 < \alpha < \alpha_\Gamma, \beta_0(\alpha) < \beta < \beta_{-1}(\alpha)\},$$
$$\mathcal{R}_1 = \{(\alpha, \beta) : 0 < \alpha < \alpha_1, 0 < \beta < \beta_0(\alpha)\},$$
$$\mathcal{R}_2 = \{(\alpha, \beta) : 0 < \alpha \leq \alpha_\Gamma, 0 < \beta < \beta_0(\alpha)\},$$
$$\mathcal{R}_3 = \{(\alpha, \beta) : \alpha_\Gamma < \alpha < \alpha_2, 0 < \beta < \beta_{-1}(\alpha)\},$$
$$\mathcal{S}_1 = \{(\alpha, \beta) : 0 < \alpha \leq \alpha_2, \beta > \beta_{-1}(\alpha)\},$$
$$\mathcal{S}_2 = \{(\alpha, \beta) : \alpha > \alpha_2, \beta > 0\},$$

we have thus completed the proofs of the following two lemmas.

Lemma 1. *If $h \in \left(0, 2(\sqrt{2} - 1)\right)$, $\alpha_1 = \sqrt{\frac{1}{1-h}}$, and $\alpha_2 = \sqrt{\frac{2(h+2)}{(2-h)h}}$, then the unique equilibrium point $\bar{z} = \left(\frac{\alpha}{\beta + \alpha^2}, \alpha\right)$ of System (1) is as follows:*

1. *Locally asymptotically stable if*

$$0 < h < 2(\sqrt{2} - 1) \text{ and } (\alpha, \beta) \in \mathcal{L}_1 \cup \mathcal{L}_2$$

   or

$$h = 2(\sqrt{2} - 1) \text{ and } (\alpha, \beta) \in \mathcal{L}_1;$$

2. *A repeller if $(\alpha, \beta) \in \mathcal{R}_1$;*
3. *A saddle point if $(\alpha, \beta) \in \mathcal{S}_1 \cup \mathcal{S}_2$;*
4. *A non-hyperbolic with*
   (a) *λ_1 and λ_2 being conjugated complex, and $|\lambda_1| = |\lambda_2| = 1$ if $\alpha \in (0, \alpha_1)$ and $\beta = \beta_0(\alpha)$;*
   (b) *$\lambda_1 = -1$ and $|\lambda_2| \neq 1$ if $\alpha \in (0, \alpha_2)$ and $\beta = \beta_{-1}(\alpha)$.*

Lemma 2. *If $h \in \left(2(\sqrt{2} - 1), 1\right)$, $\alpha_1 = \sqrt{\frac{1}{1-h}}$, $\alpha_2 = \sqrt{\frac{2(h+2)}{(2-h)h}}$, $\alpha_\Gamma = \frac{\sqrt{2}(2-h)}{h^2}$, and $\beta_\Gamma = \frac{2(h^2 + 4h - 4)}{h^4}$, then the equilibrium point $\bar{z} = \left(\frac{\alpha}{\beta + \alpha^2}, \alpha\right)$ of System (1) is as follows:*

1. *Locally asymptotically stable if $(\alpha, \beta) \in \mathcal{L}_3$;*
2. *A repeller if $(\alpha, \beta) \in \mathcal{R}_2 \cup \mathcal{R}_3$;*

3. A saddle point if $(\alpha, \beta) \in \mathcal{S}_1 \cup \mathcal{S}_2$;
4. A non-hyperbolic with
   (a) λ_1 and λ_2 being conjugated complex, and $|\lambda_1| = |\lambda_2| = 1$ if $\alpha \in (0, \alpha_\Gamma)$ and $\beta = \beta_0(\alpha)$;
   (b) $\lambda_1 = -1$ and $|\lambda_2| \neq 1$ if $\alpha \in (0, \alpha_2)$, $\alpha \neq \alpha_\Gamma$, and $\beta = \beta_{-1}(\alpha)$;
   (c) The characteristic polynomial of the form $\varphi(\lambda) = (\lambda + 1)^2$ at the point $\Gamma(\alpha_\Gamma, \beta_\Gamma) = \left(\frac{\sqrt{2}(2-h)}{h^2}, \frac{2(h^2+4h-4)}{h^4} \right)$, so the eigenvalues are $\lambda_{1,2} = -1$.

See Figure 3.

3. Li–Yorke Chaos for $h = \frac{7}{10} < 2(\sqrt{2} - 1)$

In order to prove the existence of Li–Yorke chaos, we will consider the corresponding eigenvalues with a modulus greater than one for $h < 2(\sqrt{2} - 1)$ and the set

$$\mathcal{R}_1 = \{(\alpha, \beta) : 0 < \alpha < \alpha_1,\ 0 < \beta < \beta_0(\alpha)\} = \left\{ (\alpha, \beta) : \alpha \in \left(0, \frac{1}{\sqrt{1-h}}\right),\ \beta \in (0, \beta_h) \right\},$$

and

$$\beta_h = \frac{-2\alpha^2(1-h) - 1 + \sqrt{8\alpha^2(1-h) + 1}}{2(1-h)}. \tag{6}$$

We prove that the positive equilibrium point $\bar{z} = \left(\frac{\alpha}{\beta + \alpha^2}, \alpha \right)$ of System (1) is a snap-back repeller. The next step is to determine a neighborhood $U_{\bar{z}}$ of $\bar{z} = (\bar{x}, \bar{y})$ in which the norms of eigenvalues exceed one for all $(x, y) \in U_{\bar{z}}$. It means that we need to solve the following system of inequalities, $\varphi(1, x, y, \beta, h) > 0$, $\varphi(-1, x, y, \beta, h) > 0$, and $\varphi(0, x, y, \beta, h) > 1$, where

$$\varphi(\lambda, x, y, \beta, h) = \lambda^2 + \left(hy^2 - 2hxy + h\beta + h - 2 \right)\lambda - h(1-h)y^2 + 2hxy + (1-h)(1-h\beta)$$

is the characteristic polynomial of (3), i.e., we will solve the following system of inequalities:

$$\left. \begin{array}{l} \varphi(1, x, y, \beta, h) = h^2(y^2 + \beta) > 0, \\ \varphi(-1, x, y, \beta, h) = -y^2 h(2-h) + 4hxy + (2-h)(2-h\beta) > 0, \\ \varphi(0, x, y, \beta, h) - 1 = h\left[-(1-h)y^2 + 2xy + (h\beta - \beta - 1) \right] > 0. \end{array} \right\} \tag{7}$$

The first inequality in (7) is always satisfied. Curves $\mathcal{C}_1$ and $\mathcal{C}_2$, where

$$\mathcal{C}_1 = \{(x, y) : \varphi(-1, x, y, \beta, h) = 0\} \text{ and } \mathcal{C}_2 = \{(x, y) : \varphi(0, x, y, \beta, h) - 1 = 0\}$$

are hyperbolas that intersect in the first quadrant at the point

$$P = \left(\frac{(h-2)^2}{2h\sqrt{4 - h^2\beta}}, \frac{\sqrt{4 - h^2\beta}}{h} \right)$$

for $\beta < \frac{4}{h^2}$. The assumptions $0 < h < 2(\sqrt{2} - 1)$ and $0 < \alpha < \frac{1}{\sqrt{1-h}}$ imply that $\beta_h < \frac{4}{h^2}$. Namely,

$$\frac{-2\alpha^2(1-h) - 1 + \sqrt{8\alpha^2(1-h) + 1}}{2(1-h)} < \frac{4}{h^2}$$

is equivalent to

$$\frac{4(h-1)\left[h^4(h-1)\alpha^4 + h^2(h^2 + 8h - 8)\alpha^2 - 4(h-2)^2 \right]}{h^4} > 0$$

which is satisfied if

$$h^4(h-1)\alpha^4 + h^2\left(h^2 + 8h - 8\right)\alpha^2 - 4(h-2)^2 < 0. \tag{8}$$

Since $0 < h < 2\left(\sqrt{2}-1\right)$, it follows that $h^2 + 8h - 8 < 0$, so inequality (8) is true.

Notice that

$$\varphi(0,x,y,\beta,h) - 1 = 0 \Longrightarrow x = \frac{y^2(1-h) + (1-h)\beta + 1}{2y},$$

and

$$\varphi(-1,x,y,\beta,h) = 0 \Longrightarrow x = \frac{(2-h)\left(hy^2 + h\beta - 2\right)}{4hy},$$

so a neighborhood $U_{\bar{z}}$ of $\bar{z} = (\bar{x},\bar{y})$, in which the norms of eigenvalues exceed one for all $(x,y) \in U_{\bar{z}}$, is determined with $U_{\bar{z}} = (U_{\bar{z}})_1 \cup (U_{\bar{z}})_2$, where

$$(U_{\bar{z}})_1 = \left\{(x,y) : x \in \left(\frac{y^2(1-h) + (1-h)\beta + 1}{2y}, +\infty\right), y \in \left(0, \frac{\sqrt{4-h^2\beta}}{h}\right)\right\}, \tag{9}$$

and

$$(U_{\bar{z}})_2 = \left\{(x,y) : x \in \left(\frac{(2-h)(hy^2 + h\beta - 2)}{4hy}, +\infty\right), y \in \left[\frac{\sqrt{4-h^2\beta}}{h}, +\infty\right)\right\} \tag{10}$$

for $h < 2\left(\sqrt{2}-1\right)$.

In this way, we obtained the following result.

Lemma 3. *Let $0 < h < 2\left(\sqrt{2}-1\right)$, $0 < \alpha < \frac{1}{\sqrt{1-h}}$, and $0 < \beta < \beta_h$, where β_h is given by (6). Then, $U_{\bar{z}} = (U_{\bar{z}})_1 \cup (U_{\bar{z}})_2$, where $(U_{\bar{z}})_{1,2}$ is defined by (9) and (10) is a repelling area of the equilibrium point $\bar{z}$.*

To continue investigating the conditions under which the equilibrium point $\bar{z}$ will be a snap-back repeller, we will take a fixed value of the parameter h, for example, $h = \frac{7}{10}$.

Now, if $h = \frac{7}{10}$, then $\alpha < \frac{1}{\sqrt{1-\frac{7}{10}}} = \sqrt{\frac{10}{3}} \approx 1.8257$ and $\beta < \beta_{\frac{7}{10}} = \frac{1}{3}\sqrt{5(12\alpha^2 + 5)} - \alpha^2 - \frac{5}{3}$. A repelling area of the equilibrium point $\bar{z}$ is $U_{\bar{z}} = (U_{\bar{z}})_1 \cup (U_{\bar{z}})_2$, where

$$(U_{\bar{z}})_1 = \left\{(x,y) : x \in \left(\frac{3y^2 + 3\beta + 10}{20y}, +\infty\right), y \in \left(0, \frac{\sqrt{400-49\beta}}{7}\right)\right\},$$

$$(U_{\bar{z}})_2 = \left\{(x,y) : x \in \left(\frac{91y^2 + 91\beta - 260}{280y}, +\infty\right), y \in \left[\frac{\sqrt{400-49\beta}}{7}, +\infty\right)\right\}.$$

To prove that the equilibrium point $\bar{z} = (\bar{x},\bar{y})$ is a snap-back repeller for $M = 2$, we need to find points $z_0 = (x_0,y_0) \in U_{\bar{z}}$ and $z_1 = (x_1,y_1) \notin U_{\bar{z}}$ such that

$$z_1 = T(z_0), \ z_2 = T(z_1) = T^2(z_0) = \bar{z} \text{ and } \det J_T(z_1) \neq 0.$$

By calculating the inverse iterations of the fixed point $\bar{z}$ twice, we are looking for the point $z_0 = (x_0,y_0)$, $x_0 > 0$, $y_0 > 0$, as the solution of the following system:

$$\left.\begin{array}{l} x + \frac{7}{10}(\alpha - \beta x - xy^2) = x_1 \\ y + \frac{7}{10}(\beta x + xy^2 - y) = y_1 \end{array}\right\} \tag{11}$$

for $\mathbf{z}_1 = (x_1, y_1)$ which is the solution of the system

$$\left. \begin{array}{r} x + \frac{7}{10}\left(\alpha - \beta x - xy^2\right) = \frac{\alpha}{\alpha^2 + \beta} \\ y + \frac{7}{10}\left(\beta x + xy^2 - y\right) = \alpha \end{array} \right\} . \tag{12}$$

The solutions of System (12) are

$$(\mathbf{z}_1)_\pm = ((x_1)_\pm, (y_1)_\pm),$$

where

$$(x_1)_\pm = \frac{-5\alpha \pm \frac{1}{7}Q}{10(\alpha^2 + \beta)} + \frac{10\alpha + 3\alpha(\alpha^2 + \beta)}{10(\alpha^2 + \beta)}, \quad (y_1)_\pm = \frac{5\alpha \mp \frac{1}{7}Q}{3(\alpha^2 + \beta)},$$

and

$$Q = \sqrt{7Q_1} > 0, \ Q_1 = -3\alpha^4(21\beta - 100) + \alpha^2\left(390\beta - 126\beta^2 + 175\right) - 9\beta^2(7\beta - 10).$$

By using $\beta < \beta_{\frac{7}{10}}$, it is easy to see that $Q_1 > 0$.

Now, we prove that $\det J((\mathbf{z}_1)_\pm) \neq 0$ considering that

$$\det J((\mathbf{z}_1)_+) = \frac{Q(-Q - 7\alpha(3(\alpha^2 + \beta) - 5))}{1050(\alpha^2 + \beta)^2},$$

$$\det J((\mathbf{z}_1)_-) = \frac{Q(-Q + 7\alpha(3(\alpha^2 + \beta) - 5))}{1050(\alpha^2 + \beta)^2}.$$

Suppose that $\det J((\mathbf{z}_1)_\pm) = 0$. Then,

$$\det J((\mathbf{z}_1)_\pm) = 0 \iff Q = \mp 7\alpha\left(3\left(\alpha^2 + \beta\right) - 5\right).$$

If $\alpha(3(\alpha^2 + \beta) - 5) = 0$, we have a contradiction with $Q > 0$, such that $\det J((\mathbf{z}_1)_\pm) \neq 0$. However, if $\alpha(3(\alpha^2 + \beta) - 5) > 0$, since $Q > 0$, we have that

$$Q = 7\alpha\left(3\left(\alpha^2 + \beta\right) - 5\right) \iff 21\beta^2 + \beta\left(42\alpha^2 - 30\right) + \alpha^2\left(21\alpha^2 - 170\right) = 0,$$

which for $\alpha^2 < \frac{10}{3}$ has only one positive solution

$$\beta_+ = \frac{-(21\alpha^2 - 15) + \sqrt{15(196\alpha^2 + 15)}}{21}.$$

This implies that $\beta_+ \notin \left(0, \beta_{\frac{7}{10}}\right)$, which is a contradiction. Therefore, it is true that $\det J((\mathbf{z}_1)_\pm) \neq 0$ if $\alpha(3(\alpha^2 + \beta) - 5) > 0$.

Similarly, we conclude that $\det J((\mathbf{z}_1)_\pm) \neq 0$ if $\alpha(3(\alpha^2 + \beta) - 5) < 0$.

Now, note the following fact: for $\beta < \beta_{\frac{7}{10}}$, we have

$$Q \neq \mp 7\alpha\left(3\left(\alpha^2 + \beta\right) - 5\right). \tag{13}$$

In the next step, we will solve System (11) for $\mathbf{z}_1 = (x_1, y_1) = ((x_1)_-, (y_1)_-)$. From the second equation in System (11), we obtain

$$x = \frac{-3y + 10(y_1)_-}{7(\beta + y^2)} = \frac{10Q + 350\alpha - 63y(\beta + \alpha^2)}{147(y^2 + \beta)(\alpha^2 + \beta)}.$$

This implies $-3y + 10(y_1)_- > 0 \iff y < \frac{10}{3}(y_1)_-$, i.e., $y < \frac{50\alpha + \frac{10}{7}Q}{9(\alpha^2+\beta)}$. After substituting x in the first equation of System (11), we obtain

$$\frac{-3y + 10(y_1)_-}{7(\beta + y^2)} + \frac{7}{10}\left(\alpha - \beta\left(\frac{-3y + 10(y_1)_-}{7(\beta + y^2)}\right) - \left(\frac{-3y + 10(y_1)_-}{7(\beta + y^2)}\right)y^2\right) - (x_1)_- = 0.$$

Let

$$H(\beta, y) = \frac{-3y + 10(y_1)_-}{7(\beta + y^2)} + \frac{7}{10}\left(\alpha - \left(\frac{-3y + 10(y_1)_-}{7(\beta + y^2)}\right)(\beta + y^2)\right) - (x_1)_-,$$

i.e.,

$$H(\beta, y) = \frac{21y^3 - 7(10(x_1)_- + 10(y_1)_- - 7\alpha)y^2 + 3(7\beta - 10)y + 100(y_1)_- - 7\beta(10(x_1)_- + 10(y_1)_- - 7\alpha)}{70(y^2 + \beta)}. \quad (14)$$

By using the facts

$$(x_1)_- = \frac{-5\alpha - \frac{1}{7}Q}{10(\alpha^2 + \beta)} + \frac{10\alpha + 3\alpha(\alpha^2 + \beta)}{10(\alpha^2 + \beta)}, \quad (y_1)_- = \frac{5\alpha + \frac{1}{7}Q}{3(\alpha^2 + \beta)},$$

and $\bar{y} = \alpha$, we obtain

$$H(\beta, \bar{y}) = 0 \iff \frac{(100 - 49(\alpha^2 + \beta))(Q - 7\alpha(3\alpha^2 + 3\beta - 5))}{1470(\alpha^2 + \beta)^2} = 0. \quad (15)$$

Considering (13), Equation (15) is satisfied if $49(\alpha^2 + \beta) = 100$, or, equivalently,

$$\beta = \frac{100 - 49\alpha^2}{49}.$$

It implies that $100 - 49\alpha^2 > 0$, i.e., $\alpha < \frac{10}{7} \approx 1.4286$. On the other hand,

$$\beta < \beta_{\frac{7}{10}} \iff \frac{100 - 49\alpha^2}{49} < \frac{1}{3}\sqrt{5(12\alpha^2 + 5)} - \alpha^2 - \frac{5}{3}$$

which implies $\alpha > \sqrt{\frac{3950}{2401}} \approx 1.2826$. If $\alpha \in \left(\sqrt{\frac{3950}{2401}}, \frac{10}{7}\right)$, we denote

$$\beta_* = \frac{100 - 49\alpha^2}{49}.$$

Now, from (14) we obtain

$$\frac{\partial H(\beta, y)}{\partial y} = \frac{21(\beta + y^2)^2 + 30(y^2 - \beta) - 200y(y_1)_-}{70(y^2 + \beta)^2}.$$

By using the fact that $(y_1)_- = \frac{5\alpha + \frac{1}{7}Q}{3(\alpha^2+\beta)}$ and $\bar{y} = \alpha$, we have that

$$\frac{\partial H(\beta, \alpha)}{\partial y} = \frac{7(63\beta^3 + 9(21\alpha^2 - 10)\beta^2 + \alpha^2(63\alpha^4 + 90\alpha^2 + 189\alpha^2\beta - 1000)) - 200\alpha Q}{1470(\alpha^2 + \beta)^3}.$$

Let us show that $\frac{\partial H(\beta_*, \bar{y})}{\partial y} \neq 0$. Otherwise, if $\frac{\partial H(\beta_*, \bar{y})}{\partial y} = 0$, then

$$2700 - 10633\alpha^2 = 96040\alpha^2 Q^2.$$

Since $\alpha \in \left(\sqrt{\frac{3950}{2401}}, \frac{10}{7}\right)$, the left side of the past equality is negative, which is impossible. It means that $\frac{\partial H(\beta_*, \bar{y})}{\partial y} \neq 0$ holds.

Therefore, under certain conditions on the parameters, we have that

1° $\beta_* = \frac{100 - 49\alpha^2}{49} \in \left(0, \frac{950}{2401}\right)$ for $\alpha \in \left(\sqrt{\frac{3950}{2401}}, \frac{10}{7}\right)$;

2° $H(\beta_*, \bar{y}) = 0$;

3° $H(\beta, y)$ is continuous for $\beta < \beta_*$ and $y < \frac{50\alpha + \frac{10}{7}Q}{9(\alpha^2 + \beta)}$;

4° $\frac{\partial H(\beta_*, \bar{y})}{\partial y} \neq 0$.

By the Implicit Function Theorem, there exists a unique function $y = y_0(\beta)$ and $\delta > 0$ such that

(i) $y_0(\beta_*) = \bar{y}$.
(ii) $H(\beta, y_0(\beta)) = 0$ for $\beta \in (\beta_* - \delta, \beta_* + \delta)$.
(iii) $y = y_0(\beta)$ is continuous in $\beta \in (\beta_* - \delta, \beta_* + \delta)$.

Figure 4 shows the area of the parameters for which the equilibrium point is a repeller and the set $\mathcal{B} = \left\{(\alpha, \beta) : \alpha \in \left(\sqrt{\frac{3950}{2401}}, \frac{10}{7}\right), \beta = \beta_*\right\} \subset \mathcal{R}_1$ in the (α, β)-plane.

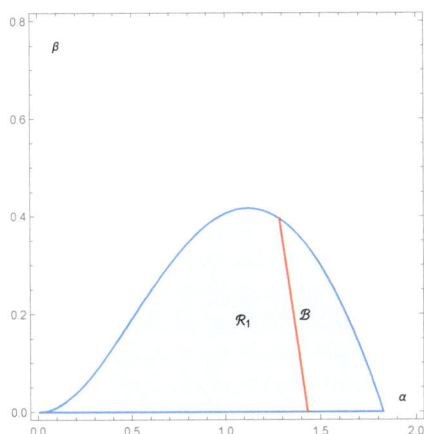

Figure 4. The area of the parameters for which the equilibrium point is a repeller and the set $\mathcal{B}$ (red) is shown (in the (α, β)-plane for $h = 0.7$).

Let $M = 2$ and $z_0 = (x_0, y_0) = \left(\frac{10Q + 350\alpha - 63y_0(\alpha^2 + \beta)}{147(\beta + y_0^2)(\alpha^2 + \beta)}, y_0\right)$ for $y_0 < \frac{50\alpha + \frac{10}{7}Q}{9(\alpha^2 + \beta)}$. Then, z_0 belongs to $U_{\bar{z}}$ for a small enough $\beta - \beta_*$. Assume that $\epsilon > 0$ is arbitrary and let

$$x^* = \max\{\bar{x} + \epsilon, x_0 + \epsilon\}.$$

Finally, let

$$U_{\bar{z}}^* = (U_1)^* \cup (U_2)^*,$$

where

$$(U_1)^* = \left\{(x, y) : x \in \left(\frac{3y^2 + 3\beta + 10}{20y}, x^*\right), y \in \left(y_1^*, \frac{\sqrt{400 - 49\beta}}{7}\right)\right\},$$

and
$$(U_2)^* = \left\{(x,y) : x \in \left(\frac{91y^2 + 91\beta - 260}{280y}, x^*\right), y \in \left[\frac{\sqrt{400 - 49\beta}}{7}, y_2^*\right)\right\}.$$

Also, y_1^* and y_2^* are the second coordinates of the intersection points of the line given by the equation $x = x^*$ with the curves C_2 and C_1, respectively.

Theorem 2. *Assume that* $h = \frac{7}{10}$, $\alpha \in \left(\sqrt{\frac{3950}{2401}}, \frac{10}{7}\right)$ *and* $\beta_* = \frac{100 - 49\alpha^2}{49}$. *Then, there exists* β *near* β_* *such that* $\bar{z} = (\bar{x}, \bar{y}) = \left(\frac{\alpha}{\alpha^2 + \beta}, \alpha\right)$ *is a snap-back repeller of System (1) and, consequently, System (1) is chaotic in the sense of Li–Yorke.*

4. Numerical Simulations

In many articles, the appearance of chaos is established by the existence of positive Lyapunov coefficients (e.g., [15]). Although we proved the existence of chaos in the previous section using the Marotto method, we will make several corresponding numerical simulations by calculating the Lyapunov coefficients. Most of the experimentalists in dynamical systems theory take the existence of positive Lyapunov coefficients as enough evidence for the existence of chaos (see [23–26]). In that case, different software packages, such as *Dynamica* in [19] or *Chaos* in [25,26], are used to justify the use of the word chaos. Also, see the references in [23].

If $\alpha = \frac{7}{5} = 1.4$, then
$$\beta_* = \frac{100 - 49\left(\frac{7}{5}\right)^2}{49} = \frac{99}{1225} \approx 0.080816.$$

Let us choose $\beta = \frac{8}{100}$ close to $\beta_* = \frac{99}{1225}$. Now, $U_{\bar{z}} = (U_{\bar{z}})_1 \cup (U_{\bar{z}})_2$, where
$$(U_{\bar{z}})_1 = \left\{(x,y) : x \in \left(\frac{75y^2 + 256}{500y}, +\infty\right), y \in \left(0, \frac{\sqrt{9902}}{35}\right)\right\},$$

and
$$(U_{\bar{z}})_2 = \left\{(x,y) : x \in \left(\frac{2275y^2 - 6318}{7000y}, +\infty\right), y \in \left[\frac{\sqrt{9902}}{35}, +\infty\right)\right\}.$$

See Figure 5a.

The solutions of System (12) are the equilibrium point and
$$(z_1)_\pm = ((x_1)_\pm, (y_1)_\pm),$$

where
$$((x_1)_\pm, (y_1)_\pm) = \left(\frac{973}{1275} \pm \frac{\sqrt{7}\sqrt{24\,003\,649}}{17\,850}, \frac{175}{153} \mp \frac{\sqrt{7}\sqrt{24\,003\,649}}{5355}\right).$$

The solution of System (11) for $(x_1, y_1) = ((x_1)_-, (y_1)_-)$ which belongs to $U_{\bar{z}}$ is
$$(x_0, y_0) = (2.2013061560494975', 1.400206800960196').$$

Therefore,
$$\begin{aligned} z_0 &= (x_0, y_0) = (2.2013061560494975', 1.400206800960196') \\ z_1 &= (x_1, y_1) = T(x_0, y_0) = \left(\frac{973}{1275} - \frac{\sqrt{7}\sqrt{24\,003\,649}}{17\,850}, \frac{175}{153} + \frac{\sqrt{7}\sqrt{24\,003\,649}}{5355}\right) \\ \bar{z} &= (\bar{x}, \bar{y}) = T(x_1, y_1) = T^2(x_0, y_0) = \left(\frac{35}{51}, \frac{7}{5}\right). \end{aligned} \quad (16)$$

The Jacobian matrix of T at the point $\bar{z} = (\bar{x}, \bar{y})$ has an eigenvalue $\lambda_{\pm} = 0.60855 \mp 0.91998i$ with $|\lambda_{\pm}| = 1.103$, at point (x_0, y_0) has eigenvalues $\lambda_1 = 2.5357$ and $\lambda_2 = 1.6511$, and at point (x_1, y_1) has eigenvalues $\lambda_1 = -7.7491$ and $\lambda_2 = 0.28397$.

For $\epsilon = 0.5$, we have that

$$x^* = \max\{\bar{x} + \epsilon, x_0 + \epsilon\} \approx 2.7013.$$

Next, $y_1^* \approx 0.19158$ and $y_2^* \approx 8.6334$ are the second coordinates of the intersection points of the line given by the equation $x = 2.7013$ with the curves $\mathcal{C}_2$ and $\mathcal{C}_1$, respectively. Then,

$$U_{\bar{z}}^* = U_1 \cup U_2,$$

where

$$U_1^* = \left\{ (x, y) : x \in \left(\frac{75y^2 + 256}{500y}, 2.7013 \right), y \in \left(0.19158, \frac{\sqrt{9902}}{35} \right) \right\},$$

and

$$U_2^* = \left\{ (x, y) : x \in \left(\frac{2275y^2 - 6318}{7000y}, 2.7013 \right), y \in \left[\frac{\sqrt{9902}}{35}, 8.6334 \right) \right\}.$$

See Figure 5b.

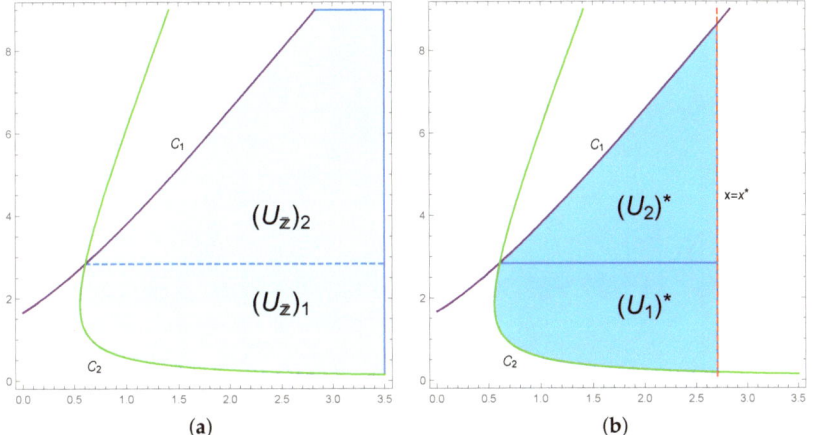

Figure 5. Repelling area $U_{\bar{z}}$ (**a**) and neighborhood $U_{\bar{z}}^*$ (**b**) of the snap-back repeller $\bar{z}$ (for $\alpha = 1.4$, $\beta = 0.08$, and $h = 0.7$).

Figure 6 represents the phase portrait with 30 iterations with repelling area $U_{\bar{z}}$ and neighborhood $U_{\bar{z}}^*$ of the snap-back repeller $\bar{z}$. Furthermore, Figure 6 shows the points in (16).

Now, assume that $\alpha = 0.6 \notin \left(\sqrt{\frac{3950}{2401}}, \frac{10}{7} \right)$ and $\beta = 0.001 < \beta_{\frac{7}{10}} = 0.24881$. Then, there exists $M > 2$ such that $T^M(\bar{z}_0) = \bar{z}$. In that case, if $M = 17$, the region $U_{\bar{z}}^*$ is a circle.

Figure 7 represents a phase portrait with 30 iterations and the snap-back repeller $\bar{z}$. Here,

$$z_1 = T(z_0), z_2 = T^2(z_0), \ldots, z_{18} = T^{17}(z_0) = \bar{z},$$

where

$$\begin{aligned}
&\mathbf{z}_0 = (1.7658, 0.52217), & &\mathbf{z}_1 = (1.84754, 0.494912), & &\mathbf{z}_2 = (1.94947, 0.46654),\\
&\mathbf{z}_3 = (2.07108, 0.438351), & &\mathbf{z}_4 = (2.21106, 0.411529), & &\mathbf{z}_5 = (2.36739, 0.387125),\\
&\mathbf{z}_6 = (2.53738, 0.366149), & &\mathbf{z}_7 = (2.71748, 0.349742), & &\mathbf{z}_8 = (2.9029, 0.339506),\\
&\mathbf{z}_9 = (3.08665, 0.338104), & &\mathbf{z}_{10} = (3.25749, 0.350585), & &\mathbf{z}_{11} = (3.39495, 0.387721),\\
&\mathbf{z}_{12} = (3.45532, 0.475941), & &\mathbf{z}_{13} = (3.32502, 0.693091), & &\mathbf{z}_{14} = (2.62461, 1.32833),\\
&\mathbf{z}_{15} = (-0.198952, 3.64206), & &\mathbf{z}_{16} = (2.0685, -0.754833), & &\bar{\mathbf{z}} = (1.66205, 0.6).
\end{aligned}$$

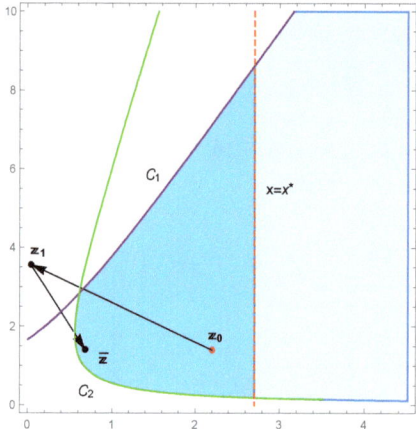

Figure 6. The snap-back repeller for $\alpha = 1.4$, $\beta = 0.08$, and $h = 0.7$.

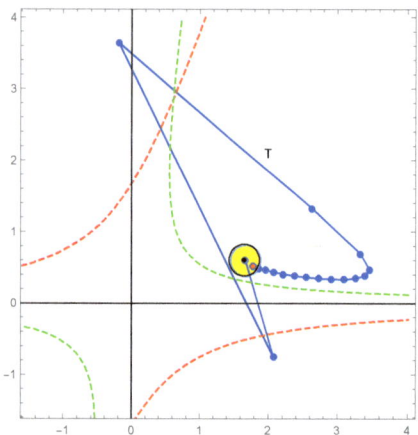

Figure 7. The snap-back repeller for $\alpha = 0.6$, $\beta = 0.001$, and $h = 0.7$.

If we suppose that $\alpha = 0.6$ and $\beta = 0.12 < \beta_{\frac{7}{10}} = 0.24881$, then Figure 8a shows a snap-back repeller with

$$\begin{aligned}
\mathbf{z}_0 &= (1.4605157298915394', 1.424776880514991'),\\
\mathbf{z}_1 &= (-0.31754936043512777', 2.6254981544811646'),\\
\mathbf{z}_2 &= (1.6613856774674765', -0.7712855915582548')\\
\bar{\mathbf{z}} &= (1.25, 0.6).
\end{aligned}$$

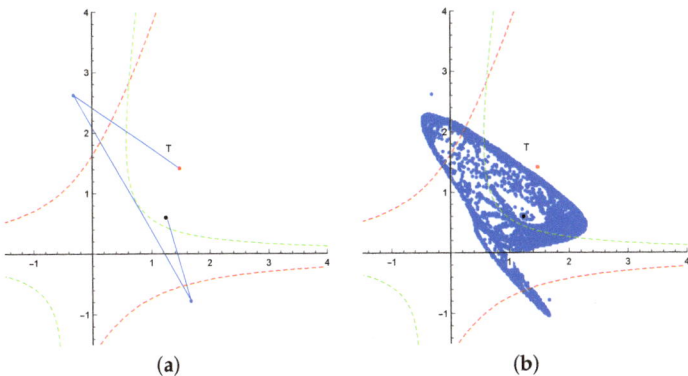

Figure 8. The snap-back repeller for $\alpha = 0.6$, $\beta = 0.12$, and $h = 0.7$.

The graph represents a phase portrait with 70 iterations. Figure 8b represents a phase portrait with 11170 iterations (we obtained a chaotic attractor due to the accumulation of rounding errors). In Figures 9a and 10a, the bifurcation diagrams are generated by code Bif2D from [23], and in Figures 9b and 10b corresponding Lyapunov coefficients are generated by the code in [24].

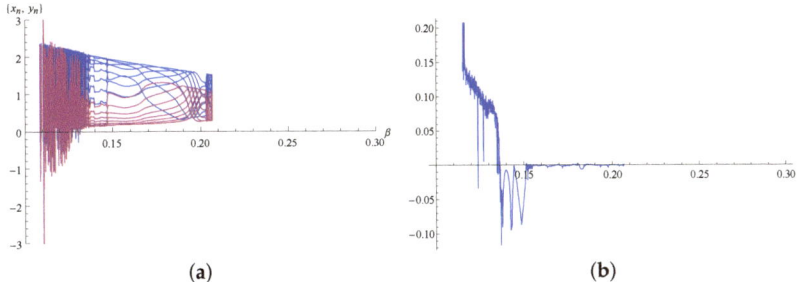

Figure 9. (a) Bifurcation diagram for $\alpha = 0.60$, $\beta \in (0.10, 0.30)$, $h = 0.7$, $\bar{z} = (1.25, 0.6)$, and initial point $z_0 = (1.4605157298915394, 1.424776880514991)$; (b) corresponding Lyapunov coefficients.

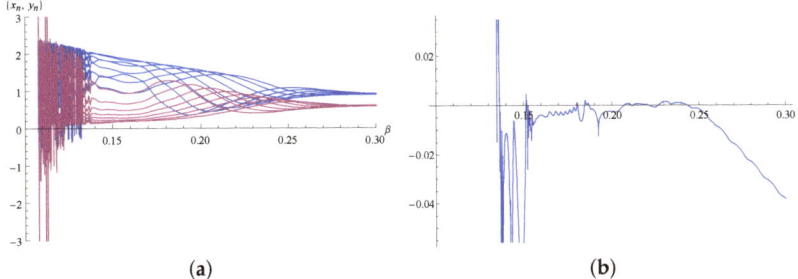

Figure 10. (a) Bifurcation diagram for $\alpha = 0.60$, $\beta \in (0.10, 0.30)$, $h = 0.7$, $\bar{z} = (1.25, 0.6)$, and initial point $z_0 = (1.40, 0.65)$; (b) corresponding Lyapunov coefficients.

5. Conclusions

We consider a chaotic dynamic of System (1), which is the Euler discretization of System (2), which was used as the model for glycolysis decomposition in [9]. System

(1) has a unique positive equilibrium, which locally can have any character depending on the parameter region. That is, this unique equiibrium solution can be either locally symptotically stable or repeller, saddle point, or non-hyperbolic. The global dynamics of such a system can be quite complicated and could include the existence of an infinite number of period-two solutions or equilibrium solutions, as we have shown in a series of papers [13]. In this paper, we focus on the case when this equilibrium is a repeller and prove that in this case there exists a region of parameters where System (1) exhibits chaos. The quite challenging problem is whether the local stability of System (1) implies the global stability of such a system and, in general, if System (1) is structurally stable. At this time, we are leaving these problems for future research.

Author Contributions: This research was carried out in equal parts by the four authors. All authors have read and agreed to the published version of the manuscript.

Funding: This research received no external funding.

Data Availability Statement: Data are contained within the article.

Conflicts of Interest: The authors declare no conflicts of interest.

Abbreviations

The following abbreviations are used in this manuscript:

DOAJ   Directory of open access journals.
TLA   Three-letter acronym.
LD   Linear dichroism.

References

1. Li, T.Y.; Yorke, J.A. Period Three Implies Chaos. *Am. Math. Mon.* **1975**, *82*, 985–992. [CrossRef]
2. Marotto, F.R. Snap-Back Repellers Imply Chaos in $\mathbb{R}^n$. *J. Math. Anal. Appl.* **1978**, *63*, 199–223. [CrossRef]
3. Marotto, F.R. Perturbations of stable and chaotic difference equations. *J. Math. Anal. Appl.* **1979**, *72*, 716–729. [CrossRef]
4. Marotto, F.R. Chaotic Behavior in the Hénon Mapping. *J. Math. Anal. Appl.* **1979**, *68*, 187–194. [CrossRef]
5. Aulbach, B.; Kieninger, B. On three definitions of chaos. *Nonlinear Dyn. Syst. Theory* **2001**, *1*, 23–37.
6. Li, C.P.; Chen, G.R. An Improved Version of the Marotto Theorem. *Chaos Solitons Fractals* **2003**, *18*, 69–77. [CrossRef]
7. Kloeden, P.; Li, Z. Li-Yorke chaos in higher dimensions: A review. *J. Differ. Equ. Appl.* **2006**, *12*, 247–269. [CrossRef]
8. Marotto, F.R. On Redefining a Snap-Back Repeller. *Chaos Solitons Fractals* **2005**, *25*, 25–28. [CrossRef]
9. Khan, A.Q.; Abdullah, E.; Ibrahim, T.F. Supercritical Neimark-Sacker Bifurcation and Hybrid Control in a Discrete-Time Glycolyt Oscillator Model. *Math. Probl. Eng.* **2020**, *2020*, 7834076. [CrossRef]
10. Berkal, M.; Almatrafi, M.B. Bifurcation and Stability of Two-Dimensional Activator–Inhibitor Model with Fractional-Ord Derivative. *Fractal Fract.* **2023**, *7*, 344. [CrossRef]
11. Berkal, M.; Almatrafi, M.B. Bifurcation Analysis and Chaos Control for Prey-Predator Model With Allee Effect. *Int. J. An Appl.* **2023**, *21*, 131.
12. Nurkanović, Z.; Nurkanović, M.; Garić-Demirović, M. Stability and Neimark-Sacker Bifurcation of Certain Mixed Monoto Rational Second-Order Difference Equation. *Qual. Theory Dyn. Syst.* **2021**, *20*, 75. [CrossRef]
13. Bektešević, J.; Kulenović, M.R.S.; Pilav, E. Global Dynamics of Cubic Second Order Difference Equation in the First Quadra *Adv. Differ. Equ.* **2015**, *176*, 1–38. [CrossRef]
14. Bektešević, J.; Hadžiabdić, V.; Mehuljić, M.; Mujić, N. Dynamics of a two-dimensional cooperative system of polynomial differen equations with cubic terms. *Sarajevo J. Math.* **2022**, *18*, 127–160.
15. Garić-Demirović, M.; Hrustić, S.; Moranjkić, S.; Nurkanović, M.; Nurkanović, Z. The existence of Li-Yorke chaos in certain predat prey system of difference equations. *Sarajevo J. Math.* **2022**, *18*, 45–62. Available online: https://www.anubih.ba/Journals/vol. ,no-1,y22/04-M_Garic_Demirovic-S_Hrustic-S_Moranjkic-M_and_Z_Nurkanovic.pdf (accessed on 19 March 2024).
16. Li, J.; Zang, H.; Wei, X. On the construction of one-dimensional discrete chaos theory based on the improved version of Marotto theorem. *J. Comput. Appl. Math.* **2020**, *380*, 112952. [CrossRef]
17. Zhang, L.; Huang, Q. Chaos induced by snap-back repellers in non-autonomous discrete dynamical systems. *J. Differ. Equ. Ap* **2018**, *24*, 1126–1144. [CrossRef]
18. Balibrea, F.; Cascales, A. Li-Yorke chaos in perturbed rational difference equations. In *Difference Equations, Discrete Dynamic Systems and Applications*; Springer Proceedings in Mathematics & Statistics; Springer: Berlin/Heidelberg, Germany, 201 Volume 180, pp. 49–61. [CrossRef]

- Kulenović, M.R.S.; Merino, O. *Discrete Dynamical Systems and Difference Equations with Mathematica*; Chapman and Hall/CRC: Boca Raton, FL, USA; London, UK, 2002. [CrossRef]
- Elaydi, S. *An Introduction to Difference Equations*, 3rd ed.; Undergraduate Texts in Mathematics; Springer: New York, NY, USA, 2005. Available online: https://www.abebooks.co.uk/9780387230597/Introduction-Difference-Equations-Undergraduate-Texts-0387230599/plp (accessed on 19 March 2024).
- Elaydi, S. *Discrete Chaos. With Applications in Science and Engineering*, 2nd ed.; Chapman & Hall/CRC: Boca Raton, FL, USA, 2007. [CrossRef]
- Alligood, K.T.; Sauer, T.D.; Yorke, J.A. *Chaos. An Introduction to Dynamical Systems*; Textbooks in Mathematical Sciences; Springer: New York, NY, USA, 1997. [CrossRef]
- Ufuktepe, Ü.; Kapçak, S. Applications of Discrete Dynamical Systems with Mathematica. Thesis, Izmir University of Economics, Izmir, Türkiye, 2014; Volume 1909, pp. 207–216. Available online: http://hdl.handle.net/2433/223175 (accessed on 19 March 2024).
- Sandri, M. Numerical Calculation of Lyapunov Exponents. *Math. J.* **1996**, *6*, 78–84. Available online: https://www.mathematica-journal.com/issue/v6i3/article/sandri/contents/63sandri.pdf (accessed on 19 March 2024).
- Korsch, H.J.; Jodl, H.-J. *Chaos. A Program Collection for the PC*, 2nd ed.; with 1 CD-ROM (Windows 95 and NT); Springer: Berlin/Heidelberg, Germany, 1999.
- Nusse, H.E.; Yorke, J.A. *Dynamics: Numerical Explorations*, 2nd ed.; Accompanying computer program Dynamics 2 coauthored by Brian R. Hunt and Eric J. Kostelich; Applied Mathematical Sciences 101; Springer: New York, NY, USA, 1998.

Disclaimer/Publisher's Note: The statements, opinions and data contained in all publications are solely those of the individual author(s) and contributor(s) and not of MDPI and/or the editor(s). MDPI and/or the editor(s) disclaim responsibility for any injury to people or property resulting from any ideas, methods, instructions or products referred to in the content.

Article

Dynamical Behaviors of Stochastic SIS Epidemic Model with Ornstein–Uhlenbeck Process

Huina Zhang, Jianguo Sun *, Peng Yu and Daqing Jiang

School of Science, China University of Petroleum (East China), Qingdao 266580, China;
20060050@upc.edu.cn (H.Z.); s19090062@s.upc.edu.cn (P.Y.); 20140012@upc.edu.cn (D.J.)
* Correspondence: sunjg616@upc.edu.cn

Abstract: Controlling infectious diseases has become an increasingly complex issue, and vaccination has become a common preventive measure to reduce infection rates. It has been thought that vaccination protects the population. However, there is no fully effective vaccine. This is based on the fact that it has long been assumed that the immune system produces corresponding antibodies after vaccination, but usually does not achieve the level of complete protection for undergoing environmental fluctuations. In this paper, we investigate a stochastic SIS epidemic model with incomplete inoculation, which is perturbed by the Ornstein–Uhlenbeck process and Brownian motion. We determine the existence of a unique global solution for the stochastic SIS epidemic model and derive control conditions for the extinction. By constructing two suitable Lyapunov functions and using the ergodicity of the Ornstein–Uhlenbeck process, we establish sufficient conditions for the existence of stationary distribution, which means the disease will prevail. Furthermore, we obtain the exact expression of the probability density function near the pseudo-equilibrium point of the stochastic model while addressing the four-dimensional Fokker–Planck equation under the same conditions. Finally, we conduct several numerical simulations to validate the theoretical results.

Keywords: Ornstein–Uhlenbeck process; Brownian motion; stationary distribution; probability density function

MSC: 60H10; 34D05

1. Introduction

It is widely acknowledged that mathematical models describing the dynamic behaviors of infectious diseases have played a crucial role in understanding various diseases and their transmission mechanisms [1–6]. As early as 1927, Kermack and McKendrick put forward the classic susceptibility–infection–susceptibility model and established the corresponding threshold theory [1]. Since then, various ordinary differential equations have been extended to analyze and control the spread of infectious diseases [3,7–9]. Controlling infectious diseases has become an increasingly complex issue, and vaccination has become a common preventive measure to reduce infection rates [10–12]. Routine vaccinations against diseases such as measles, smallpox, and tuberculosis are now available in all countries. So, over the past few decades, some basic epidemic models with vaccination strategies have been studied. Safan and Rihan [13] considered the following *SIS epidemic model* with incomplete protection from the vaccine as follows:

$$\begin{cases} \dot{S}(t) = (1-p)A + \alpha I(t) - (\mu + \varphi)S(t) - \beta S(t)I(t) \\ \dot{I}(t) = \beta S(t)I(t) + (1-e)\beta V(t)I(t) - (\mu + \alpha + \varepsilon)I(t), \\ \dot{V}(t) = pA + \varphi S(t) - \mu V(t) - (1-e)\beta V(t)I(t) \end{cases} \quad (1)$$

where $S(t)$ denotes the number of members who are susceptible to an infection, $I(t)$ denotes the number of infected individuals, and $V(t)$ is the number of members who are immune to an infection as the result of vaccination. The definitions of the basic assumptions are as in Table 1.

Table 1. The definitions of the parameters.

Parameter	Definition
A	an input of new members into the population
p	a fraction of vaccinated newborns
μ	the natural mortality rate
β	transmission coefficient between compartments $S(t)$ and $I(t)$
φ	the proportional coefficient of vaccination for the susceptible
α	recovery rate of $I(t)$
ε	the disease-related death rate
e	the rate of protection of the vaccine against infected individuals

From the definitions, we can find that $e = 1$ indicates that the vaccine is completely effective in preventing infection, whereas $e = 0$ means that the vaccine is completely invalid.

Note that the basic regeneration number $R_0 = \frac{\beta[(1-p)\mu+(1-e)(p\mu+\varphi)]}{(\mu+\varphi)(\mu+\alpha+\varepsilon)}$ is the threshold for determining the prevalence of the disease. When $R_0 < 1$, the system has only disease-free equilibrium point $E_0 = (S_0, 0, V_0) = (\frac{(1-p)\mu}{\mu+\varphi}, 0, \frac{p\mu+\varphi}{\mu+\varphi})$, and it is globally asymptotically stable in invariant set Γ, which means that the disease will be extinct. When $R_0 > 1$, E_0 is unstable, and there is a globally asymptotically stable endemic equilibrium point $E_* = (S_*, I_*, V_*)$, which means that the disease will persist.

Due to the unstable changes in effective contact factors during epidemic diseases, the most common method to consider is introducing white noise. For a more detailed explanation, readers can refer to [14–17]. Moreover, simulating random perturbations from multiple perspectives is another important way. References [18–22] extensively research Ornstein–Uhlenbeck processes driven by Brownian motion or fractional Brownian motion. The Ornstein–Uhlenbeck process, with modifications, can stochastically model interest rates, currency exchange rates, and commodity prices. According to the work in [19], the stochastic mean-reverting process incorporates the effects of environmental fluctuations into the parameters, which is a biologically meaningful method. Yang, Zhang, and Jiang [20] analyzed the persistence and extinction of a stochastic food chain system by incorporating the Ornstein–Uhlenbeck process. However, there is little information available in the literature concerning the SIS epidemic model with the Ornstein–Uhlenbeck process. Hence, in this paper, we consider the parameter β an Ornstein–Uhlenbeck process affected by randomly varying environments. The Ornstein–Uhlenbeck process in system (1) is as follows:

$$\dot{\beta}(t) = \theta(\bar{\beta} - \beta(t)) + \sigma \dot{B}(t),$$

where $\bar{\beta}$ is the time-mean value of $\beta(t)$, θ is the speed of reversion, σ is the intensity of volatility, and $B(t)$ is standard Brownian motion.

Integrating both sides of the above equation, we can obtain

$$\beta(t) = \bar{\beta} + (\beta_0 - \bar{\beta})e^{-\theta t} + \sigma \int_0^t e^{-\theta(t-s)} dB(t),$$

where $\beta_0 = \beta(0)$.

Then, we can obtain the expectation and variance in $\beta(t)$,

$$E[\beta(t)] = \bar{\beta} + (\beta_0 - \bar{\beta})e^{-\theta t} \quad \text{Var}[\beta(t)] = \frac{\sigma^2}{2\theta}\left(1 - e^{-2\theta t}\right).$$

Motivated by the above works, in this paper, we propose the following stochastic SIS epidemic model with the Ornstein–Uhlenbeck process:

$$\begin{cases} \dot{S}(t) = (1-p)A + \alpha I(t) - (\mu + \varphi)S(t) - \overline{\beta}S(t)I(t) - m(t)S(t)I(t) \\ \dot{I}(t) = \overline{\beta}S(t)I(t) + (1-e)\overline{\beta}V(t)I(t) - (\mu + \alpha + \varepsilon)I(t) + m(t)S(t)I(t) + (1-e)m(t)V(t)I(t) \\ \dot{V}(t) = pA + \varphi S(t) - \mu V(t) - (1-e)\overline{\beta}V(t)I(t) - (1-e)m(t)V(t)I(t) \\ \dot{m}(t) = -\theta m(t) + \sigma \dot{B}(t) \end{cases} \quad (\ $$

where $m(t) = \beta(t) - \overline{\beta}$.

The rest of this paper is arranged as follows. Section 2 presents the existence and uniqueness analysis for system (2), as well as the asymptotic properties of the solution. In Section 3, we discuss the conditions for predator extinction in system (2). Furthermore, we aim to obtain the exact expression for the density function for a linearized system corresponding to stochastic system (2) around the original point in Section 4. Finally, in Section 5, we conduct several numerical simulations to validate the theoretical results.

2. Existence and Uniqueness of Global Positive Solution

Throughout this paper, let $(\Omega, \mathscr{F}, \{\mathscr{F}_t\}_{t\geq 0}, \mathbb{P})$ be a complete probability space with a filtration $\{\mathscr{F}_t\}_{t\geq 0}$ satisfying the usual conditions (i.e., it is right-continuous and $\mathscr{F}_0$ contains all $\mathbb{P}$-null sets). Define $\mathbb{R}_+^d = \{x \in \mathbb{R}^d : x_i > 0 \text{ for all } 1 \leq i \leq d\}$, $\overline{\mathbb{R}}_+^d = \{x \in \mathbb{R}^d : x_i \geq 0 \text{ for all } 1 \leq i \leq d\}$. More basic, detailed knowledge of stochastic systems, readers can refer to Mao [23].

To study the long-term dynamics of a stochastic population system, the existence and uniqueness of the global solution to the model should be considered first. In this section, we give the following conclusion, which is a fundamental condition for the follow-up behavior study of stochastic systems.

Theorem 1. *For any initial conditions $(S(0), I(0), V(0), m(0)) \in \mathbb{R}_+^3 \times \mathbb{R}$, when $t \geq 0$, system (2) has a unique global positive solution $(S(t), I(t), V(t), m(t)) \in \mathbb{R}_+^3 \times \mathbb{R}$.*

Proof. Since the coefficients of system (2) are locally Lipsitz-continuous, there exists a unique local solution $(S(t), I(t), V(t))$ on $t \in (0, \tau_0)$. For any initial value $(S(0), I(0), V(0)) \in \mathbb{R}_+^3$, τ_0 is an explosion moment. To prove that the local solution is global, we need only prove that $\tau_0 = \infty$ a.s. Let us make n_0 sufficiently large that every element of $(S(0), I(0), V(0), m(0))$ is in the interval $\left[\frac{1}{n_0}, n_0\right]$, and for every integer $n \geq n_0$, we define the stop time

$$\tau_n = \inf\left\{0 < t < \tau_0 \mid \min\{S(t), I(t), V(t)\} \leq \frac{1}{n}, \text{ or } \max\{S(t), I(t), V(t)\} \geq n\right\}.$$

In this paper, we assume that $\inf\{\varnothing\} = \infty$. Obviously, τ_n increases with $n \to \infty$. If $\tau_\infty = \lim_{n \to \infty} \tau_n$, $\tau_\infty \leq \tau_0$ a.s. If $\tau_\infty = \infty$ a.s. is true, then $\tau_0 = \infty$ a.s., which means for all $t \geq 0$, $(S(t), I(t), V(t)) \in \mathbb{R}_+^3$ a.s. is true.

If $\tau_0 < \infty$ a.s. is true, then there exist two constants, $T \geq 0$ and $\varepsilon \in (0,1)$, such that $\mathbb{P}\{\tau_\infty \leq T\} > \varepsilon$. So, there is an integer $n_1 \geq n_0$, for all $n \geq n_1$, that satisfies

$$\mathbb{P}\{\tau_n \leq T\} \geq \varepsilon. \tag{3}$$

We construct the Lyapunov function $W_0 : \mathbb{R}_+^3 \times \mathbb{R} \to \mathbb{R}_+$, as follows:

$$W_0(S, I, V, m) = S - 1 - \ln S + V - 1 - \ln V + V - 1 - \ln V + \frac{m^2}{2}. \tag{4}$$

According to the property $\mu - 1 - \ln \mu \geq 0$ when $\mu > 0$, we can obtain that $W_0(S, I, V, m)$ is a non-negative C^2-function.

When we apply Ito's formula, we have

$$dW_0(S, I, V, m) = \mathcal{L}W_0(S, I, V, m)dt + \sigma m dt, \tag{5}$$

where

$$\pounds W_0(S, I, V, m) = (1 - \frac{1}{S})[(1-p)\mu + \alpha I - (\mu + \varphi)S - \bar{\beta}SI - mSI]$$
$$+ (1 - \frac{1}{I})[\bar{\beta}SI + (1-e)\bar{\beta}VI + mSI + (1-e)mVI - (\mu + \alpha + \varepsilon)I]$$
$$+ (1 - \frac{1}{V})[p\mu + \varphi S - \mu V - (1-e)\bar{\beta}VI - (1-e)mVI] \tag{6}$$
$$- \theta m^2 + \frac{\sigma^2}{2}$$
$$\leq 4\mu + \varphi + \alpha + \varepsilon + (2-e)\bar{\beta}\bar{K} + \frac{\sigma^2}{2} + (4-2e)\bar{K}|m| - \theta m^2$$
$$\leq 4\mu + \varphi + \alpha + \varepsilon + (2-e)\bar{\beta}\bar{K} + \frac{\sigma^2}{2} + \frac{(2-e)^2 \bar{K}^2}{\theta} := K,$$

and K is a constant. We can obtain $dW_0(S, I, V, m) = Kdt + \sigma m dB(t)$.
Integrating from 0 to $\tau_n \wedge T$ and taking the expectation, we have

$$EW_0(S(\tau_n \wedge T), I(\tau_n \wedge T), V(\tau_n \wedge T), m(\tau_n \wedge T))$$
$$\leq KE(\tau_n \wedge T) + W_0(S(0), I(0), V(0), m(0)) \tag{7}$$
$$\leq KT + W_0(S(0), I(0), V(0), m(0)).$$

Let $\Omega_n = \{\tau_n \leq T\}$, for $n \geq n_1$. By (3), $P(\Omega_n) \geq \epsilon$. Notice that for any $\omega \in \Omega_n$, at least one of $S(\tau_n \wedge T), I(\tau_n \wedge T), V(\tau_n \wedge T)$ is equal to $\frac{1}{n}$ or n. Therefore, $W_0(S(\tau_n \wedge T), I(\tau_n \wedge T), V(\tau_n \wedge T))$ are not less than $n - 1 - \ln n$ or $\frac{1}{n} - 1 + \ln n$. So,

$$KT + W_0(S(0), I(0), V(0), m(0)) \geq E[I_{\Omega_n}(\omega) W_0(S(\tau_n, \omega), I(\tau_n, \omega), V(\tau_n, \omega), m(\tau_n, \omega))]$$
$$\geq \epsilon \left\{ [n - 1 - \ln n] \wedge \left[\frac{1}{n} - 1 + \ln n\right] \right\}, \tag{8}$$

where $I_{\Omega_n}(\cdot)$ is the indicative function of Ω_n. $n \to \infty$ leads to the contradiction

$$\infty = KT + W_0(S(0), I(0), V(0), m(0)) < \infty.$$

Therefore, τ_∞ a.s. This means that the SDE system (2) exists a unique global positive solution. □

3. Extinction of Stochastic System (2)

The states of symbiosis and extinction due to various disturbances in the environment are the major research topics in the SIS epidemic model. In this section, we give the results of extinction among predators in SIS epidemic system (2). Before giving the main result, we first present the following Lemma [20]:

Lemma 1. *There exists a bounded domain $\mathbb{D} \subset \Omega_d$ with a regular boundary $\partial \mathbb{D}$ such that*
($\mathcal{A}1$): there is a positive number δ such that $\sum_{i,j=1}^d a_{ij}(x)\xi_i\xi_j \geq \delta|\xi|^2$, $x \in \mathbb{D}$, $\xi \in R_d$.
($\mathcal{A}2$): there exists a non-negative C^2-function V such that $\pounds V \geq -1$ for any $x \in \Omega_d \backslash \mathbb{D}$.
Then, the Markov process $X(t)$ has a unique ergodic stationary distribution $\pi(\cdot)$, and

$$P\left\{ \lim_{T \to \infty} \frac{1}{T} \int_0^T f(X(t))dt = \int_{\Omega_d} f(x)\pi(dx) = 1 \right\} \tag{9}$$

holds for all $x \in \Omega_d$, where $f(\cdot)$ is an integrable function with respect to the measure π.

Theorem 2. Assuming $R_1 = R_0 - \frac{(2+c_1+c_2-c_2e-e)\sigma}{\sqrt{2\theta(\mu+\alpha+\varepsilon)}} > 1$, then the solution $(S(t), I(t), V(t), m(t))$ of system (2) has a stationary distribution $\pi(\cdot)$ with the initial value $(S(0), I(0), V(0), m(0)) \in \Gamma$.

Proof. Obviously, system (2) does not satisfy assumption $(\mathcal{A}1)$ of Lemma 1. Hence, ergodicity and uniqueness cannot be obtained. However, to prove Theorem 2, we need to verify assumption $(\mathcal{A}2)$ of Lemma 1. We expect to construct a neighborhood $\mathbb{D}_{\epsilon_0}$ and a non-negative C^2-function $W_1(S, I, V, m)$ such that $\pounds W_1 \leq -1$ for any $(S, I, V, m) \in \Gamma \setminus \mathbb{D}_{\epsilon_0}$. We consider an appropriate Lyapunov function form,

$$\overline{W}(S, I, V, m) = M(-\ln I - c_1 S - c_2 V + \frac{b}{2}m^2) - \ln S - \ln V + \frac{m^2}{2} - \ln(1 - S - I - V) \quad (10)$$

where b, c_1, c_2, and M are all undetermined positive constants.

We can simply define that

$$V_1 = -\ln I - c_1 S - c_2 V + \frac{b}{2}m^2,$$
$$V_2 = -\ln S,$$
$$V_3 = -\ln V,$$
$$V_4 = \frac{m^2}{2},$$
$$V_5 = -\ln(1 - S - I - V).$$

Applying *Ito's* formula to V_1 and scaling it, we have

$$\begin{aligned}\pounds V_1 =& -\bar{\beta}S - (1-e)V - mS - (1-e)mV + \mu + \alpha + \varepsilon \\ & - c_1[(1-p)\mu + \alpha I - (\mu+\varphi)S - \bar{\beta}SI - mSI] \\ & - c_2[p\mu + \varphi S - \mu V - (1-e)\bar{\beta}VI - (1-e)mVI] - b\theta m^2 + \frac{b}{2}\sigma^2 \\ \leq & [c_1(\mu+\varphi) - c_2\varphi - \bar{\beta}]S + [c_2\mu - (1-e)\bar{\beta}]V - c_1(1-p)\mu - c_2p\mu + \mu + \alpha + \varepsilon \\ & + (2 + c_1 + c_2 - c_2e - e)|m| - b\theta m^2 + \frac{b}{2}\sigma^2 + [c_1(\bar{\beta}-\alpha) + c_2(1-e)\bar{\beta}]I.\end{aligned} \quad (11)$$

Let $c_1(\mu+\varphi) - c_2\varphi - \bar{\beta} = 0$. We have

$$c_1 = \frac{\bar{\beta}[\mu + (1-e)\varphi]}{\mu(\mu+\varphi)} > 0,$$
$$c_2 = \frac{(1-e)\bar{\beta}}{\mu} > 0.$$

By $(2 + c_1 + c_2 - c_2e - e)|m| - b\theta m^2 \leq \frac{(2+c_1+c_2-c_2e-e)^2}{4b\theta}$, then

$$\pounds V_1 \leq -(\mu+\alpha+\varepsilon)(R_0 - 1) + \frac{(2+c_1+c_2-c_2e-e)^2}{4b\theta} + \frac{b}{2}\sigma^2 + [c_1(\bar{\beta}-\alpha) + c_2(1-e)\bar{\beta}]I. \quad (12)$$

Taking $b = \frac{2+c_1+c_2-c_2e-e}{\sigma\sqrt{2\theta}}$, we can obtain

$$\begin{aligned}\pounds V_1 \leq & -(\mu+\alpha+\varepsilon)(R_0 - 1) + \frac{(2+c_1+c_2-c_2e-e)\sigma}{\sqrt{2\theta}} + [c_1(\bar{\beta}-\alpha) + c_2(1-e)\bar{\beta}]I \\ =& -(\mu+\alpha+\varepsilon)(R_1 - 1) + [c_1(\bar{\beta}-\alpha) + c_2(1-e)\bar{\beta}]I,\end{aligned} \quad (13)$$

where $R_1 = R_0 - \frac{(2+c_1+c_2-c_2e-e)\sigma}{\sqrt{2\theta(\mu+\alpha+\varepsilon)}}$.

Applying Itô's formula to V_2, V_3, V_4, and V_5 and scaling them, we have

$$£V_2 = -\frac{(1-p)\mu}{S} - \frac{\alpha I}{S} + \mu + \varphi + \bar{\beta}I + mI$$
$$\leq -\frac{(1-p)\mu}{S} + \mu + \varphi + \bar{\beta}I + |m|. \tag{14}$$

$$£V_3 = -\frac{p\mu}{V} - \frac{\varphi S}{V} + \mu + (1-e)\bar{\beta}I + (1-e)mI$$
$$\leq -\frac{p\mu}{V} + \mu + (1-e)\bar{\beta}I + (1-e)|m|. \tag{15}$$

$$£V_4 = -\theta m^2 + \frac{\sigma^2}{2}, \tag{16}$$

$$£V_5 = -\frac{\varepsilon I}{1-(S+I+V)}. \tag{17}$$

Moreover, notice that $\overline{W}(S, I, V, m)$ is a continuous function, which satisfies that

$$\lim_{S+I+V \to 1} \inf \overline{W}(S, I, V, m) = +\infty. \tag{18}$$

Hence, there is a minimum $\overline{W}_{min}$ of $\overline{W}(S, I, V, m)$.
We define a non-negative C^2 function $W_1(S, I, V, m) : R_+^3 \times R \to R$ by

$$W_1(S, I, V, m) = \overline{W}(S, I, V, m) - \overline{W}_{min}. \tag{19}$$

Combining (13)–(17), it can be shown that

$$£W_1 \leq -M(R_1 - 1)(\mu + \alpha + \varepsilon) + 3\mu + \varphi + \frac{(2-e)^2}{4\theta} + \frac{\sigma^2}{2}$$
$$+ \lambda I - \frac{(1-p)\mu}{S} - \frac{p\mu}{V} - \frac{\varepsilon I}{1-(S+I+V)}, \tag{20}$$

where $\lambda = M[c_{\bar{\beta}-\alpha} + c_2(1-e)\bar{\beta}] + (2-e)\bar{\beta}$.
We set $-M(R_1 - 1)(\mu + \alpha + \varepsilon) + 3\mu + \varphi + \frac{(2-e)^2}{4\theta} + \frac{\sigma^2}{2} = -2$. Then,

$$M = \frac{2 + 3\mu + \varphi + \frac{(2-e)^2}{4\theta} + \frac{\sigma^2}{2}}{(R_1 - 1)(\mu + \alpha + \varepsilon)}. \tag{21}$$

In this way, we obtain

$$£W_1 \leq -2 + \lambda I - \frac{(1-p)\mu}{S} - \frac{p\mu}{V} - \frac{\varepsilon I}{1-(S+I+V)}. \tag{22}$$

Next, the corresponding compact subset is constructed as follows:

$$\mathbb{D}_\epsilon = \left\{ (S, I, V, m) \in R_+^3 \times R | S \geq \epsilon, I \geq \epsilon, V \geq \epsilon, S+I+V \leq 1-\epsilon^2 \right\}, \tag{23}$$

where ϵ is a sufficiently small positive constant.

For convenience, we consider four subsets of $R_+^3 \times R \setminus \mathbb{D}_\epsilon$ as follows:

$$\mathbb{D}_{1,\epsilon}^c = \{(S, I, V, m) \in R_+^3 \times R | S < \epsilon\},$$

$$\mathbb{D}_{2,\epsilon}^c = \{(S, I, V, m) \in R_+^3 \times R | I < \epsilon\},$$

$$\mathbb{D}_{3,\epsilon}^c = \{(S, I, V, m) \in R_+^3 \times R | V < \epsilon\},$$

$$\mathbb{D}_{4,\epsilon}^c = \{(S, I, V, m) \in R_+^3 \times R | S + I + V > 1 - \epsilon_2, I > \epsilon\}.$$

In the following study, we will show that $£W_1 \leq -1$, for any $(S, I, V, m) \in \mathbb{D}_{i,\epsilon}^c$ ($i = 1, 2, 3, 4$).

Case 1. If $(S, I, V, m) \in \mathbb{D}_{1,\epsilon}^c$, by (22), it can be derived that

$$£W_1 < -2 - \frac{(1-p)\mu}{\epsilon} + \lambda < -1. \tag{24}$$

Case 2. If $(S, I, V, m) \in \mathbb{D}_{2,\epsilon}^c$, by (22), it can be derived that

$$£W_1 < -2 + \lambda\epsilon < -1. \tag{25}$$

Case 3. If $(S, I, V, m) \in \mathbb{D}_{3,\epsilon}^c$, by (22), it can be derived that

$$£W_1 < -2 - \frac{p\mu}{\epsilon} + \lambda < -1. \tag{26}$$

Case 4. If $(S, I, V, m) \in \mathbb{D}_{4,\epsilon}^c$, by (22), it can be derived that

$$£W_1 < -2 - \frac{\epsilon}{\epsilon} + \lambda < -1. \tag{27}$$

It is worth noting that $R_+^3 \times R \setminus \mathbb{D}_\epsilon = \cup_{i=1}^4 \mathbb{D}_{i,\epsilon}^c$. Therefore, for any $(S, I, V, m) \in R_+^3 \times R \setminus \mathbb{D}_\epsilon$, it can be obtained equivalently that $£W_1 \leq -1$. □

The states of symbiosis and extinction due to various disturbances are the two most researched topics in the epidemic model. Furthermore, we give the extinction of SIS epidemic system (2).

Theorem 3. *For any initial value $(S(0), I(0), V(0), m(0)) \in \Gamma$, if $R_2 = R_0 + \frac{(2+c_1+c_2-c_2e-e)\sigma}{\sqrt{\pi\theta}(\mu+\alpha+\epsilon)} + \frac{c_1\alpha}{\mu+\alpha+\epsilon} < 1$, the solution $(S(t), I(t), V(t), m(t))$ of system (2) satisfies*

$$\lim_{t \to \infty} \sup \frac{\ln I(t)}{t} \leq (\mu + \alpha + \epsilon)(R_2 - 1) < 0 \quad a.s. \tag{28}$$

This implies that the epidemic of system (2) will become extinct with probability 1.

Proof. Applying Ito's formula to $\ln I(t)$, we obtain

$$d(\ln I + c_1 S + c_2 V) \leq [(\mu + \alpha + \epsilon)(R_0 - 1) + c_1\alpha + (2 + c_1 + c_2 - c_2e - e)|m|]dt \tag{29}$$

Integrating the above formula from 0 to t on both sides, then

$$\ln I(t) + c_1 S(t) + c_2 V(t) \leq \int_0^t [(\mu + \alpha + \epsilon)(R_0 - 1) + c_1\alpha + (2 + c_1 + c_2 - c_2e - e)|m|]dr + \ln I(0) + c_1 S(0) + c_2 V(0), \tag{3}$$

Dividing by t on both sides of this inequality and taking the limit as $t \to \infty$, we obtain

$$\lim_{t\to\infty} \frac{\ln I(t) + c_1 S(t) + c_2 V(t)}{t} \leq (\mu + \alpha + \varepsilon)(R_0 - 1) + c_1\alpha + \lim_{t\to\infty} \frac{\int_0^t (2 + c_1 + c_2 - c_2 e - e)|m|dr}{t}, \tag{31}$$

and

$$\lim_{t\to\infty} \frac{\ln I(t)}{t} \leq (\mu + \alpha + \varepsilon)(R_0 - 1) + c_1\alpha + \int_{-\infty}^{+\infty}(2 + c_1 + c_2 - c_2 e - e)|m|\pi(m)dm$$
$$= (\mu + \alpha + \varepsilon)(R_0 - 1) + c_1\alpha + \frac{(2 + c_1 + c_2 - c_2 e - e)\sigma}{\sqrt{\pi\theta}} \tag{32}$$
$$= (\mu + \alpha + \varepsilon)(R_2 - 1) < 0.$$

Consequently, it indicates that $\lim_{t\to\infty} I(t) = 0$ a.s. The disease will die out. □

4. Probability Density Function of Stochastic System (2)

According to Theorem 2, it is obtained that the global solution $(S(t), I(t), V(t), m(t))$ of system (2) follows a stationary distribution $\pi(\cdot)$. This section is devoted to deriving an explicit expression for the probability density function of the distribution $\pi(\cdot)$ when $R_1 > 1$. In fact, this result will provide a wide range of possibilities for the further development of epidemiological dynamics. Before this, necessary transformations (equilibrium offset transformation) for system (2) should be mentioned.

Theorem 4. *If $R_0 > 1$, a quasi-stable equilibrium point $E^* = (S^*, I^*, V^*, 0)$ is defined to satisfy the following system of equations:*

$$\begin{cases} (1-p)\mu + \alpha I^* - (\mu + \varphi)S^* - \bar{\beta}S^* I^* = 0 \\ \bar{\beta}S^* I^* + (1-e)\bar{\beta}V^* I^* - (\mu + \alpha + \varepsilon)I^* = 0, \\ p\mu + \varphi S^* - \mu V^* - (1-e)\bar{\beta}V^* I^* = 0 \end{cases} \tag{33}$$

When $R_0 > 1$, Equation (33) has a unique positive solution, and $S^* \in (\frac{\alpha}{\bar{\beta}}, S^0)$, where $S^0 = \frac{(1-p)\mu}{\mu + \varphi}$.

Proof. We assume that $\bar{\beta}S^0 > \alpha$, $R_0 > 1$. Then,

$$\begin{cases} (\mu + \varphi)(S^0 - S) + (\alpha - \bar{\beta}S^0)I = 0 \\ e\bar{\beta}S + (1-e)\bar{\beta} - (\mu + \alpha + \varepsilon) = (1-e)\bar{\beta}(1 + \frac{\varepsilon}{\mu})I \end{cases} \tag{34}$$

By Equation (34), we have

$$e\bar{\beta}(S - S^0) + (\mu + \alpha + \varepsilon)(R_0 - 1) = (1-e)\bar{\beta}(1 + \frac{\varepsilon}{\mu})I. \tag{35}$$

Substituting Equation (35) with Equation (33), we have

$$F(S) = (\mu + \varphi)(S^0 - S) + (\alpha - \bar{\beta}S)\left[\frac{e}{(1-e)(1 + \frac{\varepsilon}{\mu})}(S - S^0) + \frac{\mu + \alpha + \varepsilon}{(1-e)\bar{\beta}(1 + \frac{\varepsilon}{\mu})}(R_0 - 1)\right] = 0, \tag{36}$$

$$F(S^0) = (\alpha - \bar{\beta}S^0)\frac{\mu + \alpha + \varepsilon}{(1-e)\bar{\beta}(1 + \frac{\varepsilon}{\mu})}(R_0 - 1) < 0. \tag{37}$$

Then, by $F''(S) = \frac{-2e\bar{\beta}}{(1-e)\left(1+\frac{\varepsilon}{\mu}\right)} < 0$, we know that Equation (30) has a unique solution. Thus, $S^* \in (\frac{\alpha}{\bar{\beta}}, S^0)$, $I^* = \frac{(\mu+\varphi)(S^*-S^0)}{\alpha-\bar{\beta}S^*}$. □

To facilitate the study of the problem, we can make the following transformations. Let $x_1 = m$, $x_2 = S - S^*$, $x_3 = I - I^*$, $x_4 = N - N^*$, where $N = S + I + V$.
Denote
$$X(t) = (x_1(t), x_2(t), x_3(t), x_3(t))^T,$$

$$A = \begin{pmatrix} -\theta & 0 & 0 & 0 \\ -a_{21} & -a_{22} & -a_{23} & 0 \\ a_{31} & a_{32} & -a_{33} & a_{34} \\ 0 & 0 & -a_{43} & -a_{44} \end{pmatrix},$$

$$H = \begin{pmatrix} -\sigma & 0 & 0 & 0 \\ 0 & 0 & -0 & 0 \\ 0 & 0 & 0 & 0 \\ 0 & 0 & 0 & 0 \end{pmatrix},$$

where $a_{21} = S^*I^* > 0$, $a_{22} = \mu + \varphi + (\bar{\beta})I^* > 0$, $a_{23} = \bar{\beta}S^* - \alpha > 0$, $a_{31} = \frac{\mu+\alpha+\varepsilon}{\bar{\beta}}I^* > 0$, $a_{32} = e\bar{\beta}I^* > 0$, $a_{33} = a_{34} = (1-e)\bar{\beta}I^* > 0$, $a_{43} = \varepsilon > 0$, $a_{44} = \mu > 0$. Therefore, the linearized form of system (2) at the quasi-stable equilibrium point is

$$dX(t) = AX(t)dt + HdB(t). \tag{38}$$

The probability density function of the solution of Equation (38) satisfies the Fokker–Planck equation and is in the form of Gaussian distribution

$$\Phi(X) = C_0 e^{-\frac{1}{2}X^T M_0 X}. \tag{39}$$

Here, C_0 is the normalized constant and M_0 a real symmetric matrix, which satisfies the algebraic equation
$$M_0 H^2 M_0 + A^T M_0 + M_0 A = 0. \tag{40}$$

If M_0 is an invertible matrix, Equation (40) can be equivalent to
$$H^2 + A\Sigma + \Sigma A^T = 0, \tag{41}$$

where $\Sigma = M_0^{-1}$.
Denote
$$A = \begin{pmatrix} -\theta & 0 \\ Z & \tilde{A} \end{pmatrix},$$

$$|\lambda I - \tilde{A}| = \lambda^3 + p_1 \lambda^2 + p_2 \lambda + p_3,$$

where $p_1 = a_{22} + a_{33} + a_{44}$, $p_2 = a_{22}a_{33} + a_{22}a_{44} + a_{33}a_{44} + a_{23}a_{32} + a_{34}a_{43}$, $p_3 = a_{22}a_{33}a_{44} + a_{22}a_{34}a_{43} + a_{23}a_{32}a_{44}$. By $p_1 > 0$, $p_2 > 0$, $p_1 p_2 - p_3 > 0$, it can be concluded that $\tilde{A}$ is positive definite and the quasi-stable equilibrium is locally asymptotically stable.
Here, we provide an important Lemma [16]:

Lemma 2. *For any matrix where* $B = \begin{pmatrix} -b_{11} & 0 & 0 & 0 \\ -b_{21} & b_{22} & -b_{23} & 0 \\ 0 & b_{32} & b_{33} & b_{34} \\ 0 & 0 & b_{43} & b_{44} \end{pmatrix}$ *and* $b_{32} \neq 0$, B *can move through at most two steps and B will be similar to a standard matrix.*

Step 1. Find a matrix $G_1 = \begin{pmatrix} 1 & 0 & 0 & 0 \\ 0 & b_{32}b_{43} & b_{43}(b_{33}+b_{44}) & b_{44}^2 + b_{34}b_{43} \\ 0 & 0 & b_{43} & b_{44} \\ 0 & 0 & 0 & 0 \end{pmatrix}$ such that

$$B' = G_1 B G_1^{-1} = \begin{pmatrix} -b_{11} & 0 & 0 & 0 \\ b_{21}b_{32}b_{43} & -q_1 & -q_2 & -q_3 \\ 0 & 1 & 0 & 0 \\ 0 & 0 & 1 & 0 \end{pmatrix}.$$

Step 2. Find a matrix $G_2 = \begin{pmatrix} b_{21}b_{32}b_{43} & -q_1 & -q_2 & -q_3 \\ 0 & 1 & 0 & 0 \\ 0 & 0 & 1 & 0 \\ 0 & 0 & 0 & 1 \end{pmatrix}$ such that

$$B'' = G_2 B' G_2^{-1} = \begin{pmatrix} -(\theta+q_1) & -(\theta q_1+q_2) & -(\theta q_2+q_3) & -\theta q_3 \\ 1 & 0 & 0 & 0 \\ 0 & 1 & 0 & 0 \\ 0 & 0 & 1 & 0 \end{pmatrix}$$

is a canonical matrix.

Theorem 5. *For any initial value $(m(0), S(0), I(0), N(0)) \in R \times R_+^3$ and $N(0) \leq 1$, if $R_1 > 1$, then the stationary distribution $\pi(\cdot)$ around $(0, S_*, I_*, N_*)$ follows a unique normal probability density function $\Phi(m, S, I, N)$, which is given by*

$$\Phi(m, S, I, N) = (2\pi)^{-\frac{3}{2}} |\Sigma|^{-\frac{1}{2}} e^{-\frac{1}{2}(m,S,I,N)\Sigma^{-1}(m,S,I,N)^T}, \tag{42}$$

where Σ is a positive definite matrix, and the special form of Σ is given as follows:

$$\Sigma = (J_4 J_3 J_2 J_1)^{-1} \Sigma_4 [(J_4 J_3 J_2 J_1)^{-1}]^T \tag{43}$$

with

$$J_1 = \begin{pmatrix} 1 & 0 & 0 & 0 \\ 0 & 1 & 0 & 0 \\ 0 & -\frac{a_{31}}{a_{21}} & 1 & 0 \\ 0 & 0 & 0 & 1 \end{pmatrix},$$

$$J_2 = \begin{pmatrix} 1 & 0 & 0 & 0 \\ 0 & 1 & 0 & 0 \\ 0 & 0 & 1 & 0 \\ 0 & 0 & -\frac{a'_{42}}{a'_{32}} & 1 \end{pmatrix},$$

$$J_3 = \begin{pmatrix} 1 & 0 & 0 & 0 \\ 0 & a''_{32}a''_{43} & a''_{43}(a''_{33}+a''_{44}) & (a''_{44})^2 + a_{34}a''_{43} \\ 0 & 0 & a''_{43} & a''_{44} \\ 0 & 0 & 0 & 1 \end{pmatrix},$$

$$J_4 = \begin{pmatrix} -a_{21}a'_{32}a''_{43} & -p_1 & -p_2 & -p_3 \\ 0 & 1 & 0 & 0 \\ 0 & 0 & 1 & 0 \\ 0 & 0 & 0 & 1 \end{pmatrix},$$

$$\Sigma_4 = \frac{\sigma^2}{\eta} \begin{pmatrix} A_{11}A_{14} - A_{12}A_{13} & 0 & A_{13} & 0 \\ 0 & -A_{13} & 0 & A_{11} \\ A_{13} & 0 & -A_{11} & 0 \\ 0 & A_{11} & 0 & A_{13} - A_{11}A_{12} \end{pmatrix},$$

and $a'_{22} = -a_{22} + \frac{a_{23}a_{31}}{a_{21}}$, $a'_{32} = a_{32} + \frac{a_{33}a_{31}}{a_{21}} + \frac{a_{23}a_{31}^2}{a_{21}^2} - \frac{a_{22}a_{31}}{a_{21}}$, $a'_{33} = -a_{33} - \frac{a_{23}a_{31}}{a_{21}}$, $a'_{42} = \frac{a_{43}a_{31}}{a_{21}}$, $a''_{33} = -a'_{33} + \frac{a_{34}a'_{42}}{a'_{32}}$, $a''_{43} = -a_{43} - \frac{a'_{33}a'_{42}}{a'_{32}} - \frac{a_{44}a'_{42}}{a'_{32}} - \frac{a_{34}(a'_{42})^2}{(a'_{32})^2}$, $a''_{44} = -a_{44} - \frac{a_{34}a'_{42}}{a'_{32}}$, $A_{11} = \theta + -p_1$, $A_{12} = \theta p_1 + p_2$, $A_{13} = \theta p_2 + p_3$, and $A_{14} = \theta p_3$, $\eta = 2(A_{11}^2 A_{14} - A_{11}A_{12}A_{13} + A_{13}^2)$.

Proof. Let $y_4 = x_4$, $y_3 = b_{43}x_3 + b_{44}x_4$, and $y_2 = y'_3 = dy_3 = b_{43}dx_3 + b_{44}dx_4 = b_{32}b_{43}x_2 + (b_{33}b_{43} + b_{43}b_{44})x_3 + (b_{34}b_{43} + b_{44}^2)x_4$.

Denote
$$G_1 = \begin{pmatrix} 1 & 0 & 0 & 0 \\ 0 & b_{32}b_{43} & b_{43}(b_{33}+b_{44}) & b_{44}^2 + b_{34}b_{43} \\ 0 & 0 & b_{43} & b_{44} \\ 0 & 0 & 0 & 0 \end{pmatrix},$$

Then, we have $dY = G_1 dX = G_1 BX dt = G_1 B G_1^{-1} Y dt$.
That is,

$$dY = d\begin{pmatrix} y_1 \\ y_2 \\ y_3 \\ y_4 \end{pmatrix} = \begin{pmatrix} -b_{11} & 0 & 0 & 0 \\ b_{21}b_{32}b_{43} & -q_1 & -q_2 & -q_3 \\ 0 & 1 & 0 & 0 \\ 0 & 0 & 1 & 0 \end{pmatrix} \begin{pmatrix} y_1 \\ y_2 \\ y_3 \\ y_4 \end{pmatrix} dt. \quad (44)$$

Let $z_4 = y_4$, $z_3 = y'_4 = z'_4 = y_3$, $z_2 = y'_3 = z'_3 = y_2$, and $z_1 = y'_2 = z'_2 = b_{21}b_{32}b_{43}y_1 - q_1y_2 - q_2y_3 - q_3y_4$.

Denote
$$G_2 = \begin{pmatrix} b_{21}b_{32}b_{43} & -q_1 & -q_2 & -q_3 \\ 0 & 1 & 0 & 0 \\ 0 & 0 & 1 & 0 \\ 0 & 0 & 0 & 1 \end{pmatrix},$$

Then, we have $dZ = G_2 dY = G_2 B'Y dt = G_2 B' G_2^{-1} Z dt$.
That is,

$$dZ = d\begin{pmatrix} z_1 \\ z_2 \\ z_3 \\ z_4 \end{pmatrix} = \begin{pmatrix} -(\theta + q_1) & -(\theta q_1 + q_2) & -(\theta q_2 + q_3) & -\theta q_3 \\ 1 & 0 & 0 & 0 \\ 0 & 1 & 0 & 0 \\ 0 & 0 & 1 & 0 \end{pmatrix} \begin{pmatrix} z_1 \\ z_2 \\ z_3 \\ z_4 \end{pmatrix} dt. \quad (45)$$

Now, let us solve the density function of Equation (38). Firstly, let $A_1 = J_1 A J_1^{-1}$, where

$$J_1 = \begin{pmatrix} 1 & 0 & 0 & 0 \\ 0 & 1 & 0 & 0 \\ 0 & -\frac{a_{31}}{a_{21}} & 1 & 0 \\ 0 & 0 & 0 & 1 \end{pmatrix},$$

Then,
$$A_1 = \begin{pmatrix} -\theta & 0 & 0 & 0 \\ -a_{21} & a'_{22} & -a_{23} & 0 \\ 0 & a'_{32} & a'_{33} & a_{34} \\ 0 & a'_{42} & -a_{43} & -a_{44} \end{pmatrix},$$

where $a'_{22} = -a_{22} + \frac{a_{23}a_{31}}{a_{21}}$, $a'_{32} = a_{32} + \frac{a_{33}a_{31}}{a_{21}} + \frac{a_{23}a_{31}^2}{a_{21}^2} - \frac{a_{22}a_{31}}{a_{21}}$, $a'_{33} = -a_{33} - \frac{a_{23}a_{31}}{a_{21}}$,
and $a'_{42} = \frac{a_{43}a_{31}}{a_{21}}$.

Secondly, let $A_2 = J_2 A_1 J_2^{-1}$, where

$$J_2 = \begin{pmatrix} 1 & 0 & 0 & 0 \\ 0 & 1 & 0 & 0 \\ 0 & 0 & 1 & 0 \\ 0 & 0 & -\frac{a'_{42}}{a'_{32}} & 1 \end{pmatrix},$$

Then,

$$A_2 = \begin{pmatrix} -\theta & 0 & 0 & 0 \\ -a_{21} & a'_{22} & -a_{23} & 0 \\ 0 & a'_{32} & a''_{33} & a_{34} \\ 0 & 0 & -a''_{43} & -a''_{44} \end{pmatrix},$$

where $a''_{33} = -a'_{33} + \frac{a_{34}a'_{42}}{a'_{32}}$, $a''_{43} = -a_{43} - \frac{a'_{33}a'_{42}}{a'_{32}} - \frac{a_{44}a'_{42}}{a'_{32}} - \frac{a_{34}(a'_{42})^2}{(a'_{32})^2}$, $a''_{44} = -a_{44} - \frac{a_{34}a'_{42}}{a'_{32}}$.

Thirdly, by Lemma 2, let $A_3 = J_3 A_2 J_3^{-1}$, where

$$J_3 = \begin{pmatrix} 1 & 0 & 0 & 0 \\ 0 & a'_{32}a''_{43} & a''_{43}(a''_{33} + a''_{44}) & (a''_{44})^2 + a_{34}a''_{43} \\ 0 & 0 & a''_{43} & a''_{44} \\ 0 & 0 & 0 & 1 \end{pmatrix},$$

Then,

$$A_3 = \begin{pmatrix} -\theta & 0 & 0 & 0 \\ -a_{21}a'_{32}a''_{43} & -p_1 & -p_2 & -p_3 \\ 0 & 1 & 0 & 0 \\ 0 & 0 & 1 & 0 \end{pmatrix}.$$

Finally, by Lemma 2, let $A_4 = J_4 A_3 J_4^{-1}$, where

$$J_4 = \begin{pmatrix} -a_{21}a'_{32}a''_{43} & -p_1 & -p_2 & -p_3 \\ 0 & 1 & 0 & 0 \\ 0 & 0 & 1 & 0 \\ 0 & 0 & 0 & 1 \end{pmatrix},$$

Then,

$$A_4 = \begin{pmatrix} -(\theta + p_1) & -(\theta p_1 + p_2) & -(\theta p_2 + p_3) & -\theta p_3 \\ 1 & 0 & 0 & 0 \\ 0 & 1 & 0 & 0 \\ 0 & 0 & 1 & 0 \end{pmatrix}.$$

Let $A_{11} = \theta + -p_1$, $A_{12} = \theta p_1 + p_2$, $A_{13} = \theta p_2 + p_3$, and $A_{14} = \theta p_3$. By Equation (41), we can solve that

$$\Sigma_4 = \frac{\sigma^2}{\eta} \begin{pmatrix} A_{11}A_{14} - A_{12}A_{13} & 0 & A_{13} & 0 \\ 0 & -A_{13} & 0 & A_{11} \\ A_{13} & 0 & -A_{11} & 0 \\ 0 & A_{11} & 0 & A_{13} - A_{11}A_{12} \end{pmatrix} \quad (46)$$

where $\eta = 2(A_{11}^2 A_{14} - A_{11}A_{12}A_{13} + A_{13}^2)$. Obviously, matrix Σ_4 is positive definite. Then, $\Sigma = (J_4 J_3 J_2 J_1)^{-1} \Sigma_4 [(J_4 J_3 J_2 J_1)^{-1}]^T$. □

5. Examples and Numerical Simulations

In this section, we will introduce some examples and numerical simulations to demonstrate the above theoretical results. By means of the higher-order method developed by Milstein, the corresponding discretization equation of system (2) is obtained in the form

$$\begin{cases} S(k+1) = S(k) + \Delta t[(1-p)\mu + \alpha I(k) - (\mu+\varphi)S(k) - \overline{\beta}S(k)I(k) - m(k)S(k)I(k)] \\ I(k+1) = I(k) + \Delta t[\overline{\beta}S(k)I(k) + (1-e)\overline{\beta}V(k)I(k) - (\mu+\alpha+\varepsilon)I(k) + m(k)S(k)I(k) \\ \qquad + (1-e)m(k)V(k)I(k)] \\ V(k+1) = V(k) + \Delta t[p\mu + \varphi S(k) - \mu V(k) - (1-e)\overline{\beta}V(k)I(k) - (1-e)m(k)V(k)I(k)] \\ m(k+1) = m(k) - \Delta t\theta m(k) + \sigma m(k)\sqrt{\Delta t}\xi_k + \dfrac{\sigma^2 m(k)}{2}\Delta t(\xi_k^2 - 1) \end{cases} \quad (4)$$

where Δt is the time increment, and ξ is the Gaussian random variables which follow the distribution $N(0,1)$, $k = 1,2,3\ldots$.

Example 1. *In order to check the existence of a stationary distribution, we choose the values of the system parameters as follows: $(p, \mu, \alpha, \varphi, \beta, e, \varepsilon, \theta) = (0.4, 0.2, 0.1, 0.1, 0.8, 0.8, 0.05, 0.5)$, and the environmental noise intensities $\sigma = 0.01$. Then, $R_1 = 1.07 > 1$, where R_1 is defined in Theorem 2. Therefore the conditions of Theorem 2 hold, and there is a stationary distribution $\pi(\cdot)$ of system (2) in left hand column in Figure 1.*

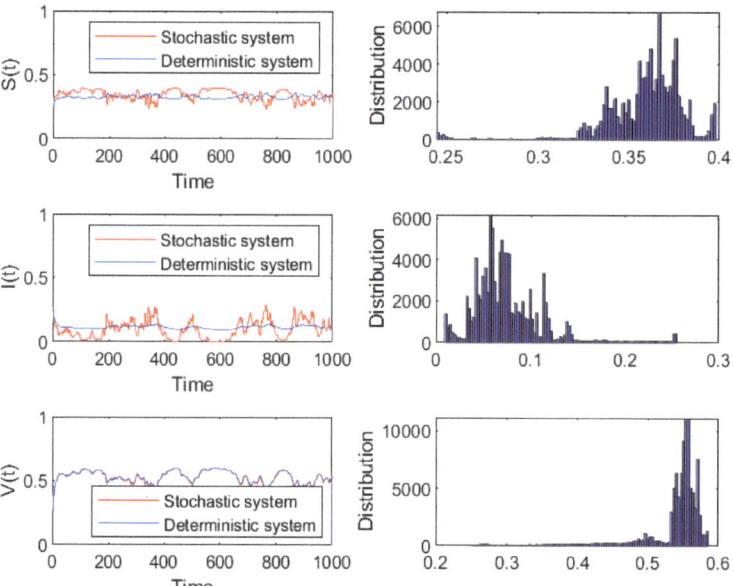

Figure 1. The left-hand column shows the simulation of compartments $S(t)$, $V(t)$, and $I(t)$ in deterministic system (1) and stochastic system (2) with parameters $(p, \mu, \alpha, \varphi, \beta, e, \varepsilon, \theta) = (0.4, 0.2, 0.1, 0.1, 0.8, 0.8, 0.05, 0.5)$. The right-hand column shows the distribution of stochastic system (2). When $R_1 > 1$, the disease will persist for a long time.

Example 2. *In order to check the existence of a stationary distribution, we choose the values of the system parameters as follows: $(p, \mu, \alpha, \varphi, \beta, e, \varepsilon, \theta) = (0.4, 0.2, 0.1, 0.1, 0.1, 0.8, 0.05, 0.5)$, and the environmental noise intensities $\sigma = 0.01$, in right hand column in Figure 1. Then, $R_2 = 0.4 < 1$, where R_2 is defined in Theorem 3, in left hand column in Figure 2. Therefore, the conditions of Theorem 3 hold, and the disease will be extinct in a long time, in right hand column in Figure 2.*

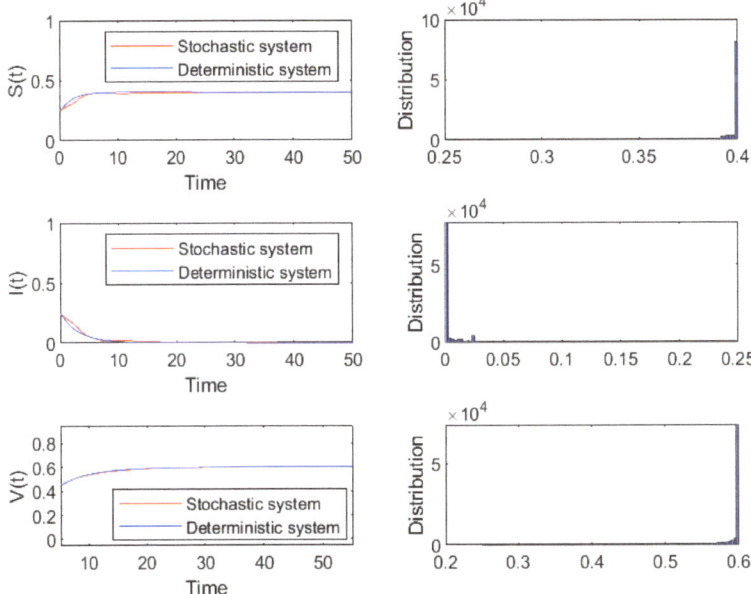

Figure 2. The left-hand column shows the simulation of compartments $S(t)$, $V(t)$, and $I(t)$ in deterministic system (1) and stochastic system (2) with parameters $(p, \mu, \alpha, \varphi, \beta, e, \varepsilon, \theta) = (0.4, 0.2, 0.1, 0.1, 0.1, 0.8, 0.05, 0.5)$. The right-hand column shows the distribution of stochastic system (2). When $R_2 < 1$, the disease will be extinct in a long time.

6. Discussion and Conclusions

In this paper, we investigate the dynamic behavior of a stochastic SIS model with imperfect vaccination, where the population is demographically static and growing with an infection-induced mortality rate. We introduce the Ornstein–Uhlenbeck process to simulate random disturbances in the environment and obtain a more biologically meaningful stochastic SIS epidemic model. To the best of our knowledge, few papers currently study SIS epidemic models with Ornstein–Uhlenbeck processes.

In this paper, we investigate the dynamic effects of the Ornstein–Uhlenbeck process on SIS epidemic models under standard incidence. We construct several different and suitable Lyapunov functions to prove our conclusions. We obtain the existence and uniqueness of the global solution to the SIS epidemic model (2). Furthermore, we establish sharp sufficient criteria for the existence of stationary distribution and reveal the effects of the Ornstein–Uhlenbeck process on the existence of stationary distribution. Specifically, if $R_1 > 1$ and the parameters β of the Ornstein–Uhlenbeck process meet certain conditions, then system (2) exists with a stable distribution. Otherwise, if $R_2 < 1$, the epidemic of system (2) will become extinct with probability 1. The innovation of this paper is that we obtain a mathematical analysis result of the density function of four-dimensional stochastic model (2), which is quite challenging. Numerically, we simulate the effects of the intensities of white noise on the stationary distribution and show that the degree of volatility will increase. Additionally, it is worth noting that the same methods are used in the survival analysis of the high-dimensional SIS epidemic model in our following research.

The numerical simulation example reveals that there exist periodic regimes in the deterministic system and metastable periodic regimes in the corresponding stochastic system, which is the subject of our future research. External interference will affect the balance of the SIS epidemic model. Therefore, it will be of extraordinary significance to minimize human interference and damage to the environment and organisms.

Author Contributions: Writing—original draft preparation, H.Z.; writing—review and editing, J.S. and P.Y.; funding acquisition, H.Z. and D.J. All authors have read and agreed to the published version of this manuscript.

Funding: The authors were supported by the Shandong Provincial Natural Science Foundation (No. ZR2021MA052).

Data Availability Statement: Data openly available in a public repository.

Conflicts of Interest: The authors declare no conflicts of interest.

References

1. Kermack, W.O.; Mckendrick, A.G. Contributions to the mathematical theory of epidemics (part i). *Proc. Soc. London Ser. A* 19?, *115*, 700–721.
2. Settati, A.; Lahrouz, A. Stationary distribution of stochastic population systems under regime switching. *Appl. Math. Comp* 2014, *244*, 235–243. [CrossRef]
3. Zhao, Y.; Jiang, D. The threshold of a stochastic SIRS epidemic model with saturated incidence. *Appl. Math. Lett.* 2014, *34*, 90– [CrossRef]
4. Ma, Z.; Zhou, Y.; Wu, J. *Modeling and Dynamics of Infectious Diseases*; Higher Education Press: Beijing, China, 2009.
5. Zhang, Y.; Fan, K.; Gao, S.; Liu, Y.; Chen, S. Ergodic stationary distribution of a stochastic SIRS epidemic model incorporatir media coverage and saturated incidence rate. *Physica A* 2019, *514*, 671–685. [CrossRef]
6. Muroya, Y.; Kuniya, T.; Wang, J. Stability analysis of a delayed multi-group SIS epidemic model with nonlinear incidence rat and patch structure. *J. Math. Anal. Appl.* 2015, *425*, 415–439. [CrossRef]
7. Wang, W.; Cai, Y.; Ding, Z.; Gui, Z. A stochastic differential equation SIS epidemic model incorporating Ornstein-Uhlenbe process. *Physica A* 2018, *509*, 921–936. [CrossRef]
8. Shang, J.; Li, W. Dynamical behaviors of a stochastic SIRV epidemic model with the Ornstein-Uhlenbeck process. *Adv. Cont Discret. Model.* 2024, *2024*, 9. [CrossRef]
9. Zhu, C.; Yin, G. Asymptotic properties of hybrid diffusion systems. *SIAM J. Control Optim.* 2007, *46*, 1155–1179. [CrossRef]
10. Hu, J.; Li, Z.; Zeng, T.; Teng, Z. A note on the stationary distribution of stochastic SIS epidemic model with vaccination und regime switching. *Filomat* 2018, *32*, 4773–4785. [CrossRef]
11. Zhao, Y.; Jiang, D. The threshold of a stochastic SIS epidemic model with vaccination. *Appl. Math. Comput.* 2014, *243*, 718–7? [CrossRef]
12. Yao, H. Mathematical analysis of an SIR network model with imperfect vaccination and varying size of population. In Proceedin of the International Conference on Computer Modeling Simulation ACM, Canberra, Australia, 20–23 January 2017.
13. Safan, M.; Rihan, F. Mathematical analysis of an SIS model with imperfect vaccination and backfward bifurcation. *Math. Comp Simul.* 2014, *96*, 195–206. [CrossRef]
14. Lahrouz, A.; Settati, A.; El Fatini, M.; Tridane, A. The effect of a generalized nonlinear incidence rate on the stochastic S epidemic model. *Math. Methods Appl. Sci.* 2021, *44*, 1137–1146. [CrossRef]
15. Qi, H.; Liu, L.; Meng, X. Dynamics of a nonautonomous stochastic SIS epidemic model with double epidemic hypothes *Complexity* 2017, *2017*, 14. [CrossRef]
16. Zhou, B.; Zhang, X.; Jiang, D. Dynamics and density function analysis of a stochastic SVI epidemic model with half saturate incidence rate. *Chaos Solitons Fract.* 2020, *137*, 109865. [CrossRef]
17. Guo, W.; Ye, M.; Zhang, Q. Stability in distribution for age-structured HIV model with delay and driven by Ornstein-Uhlenbe process. *Stud. Appl. Math.* 2021, *147*, 792–815. [CrossRef]
18. Steven, F. Ornstein-Uhlenbeck Process. *Stoch. Diff. Eq.* 2004, *25*, 61.
19. Trost, D.C.; Overman, I.I.; Ostroff, E.A.; Xiong, J.H. A model for liver homeostasis using modified meanreverting Ornstei Uhlenbeck process. *Comput. Math. Methods Med.* 2010, *11*, 27–47. [CrossRef]
20. Yang, Q.; Zhang, X.; Jiang, D. Dynamical Behaviors of a Stochastic Food Chain System with Ornstein-Uhlenbeck Process. *Nonlinear Sci.* 2022, *32*, 34. [CrossRef]
21. Laaribi, A.; Boukanjime, B.; El Khalifi, M.; Bouggar, D.; El Fatini, M. A generalized stochastic SIRS epidemic model incorporatir mean-reverting Ornstein-Uhlenbeck process. *Physica A* 2023, *615*, 128609. [CrossRef]
22. Zuo, W.; Zhou, Y. Density function and stationary distribution of a stochastic SIR model with distributed delay. *Appl. Math. Le* 2022, *129*, 107931. [CrossRef]
23. Mao, X. *Stochastic Differential Equations and Applications*; Horwood: Chichester, UK, 1997.

Disclaimer/Publisher's Note: The statements, opinions and data contained in all publications are solely those of the individu author(s) and contributor(s) and not of MDPI and/or the editor(s). MDPI and/or the editor(s) disclaim responsibility for any injury people or property resulting from any ideas, methods, instructions or products referred to in the content.

Robust State Feedback Control with D-Admissible Assurance for Uncertain Discrete Singular Systems

Chih-Peng Huang

Department of Computer Science, University of Taipei, Taipei 100, Taiwan; cphuang@utaipei.edu.tw or ponytony@seed.net.tw

Abstract: This study addresses the state feedback control associated with D-admissible assurance for discrete singular systems subjected to parameter uncertainties in both the difference term and system matrices. Firstly, a refined analysis criterion of D-admissible assurance is presented, where the distinct form embraces multiple slack matrices and has lessened linear matrix inequalities (LMIs) constraints, which may be beneficial for reducing the conservatism of admissibility analysis. In consequence, by hiring the state feedback control, controller design issues with pole locations, which directly dominate the system performance, are mainly treated. For all the presented criteria can be formulated by the strict LMIs, they are thus suitably solved via current LMI solvers to conduct a state feedback controller with specific poles' locations of system's performance requirements. Finally, two numerical examples illustrate that the presented results are efficient and practicable.

Keywords: uncertain systems; discrete singular systems; D-admissibility; linear matrix inequality (LMI)

MSC: 93C90; 93C05; 93D12; 93B52

1. Introduction

Singular systems have become an extended form of the traditional state-space systems, where, besides the dynamic behaviors, they can further integrate algebraic constraints into the systems. They are more ingeniously applicable in miscellaneous systems, e.g., economic model systems [1,2], circuit systems [3], chemical response processes [4], and power systems [5]. However, the stability analysis and controller design issues of singular systems are more intricate than traditional ones [6–8]. Since they usually embrace rank insufficient derivative term matrices (or difference term matrices, for discrete system cases) in the models, besides the stability verification, we must ensure the regularity and impulse immunity (or causality, for discrete system cases) simultaneously. Furthermore, the practical system models need to accommodate parameter uncertainties of circumstance variation, component aging, measuring inaccuracy, and so on. Thus, the robust admissible analysis and/or robust control for singular systems were deeply investigated in the past (see, e.g., [9–15] and the references therein). For practical implementation, digital signals are indispensable in real-time control or monitoring systems. Using signal transformation, discrete difference models with highly accurate forms could be attained [16]. Thus, many works have been inspired to cope with discrete singular systems subjected to various uncertainties (see, e.g., [17–19] and the references therein).

Moreover, when implementing a control system, stability is the minimum requirement of the system's behavior. The system's performance is directly dominated by the pole locations in the complex plane of a state-space system's model [20–24]. Subsequently, the D-admissible analysis and controller design issues for discrete singular systems have also been discussed recently ([25–29] and the references therein). By examining past results, they considered the difference term matrix of the discrete singular systems that needed to be fixed. Then, they could attain some explicit admissible analysis and controller design criteria. However, for system modeling from a practical system, the parameter variations usually have individually varying durations and can be meaningfully embraced by both the derivative term (or difference term for discrete system cases) and system matrices with structural uncertainties [15,30–34]. For discrete singular systems, the robust D-admissibility issues with perturbation in both the difference term and the system's matrices have been previously investigated [33]. However, the proposed conditions involved a large number of LMI constraints, which not only cause computing exertion but also may introduce conservatism for the proposed criteria. In the work [35], the D-admissibility and controller design issues were discussed for uncertain discrete singular systems with state delay. However, the results are based on the augmented system's approach, which makes it challenging to tackle the uncertainties that exist in the difference term matrix. Concluding the aforementioned exploration, it seems that relatively few results deal with the state feedback control with D-admissible assurance for uncertain discrete singular systems subjected to parametric perturbation in both the difference term and system matrices, which inspired us to undertake this topic.

This study is devoted to the state feedback control with D-admissible assurance for discrete singular systems subjected to uncertainties in both the difference term and system matrices. Using matrix algebra and LMI techniques [36,37], we first present a distinct D-admissibility criterion of the considered systems. The new form not only has less LMI constraints but also involves some slack metrics, which may be beneficial for reducing the conservatism of analysis criteria. By hiring the state feedback control, the controller design issues associated with prescribed pole locations for the closed-loop singular system are further treated. All of the presented conditions can be expressed in terms of the strict LMI constraints, which can be easily evaluated by current LMI solvers [37] for the admissible analysis or by systematically conducting state feedback control. Ultimately, two examples illustrate the feasibility and applicability of the derived results. By comparing with the previous results, the contributions of our work are summarized in the following points:

1. To the best of our knowledge, few works focus on the state feedback control with D-admissible assurance for uncertain discrete singular systems subjected to parameter uncertainties in both the difference term and system matrices. This work is mainly devoted to the state feedback control with D-admissible issues for the considered systems.
2. For all of the design criteria that can be derived in terms of the strict LMIs, a state feedback controller with prescribed performance requirements can be readily conducted via current LMI tools.

The remaining information is outlined as follows. Section 2 introduces preliminary results and definitions for discrete singular systems. The D-admissibility and the state feedback control are mainly addressed in Section 3. Two numerical examples are involved to illustrate the feasibility and effectiveness of the proposed results in Section 4. Finally, we make some concluding remarks on this study in Section 5.

2. Preliminaries on Discrete Singular Systems

Consider an uncertain discrete singular model described by

$$\widetilde{E}x(k+1) = (A + \Delta A)x(k) + (B + \Delta B)u(k), \ k > 0, \quad (1)$$

where $x(\cdot) \in R^n$ and $u(\cdot) \in R^r$ are the state vector and the control input, respectively. The uncertain difference term matrix $\widetilde{E}$ with $rank(\widetilde{E}) = m \leq n$ can be denoted by a polytopic form as

$$\Omega_E \equiv \left\{ \widetilde{E} : \widetilde{E} = \sum_{i=1}^{q_E} e_i E_i, \ e_i \geq 0, \ \sum_{i=1}^{q_E} e_i = 1 \right\}, \quad (2)$$

where q_E is the total number of the matrices' vertices, E_i. The nominal system matrices A and B have compatible dimensions and the uncertainties terms ΔA and ΔB are assumed to be norm-bounded with constant matrices M, N_A, N_B, and matrix Λ, $\Lambda^T \Lambda \leq I$, satisfying

$$[\Delta A \quad \Delta B] = M\Lambda[N_A \quad N_B]. \tag{3}$$

Remark 1. *The considered descriptor system in (1) involves both the uncertainties in (2) and (3) with distinct forms. They can be reasonably analyzed due to their inherited characteristics, including uncertain parameters that exist in the difference term and system matrices [34].*

Lemma 1 [38]. *Denote a matrix $\Omega = \Omega^T$, with compatible matrices M and N, such that*

$$\Omega + M\Lambda N + N^T \Lambda^T M^T < 0$$

where Λ satisfies $\Lambda\Lambda^T \leq I$, if and only if there exists a positive number α satisfying

$$\Omega + \alpha M M^T + \alpha^{-1} N^T N < 0.$$

To cope with the control issues of the discrete singular system (1), some definitions for the nominal form, $Ex(k+1) = Ax(k)$, are given as follows.

Definition 1 [8,33,35].

1. *The matrix pair (E, A) is asserted to be regular if $\det(zE - A) \neq 0$.*
2. *The matrix pair (E, A) is asserted to be causal if $\det(zE - A) \neq 0$ and $\deg[\det(zE - A)] = \text{rank}(E)$.*
3. *Let the characteristic polynomial of the nominal system $Ex(k+1) = Ax(k)$ be $F(z) = \det(zE - A)$. The nominal system is asserted to be D-admissible, if it is regular, causal, and all of the finite solutions of $F(z) = 0$ satisfy $z \in D(a, r) = \{z : |z - a| < r\}$, where $|a| + r < 1$. And, the nominal system is asserted to be admissible, if it is regular, causal, and all of the finite solutions of $F(z) = 0$ satisfy $z \in D(0, 1)$.*

Some previous results are introduced below.

Lemma 2 [10]. *The nominal system, $Ex(k+1) = Ax(k)$, is admissible if and only if there exist two matrices, $P > 0$ and Q, satisfying*

$$A^T PA - E^T PE + QS^T A + A^T SQ^T < 0 \tag{4}$$

where $S \in R^{n \times (n-m)}$ with $E^T S = 0$ and $\text{rank}(S) = n - m$.

Lemma 3 [33]. *The nominal system, $Ex(k+1) = Ax(k)$, is D-admissible if and only if there exist two matrices, $P > 0$ and Q, satisfying*

$$\frac{(A - aE)^T}{r} P \frac{(A - aE)}{r} - E^T PE + QS^T A + A^T SQ^T < 0 \tag{5}$$

where $S \in R^{n \times (n-m)}$ with $E^T S = 0$ and $\text{rank}(S) = n - m$.

Deducing from the equivalent admissibility issues of the symmetric form of (E, A) [39], we can replace (E, A) in Equation (5) by the transpose pair (E^T, A^T) and obtain a symmetric manner as follows.

Corollary 1. *The nominal system, $Ex(k+1) = Ax(k)$, is D-admissible if and only if there exist two matrices, $P > 0$ and Q, satisfying*

$$\frac{(A-aE)}{r} P \frac{(A-aE)^T}{r} - EPE^T + QS^T A^T + ASQ^T < 0 \qquad (6)$$

where $S \in R^{n \times (n-m)}$ with $ES = 0$ and $rank(S) = n - m$.

For the controller design issue, we present a distinct form by replacing the matrix S by PS with the nonsingular matrix P.

Corollary 2. *The nominal system, $Ex(k+1) = Ax(k)$, is D-admissible if and only if there exist two matrices, $P > 0$ and Q, satisfying*

$$\frac{(A-aE)}{r} P \frac{(A-aE)^T}{r} - EPE^T + QS^T PA^T + APSQ^T < 0 \qquad (7)$$

where $S \in R^{n \times (n-m)}$ with $EPS = 0$ and $rank(S) = n - m$.

3. D-Admissibility and State Feedback Control

A refined robust admissible analysis criterion for the uncertain discrete singular system (1) with (2) and (3) is derived as follows.

Theorem 1. *The system (1) subjected to the uncertainties (2) and (3) with free input is D-admissible, if there exist a set of matrices $P > 0$, Q_i, $i = 1, 2, \ldots, q_E$, and scalars $\alpha_{ij} > 0$, $\forall i \leq j$, satisfying*

$$\begin{bmatrix} ASQ_i^T + Q_i S^T A^T - E_i P E_i^T + \alpha_{ii} MM^T & (A - aE_i)P & Q_i S^T N_A^T \\ P(A - aE_i)^T & -r^2 P & P N_A^T \\ N_A S Q_i^T & N_A P & -\alpha_{ii} I \end{bmatrix} < 0, \forall i, \qquad (8)$$

$$\begin{bmatrix} AS(Q_i+Q_j)^T + (Q_i+Q_j)S^T A^T - E_i PE_j^T - E_j PE_i^T + \alpha_{ij} MM^T & (2A - aE_i - aE_j)P & (Q_i+Q_j)S^T N_A^T \\ P(2A - aE_i - aE_j)^T & -2r^2 P & 2P N_A^T \\ N_A S(Q_i+Q_j)^T & 2N_A P & -\alpha_{ij} I \end{bmatrix} < 0, \qquad (9)$$
$$\forall i < j,$$

where $S \in R^{n \times (n-m)}$ with $E_i S = 0$, $\forall i$, and $rank(S) = n - m$.

Proof. Based on Corollary 1 associated with the Schur complement [36], Equation (6) can be equivalent to

$$\begin{bmatrix} ASQ^T + QS^T A^T - EPE^T & (A - aE)P \\ P(A - aE)^T & -r^2 P \end{bmatrix} < 0.$$

Assume that matrices $P > 0$ and Q_i, $i = 1, 2, \ldots, q_E$, and scalars $\alpha_{ij} > 0$, $\forall i \leq j$ satisfy the inequalities (8) and (9). Based on Corollary 1 with the above equation for the system (1) with uncertainties (2) and (3), and letting $\tilde{Q} \equiv \sum_i e_i Q_i$, we can verify the D-admissibility by

$$
\begin{aligned}
&\begin{bmatrix} (A+\Delta A)S\tilde{Q}^T + \tilde{Q}S^T(A+\Delta A)^T - \tilde{E}P\tilde{E}^T & (A+\Delta A - a\tilde{E})P \\ P(A+\Delta A - a\tilde{E})^T & -r^2 P \end{bmatrix} \\
&= \begin{bmatrix} (A+\Delta A)S\left(\sum_i e_i Q_i\right)^T + \left(\sum_i e_i Q_i\right)S^T(A+\Delta A)^T - \left(\sum_i e_i E_i\right)P\left(\sum_i e_i E_i\right)^T & \left(A+\Delta A - a\left(\sum_i e_i E_i\right)\right)P \\ P\left(A+\Delta A - a\left(\sum_i e_i E_i\right)\right)^T & -r^2 P \end{bmatrix} \\
&= \sum_i e_i^2 \begin{bmatrix} (A+\Delta A)SQ_i^T + Q_i S^T (A+\Delta A)^T - E_i PE_i^T & (A+\Delta A - \alpha E_i)P \\ P(A+\Delta A - \alpha E_i)^T & -r^2 P \end{bmatrix} \\
&+ \sum_{i<j} e_i e_j \begin{bmatrix} (A+\Delta A)S(Q_i+Q_j)^T + (Q_i+Q_j)S^T(A+\Delta A)^T - E_i PE_j^T - E_j PE_i^T & (2A+2\Delta A - aE_i - aE_j)P \\ P(2A+2\Delta A - aE_i - aE_j)^T & -2r^2 P \end{bmatrix} \\
&< 0.
\end{aligned}
$$

Substituting $\Delta A = M\Lambda N_A$ into the first terms of the above leads to

$$
\begin{aligned}
&\begin{bmatrix} (A+\Delta A)SQ_i^T + Q_i S^T(A+\Delta A)^T - E_i PE_i^T & (A+\Delta A - aE_i)P \\ P(A+\Delta A - aE_i)^T & -r^2 P \end{bmatrix} \\
&= \begin{bmatrix} ASQ_i^T + Q_i S^T A^T - E_i PE_i^T & (A - aE_i)P \\ P(A - aE_i)^T & -r^2 P \end{bmatrix} + \begin{bmatrix} \Delta A SQ_i^T + Q_i S^T \Delta A^T & \Delta A P \\ P\Delta A^T & 0 \end{bmatrix} \\
&= \begin{bmatrix} ASQ_i^T + Q_i S^T A^T - E_i PE_i^T & (A - aE_i)P \\ P(A - aE_i)^T & -r^2 P \end{bmatrix} + \begin{bmatrix} M \\ 0 \end{bmatrix} \Lambda \begin{bmatrix} N_A SQ_i^T & N_A P \end{bmatrix} + \begin{bmatrix} Q_i S^T N_A^T \\ PN_A^T \end{bmatrix} \Lambda^T \begin{bmatrix} M^T & 0 \end{bmatrix}, \forall i
\end{aligned}
$$

And according to Lemma 1, the above can be equivalent to

$$
\Rightarrow \begin{bmatrix} ASQ_i^T + Q_i S^T A^T - E_i PE_i^T & (A - aE_i)P \\ P(A - aE_i)^T & -r^2 P \end{bmatrix} + \alpha_{ii} \begin{bmatrix} M \\ 0 \end{bmatrix}\begin{bmatrix} M^T & 0 \end{bmatrix} + \alpha_{ii}^{-1} \begin{bmatrix} Q_i S^T N_A^T \\ PN_A^T \end{bmatrix}\begin{bmatrix} N_A SQ_i^T & N_A P \end{bmatrix}, \forall i
$$

Thus, by the Schur complement, they lead to

$$
\Rightarrow \begin{bmatrix} ASQ_i^T + Q_i S^T A^T - E_i PE_i^T + \alpha_{ii} MM^T & (A - aE_i)P & Q_i S^T N_A^T \\ P(A - aE_i)^T & -r^2 P & PN_A^T \\ N_A SQ_i^T & N_A P & -\alpha_{ii} I \end{bmatrix}, \forall i,
$$

which are identical to (8).

Similarly, the second terms can be deduced to be

$$
\Rightarrow \begin{bmatrix} AS(Q_i+Q_j)^T + (Q_i+Q_j)S^T A^T - E_i PE_j^T - E_j PE_i^T + \alpha_{ij} MM^T & (2A - aE_i - aE_j)P & (Q_i+Q_j)S^T N_A^T \\ P(2A - aE_i - aE_j)^T & -2r^2 P & 2PN_A^T \\ N_A S(Q_i+Q_j)^T & 2N_A P & -\alpha_{ij} I \end{bmatrix}, \forall i < j,
$$

which are identical to (9). Thus, if (8) and (9) are satisfied, we can conclude that the considered system is D-admissible according to Corollary 1. □

By Theorem 1, we can simply verify the system with admissibility by letting $a = 0$ and $r = 1$, i.e., the D-admissibility with the unit circle $D(0, 1)$, as follows.

Corollary 3. *The system (1) subjected to the uncertainties (2) and (3) with free input is admissible, if there exist matrices $P > 0$ and Q_i, $i = 1, 2, \ldots, q_E$, and scalars $\alpha_{ij} > 0$, $\forall i \leq j$, satisfying*

$$\begin{bmatrix} ASQ_i^T + Q_i S^T A^T - E_i PE_i^T + \alpha_{ii} MM^T & AP & Q_i S^T N_A^T \\ PA^T & -P & PN_A^T \\ N_A S Q_i^T & N_A P & -\alpha_{ii} I \end{bmatrix} < 0, \forall i, \quad (10)$$

$$\begin{bmatrix} AS(Q_i + Q_j)^T + (Q_i + Q_j) S^T A^T - E_i PE_j^T - E_j PE_i^T + \alpha_{ij} MM^T & 2AP & (Q_i + Q_j) S^T N_A^T \\ 2PA^T & -2P & 2PN_A^T \\ N_A S (Q_i + Q_j)^T & 2N_A P & -\alpha_{ij} I \end{bmatrix} < 0, \forall i < j, \quad (11)$$

where $S \in R^{n \times (n-m)}$ with $E_i S = 0$, $\forall i$, and rank$(S) = n - m$.

Remark 2. *Comparing with the previous result [33], the LMIs' constraint number is $q_A \times (q_E + C_{q_E}^2)$. Nevertheless, in Theorem 1, the new approach can achieve a compact set of LMIs with $(q_E + C_{q_E}^2)$ and involves multiple slack matrices Q_i, $i = 1, 2, \ldots, q_E$. They both may be useful to lessen conservatism of admissible analysis.*

Subsequently, by introducing the state feedback control, i.e., the considered system with $u(k) = Kx(k)$ in (1), the control design conditions are further presented.

Theorem 2. *The system (1) with $u(k) = Kx(k)$ subjected to the uncertainties (2) and (3) is D-admissible, if there exist matrices $P > 0$ and Q_i, $i = 1, 2, \ldots, q_E$, X, and scalars $\alpha_{ij} > 0$, $\forall i \leq j$, satisfying*

$$\begin{bmatrix} \Phi_1 & (A - aE_i)P + BX & Q_i(N_A PS + N_B XS)^T \\ P(A - aE_i)^T + X^T B^T & -r^2 P & PN_A^T + X^T N_B^T \\ (N_A PS + N_B XS) Q_i^T & N_A P + N_B X & -\alpha_{ii} I \end{bmatrix} < 0, \forall i, \quad (12)$$

$$\begin{bmatrix} \Phi_2 & (2A - aE_i - aE_j)P + 2BX & (Q_i + Q_j)(N_A PS + N_B XS)^T \\ P(2A - aE_i - aE_j)^T + 2X^T B^T & -2r^2 P & 2PN_A^T + 2X^T N_B^T \\ (N_A PS + N_B XS)(Q_i + Q_j)^T & 2N_A P + 2N_B X & -\alpha_{ij} I \end{bmatrix} < 0, \forall i < j, \quad (13)$$

where

$$\Phi_1 = APSQ_i^T + Q_i S^T PA^T + BXSQ_i^T + Q_i S^T X^T B^T - E_i PE_i^T + \alpha_{ii} MM^T$$

$$\Phi_2 = APS(Q_i + Q_j)^T + (Q_i + Q_j) S^T PA^T + BXS(Q_i + Q_j)^T + (Q_i + Q_j) S^T X^T B^T - E_i PE_j^T - E_j PE_i^T + \alpha_{ij} MM^T$$

where the matrix $S \in R^{n \times (n-m)}$ with $E_i PS = 0$, $\forall i$, and rank$(S) = n - m$. Then, a state feedback gain with a prescribed pole disk $D(a, r) \subset D(0, 1)$ with the center at a and the radius r can be determined by $K = XP^{-1}$.

Proof. Deducing from Corollary 2 associated with the Schur complement, Equation (7) can be equivalent to

$$\begin{bmatrix} APSQ^T + QS^T PA^T - EPE^T & (A - aE)P \\ P(A - aE)^T & -r^2 P \end{bmatrix} < 0$$

Assume that matrices $P > 0$ and Q_i, $i = 1, 2, \ldots, q_E$, X, and scalars $\alpha_{ij} > 0$, $\forall i \leq j$ satisfy the inequalities (12) and (13). Based on Corollary 2 associated with the above for the resulting uncertain closed-loop singular system (1) with $u(t) = Kx(t)$, and letting $\widetilde{A}_C \equiv A + \Delta A + BK + \Delta BK$, $\widetilde{Q} \equiv \sum_i e_i Q_i$, we can verify the D-admissibility of (1) by

$$\begin{bmatrix} \widetilde{A}_C PS\widetilde{Q}^T + \widetilde{Q}S^T P\widetilde{A}_C^T - \widetilde{E}P\widetilde{E}^T & (\widetilde{A}_C - a\widetilde{E})P \\ P(\widetilde{A}_C - a\widetilde{E})^T & -r^2 P \end{bmatrix}$$

$$= \begin{bmatrix} \widetilde{A}_C PS\left(\sum_i e_i Q_i\right)^T + \left(\sum_i e_i Q_i\right)S^T P\widetilde{A}_C^T - \left(\sum_i e_i E_i\right)P\left(\sum_i e_i E_i\right)^T & \left(\widetilde{A}_C - a\left(\sum_i e_i E_i\right)\right)P \\ P\left(\widetilde{A}_C - a\left(\sum_i e_i E_i\right)\right)^T & -r^2 P \end{bmatrix}$$

$$= \sum_i e_i^2 \begin{bmatrix} \widetilde{A}_C PSQ_i^T + Q_i S^T P\widetilde{A}_C^T - E_i PE_i^T & (\widetilde{A}_C - aE_i)P \\ P(\widetilde{A}_C - aE_i)^T & -r^2 P \end{bmatrix}$$

$$+ \sum_{i<j} e_i e_j \begin{bmatrix} \widetilde{A}_C PS(Q_i + Q_j)^T + (Q_i + Q_j)S^T P\widetilde{A}_C^T - E_i PE_j^T - E_j PE_i^T & (2\widetilde{A}_C - aE_i - aE_j)P \\ P(2\widetilde{A}_C - aE_i - aE_j)^T & -2r^2 P \end{bmatrix}$$

$$< 0.$$

Denote $X = KP$. Substituting $\widetilde{A}_C = A + \Delta A + BK + \Delta BK$ and $[\Delta A \ \Delta B] = M\Lambda[N_A \ N_B]$ into the first terms of the above leads to

$$\begin{bmatrix} \widetilde{A}_C PSQ_i^T + Q_i S^T P\widetilde{A}_C^T - E_i PE_i^T & (\widetilde{A}_C - aE_i)P \\ P(\widetilde{A}_C - aE_i)^T & -r^2 P \end{bmatrix}$$

$$= \begin{bmatrix} APSQ_i^T + Q_i S^T A^T + BKP + PK^T B^T - E_i PE_i^T & (A - aE_i)P + BKP \\ P(A - aE_i)^T + PK^T B^T & -r^2 P \end{bmatrix}$$

$$+ \begin{bmatrix} \Delta APSQ_i^T + Q_i S^T P\Delta A^T + \Delta BKPSQ_i^T + Q_i S^T PK^T \Delta B^T & \Delta AP + \Delta BKP \\ P\Delta A^T + PK^T \Delta B^T & 0 \end{bmatrix}$$

$$= \begin{bmatrix} APSQ_i^T + Q_i S^T A^T + BX + X^T B^T - E_i PE_i^T & (A - aE_i)P + BX \\ P(A - aE_i)^T + X^T B^T & -r^2 P \end{bmatrix}$$

$$+ \begin{bmatrix} M \\ 0 \end{bmatrix} \Lambda \begin{bmatrix} N_A PSQ_i^T + N_B XSQ_i^T & N_A P + N_B X \end{bmatrix} + \begin{bmatrix} Q_i S^T PN_A^T + Q_i S^T X^T N_B^T \\ PN_A^T + X^T N_B^T \end{bmatrix} \Lambda^T \begin{bmatrix} M^T & 0 \end{bmatrix}$$

, $\forall i$.

And, from Lemma 1, the above are equivalent to

$$\Rightarrow \begin{bmatrix} APSQ_i^T + Q_i S^T A^T + BX + X^T B^T - E_i PE_i^T & (A - aE_i)P + BX \\ P(A - aE_i)^T + X^T B^T & -r^2 P \end{bmatrix}$$

$$+ \alpha_{ii} \begin{bmatrix} M \\ 0 \end{bmatrix} \begin{bmatrix} M^T & 0 \end{bmatrix} + \alpha_{ii}^{-1} \begin{bmatrix} Q_i S^T PN_A^T + Q_i S^T X^T N_B^T \\ PN_A^T + X^T N_B^T \end{bmatrix} \begin{bmatrix} N_A PSQ_i^T + N_B XSQ_i^T & N_A P + N_B X \end{bmatrix}$$

, $\forall i$.

Thus, by the Schur complement, they lead to

$$\Rightarrow \begin{bmatrix} \Phi_1 & (A - aE_i)P + BX & Q_i(N_A PS + N_B XS)^T \\ P(A - aE_i)^T + X^T B^T & -r^2 P & PN_A^T + X^T N_B^T \\ (N_A PS + N_B XS)Q_i^T & N_A P + N_B X & -\alpha_{ii} I \end{bmatrix}, \forall i,$$

which are identical to (12).

Similarly, following the same line, the second terms can lead to

$$\Rightarrow \begin{bmatrix} \Phi_2 & (2A - aE_i - aE_j)P + 2BX & (Q_i + Q_j)(N_A PS + N_B XS)^T \\ P(2A - aE_i - aE_j)^T + 2X^T B^T & -2r^2 P & 2PN_A^T + 2X^T N_B^T \\ (N_A PS + N_B XS)(Q_i + Q_j)^T & 2N_A P + 2N_B X & -\alpha_{ij} I \end{bmatrix}$$

, $\forall i < j$,

which are identical to (13). Thus, if (12) and (13) are satisfied, the considered system with $u(k) = Kx(k)$ is ensured to be D-admissible according to Corollary 2. □

Based on Theorem 2, we can simplify to conduct a state feedback control for the system (1) with admissible assurance by letting $a = 0$ and $r = 1$ in the following.

Corollary 4. *The system (1) with $u(k) = Kx(k)$ subjected to the uncertainties (2) and (3) is admissible, if there exist matrices $P > 0$ and Q_i, $i = 1, 2, \ldots, q_E$, X, and scalars $\alpha_{ij} > 0$, $\forall i \leq j$, satisfying*

$$\begin{bmatrix} \Phi_1 & AP + BX & Q_i(N_APS + N_BXS)^T \\ PA^T + X^TB^T & -P & PN_A^T + X^TN_B^T \\ (N_APS + N_BXS)Q_i^T & N_AP + N_BX & -\alpha_{ii}I \end{bmatrix} < 0, \forall i, \quad (14)$$

$$\begin{bmatrix} \Phi_2 & 2AP + 2BX & (Q_i + Q_j)(N_APS + N_BXS)^T \\ 2PA^T + 2X^TB^T & -2P & 2PN_A^T + 2X^TN_B^T \\ (N_APS + N_BXS)(Q_i + Q_j)^T & 2N_AP + 2N_BX & -\alpha_{ij}I \end{bmatrix} < 0, \forall i < j, \quad (1$$

where

$$\Phi_1 = APSQ_i^T + Q_iS^TPA^T + BXSQ_i^T + Q_iS^TX^TB^T - E_iPE_i^T + \alpha_{ii}MM^T$$

$$\Phi_2 = APS(Q_i + Q_j)^T + (Q_i + Q_j)S^TPA^T + BXS(Q_i + Q_j)^T + (Q_i + Q_j)S^TX^TB^T - E_iPE_j^T - E_jPE_i^T + \alpha_{ij}MM^T$$

where the matrix $S \in R^{n \times (n-m)}$ with $E_iPS = 0$, $\forall i$, and rank(S) = $n - m$. Then, a state feedback gain with admissible assurance can be determined by $K = XP^{-1}$.

From the proposed design criteria in Theorem 2 and Corollary 4, we summarize the design steps as follows.

Design procedure:

Step 1: Based on the descriptor system (1) with (2) and (3), denote a set of E_i by (2), and M, N_A, and N_B by (3).
Step 2: Denote a matrix S which is of full-column rank and satisfies $E_iPS = 0$, $\forall i$.
Step 3: Initially denote Q_i with a compatible dimension.
Step 4: Construct, respectively, LMI constraint sets by (12) and (13) with D-admissible assurance or (14) and (15) with admissible assurance.
Step 5: Evaluate the constructed LMIs from the LMI tool [37] for existing solutions $P > 0$, X and scalars $\alpha_{ij} > 0$.
Step 6: If the LMIs are feasible, a satisfying control gain can be evaluated by $K = XP^{-1}$; otherwise, no satisfying control gain can be obtained. End the design procedure.

4. Illustrative Examples

Two numerical examples are introduced to verify the effectiveness and applicability as follows.

Example 1. *A discrete singular system subjected to parametric perturbation is represented as*

$$\left(\begin{bmatrix} 2 & 1+w_1 & 0 \\ 0 & 1+w_2 & 0 \\ 0 & 0 & 0 \end{bmatrix}\right)x(k+1) = \left(\begin{bmatrix} 0.5 & 0.4 & 0.6 \\ 0.2 & -0.5 & 0 \\ 0.4 & -0.2 & 0.4 \end{bmatrix} + w_3 \begin{bmatrix} 0 & 0 & 0 \\ 0 & 0 & 0 \\ 0.47 & 0 & 0.36 \end{bmatrix}\right)x(k),$$

where $|w_1| \leq 0.52$, $|w_2| \leq 0.19$, and $|w_3| \leq 1$.

Since the considered singular system involves the uncertain difference term matrix $\tilde{E}$, some existing works [17,18,39] with a constant E are not applicable. Moreover, based on the previous work in [33], we first denote the matrices' vertices for the difference term and system's matrices as

$$E_1 = \begin{bmatrix} 2 & 1.52 & 0 \\ 0 & 1.19 & 0 \\ 0 & 0 & 0 \end{bmatrix}, E_2 = \begin{bmatrix} 2 & 0.48 & 0 \\ 0 & 1.19 & 0 \\ 0 & 0 & 0 \end{bmatrix},$$

$$E_3 = \begin{bmatrix} 2 & 1.52 & 0 \\ 0 & 0.81 & 0 \\ 0 & 0 & 0 \end{bmatrix}, E_4 = \begin{bmatrix} 2 & 0.48 & 0 \\ 0 & 0.81 & 0 \\ 0 & 0 & 0 \end{bmatrix},$$

with $q_E = 4$ and

$$A_1 = \begin{bmatrix} 0.5 & 0.4 & 0.6 \\ 0.2 & -0.5 & 0 \\ 0.87 & -0.2 & 0.76 \end{bmatrix}, A_2 = \begin{bmatrix} 0.5 & 0.4 & 0.6 \\ 0.2 & -0.5 & 0 \\ -0.07 & -0.2 & 0.04 \end{bmatrix},$$

with $q_A = 2$. According to Theorem 3.1 in [33], we can form $q_A \times (q_E + C_{q_E}^2) = 20$ LMIs for analyzing the admissibility of the considered system. However, when we evaluated them using the LMI solver [37], it showed infeasibility and we could not conclude the admissibility for this system. Furthermore, when evaluating the regarding system from the proposed approach in [19], the LMI solver also showed infeasibility.

However, in this work, the uncertain term of a system matrix can be alternatively described as $\Delta A = M\Lambda N_A$ with $M = \begin{bmatrix} 0 & 0 & 1 \end{bmatrix}^T$ and $N_a = \begin{bmatrix} 0.47 & 0 & 0.36 \end{bmatrix}$. Based on Corollary 3 with a denoted matrix $S = \begin{bmatrix} 0 & 0 & 1 \end{bmatrix}^T$, $E_1 S = E_2 S = 0$, the admissible analyzing conditions for this system can be formed by the LMI constraints with the number $(q_E + C_{q_E}^2) = 10$ from (10) and (11). By evaluating the LMI, we can obtain satisfying feasible solutions such as

$$P = \begin{bmatrix} 154.8676 & -1.0631 & -125.8808 \\ -1.0631 & 20.7002 & -0.1751 \\ -125.8808 & -0.1751 & 145.8124 \end{bmatrix} \times 10^{-2} > 0, Q_1 = \begin{bmatrix} 111.1610 \\ -2.9668 \\ -60.6450 \end{bmatrix} \times 10^{-2},$$

$$Q_2 = \begin{bmatrix} 106.5411 \\ -8.5998 \\ -62.0371 \end{bmatrix} \times 10^{-2}, Q_3 = \begin{bmatrix} 83.2633 \\ -7.8827 \\ -45.4755 \end{bmatrix} \times 10^{-2}, Q_4 = \begin{bmatrix} 110.5696 \\ -9.5869 \\ -64.3897 \end{bmatrix} \times 10^{-2},$$

$$\min_{i \leq j} \alpha_{ij} = \alpha_{33} = 0.2 > 0.$$

According to Corollary 3, we thus conclude that the regarded system with uncertainties is robustly admissible.

For verification, we denote the initial condition $x(0) = \begin{bmatrix} 20 & -10 & -25 \end{bmatrix}^T$ and the uncertainties terms as $\omega_1 = 0.52 \sin k\pi$, $\omega_2 = 0.19 \cos 2k\pi$, and $\omega_3 = \sin 4k\pi$. The regarded system, subjected to the given uncertainties, is then simulated. By observing Figure 1, it is evident that the state behaviors $x(k)$ have convergent trajectories with all the allowable uncertainties.

Example 2. *A third-order singular system with parametric perturbation is described by*

$$\begin{bmatrix} 1 & 0 & 0 \\ 1+w_1 & 2 & 0 \\ 0 & 0 & 0 \end{bmatrix} x(k+1) = \left(\begin{bmatrix} 1 & 0.8 & -1 \\ -1.2 & 1.5 & 2 \\ 0.6 & 0.4 & 1 \end{bmatrix} + w_2 \begin{bmatrix} 0 & 0 & 0 \\ 0 & 1 & 1 \\ 0 & 0 & 0 \end{bmatrix} \right) x(k) + \left(\begin{bmatrix} 1 \\ 1 \\ 0 \end{bmatrix} + w_3 \begin{bmatrix} 0 \\ 1 \\ 0 \end{bmatrix} \right) u(k),$$

where the perturbed uncertainties are assumed to fulfill $|w_1| \leq 1$, $0 \leq w_2 \leq 0.6$, and $0 \leq w_3 \leq 1$.

The vertices of matrices $\widetilde{E}$ in (2) for the considered system can be denoted as

$$E_1 = \begin{bmatrix} 1 & 0 & 0 \\ 2 & 2 & 0 \\ 0 & 0 & 0 \end{bmatrix}, E_2 = \begin{bmatrix} 1 & 0 & 0 \\ 0 & 2 & 0 \\ 0 & 0 & 0 \end{bmatrix}.$$

The uncertain system matrices can be described by $[\Delta A \quad \Delta B] = M\Lambda[N_A \quad N_B]$ with $M = [0 \quad 1 \quad 0]^T$, $N_a = [0 \quad 0.6 \quad 0.6]$, and $N_b = 1$. By primary evaluation, the nominal unforced system is originally unstable, i.e., the poles of the system with free input are not within $D(0, 1)$. When letting $x(0) = [-3 \quad 7 \quad -1]^T$, the system with free input is firstly simulated, and the state behaviors are drawn in Figure 2. By observation, the state responses of the system with free input are divergent. Thus, we need to conduct a proper control law for compensation. However, the previous work [19] cannot be applied to design a practicable controller with respect to D-admissible assurance.

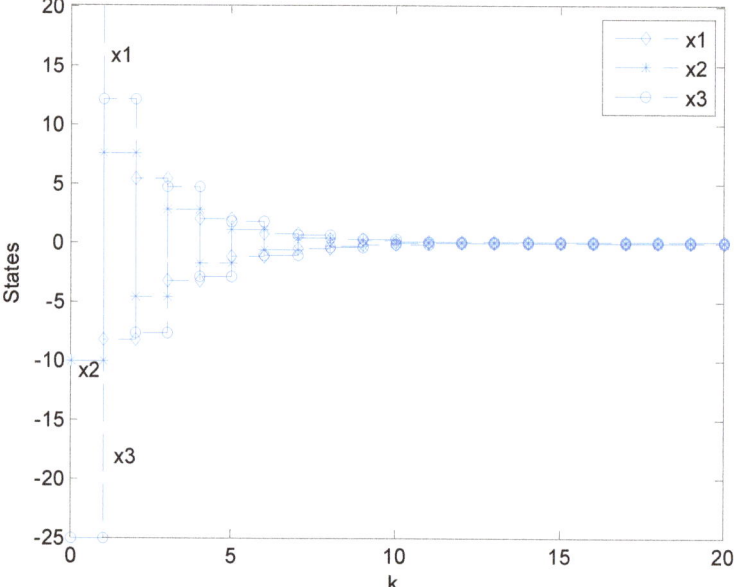

Figure 1. State responses of the considered system in Example 1.

By the design criteria of Theorem 2, we can conduct a state feedback controller with D-admissible assurance of a prescribed pole disk $D(0.2, 0.6)$. Thus, based on Equations (12) and (13), we correspondingly formulate three LMI constraints and denote

$$S = \begin{bmatrix} 0 \\ 0 \\ 1 \end{bmatrix}, Q_1 = Q_2 = -10 \times \begin{bmatrix} 1 \\ 1 \\ 1 \end{bmatrix}, P = \begin{bmatrix} P_1 & 0 \\ 0 & P_3 \end{bmatrix},$$

with $P_1 \in R^{2\times 2}$, $P_3 \in R^{1\times 1}$ satisfying $E_i PS = 0$, $\forall i$. Using the LMI solver for evaluation, a set of feasible solutions can be attained by

$$P = \begin{bmatrix} 3.3813 & -15.1082 & 0 \\ -15.1082 & 109.5238 & 0 \\ 0 & 0 & 2.0432 \end{bmatrix} \times 10^4 > 0,$$
$$X = \begin{bmatrix} 6.7012 & -48.1456 & 3.4029 \end{bmatrix} \times 10^4,$$
$$\alpha_{11} = 1.3965 \times 10^6,$$
$$\alpha_{12} = 2.5093 \times 10^6,$$
$$\alpha_{22} = 1.4135 \times 10^6.$$

Thus, a satisfying state feedback gain with the pole region $D(0.2, 0.6)$ can be determined by

$$K = XP^{-1} = \begin{bmatrix} 4.6076 & -43.3235 & 166.5498 \end{bmatrix} \times 10^{-2}.$$

When given the same initial condition $x(0) = [-3 \ 7 \ -1]^T$, the compensated system with the state feedback controller is simulated once again. Furthermore, the state behaviors $x(k)$ and the control input $u(k)$ are depicted in Figures 3 and 4, respectively. From Figure 3, all the state responses have well-convergent trajectories. Thus, the considered system with the state feedback gain is ensured to be D-admissible, where the closed-loop system can meet the prescribed performance requirement with the pole region $D(0.2, 0.6)$.

Remark 3. *Using the proposed design scheme in Theorem 2 and Corollary 4, we can conduct a conventional state feedback controller with D-admissible assurance or admissible assurance for the considered discrete singular system subjected to the uncertainties, which has the advantages of easy implementation and low cost. The given numerical examples have illustrated the feasibility and superiority of the developed methods. For nonlinear systems, we can perform the linearization by the given operating point and then can approximate to a linear form with uncertainties around the operating point. However, in the case of multiple operating points, we can incorporate the proposed results with existing intelligent control methods, such as fuzzy control systems [40,41], for further study.*

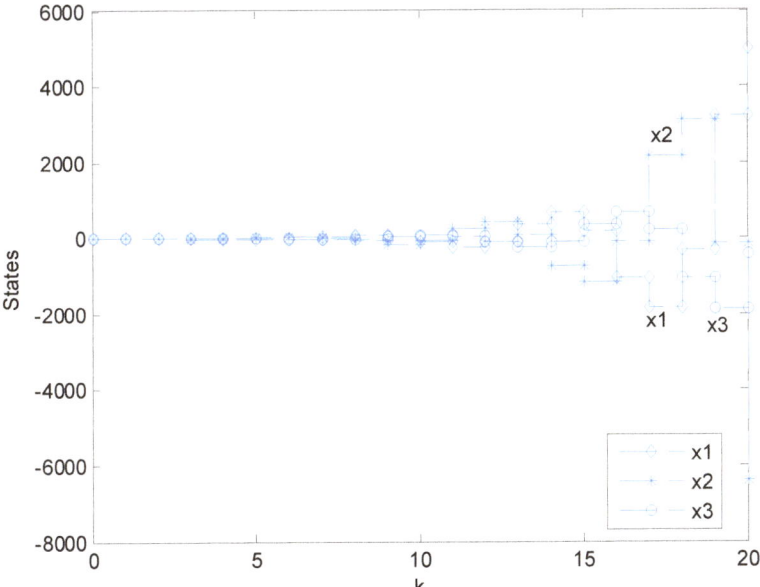

Figure 2. State responses of the open-loop system.

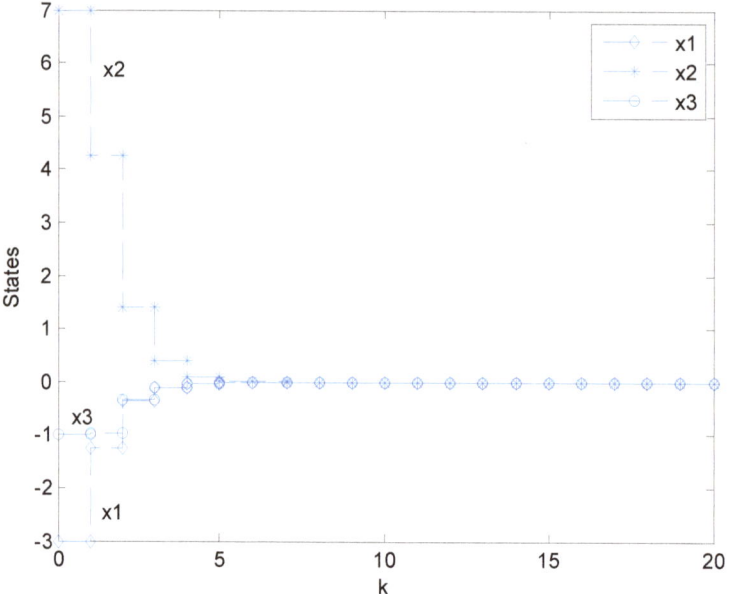

Figure 3. State responses with D-admissible assurance of the closed-loop system.

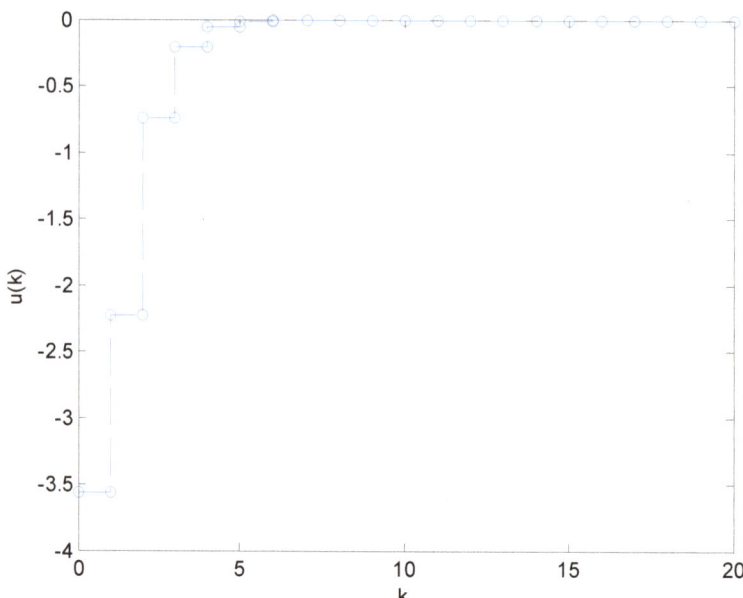

Figure 4. Control input trajectory.

5. Conclusions

In this work, we have dealt with state feedback control with D-admissible assurance for discrete singular systems subjected to the uncertain difference term and system matrices. Firstly, based on LMI techniques and matrix algebra manipulation, a refined D-admissible analysis criterion could be presented. The extended result has compact LMI constraints and involves multiple slack matrices, which help to lessen the conservatism for admissible analysis. By introducing the state feedback control, we then focused on state feedback control with D-admissible assurance for the closed-loop system. Since the proposed design criteria can be formulated in terms of the strict LMIs, they are readily evaluated by current LMI tools to construct a state feedback controller with the prescribed system's performance. Finally, two illustrative examples demonstrate the feasibility and applicability of the derived results. In the future, we will incorporate the proposed design scheme with existing intelligent control to cope with real physical systems, nonlinear systems, and/or time-delay systems.

Funding: This research received no external funding.

Data Availability Statement: Data are contained within the article.

Conflicts of Interest: The author declares no conflicts of interest.

References

1. Luenberger, D.G.; Arbel, A. Singular dynamical Leotief systems. *Econometrica* **1977**, *45*, 991–995. [CrossRef]
2. Zhang, Y.; Zhao, Y.; Li, N.; Wang, Y. Observer-based sliding mode controller design for singular bio-economic system with stochastic disturbance. *AIMS Math.* **2023**, *9*, 1472–1493. [CrossRef]
3. Newcomb, R.W. The semistate description of nonlinear time variable circuits. *IEEE Trans. Circuits Syst.* **1981**, *28*, 62–71. [CrossRef]
4. Kumar, A.; Daoutidis, P. Feedback control of nonlinear differential-algebraic-equation systems. *AIChE J.* **1995**, *41*, 619–636. [CrossRef]
5. Li, Y.; Geng, G.; Jiang, Q. A parallel contour integral method for eigenvalue analysis of power systems. *IEEE Trans. Power Syst.* **2017**, *32*, 624–632. [CrossRef]
6. Luenberger, D.G. Dynamic equations in descriptor form. *IEEE Trans. Autom. Control.* **1977**, *22*, 312–321. [CrossRef]
7. Lewis, F.L. A survey of linear singular systems. *Circuits Syst. Signal Process.* **1986**, *5*, 3–36. [CrossRef]
8. Dai, L. *Singular Control Systems. Lecture Notes in Control and Information Sciences*; Springer: New York, NY, USA, 1989; Volume 118.
9. Masubuchi, I.; Kamitane, Y.; Ohara, A.; Suda, N. H_∞ control for descriptor systems: A matrix inequalities approach. *Automatica* **1997**, *33*, 669–673. [CrossRef]
10. Xu, S.; Lam, J. Robust stability and stabilization of discrete singular systems: An equivalent characterization. *IEEE Trans. Autom. Control.* **2004**, *49*, 568–574. [CrossRef]
11. Yue, D.; Lam, J. Suboptimal robust mixed H_2/H_∞ controller design for uncertain descriptor systems with distributed delays. *Comput. Math. Appl.* **2004**, *47*, 1041–1055. [CrossRef]
12. Zhang, G.; Xia, Y.; Shi, P. New bounded real lemma for discrete-time singular systems. *Automatica* **2008**, *44*, 886–890. [CrossRef]
13. Chen, Y.; Xu, T.; Zeng, C.; Zhou, Z.; Zhang, Q. Simultaneous stabilization for uncertain descriptor systems with input saturation. *Int. J. Robust Nonlinear Control.* **2012**, *22*, 1938–1951. [CrossRef]
14. Zaghdoud, R.; Salhi, S.; Ksouri, M. State derivative feedback for singular systems. *IMA J. Math. Control. Inf.* **2018**, *35*, 611–626. [CrossRef]
15. Liu, R.R.; Xiong, J.; Zhang, Z. Reliable induced L_∞ control for polytopic uncertain continuous-time singular systems with dynamic quantization. *Appl. Math. Comput.* **2023**, *443*, 127765. [CrossRef]
16. Zhang, T.; Li, Y. Exponential Euler scheme of multi-delay Caputo–Fabrizio fractional-order differential equations. *Appl. Math. Lett.* **2022**, *124*, 107709. [CrossRef]
17. Belov, A.A.; Andrianova, O.G. Robust state feedback H_∞ control for discrete-time descriptor systems with norm-bounded parametric uncertainties. *Int. J. Syst. Sci.* **2019**, *50*, 1303–1312. [CrossRef]
18. Wang, J.; Wu, H.; Ji, X.; Liu, X. Robust finite-time stabilization for uncertain discrete-time linear singular systems. *IEEE Access* **2020**, *8*, 100645–100651. [CrossRef]
19. Huang, C.P. Admissibility analysis and controller design for discrete singular time-delay systems embracing uncertainties in the difference and systems' matrices. *Math. Probl. Eng.* **2021**, *2021*, 8845558. [CrossRef]
20. Chilali, M.; Gahinet, P. H_∞ design with pole placement constraints: An LMI approach. *IEEE Trans. Autom. Control.* **1996**, *41*, 358–367. [CrossRef]
21. Luo, J.S.; Bosch, P.P.J.; Weiland, S. New sufficient condition for robust root clustering of linear state space models with structured uncertainty. *IEE Proc.-Control. Theory Appl.* **1996**, *143*, 244–246. [CrossRef]
22. Chen, S.J.; Lin, J.L. Robust D-stability of discrete and continuous time interval systems. *J. Frankl. Inst.* **2004**, *341*, 505–517. [CrossRef]
23. Goncalves, E.N.; Palhares, R.M.; Takahashi, R.H.C.; Mesquita, R.C. New approach to robust D-stability analysis of linear time-invariant systems with polytope-bounded uncertainty. *IEEE Trans. Autom. Control.* **2006**, *51*, 1709–1714. [CrossRef]
24. Maamri, N.; Bachelier, O.; Mehdi, D. Pole placement in a union of regions with prespecified subregion allocation. *Math. Comput. Simul.* **2006**, *72*, 38–46. [CrossRef]

25. Xu, S.; Lam, J.; Zheng, L. Robust D-stability analysis for uncertain discrete singular systems with state delay. *IEEE Trans. Circu. Syst. I Fundam. Theory Appl.* **2002**, *49*, 551–555.
26. Chen, S.J. Robust D-stability analysis for linear discrete singular time-delay systems with structured and unstructured paramet uncertainties. *IMA J. Math. Control. Inf.* **2003**, *20*, 153–165. [CrossRef]
27. Chen, S.H.; Chou, J.H. Robust D-stability analysis for linear uncertain discrete singular systems with state delay. *Appl. Math. Le* **2006**, *19*, 197–205. [CrossRef]
28. Chen, S.H.; Chou, J.H. Robust eigenvalue-clustering in a specified circular region for linear uncertain discrete singular system with state delay. *Appl. Math. Comput.* **2007**, *186*, 1660–1670. [CrossRef]
29. Sari, B.; Bachelier, O.; Bosche, J.; Maamri, N.; Mehdi, D. Pole placement in non connected regions for descriptor models. *Ma Comput. Simul.* **2011**, *81*, 2617–2631. [CrossRef]
30. Lin, C.; Wang, J.L.; Yang, G.H.; Lam, J. Robust stabilization via state feedback for descriptor systems with uncertainties in t derivative matrix. *Int. J. Control.* **2000**, *73*, 407–415. [CrossRef]
31. Lin, C.; Lam, J.; Wang, J.; Yang, G.H. Analysis on robust stability for interval descriptor systems. *Syst. Control. Lett.* **2001**, *42*, 267–2. [CrossRef]
32. Lin, C.; Wang, Q.G.; Lee, T.H. Robust normalization and stabilization of uncertain descriptor systems with norm-bounde perturbations. *IEEE Trans. Autom. Control.* **2005**, *50*, 515–520.
33. Huang, C.P. Analysing robust D-admissibility for discrete singular systems subjected to parametric uncertainties in the differen matrix. *IMA J. Math. Control. Inf.* **2011**, *28*, 279–289. [CrossRef]
34. Huang, C.P. Specific D-admissibility and design issues for uncertain descriptor systems with parametric uncertainty in t derivative matrix. *Math. Probl. Eng.* **2016**, *2016*, 6142848. [CrossRef]
35. Mao, W.J. An LMI approach to D-stability and D-stabilization of linear discrete singular systems with state delay. *Appl. Ma Comput.* **2011**, *218*, 1694–1704. [CrossRef]
36. Boyd, S.; Ghaouim, L.E.; Feron, E.; Balakrishnan, V. *Linear Matrix Inequalities in Systems and Control Theory*; SIAM: Philadelph PA, USA, 1994.
37. Gahinet, P.; Nemirovski, A.; Jaub, A.J.; Chilali, M. *LMI Control Toolbox User's Guide*; The Mathworks Partner Series; The Mathwork Inc.: Natick, MA, USA, 1995.
38. Petersen, I.R. A stabilization algorithm for a class of uncertain linear systems. *Syst. Control. Lett.* **1987**, *8*, 351–357. [CrossRef]
39. Sun, X.; Zhang, Q.; Yang, C.; Su, Z. Stability analysis and stabilization for discrete-time singular delay systems. *J. Syst. En Electron.* **2011**, *22*, 482–487. [CrossRef]
40. Saravanakumar, T.; Lee, T.H. Hybrid-driven-based resilient control for networked T-S fuzzy systems with time-delay ar cyber-attacks. *Int. J. Robust Nonlinear Control.* **2023**, *33*, 7869–7891. [CrossRef]
41. Tharanidharan, V.; Saravanakumar, T.; Anthoni, S.M. Robust and quantized repetitive tracking control for fractional-order fuz. large-scale systems. *Int. J. Adapt. Control. Signal Process.* **2024**, *38*, 1496–1511. [CrossRef]

Disclaimer/Publisher's Note: The statements, opinions and data contained in all publications are solely those of the individu author(s) and contributor(s) and not of MDPI and/or the editor(s). MDPI and/or the editor(s) disclaim responsibility for any injury people or property resulting from any ideas, methods, instructions or products referred to in the content.

Article

Parameters Determination via Fuzzy Inference Systems for the Logistic Populations Growth Model

Yuney Gorrin-Ortega [1], Selene Lilette Cardenas-Maciel [1,*], Jorge Antonio Lopez-Renteria [2] and Nohe Ramon Cazarez-Castro [1,3,*]

[1] Instituto Tecnologico de Tijuana, Tecnologico Nacional de Mexico, Tijuana 22414, BC, Mexico; yuney.gorrin@tectijuana.edu.mx
[2] CONAHCYT—Tecnológico Nacional de México/Instituto Tecnológico de Tijuana, Tijuana 22414, BC, Mexico; jorge.lopez@tectijuana.edu.mx
[3] Facultad de Ingenieria Quimica, Universidad Michoacana de San Nicolas de Hidalgo, Morelia 58030, MC, Mexico
* Correspondence: lilettecardenas@ieee.org (S.L.C.-M.); nohe@ieee.org (N.R.C.-C.)

Abstract: This study addresses the fuzzy parameters (coefficient) determination for the logistic population growth model, proposing a novel methodology based on fuzzy logic concepts. Population dynamics are often modeled using differential equations whose parameters represent critical ecological information, where the parameters determination is a problem itself. Unlike those approaches, the proposed methodology leverages ecosystem variables as inputs to a fuzzy inference system, which then generates fuzzy coefficients that better capture the inherent uncertainties in population dynamics. The approach was tested on a case study involving marine fish populations, where the fuzzy coefficients for growth rate and carrying capacity were calculated and integrated into the logistic model. The results illustrate that the fuzzy model with the proposed coefficients provide a robust framework for modeling population growth, preserving the increasing trajectory of the population under different scenarios. This method allows for the incorporation of expert knowledge and linguistic variables into the model, offering a more flexible and accurate representation of real-world ecosystems. The study concludes that this methodology significantly enhances the model's applicability and predictive power, particularly in situations where precise data are not available.

Keywords: fuzzy differential equations; verhulst model; fuzzy coefficients; population dynamics; expert knowledge

MSC: 34A07; 62F86; 62J12; 28E10; 41A25

1. Introduction

Mathematical modeling plays a crucial role in understanding various natural phenomena. One of the well-established areas within mathematical modeling is population growth dynamics, where models help to predict and analyze the behavior of populations over time [1]. Among the most notable models in this field is the Verhulst logistic model, which describes population growth by considering both exponential growth and the limitations imposed by environmental factors. The Verhulst equation has been widely applied to real-world problems, providing valuable insights into ecological systems and population dynamics [2,3]. This model is particularly useful when studying populations constrained by resources, as it introduces the concept of carrying capacity, which is the maximum population size that an environment can sustain [4–6].

The main tool to model these kind of phenomena are the differential equations (DEs). Nevertheless, in many practical scenarios, the parameters that define these differential equations, such as growth rate and carrying capacity, are not precisely known due to data variability or measurement uncertainties. To address this issue, fuzzy differential equations (FDEs) have been introduced, offering a robust mathematical framework for handling uncertainty in initial conditions and model parameters. The FDEs have been successfully applied to various fields, extending classical differential equations into the fuzzy domain, where uncertainties are represented by fuzzy numbers [7–9].

An extension of the Verhulst logistic model into the fuzzy domain, known as the fuzzy Verhulst model, allows for more realistic representations of populations where parameters, like growth rate and carrying capacity, are not fixed but vary within certain bounds [10]. This approach captures the inherent uncertainties in ecological systems, where factors such as resource availability or environmental conditions fluctuate over time [11]. The fuzzy Verhulst model thus provides a more flexible tool for population modeling especially when precise data are unavailable.

Parameter estimation in both classical and FDEs is a critical task, as the accuracy of the model heavily depends on the proper determination of these coefficients [12–15]. In the classical framework, statistical or numerical methods are often employed to estimate parameters based on historical data [16]. However, when dealing with fuzzy models, parameter estimation becomes more complex due to the uncertainty in both the data and the model structure itself. Several approaches, including fuzzy regression techniques, have been developed to estimate parameters in FDEs, such as the fuzzy least absolute regression model, which incorporates probabilistic linguistic term sets for handling fat-tailed or outlier-prone data [17], and the Intuitionistic Fuzzy Logistic Regression model, which deals with imprecise parameters due to vagueness and hesitation in datasets [18]. In [19], the authors introduce a fuzzy autoregression model to predict wind speed and direction. The model uses fuzzy numbers for regression coefficients, which effectively manage the inherent variability and uncertainty in wind patterns. These accurate predictions can enhance power system reliability by optimizing wind power integration into the grid.

As seen, most of the solution techniques for DEs in the domain of real numbers can be adapted and used in the study of the FDE. The calculation of coefficients for DE models can be divided into two main classes: (1) techniques using historical data and (2) techniques without using data. Numerical–statistical methods or evolutionary methods belong to the first class, and coefficients proposed by the expert are representative of the second.

As part of the fuzzy mathematics and systems theory, let us consider the concept of a fuzzy inference system (FIS), first introduced by Zadeh [20,21], that allows dealing with situations where the information is vague or imprecise and allows considering experts' knowledge for the design of causal experts systems. A lot of theory has been developed around this type of system, as well as a large number of applications, some of which are related to control [22–33], forescasting [34–38], and classification [39–43], to name a few. These characteristics of the FIS are used to design the coefficients for the FDEs.

The motivation for this research stems from the need to develop an alternative method for estimating the coefficients of the fuzzy Verhulst model, specifically considering fuzzy coefficients, without relying on traditional datasets. The proposed approach leverages an FIS closely related to the phenomenon under study. By utilizing linguistic variables within the FIS and performing arithmetic operations, the model's coefficients are calculated based entirely on expert knowledge. This methodology provides a robust alternative to numerical or statistical methods, which typically require large volumes of data and extensive processing time. Instead, it offers a practical solution that effectively models complex systems governed by well-defined rules, integrating fuzzy coefficients without requiring extensive data processing.

Therefore, the problem statement is centered on the estimation of fuzzy coefficients in the Verhulst model, which traditionally relies on large datasets and statistical methods. However, in scenarios where data are limited or unavailable, these traditional methods become impractical. Additionally, adapting fuzzy techniques to handle fuzzy coefficients without relying on data remains a significant challenge. This study addresses this issue by developing an approach based on an FIS that leverages expert knowledge to calculate the model's coefficients, thereby eliminating the need for historical data.

The remainder of this paper is organized as follows: Section 2 is about the preliminaries; in Section 3, the materials and methods for the determination of fuzzy coefficients are presented; in Section 4, the results are shown; Section 5 presents the discussion; and in Section 6, the conclusions are stated.

2. Preliminaries

In this section, the main preliminaries are presented for the development of the rest of the article.

2.1. Necessary Knowledge About Fuzzy Inference Systems

Consider the following definitions:

Definition 1 ([20]). *A fuzzy set A is a tuple of two elements defined as $A = \{(x, \mu_A(x)) | x \in \mathbb{R}, \mu_A(x) \in [0,1]\}$, where $\mu_A(x)$ is the membership function of the fuzzy set A.*

So, the membership function is defined as

Definition 2 ([20]). *Given X any set. The membership function μ_A of a non-empty fuzzy set A is a function $\mu_A : X \to [0,1]$. The function μ_A is interpreted as the degree of membership of each element x to the fuzzy set A for each $x \in X$.*

The $\alpha - cut$ operation is very useful because it allows writing some fuzzy sets in intervals, and in this way, it is easier to execute arithmetic operations [44]. The $\alpha - cut$ operation of a fuzzy set A denoted by $[A]^\alpha$ is defined as

Definition 3 ([20]). *Let $\mu : \mathbb{R} \to [0,1]$, the membership function of a fuzzy set over $\mathbb{R}$, the $\alpha - cut$ or $\alpha - level$ is defined as the set $[A]^\alpha = \{x \in \mathbb{R} : \mu_A(x) \geq \alpha\}$ for each $0 < \alpha \leq 1$.*

In the context of fuzzy systems, the inaccurate or uncertain information can be represented as a linguistic variable (LV). An LV is characterized by a tuple (N, T, M, U), in which N is the name of the variable; T is the set of linguistic labels (each label is represented by a fuzzy set); M is the set of semantic rules that assign each label its meaning; and U is a universe of discourse (finite or infinite set).

Linguistic variables are important concepts in fuzzy logic, these variables are part of the FIS, and the FIS is a well-studied and applied form of knowledge representation.

The LVs are constituted by linguistic labels that allow the association of linguistic meaning to subintervals in the domain of each variable. A variable can have one or more linguistic labels; mathematically, these are represented through membership functions and consequently by fuzzy sets.

An FIS in general is a multivalued function where the inputs correspond to outputs and the function that makes this relationship is based on rules [45].

Specifically, the FIS has an inference engine that is responsible for performing the operations that relate to the inputs and outputs. Within this inference machine, there are three main modules (see Figure 1).

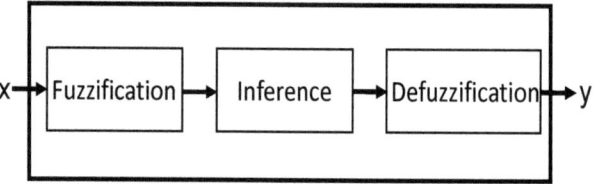

Figure 1. Structure of an FIS.

Fuzzification is the process of converting crisp, precise inputs into degrees of membership for fuzzy sets. The goal here is to map input values into fuzzy sets, where each fuzzy set represents a linguistic variable, for example, low, medium or high.

The inference engine processes the fuzzified inputs and applies fuzzy logic rules to produce fuzzy outputs. These rules are typically in the form of IF–THEN statements and operate on the fuzzified input data.

Defuzzification is the process of converting the fuzzy output obtained from the inference module into a crisp, actionable value. This step translates fuzzy conclusions into a real-world decision or action so that the output of this module is the output of the FIS itself.

There are several types of FIS, the more known are Takagi–Sugeno [46], Tsukamoto [47] and Mamdani [48]. A Mamdani-type fuzzy inference system (MFIS) is represented as a 4-tuple $M = (I, R, O, f)$ where the following apply:

- I is the set of linguistic variables of the inputs;
- R set of rules that relate the inputs to outputs;
- O set of linguistic variables of the outputs;
- f is a defuzzification method.

The relationship between the input and output linguistic variables is made through IF–THEN rules. These rules have the following form:

$$R_i : \text{IF } x_1 \text{ is } M_{p1}, x_2 \text{ is } M_{p2}, \ldots, x_n \text{ is } M_{pk}, \text{THEN } y_1 \text{ is } N_{l1}, y_2 \text{ is } N_{l2}, \ldots, y_m \text{ is } N_{lj}, \quad (1)$$

where $R_1, R_2, \ldots, R_i \in R$ represents the rules; $x_1, x_2, \ldots, x_n \in I$ are the linguistic variables of the inputs; $M_{p1}, M_{p2}, \ldots, M_{pk}$ are the labels of the input variables; $y_1, y_2, \ldots, y_m \in O$ are the output variables and $N_{l1}, N_{l2}, \ldots, N_{lj}$ are their respective linguistic labels [49].

There are various defuzzification methods. The most used are the center of area, bisector of area, last of maximum, first of maximum, middle of maximum and weighted average [50].

2.2. Foundations on Fuzzy Differential Equations

In this section, definitions to generalize the concept of derivatives and elements to solve FDEs are presented. The definition of a fuzzy number is presented to move toward the derivative definition.

Definition 4 ([51])**.** *Let μ be the membership function of a fuzzy set. It is said that μ is a fuzzy number if $\mu : \mathbb{R} \to [0,1]$ and satisfies the following conditions:*

(i) μ *is normal; i.e., there exists al least one $x^* \in \mathbb{R}$ such that $\mu(x^*) = 1$;*
(ii) $[\mu]^\alpha$ *is closed $\forall \alpha \in (0,1]$; and*

(iii) $[\mu]^0$ is bounded.

One way to obtain better representations and be able to operate fuzzy numbers arithmetically is through interval algebra. Therefore, a fuzzy number can be represented as an interval in the following way:

Definition 5 ([52]). *Given $\mu(x)$ with $x \in \mathbb{R}$ as the membership function of a fuzzy number, then there exist continuous functions $\mu_L(\alpha)$ and $\mu_R(\alpha)$ called, respectively, the left membership function and right membership function, such that*

$$\mu(x) = [\mu_L(\alpha), \mu_R(\alpha)], \forall \alpha \in [0,1] \quad (2)$$

with $\mu_L(\alpha) \leq \mu_R(\alpha)$.

For arithmetic intervals, it is possible to define the basic operations, where subindexes L and R represent the extreme left and right of the interval, respectively.

Definition 6 ([44,53]). *Given $[S_L, S_R]$ and $[T_L, T_R]$ arithmetic intervals, $\lambda \in \mathbb{R}$ (a scalar number), the following operations are defined:*

(i) Addition:
$$[S_L, S_R] + [T_L, T_R] = [S_L + T_L, S_R + T_R].$$
(ii) Subtraction:
$$[S_L, S_R] - [T_L, T_R] = [S_L - T_L, S_R - T_R].$$
(iii) Reciprocal:
if $0 \notin [S_L, S_R]$ then $[S_L, S_R]^{-1} = [1/S_L, 1/S_R]$;
if $0 \in [S_L, S_R]$ then $[S_L, S_R]^{-1}$ is undefined.
(iv) Multiplication:
$$[S_L, S_R] \cdot [T_L, T_R] = [U_L, U_R],$$
where:
$$U_L = \min\{S_L \cdot T_L, S_L \cdot T_R, S_R \cdot T_L, S_R \cdot T_R\},$$
$$U_R = \max\{S_L \cdot T_L, S_L \cdot T_R, S_R \cdot T_L, S_R \cdot T_R\}.$$
(v) Division:
$$[S_L, S_R] / [T_L, T_R] = [S_L, S_R] \cdot [T_L, T_R]^{-1}.$$
(vi) Multiplication by a scalar:
$$\lambda[S_L, S_R] = [\lambda S_L, \lambda S_R].$$

The definition of differentiability in the fuzzy sense was first introduced by [54] as

Definition 7 ([54]). *Let $u, v \in \mathcal{F}_\mathbb{R}$ (fuzzy number on reals). If there exists $w \in \mathcal{F}_\mathbb{R}$ such that $u = v \oplus w$, then w is called the H-difference of u and v, and it is denoted by $u \ominus v$.*

Observe that $\ominus$ means the H-difference in this context, and $\oplus$ is the opposite of this. Fuzzy differentiability is based in terms of limits, similar to classical derivative, and it is defined as

Definition 8 ([54]). *Let $F : T \to \mathcal{F}_\mathbb{R}$ and $t_0 \in T \subseteq \mathbb{R}$. The function F is said to be differentiable on t_0 if*

(I) There exists an element $\dot{F}(t_0) \in \mathcal{F}_\mathbb{R}$ such that for all $h > 0$ sufficiently close to zero, there exist $F(t_0 + h) \ominus F(t_0)$, $F(t_0) \ominus F(t_0 - h)$ and limits

$$\lim_{h \to 0^+} \frac{F(t_0 + h) \ominus F(t_0)}{h} = \lim_{h \to 0^+} \frac{F(t_0) \ominus F(t_0 - h)}{h}$$

are equal to $\dot{F}(t_0)$, or

(II) There exists an element $\dot{F}(t_0) \in \mathcal{F}_\mathbb{R}$ such that for all $h < 0$ sufficiently close to zero, there exist $F(t_0 + h) \ominus F(t_0)$, $F(t_0) \ominus F(t_0 - h)$ and limits

$$\lim_{h \to 0^-} \frac{F(t_0 + h) \ominus F(t_0)}{h} = \lim_{h \to 0^-} \frac{F(t_0) \ominus F(t_0 - h)}{h}$$

are equal to $\dot{F}(t_0)$.

It should be noted that if F is differentiable in the first form (I), then it is not differentiable in the second form (II), and vice versa, which is summarized in the following theorem:

Theorem 1 ([51]). *Let $F : T \to \mathcal{F}_\mathbb{R}$, and $[F(t)]^\alpha = [F_L^\alpha(t), F_R^\alpha(t)]$, for each $\alpha \in [0,1]$. Then*

(i) *If F is differentiable from Form-I, then $F_L^\alpha(t)$ and $F_R^\alpha(t)$ are differentiable functions and*

$$[\dot{F}(t)]^\alpha = [(\dot{F}_L^\alpha(t)), (\dot{F}_R^\alpha(t))], \tag{3}$$

or

(ii) *If F is differentiable from Form-II then $F_L^\alpha(t)$ y $F_R^\alpha(t)$ are differentiable functions and*

$$[\dot{F}(t)]^\alpha = [(\dot{F}_R^\alpha(t)), (\dot{F}_L^\alpha(t))] \tag{4}$$

where L and R are subindexes that represent the left and right extremes in interval algebra, respectively. The superindex α represents the function expressed in the α-cut.

The previous theorem constitutes a tool that allows writing the FDE in terms of standard equations in real numbers using the interval arithmetic. The way for doing this is through the equality of intervals, which can be seen in

Definition 9 ([45]). *Two intervals $[S_L, S_R]$ and $[T_L, T_R]$ are said to be equal if and only if $S_L = T_L$ and $S_R = T_R$.*

Another definition that is important to resolve the FDE is the initial value problem:

Definition 10 ([55]). *Let us consider the first-order linear fuzzy differential equation $\dot{\tilde{x}} = \tilde{f}(\tilde{x})$, where $\tilde{f}(\tilde{x})$ is a fuzzy function of $\tilde{x}$, and $\dot{\tilde{x}}$ is the H-derivative of $\tilde{x}$; if an initial value $\tilde{x}(0) = \tilde{x}_0$ is given, then this is a fuzzy initial value problem (FIVP).*

2.3. Verhulst Logistic Model Expressed as Fuzzy Differential Equation

We assume the basic law of growth expressed as the form $\dot{x} = xf(x)$, where $x \in \mathbb{R}$ and $f(x)$ is some function [56,57]. If this function is sufficiently smooth, it can be represented with an approximation of $f(x)$ through the expansion of the Taylor series around $x = 0$:

$$f(x) \approx f(0) + \frac{f'(0)}{1!}x + \frac{f''(0)}{2!}x^2 + \ldots + \frac{f^n(0)}{n!}x^n, \tag{5}$$

where $n \in \mathbb{N}$ [58–60]. Note that if in the Taylor series, only the constant term is kept, then from $\dot{x} = xf(x) = x(f(0)) = rx$ is obtained exactly the equation $\dot{x} = rx$, where $r = f(0)$, and it is known as the growth rate. This equation means that the population growth is proportional to the r coefficient; this is named the Malthus equation [61–63]. If two terms of the Taylor series expasion are kept, then the equation $\dot{x} = xf(x) = x(f(0) + f'(0)x) = rx\left(1 - \frac{x}{C}\right)$ is obtained, which is the logistic equation, where $f(0)$ and $f'(0)$ are connected to r and C, respectively, and the parameter C is the carrying capacity.

With this aim in mind, the classic Verhulst logistic model within the real domain has been discussed. But there are several ways to represent this model or any other as an FDE. In this work, all the coefficients of the model are considered as fuzzy numbers such that the model can be seen as

$$\dot{\tilde{x}} = \tilde{r}\tilde{x}\left(\tilde{1} - \frac{\tilde{x}}{\tilde{C}}\right), \tag{6}$$

where $\tilde{x}, \tilde{r}, \tilde{C} \in \mathcal{F}_{\mathbb{R}}$ and the fuzzy numbers are represented with a tilde above.

On the other hand, when Theorem 1 is applied, it can be represented (6) with interval algebra as

$$[\dot{x}_L, \dot{x}_R] = [r_L, r_R][x_L, x_R]\left([1,1] - \frac{[x_L, x_R]}{[C_L, C_R]}\right). \tag{7}$$

The subindex L and R represent the extremes of the left and right intervals, respectively [64].

3. Determination of Fuzzy Coefficients

For solving the problem stated, the following methodology is defined.

Let an FIS describe population dynamics, then the FIS makes up the input for the methodology. For this, the FIS can be taken from one previously built. Then, using the linguistic variables of the inputs, it is necessary to propose the modeling functions to calculate the coefficients $\tilde{r}$ and $\tilde{C}$ in (6). So, this section will also show the structure for the modeling functions. The diagram in Figure 2 represents the methodology to build $\tilde{r}$ and $\tilde{C}$ coefficients. For better understanding, the diagram was divided into stages.

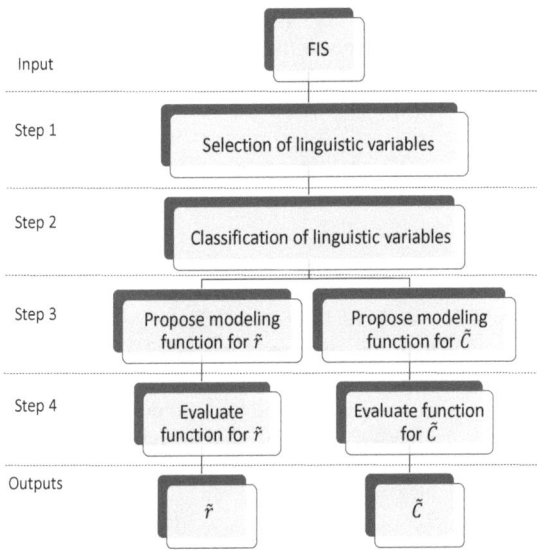

Figure 2. Methodology through modeling functions.

In the input stage, it is necessary to have an FIS related to the model whose coefficients will be calculated. Therefore, the FIS must be made up of linguistic variables corresponding to the case study.

Considering the input, as step 1, it is established that the selection process consists of the following. From the linguistic variables in the FIS, the expert has to choose which of these variables are relevant for the construction of the coefficients. The relevance criterion can be based on modeling in real numbers or on the expert knowledge. The selected variables will be denoted as set E.

Step 2 consists of classifying the variables from step 1 into two subsets according to the expert knowledge about which variables could be important in the design of a specific coefficient. Therefore, each subset contains the linguistic variables to design each coefficient. These subsets will be denoted as E_i, where $E_{i \in \{r,c\}}$ is the subset of linguistic variables corresponding to each coefficient as a result of this step.

In step 3, the modeling functions are designed by the expert from the sets obtained in step 2. For this, a structure of modeling functions for calculating $\tilde{r}$ and $\tilde{C}$ is proposed as

$$\tilde{r} = \tilde{f}_r(E_r) \tag{8}$$

and

$$\tilde{C} = \tilde{f}_c(E_c), \tag{9}$$

where $\tilde{f}_r$ and $\tilde{f}_c$ are fuzzy functions that the expert must propose depending on the nature of the problem under study. These functions receive E_i as a parameter, where E_i is the set of linguistic variables determined in step 2 of the methodology.

As step 4, the modeling functions are evaluated with E_i from the previous step.

Finally, numerical values for the coefficients are obtained in the output stage. The methodology presented for determining fuzzy coefficients offers significant advantages, particularly in handling the inherent uncertainties of ecological data. Traditional methods often rely on precise data, which can be difficult to obtain or may not accurately reflect the variability found in real-world scenarios. In contrast, our approach leverages expert knowledge through an FIS, enabling the integration of linguistic variables directly related to the phenomenon under study. This not only enhances the flexibility and robustness of the logistic growth model but also introduces a novel way of addressing data imprecision in population dynamics. By proposing fuzzy coefficients, it provides a framework that better captures the complexities and uncertainties of real ecosystems, thus improving the model's applicability and predictive power in diverse environmental contexts.

An example will be presented in the next section.

4. Experimental Results

This case study will show how to determine the fuzzy coefficients for the logistic model using the methodology above described. For this, it will be using an FIS, and the model to calculate its coefficients is (6). This FIS is taken from [65], and it estimates the intrinsic extinction vulnerabilities of marine fishes to fishing. The FIS's linguistic variables are used to design the functions $\tilde{f}_r$ and $\tilde{f}_c$ and therefore calculate the coefficients $\tilde{r}$ and $\tilde{C}$, respectively. Finally, the coefficients will be incorporated into (6), and this will be solved using an initial condition.

4.1. FIS That Estimates Vulnerabilities of Marine Fishes

In their study, the authors of [65] aimed to address the timely identification of vulnerable species for conservation efforts, despite incomplete information on most species that makes it challenging to establish an index of extinction vulnerability. To overcome this challenge, the authors developed a fuzzy inference system that assesses the intrinsic vulnerability of marine fishes. This system considers the fish's life history and ecological traits, which contribute to their susceptibility to fishing. The maximum rate of population growth and strength of density dependence are important factors in assessing intrinsic vulnerability. Using life history and ecological characteristics as "rules-of-thumb", the authors identified certain relationships commons for all species, and using that knowledge, the fuzzy system was developed.

The FIS developed in [65] is of the Mamdani type. This has eight inputs and one output, which are presented in Figures 3–11, where Figures 3–10 corresponds to the input variables and Figure 11 corresponds to the output variable. The defuzzification method used is the weighted average [66]. The rules are shown in Table 1, and they are grouped according to the linguistic variable in the antecedent.

To construct the main linguistic variables that form the FIS, the article used as a reference is based on the biological and ecological characteristics of marine species, which are crucial for determining their intrinsic vulnerability to fishing. These characteristics include the maximum population growth rate, longevity, age at sexual maturity, and fecundity, among other parameters. These variables are combined using fuzzy set theory, which allows for the management of the inherent uncertainty in biological and ecological knowledge, as well as the challenges in strictly classifying species parameters. Fuzzy membership functions are employed to assign degrees of membership to different categories, such as low, medium or high, among others.

This figure illustrates the fuzzy membership functions for categorizing fish age at first maturity into four levels: Low (Lw), Medium (M), High (H), and Very High (VH). The X-axis represents the age at first maturity in years, while the Y-axis shows the membership degree from 0 to 1. Each color line corresponds to a category, demonstrating the gradual transitions and overlaps typical of fuzzy logic, which enables more nuanced classifications compared to binary categorization.

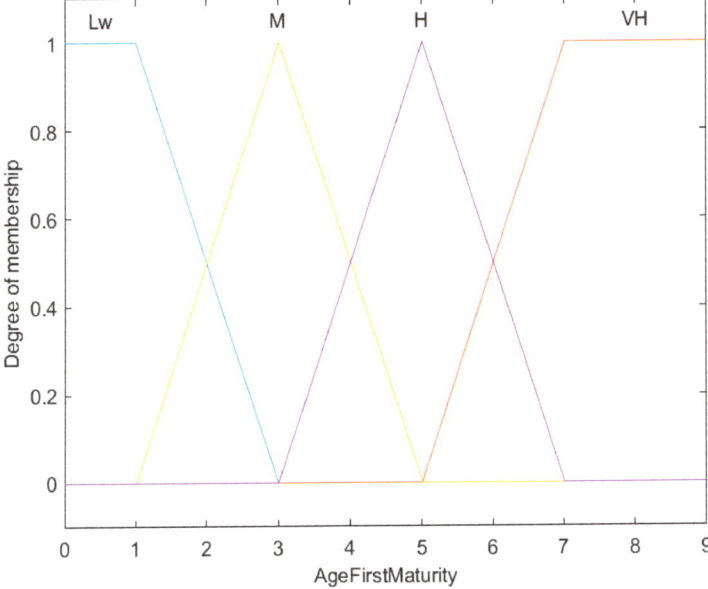

Figure 3. Fuzzy membership functions for fish age at first maturity (T_m).

Depicted here are the fuzzy membership functions categorizing fish fecundity into three levels: Very Low (VLw), Low (Lw), and Not Low (NLw). On the X-axis, fecundity is quantified by the number of eggs, and the Y-axis represents the membership degree from 0 to 1. Each color represents a specific fecundity level, showcasing the utility of fuzzy logic for managing overlapping categories.

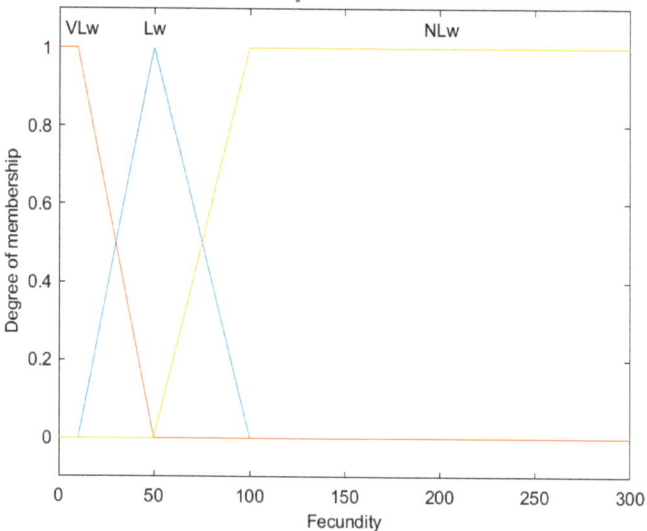

Figure 4. Fuzzy membership functions for fish fecundity (F).

Illustrating the classification of fish geographic ranges, the graph uses fuzzy membership functions to sort ranges into Very Restricted (VR), Restricted (R), and Not Restricted (NR). The X-axis displays geographic range values in square kilometers, while the Y-axis assesses the membership degree, ranging from 0 to 1.

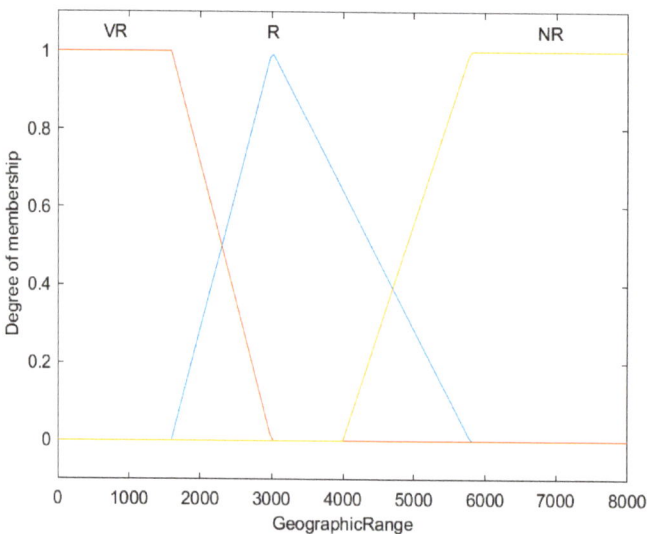

Figure 5. Fuzzy membership functions for geographic range of fish species (R).

The graph delineates fuzzy membership functions that categorize the maximum length of fish into Small (S), Medium (M), Large (L), and Very Large (VL). The X-axis measures the maximum length in centimeters, and the Y-axis plots the membership degree from 0 to 1.

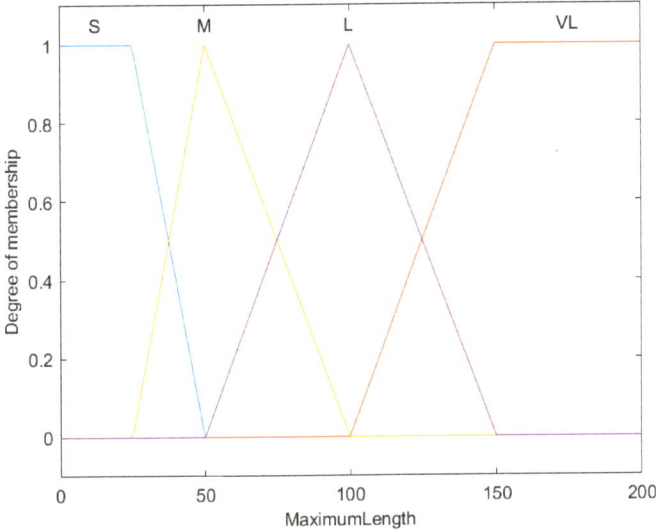

Figure 6. Fuzzy membership functions for maximum length of fish (L_{max}).

This graph categorizes the maximum age of fish using fuzzy membership functions across four classifications: Low (Lw), Medium (M), High (H), and Very High (VH). The X-axis presents the maximum age in years, and the Y-axis indicates the degree of membership, which is scaled from 0 to 1.

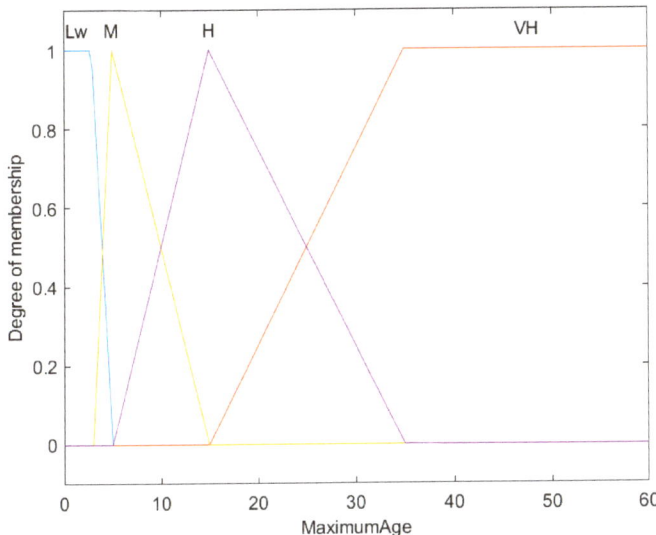

Figure 7. Fuzzy membership functions for maximum age of fish (T_{max}).

Portrayed in this graph are the fuzzy membership functions that segment natural mortality rates in fish into four categories: Very Low (VLw), Low (Lw), Medium (M), and High (H). The X-axis details the natural mortality rates per year, and the Y-axis reflects the membership degree from 0 to 1.

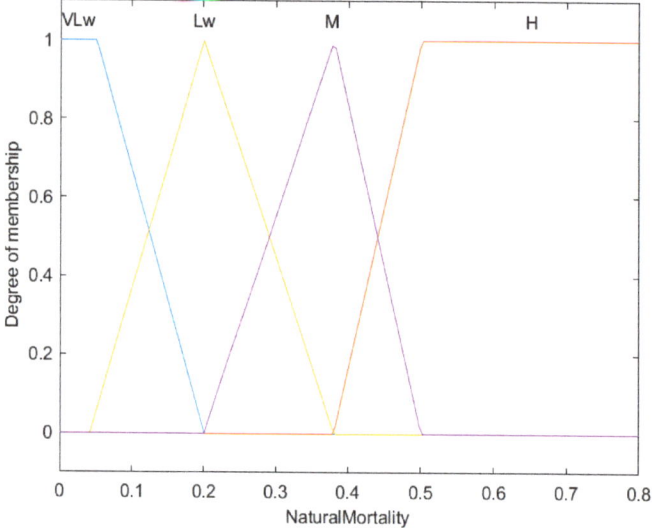

Figure 8. Fuzzy membership functions for natural mortality rates in fish (M).

This graph elucidates the fuzzy membership functions applied to evaluate the spatial behavior strength of fish, which are segmented into four categories: Low (Lw), Medium (M), High (H), and Very High (VH). The X-axis represents the spatial behavior strength score, scaling from 0 to 100, while the Y-axis depicts the degree of membership, ranging from 0 to 1.

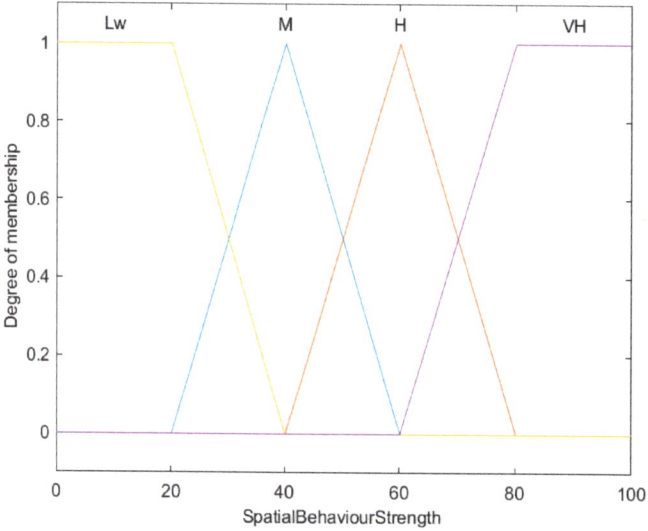

Figure 9. Fuzzy membership functions for spatial behavior strength in fish (B).

This chart illustrates the fuzzy membership functions used to categorize the von Bertalanffy growth factor (VBGFk) of fish, defining four levels: Very Low (VLw), Low (Lw), Medium (M), and High (H). The X-axis measures VBGFk values, while the Y-axis quantifies membership degrees from 0 to 1.

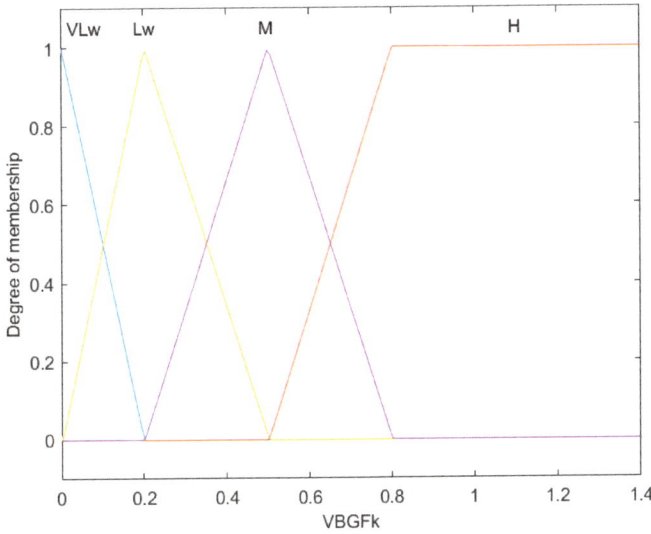

Figure 10. Fuzzy membership functions for the natural growth (K).

This graph presents the fuzzy membership functions that classify the intrinsic vulnerability of fish into four categories: Low, Moderate, High, and Very High. The X-axis depicts the intrinsic vulnerability score, ranging from 0 to 100, while the Y-axis represents the degree of membership from 0 to 1, as usual.

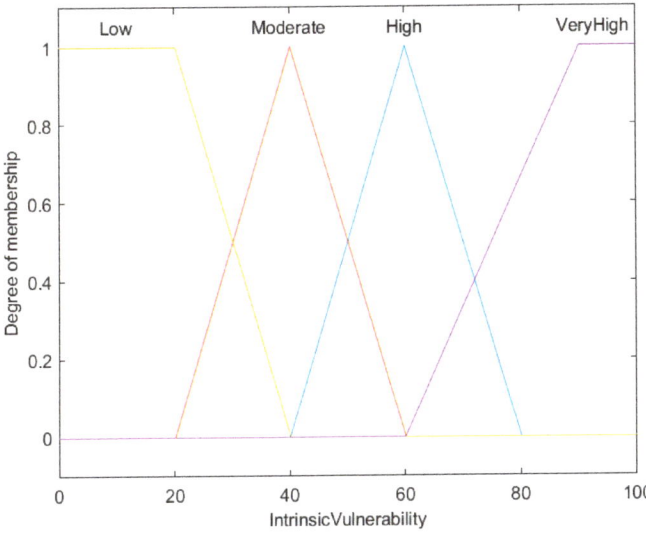

Figure 11. Fuzzy membership functions for intrinsic vulnerability (V).

Table 1. Heuristic rules defined in the fuzzy system to assign relative vulnerabilities to fishes.

Rule		Conditions		Consequences
1	IF	Maximum length is very large	THEN	Vulnerability is very high
2	IF	Maximum length is large	THEN	Vulnerability is high
3	IF	Maximum length is medium	THEN	Vulnerability is moderate
4	IF	Maximum length is small	THEN	Vulnerability is low
5	IF	Age at first maturity is very high	THEN	Vulnerability is very high
6	IF	Age at first maturity is high	THEN	Vulnerability is high
7	IF	Age at first maturity is medium	THEN	Vulnerability is moderate
8	IF	Age at first maturity is low	THEN	Vulnerability is low
9	IF	Maximum age is very high	THEN	Vulnerability is very high
10	IF	Maximum age is high	THEN	Vulnerability is high
11	IF	Maximum age is medium	THEN	Vulnerability is moderate
12	IF	Maximum age is low	THEN	Vulnerability is low
13	IF	VBGF K is very low OR IF Natural mortality is very low	THEN	Vulnerability is very high
14	IF	VBGF K is low OR IF Natural mortality is low	THEN	Vulnerability is high
15	IF	VBGF K is medium OR IF Natural mortality is medium	THEN	Vulnerability is medium
16	IF	VBGF K is high OR IF Natural mortality is high	THEN	Vulnerability is low
17	IF	Geographic range is restricted	THEN	Vulnerability is high
18	IF	Geographic range is very restricted	THEN	Vulnerability is very high
19	IF	Fecundity is low	THEN	Vulnerability is high
20	IF	Fecundity is very low	THEN	Vulnerability is very high
21	IF	Spatial behaviour strength is low	THEN	Vulnerability is low
22	IF	Spatial behaviour strength is moderate	THEN	Vulnerability is moderate
23	IF	Spatial behaviour strength is high	THEN	Vulnerability is high
24	IF	Spatial behaviour strength is very high	THEN	Vulnerability is very high
25	IF	Spatial behaviour is related to feeding aggregation	THEN	Vulnerability resulted from spatial behaviour decreases
26	IF	Spatial behaviour is related to spawning aggregation	THEN	Vulnerability resulted from spatial behaviour increases

4.2. Proposal of Coefficients $\tilde{r}$ and $\tilde{C}$

The FIS presented in Section 4.1 will be the input for the methodology described in Section 3.

In step 1, the set of linguistic variables considered important to calculate the coefficients of the model under study is selected. The linguistic variables in

$$E = \{L_{max}, T_m, K, M, T_{max}, R, F\}, \tag{10}$$

where L_{max} means maximum length (for a fish); T_m is the age at first maturity, K is the VBGF parameter (growth of fish [67]), M is the natural mortality rate, T_{max} is the maximum age, R is the geographic range and F is the fecundity; all of them are features of a certain fish population, and these can be used in the calculation of the coefficients for the growth model.

Then, in step 2, the variables from the set E are classified as

$$E_r = \{T_m, K, M, T_{max}, F\} \tag{11}$$

and

$$E_c = \{L_{max}, R\}. \tag{12}$$

Note that in (11), the age at first maturity (T_m), natural growth (K), the natural mortality rate (M), the maximum age (T_{max}), and fecundity (F) are variables that directly influence r, which is similar to biological modeling rules on real numbers. In (12), variables such as

L_{max} means the maximum length of a fish's body and R represents the geographic range; these are linked to the coefficient C.

Step 3 consists of designing the modeling functions (8) and (9); therefore, $\tilde{f}_r$ is proposed as the addition of natural growth, fecundity and the reciprocal of age at first maturity because those variables contribute to population growth; and the natural mortality rate and the reciprocal of maximum age are subtracted because they negatively influence the growth. The reciprocal expression for $\tilde{T}_m$ and $\tilde{T}_{max}$ is due to unit measure; observe, the before variables are in *year* and the others are in $year^{-1}$. From this logic,

$$\tilde{r} = \tilde{f}_r(E_r) = \tilde{K} + \tilde{F} + \frac{1}{\tilde{T}_m} - \tilde{M} - \frac{1}{\tilde{T}_{max}} \quad (13)$$

is designed.

Similarly to the real model, $\tilde{C}$ represents the carrying capacity in the ecosystem. Then,

$$\tilde{C} = \tilde{f}_c(E_c) = \frac{\tilde{R}}{(\frac{\tilde{L}_{max}}{100,000})^2} \quad (14)$$

is explained as follows. The denominator expresses the square space required for a fish, where the constant 100,000 is a conversion factor between units of measurement. The idea is to know how many fishes can live in a certain region, and for this, it is necessary to divide $\tilde{R}$ between the space required for each fish. In this way, the ecosystem capacity is calculated.

As step 4 of the methodology, to evaluate (13) and (14) and obtain the outputs, a combination of linguistic labels is taken for the linguistic variables selected in (10). Table 2 presents the linguistic label together with the respective linguistic variable, and also the numeric value in interval form is shown. This combination of linguistic labels is chosen because it yields a low vulnerability value when it is evaluated in the FIS.

It is important to mention that each linguistic label is a fuzzy number, and these are used to obtain $\tilde{r}$ and $\tilde{C}$. When (13) and (14) are evaluated, then [50.25 300.60] and [1.63 326,530,612.24] are obtained, respectively, for $\tilde{r}$ and $\tilde{C}$ expressed as intervals.

Table 2. Linguistic labels for evaluate (13) and (14).

Linguistic Variables	Linguistic Labels	Values
L_{max} (Maximum length)	S (Small)	[0 50]
T_m (Age at first maturity)	Lw (Low)	[0 3]
K (von Bertalanffy growth parameter)	H (High)	[0.5 1.4]
M (Natural mortality rate)	H (High)	[0.38 0.8]
T_{max} (Maximum age)	Lw (Low)	[0 5]
R (Geographic range)	NR (Not Restricted)	[4000 8000]
F (Fecundity)	NLw (Not Low)	[50 300]

4.3. Solutions for the Fuzzy Verhulst Logistic Model

To solve (7), it is necessary to consider an FIVP. Consider that the initial condition is [9,000,000 9,100,000], where X represents the number of fishes at a given time. Figure 12 shows the trajectories of the Form-I and Form-II solutions, X_L and X_R represent the extremes of the arithmetic interval corresponding to the solutions, and the green area is the uncertainty or membership value in the solutions.

All the calculations and solutions of the equation were programmed in a MatLab® script (R2019a). Matlab's ode45 numerical method is used to solve the model expressed as an FIVP.

The experimental results demonstrate the effectiveness of the proposed fuzzy coefficients in the logistic population growth model. The fuzzy model maintained stable and accurate growth trajectories, even under varying scenarios, highlighting its robustness in handling data uncertainties. Unlike traditional methods, this approach integrates expert knowledge without requiring extensive historical data, making it particularly useful in fields with limited or imprecise data. This shows that incorporating fuzzy logic enhances the model's applicability and predictive power in complex environments.

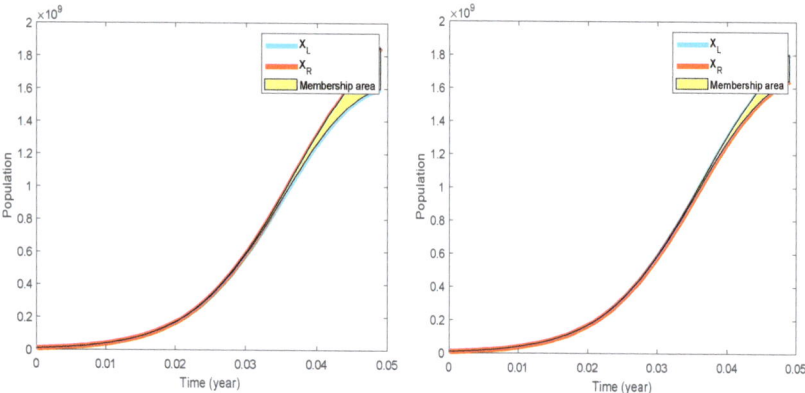

Figure 12. Form-I solution (left) and Form-II solution (right) for (7).

5. Discussion

We used linguistic variables to evaluate the modeling functions. If, for example, the kernels are taken as representatives to evaluate numerically the FIS presented in Section 4.1, then we only need the value for the input corresponding to spatial behavior strength, because it was not used in the methodology. Even so, evaluating the FIS for the mentioned values and with all values on spatial behavior strength, the result of the intrinsic vulnerability index is in the range between 15.29 and 47.61; this means that the result is a low intrinsic vulnerability index. On the other hand, it can be appreciated that the solution curves for the model are increasing; here, an inversely proportional relationship can be established, given that when there is a low vulnerability, a population increase occurs.

6. Conclusions

In this work, a methodology for the construction of coefficients of Verhulst models expressed in differential equations was presented. The methodology was tested to calculate the fuzzy coefficients that represents the growth rate and the carrying capacity in the Verhulst model. The resolution of the Verhulst model that used the calculated coefficients and initial condition both defined as fuzzy numbers yielded a family of solutions that preserve the trajectories of increasing for the Form-I and Form-II solutions. It can be seen that there is an inverse relationship between the solutions and vulnerability with low vulnerability corresponding to a high growth.

The results obtained show that the proposed methodology to build coefficients, based on expert knowledge represented through fuzzy systems, could help to incorporate smoothly and easily the uncertainties and inaccuracies present in the parameters of the Verhulst model because the methodology is based on linguistic variables proposed by an expert that it is related to the nature of the model.

In comparison to existing models and methods for determining fuzzy coefficients, such as fuzzy regression techniques or evolutionary algorithms, the method applied in this study leverages a pre-existing FIS to calculate coefficients without relying extensively on large datasets. Traditional methods, such as statistical or evolutionary approaches, often require significant amounts of historical data, which can be limiting in ecological applications. In contrast, this study integrates the FIS from previous research, allowing for a flexible and adaptable calculation of fuzzy coefficients based on expert knowledge. While traditional methods are effective in certain contexts, the use of a pre-established FIS provides an efficient alternative for handling uncertainty and vagueness, particularly when precise data are not available.

This study offers valuable insights into the modeling of population dynamics using fuzzy logic, particularly in scenarios where precise data are unavailable or uncertainty is inherent. The methodology introduced for determining fuzzy coefficients in the logistic population growth model can be extended to a wide range of biomathematical applications, such as modeling species interactions, epidemiological models, and ecological sustainability assessments. By incorporating expert knowledge through FIS, this approach enhances the flexibility and realism of traditional population models, making it particularly useful in fields like conservation biology, ecological forecasting, and resource management, where accurate predictions are critical but data are often incomplete or imprecise.

Future work could explore the application of this methodology to other mathematical models in population dynamics, such as predator–prey models, age-structured population models, or spatial models that consider habitat fragmentation. Expanding beyond population dynamics, this approach could also be applied to fields like automatic control systems, where uncertainty plays a significant role in system behavior. By incorporating fuzzy logic into control theory models, such as in the regulation of biological processes or environmental systems, the robustness and adaptability of control mechanisms could be improved. Additionally, integrating this methodology with real-world case studies from both ecological and engineering fields could further validate its effectiveness and extend its utility across diverse scientific and industrial applications.

Author Contributions: Conceptualization, N.R.C.-C.; Methodology, Y.G.-O., S.L.C.-M., J.A.L.-R. and N.R.C.-C.; Software, Y.G.-O. and N.R.C.-C.; Validation, Y.G.-O., S.L.C.-M., J.A.L.-R. and N.R.C.-C.; Formal analysis, S.L.C.-M., J.A.L.-R. and N.R.C.-C.; Investigation, Y.G.-O., S.L.C.-M., J.A.L.-R. and N.R.C.-C.; Resources, S.L.C.-M. and N.R.C.-C.; Data curation, Y.G.-O., S.L.C.-M., J.A.L.-R. and N.R.C.-C.; Writing—original draft, Y.G.-O.; Writing—review & editing, N.R.C.-C.; Visualization, Y.G.-O.; Supervision, N.R.C.-C.; Project administration, N.R.C.-C.; Funding acquisition, S.L.C.-M., J.A.L.-R. and N.R.C.-C. All authors have read and agreed to the published version of the manuscript.

Funding: This research was funded by Tecnológico Nacional de México, grant number 18009.23-P, 18302.23-P. Yuney Gorrin-Ortega thanks CONAHCyT for the scholarship awarded to carry out doctoral studies.

Data Availability Statement: Data are contained within the article.

Conflicts of Interest: The authors declare no conflicts of interest.

Abbreviations

The following abbreviations are used in this manuscript:

Lw	Low
M	Medium
H	High
VH	Very High

NLw	Not Low
VR	Very Restricted
R	Restricted
NR	Not Restricted
S	Small
VL	Very Large
VLw	Very Low

References

1. Banerjee, S. *Mathematical Modeling: Models, Analysis and Applications*; Chapman and Hall/CRC: Boca Raton, FL, USA, 2021.
2. Kalman, D. Verhulst Discrete Logistic Growth. *Math. Mag.* **2023**, *96*, 244–258. [CrossRef]
3. Morales-Erosa, A.; Reyes-Reyes, J.; Astorga-Zaragoza, C.M.; Osorio-Gordillo, G.L.; García-Beltrán, C.D.; Madrigal-Espinosa, G. Growth modeling approach with the Verhulst coexistence dynamic properties for regulation purposes. *Theory Biosci.* **2023**, *142*, 221–234. [CrossRef] [PubMed]
4. İskender, C. Mathematical Study of the Verhulst and Gompertz Growth Functions and Their Contemporary Applications. *EKOIST J. Econom. Stat.* **2021**, *34*, 73–102. [CrossRef]
5. Adeyeye, O.; Omar, Z. Investigating accuracy of multistep block methods based on step-length values for solving Malthus and Verhulst growth models. In *AIP Conference Proceedings*; AIP Publishing: Melville, NY, USA, 2022; Volume 2472.
6. Naso, P.; Lanz, B.; Swanson, T. The return of Malthus? Resource constraints in an era of declining population growth. *Eur. Econ. Rev.* **2020**, *128*, 103499. [CrossRef]
7. Zwillinger, D.; Dobrushkin, V. *Handbook of Differential Equations*; Chapman and Hall/CRC: Boca Raton, FL, USA, 2021.
8. Suhhiem, M.H. Legendre Operational Differential Matrix for Solving Fuzzy Differential Equations with Trapezoidal Fuzzy Function Coefficients. *J. Kufa Math. Comput.* **2024**, *11*, 31–48.
9. Thangathamizh, R. A Revised Fuzzy Differential Equations Using Weakly Compatible Self-Mappings in Revised Fuzzy Metric Spaces. *Adv. Nonlinear Var. Inequalities* **2024**, *27*, 233–254. [CrossRef]
10. Shiri, B.; Alijani, Z.; Karaca, Y. A power series method for the fuzzy fractional logistic differential equation. *Fractals* **2023**, *31*, 2340086. [CrossRef]
11. Cecconello, M.; Dorini, F.; Haeser, G. On fuzzy uncertainties on the logistic equation. *Fuzzy Sets Syst.* **2017**, *328*, 107–121. [CrossRef]
12. Ghosh, D.; Mandal, C. Clustering Based Parameter Estimation of Thyroid Hormone Pathway. *IEEE/ACM Trans. Comput. Biol. Bioinform.* **2022**, *19*, 343–354. [CrossRef] [PubMed]
13. Guan, Y.; Li, Y.; Ke, Z.; Peng, X.; Liu, R.; Li, Y.; Du, Y.P.; Liang, Z.P. Learning-Assisted Fast Determination of Regularization Parameter in Constrained Image Reconstruction. *IEEE Trans. Biomed. Eng.* **2024**, *71*, 2253–2264. [CrossRef]
14. Cui, J.; Chen, R.; Feng, F.; Wang, J.; Zhang, J.; Liu, W.; Ma, K.; Zhang, Q.J. Advanced Bayesian-Inspired Multilayer Effective Parameter Determination Method for Automated ANN Model Generation of Microwave Components. *IEEE Trans. Microw. Theory Tech.* **2024**, *72*, 4408–4420. [CrossRef]
15. He, P.; Liu, Y.; Zhang, B.; He, J. Determination of Parameters for Space Charge Simulation Based on Bipolar Charge Transport Model Under a Divergent Electric Field. *IEEE Trans. Dielectr. Electr. Insul.* **2024**, *31*, 1376–1385. [CrossRef]
16. Pardoe, I. *Applied Regression Modeling*; John Wiley & Sons: Hoboken, NJ, USA, 2020.
17. Jiang, L.; Liao, H. Mixed fuzzy least absolute regression analysis with quantitative and probabilistic linguistic information. *Fuzzy Sets Syst.* **2020**, *387*, 35–48. [CrossRef]
18. Ahmadini, A.A.H. A novel technique for parameter estimation in intuitionistic fuzzy logistic regression model. *Ain Shams Eng.* **2022**, *13*, 101518. [CrossRef]
19. Khasanzoda, N.; Zicmane, I.; Beryozkina, S.; Safaraliev, M.; Sultonov, S.; Kirgizov, A. Regression model for predicting the speed wind flows for energy needs based on fuzzy logic. *Renew. Energy* **2022**, *191*, 723–731. [CrossRef]
20. Zadeh, L. Fuzzy sets. *Inf. Control* **1965**, *8*, 338–353. [CrossRef]
21. Zadeh, L. The concept of a linguistic variable and its application to approximate reasoning-I. *Inf. Sci.* **1975**, *8*, 199–249. [CrossRef]
22. Zhang, T.; Qu, H.; Zhou, J. Asymptotically almost periodic synchronization in fuzzy competitive neural networks with Caputo-Fabrizio operator. *Fuzzy Sets Syst.* **2023**, *471*, 108676. [CrossRef]
23. Cazarez-Castro, N.R.; Aguilar, L.T.; Castillo, O. Fuzzy logic control with genetic membership function parameters optimization for the output regulation of a servomechanism with nonlinear backlash. *Expert Syst. Appl.* **2010**, *37*, 4368–4378. [CrossRef]
24. Cazarez-Castro, N.R.; Aguilar, L.T.; Castillo, O. Designing Type-1 and Type-2 Fuzzy Logic Controllers via Fuzzy Lyapunov Synthesis for nonsmooth mechanical systems. *Eng. Appl. Artif. Intell.* **2012**, *25*, 971–979. [CrossRef]

Article

Dynamics of a Fractional-Order Eco-Epidemiological Model with Two Disease Strains in a Predator Population Incorporating Harvesting

Moustafa El-Shahed [1,*] and Mahmoud Moustafa [2,*]

1. Department of Mathematics, College of Science, Qassim University, P.O. Box 6644, Buraydah 51452, Saudi Arabia
2. Department of Computer Science, College of Engineering and Information Technology, Onaizah Colleges, Unaizah 56447, Saudi Arabia
* Correspondence: m.elshahed@qu.edu.sa (M.E.-S.); m.mahmoud@oc.edu.sa (M.M.)

Abstract: In this paper, a fractional-order eco-epidemiological model with two disease strains in the predator population incorporating harvesting is formulated and analyzed. The model assumes that the population is divided into a prey population, a susceptible predator population, a predator population infected by the first disease, and a predator population infected by the second disease. A mathematical analysis and numerical simulations are performed to explain the dynamics and properties of the proposed fractional-order eco-epidemiological model. The positivity, boundedness, existence, and uniqueness of the solutions are examined. The basic reproduction number and some sufficient conditions for the existence of four equilibrium points are obtained. In addition, some sufficient conditions are proposed to ensure the local and global asymptotic stability of the equilibrium points. Theoretical results are illustrated through numerical simulations, which also highlight the effect of the fractional order.

Keywords: eco-epidemiological model; local stability; global stability; numerical simulations

MSC: 92D25; 26A33; 34D23

1. Introduction

The relationship between predators and their prey is a fundamental topic in mathematical ecology due to its widespread occurrence and ecological significance [1]. The interactions between prey and predators were studied for the first time by the famous mathematicians Lotka and Volterra [2]. After that, many predator–prey models have been established and studied by mathematicians and ecologists, for example [3–7].

Investigating the spread of infections within populations is a crucial area of mathematical biology, offering insights into predicting the impacts of such infections [8–10]. An eco-epidemiological model studies the dynamics of predator–prey interactions in the context of infectious diseases, which may affect either the prey population only [11,12], the predator population only [13–15], or both simultaneously [16,17].

Fractional-order differential equations are a generalized form of classical ordinary differential equations, extending their order to non-integer values [18]. Fractional-order models offer advantages over integer-order models, including memory effects and hereditary dynamics, which better capture complex system behaviors [19]. Models based on fractional-order differential equations may offer a more accurate representation of complex systems and elucidate the interactions between prey and predator species, particularly in

https://doi.org/10.3390/axioms14010053

the context of infectious diseases affecting the predator population [20]. Fractional-order derivatives have found widespread application across various scientific and engineering disciplines [21]. For a more comprehensive understanding of fractional-order differential equations, one can refer to [22–28] and the references contained therein. These references explore the application of the fractional order in ecological, epidemiological, and biological–economic models, emphasizing the analysis of stability, bifurcation, and memory effects to understand complex dynamic systems.

In this paper, a fractional-order eco-epidemiological model incorporating two disease strains within the predator population and the effects of harvesting is proposed and studied. The population is assumed to consist of prey, susceptible predators, predators infected by the first disease, and predators infected by the second disease. For instance, the black-footed ferret relies exclusively on Prairie dogs as its primary food source. This black-footed ferret population can be infected by the Sylvatic plague and the Canine distemper virus [29]. The positivity, boundedness, existence, and uniqueness of the solutions for the fractional-order model are examined. Additionally, the basic reproduction number is derived, along with sufficient conditions for the existence of four equilibrium points. The main contribution of this paper is establishing sufficient conditions to guarantee the local and global asymptotic stability of the equilibrium points in the proposed model. The theoretical findings are further illustrated through numerical simulations.

The structure of this paper is as follows. In the next section, the model formulation, positivity, boundedness, existence, and uniqueness are proposed. In Sections 3, the equilibrium points, basic reproduction number, local stability, and global stability of the proposed fractional-order model are investigated. Section 4 presents numerical simulations to illustrate the theoretical results obtained. Finally, the conclusions are provided in Section 5.

2. Model Formulation

Following [30], the eco-epidemiological model incorporating two disease strains affecting the predator population can be described as follows.

$$\begin{aligned}
\frac{dx}{dt} &= \hat{r}\left(1 - \frac{x}{\hat{k}}\right)x - \hat{a}xy, \quad x(0) = x_0, \\
\frac{dy}{dt} &= \hat{e}\hat{a}xy - \hat{\lambda}yz - \hat{\beta}yw + \hat{\gamma}z + \hat{\varphi}w - \hat{m}y, \quad y(0) = y_0, \\
\frac{dz}{dt} &= \hat{\lambda}yz - \hat{\gamma}z - \hat{d}z + \hat{\theta}w, \quad z(0) = z_0, \\
\frac{dw}{dt} &= \hat{\beta}yw - \hat{\varphi}w - \hat{v}w - \hat{\theta}w, \quad w(0) = w_0.
\end{aligned} \quad (1)$$

The model (1) categorizes the populations into four classes: the prey population $x(t)$, the susceptible predator population $y(t)$, the predator population infected with the first disease $z(t)$, and the predator population infected with the second disease $w(t)$. It is assumed that disease transmission occurs within the predator populations, while the susceptible predators feed on the prey. All parameters in model (1) are non-negative for $t \geq 0$ and are detailed in Table 1.

This paper seeks to investigate the dynamic properties of a generalization of the eco-epidemiological model described in (1) through the introduction of the Caputo fractional derivative of order q ($^cD^q$) and prey harvesting ($\hat{H}$) as follows.

2.2. Existence and Uniqueness

The existence and uniqueness of solutions for the fractional-order model (4) within the region $M \times (0, T]$, where where

$$M = \left\{(x, y, z, w) \in \mathbb{R}^4 : \max(|x|, |y|, |z|, |w|) \leq h\right\},$$

are investigated as follows:

Theorem 2. *For each $X_0 = (x_0, y_0, z_0, w_0) \in M$, there exists a unique solution $X(t) \in M$ of model (4) with the initial condition X_0, which is defined for all $t \geq 0$.*

Proof. Consider a mapping $L(X) = (L_1(X), L_2(X), L_3(X), L_4(X))$, where

$$
\begin{aligned}
L_1(X) &= r\left(1 - \frac{x}{k}\right)x - axy - Hx, \\
L_2(X) &= eaxy - \lambda yz - \beta yw + \gamma z + \varphi w - my, \\
L_3(X) &= \lambda yz - \eta z + \theta w, \\
L_4(X) &= \beta yw - \xi w,
\end{aligned}
\tag{6}
$$

For any $X, \bar{X} \in M$, it follows from (6) that

$$
\begin{aligned}
\|L(X) - L(\bar{X})\| &= |L_1(X) - L_1(\bar{X})| + |L_2(X) - L_2(\bar{X})| + |L_3(X) - L_3(\bar{X})| + |L_4(X) - L_4(\bar{X})| \\
&= \left| r\left(1 - \frac{x}{k}\right)x - axy - Hx - r\left(1 - \frac{\bar{x}}{k}\right)\bar{x} + a\bar{x}\bar{y} + H\bar{x} \right| \\
&\quad + |eaxy - \lambda yz - \beta yw + \gamma z + \varphi w - my - ea\bar{x}\bar{y} + \lambda \bar{y}\bar{z} + \beta \bar{y}\bar{w} - \gamma \bar{z} - \varphi \bar{w} + m\bar{y}| \\
&\quad + |\lambda yz - \eta z + \theta w - \lambda \bar{y}\bar{z} + \eta \bar{z} - \theta \bar{w}| + |\beta yw - \xi w - \beta \bar{y}\bar{w} + \xi \bar{w}| \\
&\leq r|x - \bar{x}| + \frac{r}{k}|x - \bar{x}||x + \bar{x}| + a(1+e)|xy - \bar{x}y + \bar{x}y - \bar{x}\bar{y}| \\
&\quad + H|x - \bar{x}| + 2\lambda|yz - \bar{y}z + \bar{y}z - \bar{y}\bar{z}| \\
&\quad + 2\beta|yw - \bar{y}w + \bar{y}w - \bar{y}\bar{w}| + \gamma|z - \bar{z}| + \varphi|w - \bar{w}| \\
&\quad + m|y - \bar{y}| + \eta|z - \bar{z}| + \theta|w - \bar{w}| + \xi|w - \bar{w}| \\
&\leq r|x - \bar{x}| + \frac{2rh}{k}|x - \bar{x}| + a(1+e)h|x - \bar{x}| \\
&\quad + a(1+e)h|y - \bar{y}| + H|x - \bar{x}| + 2\lambda h|y - \bar{y}| + 2\lambda h|z - \bar{z}| \\
&\quad + 2\beta h|y - \bar{y}| + 2\beta h|w - \bar{w}| + \gamma|z - \bar{z}| + \varphi|w - \bar{w}| \\
&\quad + m|y - \bar{y}| + \eta|z - \bar{z}| + \theta|w - \bar{w}| + \xi|w - \bar{w}| \\
&\leq \left(r + \frac{2rh}{k} + a(1+e)h + H\right)|x - \bar{x}| \\
&\quad + (a(1+e)h + 2\lambda h + 2\beta h + m)|y - \bar{y}| \\
&\quad + (2\lambda h + \gamma + \eta)|z - \bar{z}| \\
&\quad + (2\beta h + \varphi + \theta + \xi)|w - \bar{w}| \\
&\leq U\|X - \bar{X}\|,
\end{aligned}
$$

where

$$U = \max\left\{r + \frac{2rh}{k} + a(1+e)h + H,\ a(1+e)h + 2\lambda h + 2\beta h + m,\ 2\lambda h + \gamma + \eta,\ 2\beta h + \varphi + \theta + \xi\right\}.$$

Thus, $L(X)$ satisfies the Lipschitz condition, proving the existence and uniqueness of solutions for model (4) under the given initial conditions. □

3. Model Analysis

This section investigates the equilibrium points, basic reproduction number, local stability, and global stability of the fractional-order eco-epidemiological model (4).

3.1. Equilibrium Points

This subsection and the next will utilize the basic reproduction number ($\Re_0$) of model (4) to determine the existence and stability of its equilibrium points. The basic reproduction number ($\Re_0$) can be obtained by using the next-generation method [34]. One can rewrite the fractional-order model (4) as follows

$$\begin{aligned} {}^cD^q w(t) &= \beta yw - \zeta w, \\ {}^cD^q z(t) &= \lambda yz - \eta z + \theta w, \\ {}^cD^q y(t) &= eaxy - \lambda yz - \beta yw + \gamma z + \varphi w - my, \\ {}^cD^q x(t) &= r\left(1 - \frac{x}{k}\right)x - axy - Hx, \end{aligned} \quad (7)$$

where $\zeta = \varphi + v + \theta$ and $\eta = \gamma + d$. The model (7) can subsequently be expressed as follows:

$$D^q X(t) = f(X) - v(X),$$

where

$$f(X) = \begin{bmatrix} f_1 \\ f_2 \\ f_3 \\ f_4 \end{bmatrix} = \begin{bmatrix} \beta yw \\ \lambda yz \\ eaxy \\ 0 \end{bmatrix}, \quad v(X) = \begin{bmatrix} v_1 \\ v_2 \\ v_3 \\ v_4 \end{bmatrix} = \begin{bmatrix} \zeta w \\ \eta z - \theta w \\ \lambda yz + \beta yw - \gamma z - \varphi w + my \\ -r\left(1 - \frac{x}{k}\right)x + axy + Hx \end{bmatrix}.$$

The matrices $F(X)$ and $V(X)$ are defined as

$$F(X) = \begin{bmatrix} \frac{\partial f_1}{\partial w} & \frac{\partial f_1}{\partial z} & \frac{\partial f_1}{\partial y} & \frac{\partial f_1}{\partial x} \\ \frac{\partial f_2}{\partial w} & \frac{\partial f_2}{\partial z} & \frac{\partial f_2}{\partial y} & \frac{\partial f_2}{\partial x} \\ \frac{\partial f_3}{\partial w} & \frac{\partial f_3}{\partial z} & \frac{\partial f_3}{\partial y} & \frac{\partial f_3}{\partial x} \\ \frac{\partial f_4}{\partial w} & \frac{\partial f_4}{\partial z} & \frac{\partial f_4}{\partial y} & \frac{\partial f_4}{\partial x} \end{bmatrix}, \quad V(X) = \begin{bmatrix} \frac{\partial v_1}{\partial w} & \frac{\partial v_1}{\partial z} & \frac{\partial v_1}{\partial y} & \frac{\partial v_1}{\partial x} \\ \frac{\partial v_2}{\partial w} & \frac{\partial v_2}{\partial z} & \frac{\partial v_2}{\partial y} & \frac{\partial v_2}{\partial x} \\ \frac{\partial v_3}{\partial w} & \frac{\partial v_3}{\partial z} & \frac{\partial v_3}{\partial y} & \frac{\partial v_3}{\partial x} \\ \frac{\partial v_4}{\partial w} & \frac{\partial v_4}{\partial z} & \frac{\partial v_4}{\partial y} & \frac{\partial v_4}{\partial x} \end{bmatrix}.$$

Thus,

$$F(X) = \begin{bmatrix} \beta y & 0 & \beta w & 0 \\ 0 & \lambda y & \lambda z & 0 \\ 0 & 0 & aex & aey \\ 0 & 0 & 0 & 0 \end{bmatrix},$$

$$V(X) = \begin{bmatrix} \zeta & 0 & 0 & 0 \\ -\theta & \eta & 0 & 0 \\ \beta y - \varphi & \lambda y - \gamma & \beta w + \lambda z + m & 0 \\ 0 & 0 & ax & r\left(\frac{2x}{k} - 1\right) + ay + H \end{bmatrix}.$$

To obtain the eigenvalues of $F \cdot V^{-1}$, at equilibrium point $E_1\left(\frac{k(r-H)}{r}, 0, 0, 0\right)$, the equation

$$\left|F \cdot V^{-1} - \mu I\right| = 0,$$

can be solved. Based on Theorem 2 in [34], the basic reproduction number of Model 2 is given as $\Re_0 = \frac{ae(r-H)k}{rm}$. Additionally, the threshold parameters will be utilized to establish the conditions for the existence and stability of the equilibrium points of model (4):

$$\mathfrak{R}_2 = \frac{\beta(ae(r-H)k - rm)}{ea^2k\xi}, \quad \mathfrak{R}_{22} = \frac{\lambda(ae(r-H)k - rm)}{ea^2k\eta}, \quad \mathfrak{R}_3 = \frac{\beta\eta}{\xi\lambda}.$$

It is to be noted that the basic reproduction number ($\mathfrak{R}_0$) and the threshold parameters ($\mathfrak{R}_2$ and $\mathfrak{R}_{22}$) depend on the prey harvesting (H). This means that the prey harvesting (H) has a crucial effect on the existence and stability conditions of equilibrium points of model (4).

The fractional-order eco-epidemiological model (4) has four equilibrium points:

1. $E_0 = (0,0,0,0)$, which always exists.
2. $E_1 = \left(\frac{k}{r}(r-H), 0, 0, 0\right)$, which exists if $r > H$.
3. $E_2 = (x_2, y_2, 0, 0)$ where

$$x_2 = \frac{m}{ae}, \quad y_2 = \frac{ae(r-H)k - rm}{ea^2k} = \frac{rm}{ea^2k}(\mathfrak{R}_0 - 1).$$

Therefore, E_2 exists if $\mathfrak{R}_0 > 1$.

4. $E_3 = (x_3, y_3, z_3, 0)$ where

$$x_3 = \frac{k(r-H)}{r} - \frac{a\eta k}{r\lambda} = x_1 - \frac{a\eta k}{r\lambda}, \quad y_3 = \frac{\eta}{\lambda}, \quad z_3 = \frac{(\mathfrak{R}_{22} - 1)eka^2\eta^2}{r(\eta - \gamma)\lambda^2}.$$

Then, E_3 exists if $x_1 > \frac{a\eta k}{r\lambda}$ and $\mathfrak{R}_{22} > 1$.

5. $E_4 = (x_4, y_4, z_4, w_4)$ where

$$x_4 = \frac{k(\beta(r-H) - a\xi)}{r\beta}, \quad y_4 = \frac{\xi}{\beta}, \quad z_4 = \frac{ea^2k\xi^2(\mathfrak{R}_2 - 1)}{C_1}, \quad w_4 = \frac{ea^2k\lambda\xi^3}{\beta C_1}(\mathfrak{R}_2 - 1)(\mathfrak{R}_3 - 1),$$

where $C_1 = r\beta(\lambda\xi(\theta + \varphi - \xi) + \beta(\xi\eta - \gamma\theta - \eta\varphi))$. Therefore E_4 exists if $\beta > \frac{a\xi}{r-H}$, $\mathfrak{R}_2 > 1$, $\mathfrak{R}_3 > 1$ and $C_1 > 0$.

3.2. Local Stability Analysis

In the following, the asymptotic stability of equilibrium points of model (4) is studied. The Jacobian matrix ($J(x, y, z, w)$) of model (4) is as follows:

$$J(x,y,z,w) = \begin{pmatrix} r - \frac{2rx}{k} - ay - H & -ax & 0 & 0 \\ aey & aex - \lambda z - \beta w - m & \gamma - \lambda y & \varphi - \beta y \\ 0 & \lambda z & \lambda y - \eta & \theta \\ 0 & \beta w & 0 & \beta y - \xi \end{pmatrix}. \quad (8)$$

The stability analysis of the equilibrium point E_0 is not considered, as this state signifies the extinction of all populations. The E_0 is unstable.

Lemma 1. *If $\mathfrak{R}_0 < 1$, then E_1 is locally asymptotically stable.*

Proof. The $J(E_1)$ is

$$J(E_1) = \begin{pmatrix} H - r & \frac{a(H-r)k}{r} & 0 & 0 \\ 0 & (\mathfrak{R}_0 - 1)m & \gamma & \varphi \\ 0 & 0 & -\eta & \theta \\ 0 & 0 & 0 & -\xi \end{pmatrix}. \quad (9)$$

The eigenvalues of $J(E_1)$ are $\mu_1 = H - r$, $\mu_2 = (\mathfrak{R}_0 - 1)m$, $\mu_3 = -\xi$ and $\mu_4 = -\eta$. Thus $|\arg(\mu_{1,3,4})| = \pi > \frac{q\pi}{2}$. If $\mathfrak{R}_0 < 1$, then $|\arg(\mu_2)| = \pi > \frac{q\pi}{2}$ for all $q \in (0,1)$. As demonstrated in [35,36], the proof is thus complete. □

Lemma 2. *If $y_2 < \min\left\{\frac{\xi}{\beta}, \frac{\eta}{\lambda}\right\}$, then E_2 is locally asymptotically stable.*

Proof. The $J(E_2)$ is

$$J(E_2) = \begin{pmatrix} -\frac{rx_2}{k} & -ax_2 & 0 & 0 \\ aey_2 & 0 & \gamma - \lambda y_2 & \varphi - \beta y_2 \\ 0 & 0 & \lambda y_2 - \eta & \theta \\ 0 & 0 & 0 & \beta y_2 - \xi \end{pmatrix}. \tag{10}$$

The eigenvalues of $J(E_2)$ are $\mu_1 = \beta y_2 - \xi$, $\mu_2 = \lambda y_2 - \eta$, and $\mu_{3,4}$ are the solutions of:

$$\mu^2 + \frac{rx_2}{k}\mu + ea^2 x_2 y_2 = 0, \tag{11}$$

since $\frac{rx_2}{k} > 0$ and $ea^2 x_2 y_2 > 0$, the eigenvalues of Equation (11), exhibit negative real parts. If $y_2 < \min\left\{\frac{\xi}{\beta}, \frac{\eta}{\lambda}\right\}$, then $|\arg(\mu_{1,2})| = \pi > \frac{q\pi}{2}$ for all $q \in (0,1)$. As demonstrated in [35,36], the proof is thus complete. □

Lemma 3. *If $\frac{\gamma}{\lambda} < y_3 < \frac{\xi}{\beta}$, then E_3 is locally asymptotically stable.*

Proof. The $J(E_3)$ is

$$J(E_3) = \begin{pmatrix} -\frac{rx_3}{k} & -ax_3 & 0 & 0 \\ aey_3 & -\frac{\gamma z_3}{y_3} & \gamma - \lambda y_3 & \varphi - \beta y_3 \\ 0 & \lambda z_3 & 0 & \theta \\ 0 & 0 & 0 & \beta y_3 - \xi \end{pmatrix}.$$

The eigenvalues of $J(E_3)$ are $\mu_1 = \beta y_3 - \xi$, while the other three eigenvalues $\mu_{2,3,4}$ are the solutions of

$$\mu^3 + B_1 \mu^2 + B_2 \mu + B_3 = 0, \tag{12}$$

where

$$B_1 = \frac{rx_3}{k} + \frac{\gamma z_3}{y_3},$$

$$B_2 = \left(\frac{r\gamma z_3}{ky_3} + ea^2 y_3\right)x_3 + \lambda(\lambda y_3 - \gamma)z_3,$$

$$B_3 = \frac{1}{k}(r\lambda(\lambda y_3 - \gamma)x_3 z_3).$$

It is obvious that $B_1 > 0$, $B_2 > 0$, $B_3 > 0$ and $B_1 B_2 > B_3$ as long as $\lambda y_3 > \gamma$. By applying the Routh–Hurwitz criterion, it is established that all solutions of Equation (12) have negative real parts. Consequently, the equilibrium point E_3 is locally asymptotically stable when $\frac{\gamma}{\lambda} < y_3 < \frac{\xi}{\beta}$. □

The stability of the equilibrium point E_4 is now investigated. The $J(E_4)$ is

$$J(E_4) = \begin{pmatrix} -\frac{rx_4}{k} & -ax_4 & 0 & 0 \\ aey_4 & -\frac{\gamma z_4 + \varphi w_4}{y_4} & \gamma - \lambda y_4 & \varphi - \beta y_4 \\ 0 & \lambda z_4 & -\frac{\theta w_4}{z_4} & \theta \\ 0 & \beta w_4 & 0 & 0 \end{pmatrix}.$$

The eigenvalues of $J(E_4)$ are the solutions of

$$\mu^4 + A_1 \mu^3 + A_2 \mu^2 + A_3 \mu + A_4 = 0, \tag{13}$$

where

$$A_1 = \frac{rx_4}{k} + \frac{C_2}{y_4} + \frac{\theta w_4}{z_4},$$

$$A_2 = \frac{\theta(kC_2 + rx_4y_4)w_4}{ky_4z_4} + \frac{rC_2x_4}{ky_4} + ea^2x_4y_4 - \lambda C_3z_4 - \beta C_4w_4,$$

$$A_3 = \frac{1}{ky_4z_4}(r\theta C_2w_4x_4 + y_4(k\theta w_4(ea^2x_4y_4 - \beta C_4w_4) - \beta w_4(k\theta C_3 + rC_4x_4)z_4 - r\lambda C_3x_4z_4^2)),$$

$$A_4 = -\frac{r\beta\theta(C_3z_4 + C_4w_4)x_4w_4}{kz_4},$$

$$C_2 = \gamma z_4 + \varphi w_4, \; C_3 = \gamma - \lambda y_4, \; C_4 = \varphi - \beta y_4.$$

The conditions for stability at E_4 can be derived using the proposition outlined in [37].

3.3. Global Stability Analysis

The global asymptotic stability of all four equilibrium points of the fractional-order model (4) is investigated as follows.

Theorem 3. *The equilibrium point E_1 is globally asymptotically stable if $\frac{ak(r-H)}{rm} < 1$.*

Proof. A suitable positive definite Lyapunov function is considered as follows:

$$V = x - x_1 - x_1 \ln\left(\frac{x}{x_1}\right) + y + z + w.$$

By calculating the q-order derivative of V throughout the solution of (4) and applying Lemma 3.1 in [38],

$$^cD^qV \leq (x - x_1)\left(r - \frac{rx}{k} - ay - H\right) + eaxy - my - dz - vw$$

$$\leq (x - x_1)\left(\frac{rx_1}{k} - \frac{rx}{k} - ay\right) + eaxy - my - dz - vw$$

$$\leq -\frac{r}{k}(x - x_1)^2 + a(e-1)xy + (ax_1 - m)y - dz - vw.$$

Thus, $^cD^qV \leq 0$ if $\frac{ax_1}{m} < 1$ which is equivalent to $\frac{ak(r-H)}{rm} < 1$. By applying Lemma 4.6 in [39], the equilibrium point E_1 is proven to be globally asymptotically stable. □

Theorem 4. *The equilibrium point E_2 is globally asymptotically stable if $r\lambda k < 4\sigma\gamma$.*

Proof. A suitable positive definite Lyapunov function is considered as follows:

$$V = C_5\left(x - x_2 - x_2\ln\left(\frac{x}{x_2}\right)\right) + y - y_2 - y_2\ln\left(\frac{y}{y_2}\right) + z + w.$$

By calculating the q-order derivative of V throughout the solution of (4) and applying Lemma 3.1 in [38].

$$^cD^qV \leq C_5(x-x_2)\left(r - \frac{rx}{k} - ay - H\right)$$
$$+ (y-y_2)(aex - \lambda z - m) + \left(\frac{y-y_2}{y}\right)(\gamma z - \beta yw + \varphi w)$$
$$+ \lambda yz - \gamma z - dz + \theta w + \beta yw - \varphi w - vw - \theta w$$
$$\leq -\frac{rC_5}{k}(x-x_2)^2 - aC_5(x-x_2)(y-y_2)$$
$$+ ae(x-x_2)(y-y_2) + y_2\left(\lambda - \frac{\gamma}{y}\right)z$$
$$+ \left(-\frac{\varphi y_2}{y} + \beta y_2 - v\right)w - dz$$
$$\leq -\frac{rC_5}{k}(x-x_2)^2 + a(e-C_5)(x-x_2)(y-y_2)$$
$$+ y_2\left(\lambda - \frac{\gamma}{y_{max}}\right)z.$$

Suppose $C_5 = e$. Thus, $^cD^q \leq 0$ when $\lambda < \frac{\gamma}{y_{max}}$ which is equivalent to $r\lambda k < 4\sigma\gamma$. Hence, the proof is established. □

Theorem 5. *The equilibrium point E_3 is globally asymptotically stable if $aex_3 < \lambda z_3 + m$, $\lambda < \frac{\gamma}{y_{max}} + \frac{d}{y_3}$, $\beta y_3 < v$, and $my_3 + \gamma z_3 + dz_3 < aex_3y_3$.*

Proof. A suitable positive definite Lyapunov function is considered as follows:

$$V = e\left(x - x_3 - x_3\ln\left(\frac{x}{x_3}\right)\right) + y - y_3 - y_3\ln\left(\frac{y}{y_3}\right) + z - z_3 - z_3\ln\left(\frac{z}{z_3}\right) + w.$$

By calculating the q-order derivative of V throughout the solution of (4) and applying Lemma 3.1 in [38],

$$^cD^qV \leq e(x-x_3)\left(r - \frac{rx}{k} - ay - H\right) + \left(1 - \frac{y_3}{y}\right)(aexy - \lambda yz - \beta yw + \gamma z + \varphi w - my)$$
$$+ \left(1 - \frac{z_3}{z}\right)(\lambda yz - \gamma z - dz + \theta w) + \beta yw - \varphi w - vw - \theta w$$
$$\leq -\frac{re}{k}(x-x_3)^2 + (aex_3 - \lambda z_3 - m)y + d(z_3 - z)$$
$$+ \left(\lambda y_3 - \frac{\gamma y_3}{y}\right)z + (\beta y_3 - v)w + (my_3 + \gamma z_3 - aex_3y_3)$$
$$\leq -\frac{re}{k}(x-x_3)^2 + (aex_3 - \lambda z_3 - m)y$$
$$+ \left(\lambda y_3 - \frac{\gamma y_3}{y_{max}} - d\right)z + (\beta y_3 - v)w + (my_3 + \gamma z_3 + dz_3 - aex_3y_3).$$

Thus, $^cD^q \leq 0$ when $aex_3 < \lambda z_3 + m$, $\lambda < \frac{\gamma}{y_{max}} + \frac{d}{y_3}$, $\beta y_3 < v$, and $my_3 + \gamma z_3 + dz_3 < aex_3y_3$. Consequently, the theorem is proven. □

Theorem 6. *The equilibrium point E_4 is globally asymptotically stable if $aex_4 < \lambda z_4 + \beta w_4 + m$, $\lambda < \frac{\gamma}{y_{max}} + \frac{d}{y_4}$, $\beta y_4 < \frac{\varphi y_4}{y_{max}} + \frac{\theta z_4}{z_{max}} + v$, and $my_4 + \gamma z_4 + \xi w_4 + dz_4 < aex_4y_4$.*

Proof. A suitable positive definite Lyapunov function is considered as follows:

$$V = e\left(x - x_4 - x_4\ln\left(\frac{x}{x_4}\right)\right) + y - y_4 - y_4\ln\left(\frac{y}{y_4}\right) + z - z_4 - z_4\ln\left(\frac{z}{z_4}\right) + w - w_4 - w_4\ln\left(\frac{w}{w_4}\right).$$

By calculating the q-order derivative of V throughout the solution of (4) and applying Lemma 3.1 in [38],

$$^cD^qV \leq e(x-x_4)\left(r - \frac{rx}{k} - ay - H\right) + \left(1 - \frac{y_4}{y}\right)(aexy - \lambda yz - \beta yw + \gamma z + \varphi w - my)$$
$$+ \left(1 - \frac{z_4}{z}\right)(\lambda yz - \gamma z - dz + \theta w) + (w - w_4)(\beta y - \varphi - v - \theta)$$
$$\leq -\frac{re}{k}(x-x_4)^2 + (aex_4 - \lambda z_4 - \beta w_4 - m)y$$
$$+ \left(\lambda y_4 - \frac{\gamma y_4}{y}\right)z + \left(\beta y_4 - v - \frac{\varphi y_4}{y} - \frac{\theta z_4}{z}\right)w$$
$$+ (my_4 + \gamma z_4 + \zeta w_4 - aex_4 y_4) + d(z_4 - z)$$
$$\leq -\frac{re}{k}(x-x_4)^2 + (aex_4 - \lambda z_4 - \beta w_4 - m)y$$
$$+ \left(\lambda y_4 - \frac{\gamma y_4}{y_{max}} - d\right)z + \left(\beta y_4 - v - \frac{\varphi y_4}{y_{max}} - \frac{\theta z_4}{z_{max}}\right)w$$
$$+ (my_4 + \gamma z_4 + \zeta w_4 + dz_4 - aex_4 y_4).$$

Thus, $^cD^qV(x,y,z) \leq 0$, when $aex_4 < \lambda z_4 + \beta w_4 + m$, $\lambda < \frac{\gamma}{y_{max}} + \frac{d}{y_4}$, $\beta y_4 < \frac{\varphi y_4}{y_{max}} + \frac{\theta z_4}{z_{max}} + v$ and $my_4 + \gamma z_4 + \zeta w_4 + dz_4 < aex_4 y_4$. By applying Lemma 4.6 in [39], the equilibrium point E_4 is proven to be globally asymptotically stable. □

4. Numerical Simulations

This section presents numerical simulations performed using the numerical method described in [40,41]. The numerical simulations are conducted to illustrate the theoretical findings regarding the fractional order (q) and stability of model (4). The parameter values used in the simulations are detailed in Table 2, and most of them are given in [30].

Table 2. Parameter values for model (4).

Case	r	m	e	a	k	γ	φ	β	λ	d	v	H	θ	Figures
1	1	0.5	0.07	0.02	100	0.9	0.3	0.2	0.4	0.25	0.4	0.01	0.01	Figure 1
2	1	0.5	0.7	0.5	1000	0.25	0.47	0.6	0.48	0.39	0.33	0.35	0.1	Figure 2
3	1	0.05	0.7	0.2	5000	0.9	0.3	0.2	0.4	0.25	0.4	0.01	0.01	Figure 3
4	1	0.05	0.6	0.5	1000	0.25	0.3	0.6	0.48	0.39	0.33	0.1	0.1	Figure 4

In case 1 of Table 2, the fractional-order model (4) shows the equilibrium point $E_1 = (99,0,0,0)$, where all populations are healthy, and no infections exist. In this case, $\Re_0 = 0.2772 < 1$, which indicates that E_1 is locally asymptotically stable. This coincides with Lemma 1 and is indicated in Figure 1. Figure 1 demonstrates that the populations remain stable across various values of the fractional order (q), with the solutions reaching the equilibrium point $E_1 = (99,0,0,0)$.

In case 2 of Table 2, the fractional-order model (4) shows the equilibrium point $E_2 = (1.428, 1.297, 0, 0)$. In this case, $y_2 = 1.29714 < \min\left\{\frac{\zeta}{\beta} = 1.5, \frac{\eta}{\lambda} = 1.3\right\}$, which means that E_2 is locally asymptotically stable. This coincides with the result of Lemma 2 and is shown in Figure 2. It can be observed from Figure 2 that the oscillation of fractional-order model (4) decreases with decreasing the value of the fractional order (q). Figure 2 illustrates that the populations maintain stability for various values of the fractional order $(q \in (0,1))$, with the solutions reaching the equilibrium point $E_2 = (1.428, 1.297, 0, 0)$.

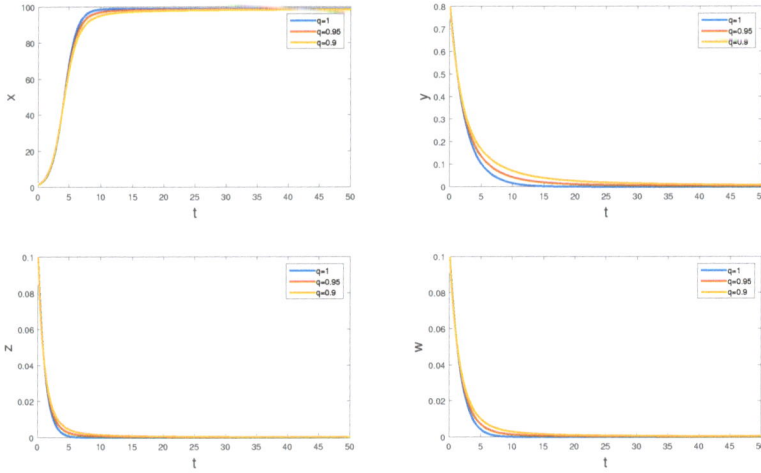

Figure 1. The local asymptotic stability of E_1 for various values of the fractional order (q).

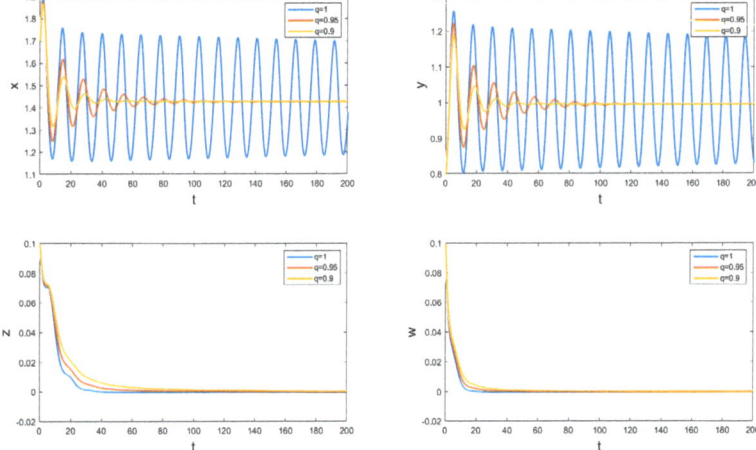

Figure 2. The local asymptotic stability of E_2 for various values of the fractional order (q).

In case 3 of Table 2, the fractional-order model (4) shows the equilibrium point $E_3 = (2075, 2.875, 3340.175, 0)$. In this case, $\frac{\gamma}{\lambda} = 2.25 < y_3 = 2.875 < \frac{\xi}{\beta} = 3.55$, which indicates that E_3 is locally asymptotically stable. This coincides with the result of Lemma 3 and is indicated in Figure 3. In order to verify the Routh–Hurwitz criteria of Lemma 3, one has $B_1 = 1046.04 > 0$, $B_2 = 934.987 > 0$, $B_3 = 138.617 > 0$ and $B_1 B_2 - B_3 = 977891 > 0$. Therefore, the fractional-order model (4) exhibits local asymptotic stability around E_3, as demonstrated in Figure 3. Figure 3 shows that the populations remain stable for different values of fractional order $(q \in (0,1))$, with the solutions reaching the equilibrium point $E_3 = (2075, 2.875, 3340.175, 0)$.

In case 4 of Table 2 the fractional-order model (4) shows the coexistence equilibrium point $E_4 = (291.667, 1.217, 185.104, 103.658)$, where all the populations in the ecosystem coexist: the prey (x), susceptible predator (y), predator infected by the first disease (z), and predator infected by the second disease (w) reach constant levels over time. In this case, the E_4 is locally asymptotically stable as shown in Figure 4. This means that the two infectious diseases will persist in the predator population. Figure 4 indicates that the populations remain stable for different values of fractional order ($q \in (0,1)$), with the solutions reaching the equilibrium point $E_4 = (291.667, 1.217, 185.104, 103.658)$. It is to be noted that the integer-order model (1) given in [30] cannot be sustained at a stable coexistence equilibrium level. However, the newly proposed fractional-order model (4) can be sustained at the stable coexistence equilibrium level as illustrated in Figure 4 and coincides with Theorem 6. Therefore, the fractional order has a stabilization effect.

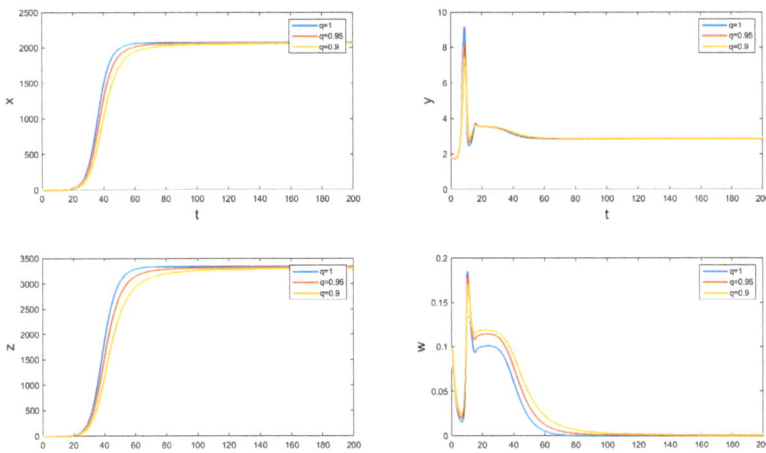

Figure 3. The local asymptotic stability of E_3 for various values of the fractional order (q).

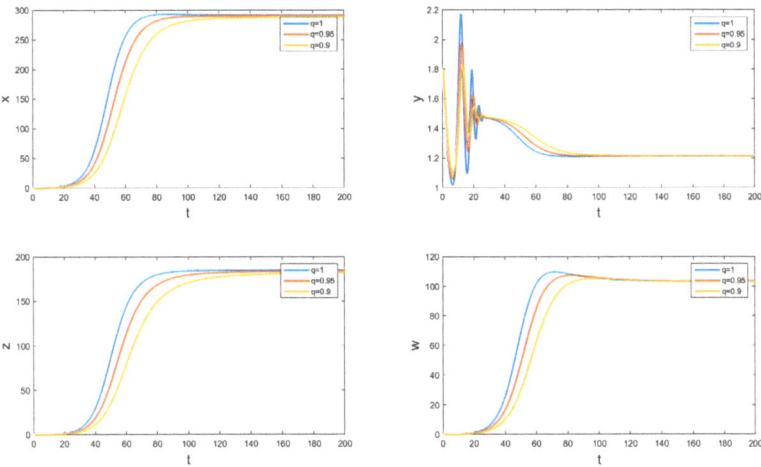

Figure 4. The local asymptotic stability of E_4 for various values of the fractional order (q).

Figure 5 shows the 3D plot of the basic reproduction number $\mathcal{R}_0$ when the predation rate of susceptible predator (a) and prey harvesting (H) varies. It is observed that as the predation rate of susceptible predator (a) increases, $\mathcal{R}_0$ will increase and cross the threshold $\mathcal{R}_0 = 1$, thus leading to the outbreak of the diseases. Moreover, when the prey harvesting (H) increases, $\mathcal{R}_0$ will increase. Therefore, one can control the reproduction $\mathcal{R}_0$ by reducing the predation rate of susceptible predator (a) and prey harvesting (H).

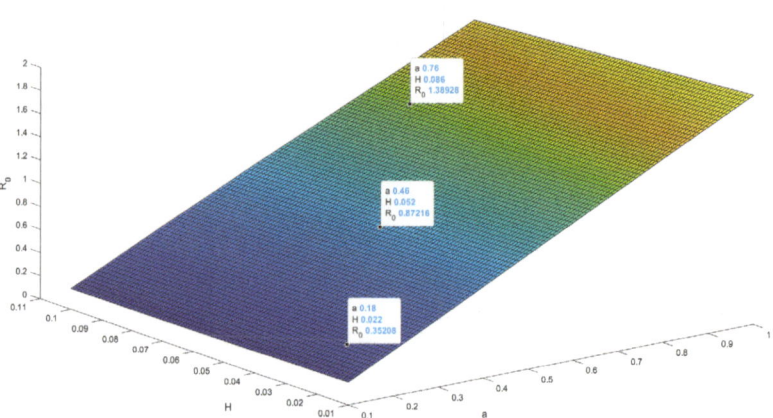

Figure 5. The 3D plot of the basic reproduction number $\mathfrak{R}_0$ when the predation rate of susceptible predator (a) and prey harvesting (H) varies.

5. Conclusions

This paper proposed and analyzed a fractional-order eco-epidemiological model incorporating two disease strains in the predator population and harvesting. The model categorizes the populations into four groups: prey (x), susceptible predators (y), predators infected by the first disease (z), and predators infected by the second disease (w). The proposed model (4) has been analyzed to investigate its dynamical behavior. The model's dynamics, including positivity, boundedness, and the existence and uniqueness of solutions, have been studied. The proposed eco-epidemiological model exhibits four non-negative equilibrium points, and the threshold parameters have been utilized to determine equilibrium existence and stability conditions. Furthermore, sufficient conditions for the locally asymptotic stability of the four equilibrium points have been derived. The global properties of the equilibrium points E_1, E_2, E_3 and E_4 have been investigated by constructing suitable Lyapunov functions. Numerical simulations have been performed to illustrate the theoretical findings, demonstrating the influence of the fractional order (q) on the stability of the equilibrium points. It has been shown that the populations remain stable for different values of fractional order ($q \in (0,1)$), though the solutions reach the obtained equilibrium points. It has been observed that the integer-order model (1) given in [30] cannot be sustained at a stable coexistence equilibrium level. However, it has been shown that the fractional-order model (4) can be sustained at the stable coexistence equilibrium level. Therefore, the fractional order has a stabilization effect. Future research will explore the inclusion of time delays in the system and analyze their potential effect.

Author Contributions: Methodology, M.E.-S.; Software, M.M.; Validation, M.E.-S.; Investigation, M.M.; Writing—original draft, M.M.; Writing—review & editing, M.E.-S.; Visualization, M.E.-S. and M.M. All authors have read and agreed to the published version of the manuscript.

Funding: This research received no external funding.

Data Availability Statement: No new data were created or analyzed in this study. Data sharing is not applicable to this article.

Acknowledgments: The researchers would like to thank the Deanship of Scientific Research, Qassim University, for funding the publication of this paper.

Conflicts of Interest: The authors declare no conflicts of interest.

References

1. Wang, Z.; Xie, Y.; Lu, J.; Li, Y. Stability and bifurcation of a delayed generalized fractional-order prey–predator model with interspecific competition. *Appl. Math. Comput.* **2019**, *347*, 360–369. [CrossRef]
2. Boccara, N. *Modeling Complex Systems*; Springer Science and Business Media: Berlin/Heidelberg, Germany, 2010.
3. Khajanchi, S. Modeling the dynamics of stage-structure predator-prey system with Monod–Haldane type response function. *Appl. Math. Comput.* **2017**, *302*, 122–143. [CrossRef]
4. Nosrati, K.; Shafiee, M. Dynamic analysis of fractional-order singular Holling type-II predator–prey system. *Appl. Math. Comput.* **2017**, *313*, 159–179. [CrossRef]
5. Zhang, F.; Chen, Y.; Li, J. Dynamical analysis of a stage-structured predator-prey model with cannibalism. *Math. Biosci.* **2019**, *307*, 33–41. [CrossRef] [PubMed]
6. Das, M.; Samanta, G.P. A prey-predator fractional order model with fear effect and group defense. *Int. J. Dyn. Control* **2021**, *9*, 334–349. [CrossRef]
7. Blackmore, D.; Chen, J.; Perez, J.; Savescu, M. Dynamical properties of discrete Lotka–Volterra equations. *Chaos Solitons Fractals* **2001**, *12*, 2553–2568. [CrossRef]
8. Biswas, S.; Sasmal, S.K.; Samanta, S.; Saifuddin, M.; Pal, N.; Chattopadhyay, J. Optimal harvesting and complex dynamics in a delayed eco-epidemiological model with weak Allee effects. *Nonlinear Dyn.* **2017**, *87*, 1553–1573. [CrossRef]
9. Samui, P.; Mondal, J.; Khajanchi, S. A mathematical model for COVID-19 transmission dynamics with a case study of India. *Chaos Solitons Fractals* **2020**, *140*, 110173. [CrossRef]
10. Gurski, K.; Peace, A.; Prosper, O.; Stepien, T.; Teboh-Ewungkem, M.I. Mathematicians Navigating Parenthood: Lessons Learned, Methodologies, and Useful Solutions That Were Beneficial During the COVID-19 Pandemic. *Not. Am. Math. Soc.* **2023**, *69*, 1918–1922.
11. Moustafa, M.; Mohd, M.H.; Ismail, A.I.; Abdullah, F.A. Dynamical analysis of a fractional order eco-epidemiological model with nonlinear incidence rate and prey refuge. *J. Appl. Math. Comput.* **2021**, *65*, 623–650. [CrossRef]
12. Moustafa, M.; Mohd, M.H.; Ismail, A.I.; Abdullah, F.A. Dynamical analysis of a fractional-order eco-epidemiological model with disease in prey population. *Adv. Differ. Equ.* **2020**, *2020*, 48. [CrossRef]
13. Bulai, I.M.; Hilker, F.M. Eco-epidemiological interactions with predator interference and infection. *Theor. Popul. Biol.* **2019**, *130*, 191–202. [CrossRef] [PubMed]
14. Moustafa, M.; Abdullah, F.A.; Shafie, S.; Ismail, Z. Dynamical behavior of a fractional-order Hantavirus infection model incorporating harvesting. *Alex. Eng. J.* **2022**, *61*, 11301–11312. [CrossRef]
15. Juneja, N.; Agnihotri, K. Global Stability of Harvested Prey–Predator Model with Infection in Predator Species. In *Information and Decision Sciences*; Springer: Berlin/Heidelberg, Germany, 2018; pp. 559–568.
16. Agnihotri, K.; Juneja, N. An eco-epidemic model with disease in both prey and predator. *IJAEEE* **2015**, *4*, 50–54.
17. Gao, X.; Pan, Q.; He, M.; Kang, Y. A predator–prey model with diseases in both prey and predator. *Phys. A Stat. Mech. Its Appl.* **2013**, *392*, 5898–5906. [CrossRef]
18. Kilbas, A.A.; Srivastava, H.M.; Trujillo, J.J. *Theory and Applications of Fractional Differential Equations*; Elsevier: Amsterdam, The Netherlands, 2006.
19. Li, H.; Muhammadhaji, A.; Zhang, L.; Teng, Z. Stability analysis of a fractional-order predator–prey model incorporating a constant prey refuge and feedback control. *Adv. Differ. Equ.* **2018**, *2018*, 325. [CrossRef]
20. Yang, Y.; Xu, L. Stability of a fractional order SEIR model with general incidence. *Appl. Math. Lett.* **2020**, *105*, 106303. [CrossRef]
21. Shi, R.; Lu, T.; Wang, C. Dynamic analysis of a fractional-order delayed model for hepatitis B virus with CTL immune response. *Virus Res.* **2020**, *277*, 197841. [CrossRef]
22. Elsadany, A.A.; Matouk, A.E. Dynamical behaviors of fractional-order Lotka–Volterra predator–prey model and its discretization. *J. Appl. Math. Comput.* **2015**, *49*, 269–283. [CrossRef]
23. Moustafa, M.; Mohd, M.H.; Ismail, A.I.; Abdullah, F.A. Dynamical analysis of a fractional-order Rosenzweig–MacArthur model incorporating a prey refuge. *Chaos Solitons Fractals* **2018**, *109*, 1–13. [CrossRef]
24. El-Saka, H.A.; Lee, S.; Jang, B. Dynamic analysis of fractional-order predator–prey biological economic system with Holling type II functional response. *Nonlinear Dyn.* **2019**, *96*, 407–416. [CrossRef]
25. Moustafa, M.; Zali, S.M.; Shafie, S. Dynamical Analysis of Eco-Epidemiological Model with Fading Memory. *J. Appl. Nonlinear Dyn.* **2024**, *13*, 191–202. [CrossRef]
26. Moustafa, M.; Mohd, M.H.; Ismail, A.I.; Abdullah, F.A. Dynamical Analysis of a Fractional-Order Hantavirus Infection Model. *Int. J. Nonlinear Sci. Numer. Simul.* **2020**, *21*, 171–181. [CrossRef]
27. Wang, X.; Wang, Z.; Xia, J. Stability and bifurcation control of a delayed fractional-order eco-epidemiological model with incommensurate orders. *J. Frankl. Inst.* **2019**, *356*, 8278–8295. [CrossRef]
28. Moustafa, M.; Abdullah, F.A.; Shafie, S.; Amirsom, N.A. Global stability of a fractional-order eco-epidemiological model with infected predator: Theoretical analysis. *Commun. Math. Biol. Neurosci.* **2023**, *56*, 1–11.

29. Thorne, E.T.; Williams, E.S. Disease and endangered species: The black-footed ferret as a recent example. *Conserv. Biol.* **1988**, *2*, 66–74. [CrossRef]
30. Roman, F.; Rossotto, F.; Venturino, E. Ecoepidemics with two strains: Diseased predators. *WSEAS Trans. Biol. Biomed.* **2011**, *8*, 73–85.
31. Das, M.; Maiti, A.; Samanta, G.P. Stability analysis of a prey-predator fractional order model incorporating prey refuge. *Eco. Genet. Genom.* **2018**, *7*, 33–46. [CrossRef]
32. Cresson, J.; Szafrańska, A. Discrete and continuous fractional persistence problems–the positivity property and applications. *Commun. Nonlinear Sci. Numer. Simul.* **2017**, *44*, 424–448. [CrossRef]
33. Choi, S.K.; Kang, B.; Koo, N. Stability for Caputo fractional differential systems. *Abstr. Appl. Anal.* **2014**, *2014*, 631419. [CrossRef]
34. Driessche, P.; Watmough, J. Reproduction numbers and sub-threshold endemic equilibria for compartmental models of disease transmission. *Math. Biosci.* **2002**, *180*, 29–48. [CrossRef] [PubMed]
35. Ahmed, E.; El-Sayed, A.; El-Saka, H.A. Equilibrium points, stability and numerical solutions of fractional-order predator–prey and rabies models. *J. Math. Anal. Appl.* **2007**, *325*, 542–553. [CrossRef]
36. Petras, I. *Fractional-Order Nonlinear Systems: Modeling, Analysis and Simulation*; Springer Science and Business Media: Berlin/Heidelberg, Germany, 2011.
37. Matouk, A.E. Stability conditions, hyperchaos and control in a novel fractional order hyperchaotic system. *Phys. Lett. A* **2009**, *373*, 2166–2173. [CrossRef]
38. Vargas-De-León, C. Volterra-type Lyapunov functions for fractional-order epidemic systems. *Commun. Nonlinear Sci. Numer. Simul.* **2015**, *24*, 75–85. [CrossRef]
39. Huo, J.; Zhao, H.; Zhu, L. The effect of vaccines on backward bifurcation in a fractional order HIV model. *Nonlinear Anal. Real World Appl.* **2015**, *26*, 289–305. [CrossRef]
40. Diethelm, K.; Ford, N.J.; Freed, A.D. A predictor-corrector approach for the numerical solution of fractional differential equations. *Nonlinear Dyn.* **2002**, *29*, 3–22. [CrossRef]
41. Li, C.; Tao, C. On the fractional Adams method. *Comput. Math. Appl.* **2009**, *58*, 1573–1588. [CrossRef]

Disclaimer/Publisher's Note: The statements, opinions and data contained in all publications are solely those of the individual author(s) and contributor(s) and not of MDPI and/or the editor(s). MDPI and/or the editor(s) disclaim responsibility for any injury to people or property resulting from any ideas, methods, instructions or products referred to in the content.

Exponential Stability for a Degenerate/Singular Beam-Type Equation in Non-Divergence Form

Mohammad Akil [1], Genni Fragnelli [2,*] and Amine Sbai [3]

[1] CERAMATHS-Laboratoire, INSA Hauts-de-France, University Polytechnique Hauts-de-France, F-59313 Valenciennes, France; mohammad.akil@uphf.fr
[2] Dipartimento di Ingegneria dell'Informazione e Scienze Matematiche, Università degli Studi di Siena, Via Roma 56, 53100 Siena, Italy
[3] MISI Laboratory, Faculty of Sciences and Technology, Hassan First University of Settat, B.P. 577, Settat 26000, Morocco; a.sbai@uhp.ac.ma
* Correspondence: genni.fragnelli@unisi.it

Abstract: The paper deals with the stability of a degenerate/singular beam equation in non-divergence form. In particular, we assume that the degeneracy and the singularity are at the same boundary point and we impose clamped conditions where the degeneracy occurs and dissipative conditions at the other endpoint. Using the energy method, we provide some conditions to obtain the stability for the considered problem.

Keywords: degenerate wave equation; singular potentials; stabilization; exponential decay

MSC: 35L80; 35L81; 93D23; 93D15

1. Introduction

This paper is devoted to studying the stability of a beam-type degenerate equation with a small singular perturbation through a linear boundary feedback. To be more precise, we consider the following problem:

$$\begin{cases} y_{tt}(t,x) + ay_{xxxx}(t,x) - \dfrac{\lambda}{d}y(t,x) = 0, & (t,x) \in (0,+\infty) \times (0,1), \\ y(t,0) = 0, \ y_x(t,0) = 0, & t > 0, \\ \beta y(t,1) - y_{xxx}(t,1) + y_t(t,1) = 0, & t > 0, \\ \gamma y_x(t,1) + y_{xx}(t,1) + y_{tx}(t,1) = 0, & t > 0, \\ y(0,x) = y_0(x), \ y_t(0,x) = y_1(x), & x \in (0,1), \end{cases} \qquad (1)$$

where β and γ are non-negative constants and the function a is such that $a(0) = 0$ and $a(x) > 0$ for all $x \in (0,1]$. In particular, for the function a, we consider two types of degeneracy according to the following definitions:

Definition 1. *The function $g \colon [0,1] \to \mathbb{R}$ is weakly degenerate, (WD) for short, at 0 if $g \in C^0[0,1] \cap C^1(0,1]$ is such that $g(0) = 0, g > 0$ on $(0,1]$, and if*

$$\sup_{x \in (0,1]} \frac{x|g'(x)|}{g(x)} := K_g, \qquad (2)$$

then $K_g \in (0,1)$.

Definition 2. *The function $g \colon [0,1] \to \mathbb{R}$ is strongly degenerate, (SD) for short, at 0 if $g \in C^1[0,1]$ is such that $g(0) = 0, g > 0$ on $(0,1]$ and in (2) we have $K_g \in [1,2)$.*

Roughly speaking, when $g(x) \sim x^K$, it is (WD) if $K \in (0,1)$ and (SD) it $K \in [1,2)$.

Problems similar to (1) are considered in several papers (see, for example, [1–7]). In particular, in [3,5], the following Euler–Bernoulli beam equation is considered:

$$my_{tt}(t,x) + EIy_{xxxx}(t,x) = 0, \quad x \in (0,1), \ t > 0, \tag{3}$$

with clamped conditions at the left end

$$y(t,0) = 0, \quad y_x(t,0) = 0, \tag{4}$$

and with dissipative conditions at the right end

$$\begin{cases} -EIy_{xxx}(t,1) + \mu_1 y_t(t,1) = 0, & \mu_1 \geq 0, \\ EIy_{xx}(t,1) + \mu_2 y_{tx}(t,1) = 0, & \mu_2 \geq 0. \end{cases} \tag{5}$$

Here, y is the vertical displacement, y_t is the velocity, y_x is the rotation, y_{tx} is the angular velocity, m is the mass density per unit length, EI is the flexural rigidity coefficient, $-EIy_{xx}$ is the bending moment, and $-EIy_{xxx}$ is the shear. In particular, the boundary conditions (5) mean that the shear is proportional to the velocity and the bending moment is negatively proportional to the angular moment. Observe that if we consider $\beta = \gamma = 0$ in (1), then we have boundary conditions analogous to those in (5). Thus, the dissipative conditions at 1 are not surprising. We remark that the conditions $\beta, \gamma \geq 0$ are necessary to study the well-posedness of the problem and to prove equivalence among all the norms introduced in this paper and that are crucial to obtain the stability result.

The qualitative behavior of (3)–(5) is studied in [4], where it is proved that if $\mu_1^2 > 0$ and $\mu_2^2 \geq 0$, the energy $E(t)$ of the vibration of the beam decays exponentially in a uniform way

$$E(t) \leq k e^{-\mu t} E(0) \tag{6}$$

for some $k, \mu > 0$.

Observe that in all the references above, the equation is non-degenerate; however, there are some papers where the equation is degenerate in the sense that a *degenerate damping* appears in the equation of (3) (see, for example, [8–10]). The first paper where the equation is degenerate in the sense that the fourth-order operator degenerates in a point as in (1) is [11]. However, to the best of our knowledge, [12] is the first paper where the *stability* for (1) with $\lambda = 0$ is considered. On the other hand, for a degenerate wave-equation, we refer to [13] (see also the arxiv version of 2015) for a problem in divergence form and to [14] for a problem in non-divergence form.

A position-dependent restoring force is introduced using the modified Euler–Bernoulli equation that includes a coefficient-dependent drift term. High stiffness, concentrated forces, or material discontinuities can be modeled by the term $\frac{\lambda}{d(x)} y$, which produces a single behavior at $x = 0$, suggesting a highly localized effect. Additionally, it denotes pre-stress or non-homogeneous stiffness, which applies to beams on uneven elastic foundations. Furthermore, if $d(x)$ is a distance function, the term affects tension in pre-stressed structures by acting like an inverse square law, similar to electrostatic or gravitational potentials. Additionally, the equation resembles singular potential quantum wave equations, which cause localized resonance effects in structural dynamics. All things considered, this formulation captures strong localized effects, pre-stress changes, and non-uniform limitations that are pertinent to practical physics and engineering (see [15]).

As far as we know, for beam-type equations simultaneously admitting degeneracy and singularity, only controllability problems have been faced (see the recent paper [16]), while nothing has been undertaken for stability. For this reason, in this paper, we focus on such a problem, proving that (1) permits boundary stabilization, provided that the singular term has a small coefficient (see Theorem 2 below). Hence, we may regard this result as a natural continuation of [12] and a perturbation of the related one in [16]. Clearly, the presence of the singular term $\frac{y}{d}$ introduces several difficulties with respect to [12], which let us treat only the case of a function d with weak degeneracy, according to the definition above. For a stability result for a degenerate/singular wave equation, we refer to [17].

Strategy method. In order to prove (6) for (1), we use a multiplier method. In particular, after defining the energy associated with the problem, we prove an estimate on it using a multiplier method (see Proposition 6). Obviously, the presence of a degenerate fourth-order operator brings more difficulties with respect to the ones for the second-order case. These difficulties are related to some new terms that we have to face; for example, we have to estimate from above $\int_s^T y^2(t,1)dt + \int_s^T y_x^2(t,1)dt$ for every $0 < s < T$ using the energy associated with the original problem. This is carried out in Proposition 7 thanks to a suitable fourth-order variational problem (see Proposition 3). Thanks to the estimates proved in Propositions 6 and 7 and using a result given in [18], we prove the main result of the paper, i.e. Theorem 2.

This paper is organized as follows: In Section 2, we give the functional setting and some preliminary results that we will use in the rest of the paper, together with the existence of solutions. In Section 3, we introduce the energy associated with a solution for the problem and we show that it decays exponentially as time diverges. In particular, we prove that if λ is small and a, d are not too degenerate (in the sense of Definitions 1 or 2), the energy satisfies (6), as in [4] for the non-degenerate and non-singular case. The last section is devoted to the conclusions and to some open problems.

2. Preliminary Results and Well-Posedness

In this section, we introduce the functional setting needed to treat (1). However, here, our assumptions are more general than those required to obtain the stability result in the next section.

We start by assuming a very modest requirement.

Hypothesis 1. *The functions $a, d \in C^0[0,1]$ are such that*
1. $a(0) = d(0) = 0, a, d > 0$ *on* $(0, 1]$,
2. *there are $K_a, K_d \in (0, 2)$ such that the functions*

$$x \longmapsto \frac{x^{K_a}}{a(x)} \qquad (7)$$

and

$$x \longmapsto \frac{x^{K_d}}{d(x)} \qquad (8)$$

are non-decreasing in a right neighborhood of $x = 0$.

It is clear that, if Hypothesis 1 holds, then

$$\lim_{x \to 0} \frac{x^\gamma}{a(x)} = 0, \qquad (9)$$

for all $\gamma > K_a$, and

$$\lim_{x \to 0} \frac{x^\gamma}{d(x)} = 0, \qquad (10)$$

for all $\gamma > K_d$.

Let us state that if a is (WD) or (SD), then (2) implies that (7) holds on the whole domain $(0, 1]$ analogously for d.

In order to treat (1), let us introduce the following Hilbert spaces with the related inner products and norms given by the following:

$$L^2_{\frac{1}{a}}(0,1) := \left\{ u \in L^2(0,1) \,\big|\, \|u\|_{\frac{1}{a}} < \infty \right\},$$

$$\langle u, v \rangle_{\frac{1}{a}} := \int_0^1 uv \frac{1}{a} dx, \quad \|u\|^2_{\frac{1}{a}} = \int_0^1 \frac{u^2}{a} dx,$$

for all $u, v \in L^2_{\frac{1}{a}}(0,1)$;

$$H^i_{\frac{1}{a}}(0,1) := L^2_{\frac{1}{a}}(0,1) \cap H^i(0,1), i = 1, 2,$$

$$\langle u, v \rangle_{i, \frac{1}{a}} := \langle u, v \rangle_{\frac{1}{a}} + \sum_{k=1}^{i} \int_0^1 u^{(k)}(x) v^{(k)}(x) dx$$

and

$$\|u\|^2_{H^i_{\frac{1}{a}}(0,1)} := \|u\|^2_{\frac{1}{a}} + \sum_{k=1}^{i} \left\|u^{(k)}\right\|^2_{L^2(0,1)},$$

$\forall\, u, v \in H^i_{\frac{1}{a}}(0,1)$, $i = 1, 2$. In addition to the previous ones, we introduce the following important Hilbert spaces:

$$H^1_{\frac{1}{a}, 0}(0,1) := \left\{ u \in H^1_{\frac{1}{a}}(0,1) : u(0) = 0 \right\} \quad \text{and}$$

$$H^2_{\frac{1}{a}, 0}(0,1) := \left\{ u \in H^1_{\frac{1}{a}, 0}(0,1) \cap H^2(0,1) : u'(0) = 0 \right\},$$

with the previous inner products $\langle \cdot, \cdot \rangle_{i, \frac{1}{a}}$ and norms $\|\cdot\|_{H^i_{\frac{1}{a}}(0,1)}$, $i = 1, 2$. Now, consider the scalar product

$$\langle u, v \rangle_{i, o} := \int_0^1 u^{(i)}(x) v^{(i)}(x) dx$$

for all $u, v \in H^i_{\frac{1}{a}}(0,1)$, which induces the norm

$$\|u\|_{i, o} := \|u^{(i)}\|_{L^2(0,1)}, \quad \forall\, u \in H^i_{\frac{1}{a}}(0,1),$$

$i = 1, 2$. Observe that, if a is continuous, $a(0) = 0$ and (7) is satisfied, then the norms $\|\cdot\|_{H^i_{\frac{1}{a}}(0,1)}$, $\|\cdot\|_i$ and $\|\cdot\|_{i, o}$ are equivalent in $H^i_{\frac{1}{a}, 0}(0,1)$. Here,

$$\|u\|^2_i := \|u\|^2_{\frac{1}{a}} + \|u^{(i)}\|^2_{L^2(0,1)}, \quad \forall\, u \in H^i_{\frac{1}{a}, 0}(0,1),$$

$i = 1, 2$ (see, e.g., [11]). Clearly, if $i = 1$, the previous equivalence is obviously satisfied. Indeed, $\|\cdot\|_{H^1_{\frac{1}{a}}(0,1)}$ and $\|\cdot\|_1$ coincide and, for ([19], Proposition 2.6), one proves that there is $C > 0$ such that

$$\int_0^1 \frac{u^2}{a} dx \leq C \int_0^1 (u')^2 dx, \tag{11}$$

for all $u \in H^1_{\frac{1}{a}, 0}(0,1)$. Let

$$C_{HP} \text{ be the best constant of (11)}. \tag{12}$$

Now, assume $i = 2$ and fix $u \in H^2_{\frac{1}{a},0}(0,1)$. Proceeding as for $i = 1$ and applying the classical Hardy's inequality to $z := u'$ (observing that $z \in H^1_{\frac{1}{a},0}(0,1)$), we have

$$\int_0^1 (u')^2 dx \leq \int_0^1 \frac{z^2}{x^2} dx \leq 4 \int_0^1 (z')^2 dx = 4 \int_0^1 (u'')^2 dx = 4\|u\|_{2,\circ}^2.$$

Hence, $\|\cdot\|_{H^2_{\frac{1}{a}}(0,1)}$ and $\|\cdot\|_2$ are equivalent in $H^2_{\frac{1}{a},0}(0,1)$ (actually, they are equivalent in $H^2_{\frac{1}{a}}(0,1)$, see, e.g., [11]). Moreover, by the previous inequality,

$$\int_0^1 \frac{u^2}{a} dx \leq C_{HP} \int_0^1 (u')^2 dx \leq 4 C_{HP} \|u\|_{2,\circ}^2 \tag{13}$$

and the thesis follows. In particular, $\|u\|_1^2 \leq (C_{HP} + 1)\|u\|_{1,\circ}^2$ for all $u \in H^1_{\frac{1}{a},0}(0,1)$ and

$$\|u\|_2^2 \leq (4C_{HP} + 1)\|u\|_{2,\circ}^2 \tag{14}$$

for all $u \in H^2_{\frac{1}{a},0}(0,1)$ (see ([12], Proposition 2.1)).

As in ([16], Proposition 2.3), one can prove the next result

Proposition 1. *Assume Hypothesis 1 and take K_a, K_d such that $K_a + K_d \leq 2$. If $u \in H^2_{\frac{1}{a},0}(0,1)$, then for $\frac{u}{\sqrt{ad}} \in L^2(0,1)$, there is a positive constant $C > 0$ such that*

$$\int_0^1 \frac{u^2(x)}{a(x)d(x)} dx \leq C \int_0^1 (u''(x))^2 dx. \tag{15}$$

Let

$$\tilde{C}_{HP} \text{ be the best constant of (15).} \tag{16}$$

As in ([20], Chapter V), we assume the next hypothesis:

Hypothesis 2. *The constant $\lambda \in \mathbb{R}$ is such that $\lambda \neq 0$ and*

$$\lambda < \frac{1}{\tilde{C}_{HP}}. \tag{17}$$

Observe that the case $\lambda = 0$ is already considered in [12]. Thus, it is not restrictive to assume $\lambda \neq 0$.

Moreover, if $\lambda \in \left(0, \frac{1}{\tilde{C}_{HP}}\right)$, we can take $\epsilon \in (0,1)$ such that

$$\lambda = \frac{1-\epsilon}{\tilde{C}_{HP}} > 0. \tag{18}$$

Hence, as a consequence of Proposition 1, one has the next estimate (see ([16], Proposition 2.4)).

Proposition 2. *Assume Hypothesis 1 and $\lambda \in \left(0, \frac{1}{\tilde{C}_{HP}}\right)$. If $u \in H^2_{\frac{1}{a},0}(0,1)$, then*

$$\int_0^1 (u''(x))^2 dx - \lambda \int_0^1 \frac{u^2(x)}{a(x)d(x)} dx \geq \epsilon \int_0^1 (u''(x))^2 dx.$$

Under Hypotheses 1 and 2, one can consider in $H^2_{\frac{1}{a},0}(0,1)$ also the product

$$\langle u,v\rangle_{2,\sim} := \langle u,v\rangle_{2,\circ} - \lambda \int_0^1 \frac{uv}{ad}dx,$$

which induces the norm

$$\|u\|^2_{2,\sim} = \|u\|^2_{2,\circ} - \lambda \int_0^1 \frac{u^2}{ad}dx.$$

By Propositions 1 and 2, one can prove the following equivalence:

Corollary 1. *Assume Hypotheses 1 and 2 and $K_a + K_d \le 2$. Then, the norms $\|\cdot\|_{H^2_{\frac{1}{a}}(0,1)}$, $\|\cdot\|_2$, $\|\cdot\|_{2,\circ}$, and $\|\cdot\|_{2,\sim}$ are equivalent in $H^2_{\frac{1}{a}}(0,1)$.*

In order to study the well-posedness of (1), we introduce the operator $A: D(A) \subset L^2_{\frac{1}{a}}(0,1) \to L^2_{\frac{1}{a}}(0,1)$ by $Au := au''''$, for all $u \in D(A) := \left\{u \in H^2_{\frac{1}{a},0}(0,1) : au'''' \in L^2_{\frac{1}{a}}(0,1)\right\}$, where the next Gauss–Green formula holds

$$\int_0^1 u''''vdx = u'''(1)v(1) - u''(1)v'(1) + \int_0^1 u''v''dx \tag{19}$$

for all $(u,v) \in D(A) \times H^2_{\frac{1}{a},0}(0,1)$ (see [12]). Moreover, consider

$$A_\lambda u := Au - \frac{\lambda}{d}u, \quad \forall u \in D(A_\lambda),$$

where

$$D(A_\lambda) := \left\{u \in H^2_{\frac{1}{a},0}(0,1) \mid A_\lambda u \in L^2_{\frac{1}{a}}(0,1)\right\}. \tag{20}$$

Observe that if $u \in H^2_{\frac{1}{a},0}(0,1)$ and $K_a + 2K_d \le 2$, one proves that $\frac{u}{d} \in L^2_{\frac{1}{a}}(0,1)$; hence, $u \in D(A_\lambda)$ if and only if $u \in D(A)$, i.e., $D(A_\lambda) = D(A)$ (for more details, we refer to [16]). For this reason, in the following, we assume the next assumption:

Hypothesis 3. *Assume Hypothesis 1 and $K_a + 2K_d \le 2$.*

Under this assumption, it is clear that d cannot be (SD). On the other hand, a can be (SD), but in this case, K_d has to be very small.

Finally, to prove the well-posedness of (1), we need to introduce the last Hilbert space $\mathcal{H}_0 := H^2_{\frac{1}{a},0}(0,1) \times L^2_{\frac{1}{a}}(0,1)$, with inner product and norm given by

$$\langle (u,v),(\tilde{u},\tilde{v})\rangle_{\mathcal{H}_0} := \langle u,\tilde{u}\rangle_{2,\circ} + \langle v,\tilde{v}\rangle_{\frac{1}{a}} + \beta u(1)\tilde{u}(1) + \gamma u'(1)\tilde{u}'(1)$$

and

$$\|(u,v)\|^2_{\mathcal{H}_0} := \|u''\|^2_{L^2(0,1)} + \|v\|^2_{\frac{1}{a}} + \beta u^2(1) + \gamma(u'(1))^2$$

for every $(u,v), (\tilde{u},\tilde{v}) \in \mathcal{H}_0$, where $\beta, \gamma \ge 0$, and the matrix operator $\mathcal{A}: D(\mathcal{A}) \subset \mathcal{H}_0 \to \mathcal{H}_0$ given by

$$\mathcal{A} := \begin{pmatrix} 0 & Id \\ -A_\lambda & 0 \end{pmatrix}$$

with domain

$$D(\mathcal{A}) := \{(u,v) \in D(A) \times H^2_{\frac{1}{a},0}(0,1) : \beta u(1) - u'''(1) + v(1) = 0,$$
$$\gamma u'(1) + u''(1) + v'(1) = 0\}.$$

Thanks to (19), one can prove the next theorem that contains the main properties of the operator $(\mathcal{A}, D(\mathcal{A}))$. Since the proof is similar to the one of [21] or [22], we omit it.

Theorem 1. *Assume a (WD) or (SD). Then, the operator $(\mathcal{A}, D(\mathcal{A}))$ is non-positive with a dense domain and generates a contraction semigroup $(S(t))_{t\geq 0}$.*

Thanks to the previous theorem, one has the next result, which can be proved as in ([16], Theorem 2.7).

Theorem 2. *Hypotheses 2 and 3 hold. If $(y_0, y_1) \in H^2_{\frac{1}{a},0}(0,1) \times L^2_{\frac{1}{a}}(0,1)$, then there is a unique mild solution*

$$y \in C^1\left([0, +\infty); L^2_{\frac{1}{a}}(0,1)\right) \cap C\left([0, +\infty); H^2_{\frac{1}{a},0}(0,1)\right)$$

of (1), which depends continuously on the initial data. In addition, if $(y_0, y_1) \in D(\mathcal{A}_1)$, then the solution y is classical in the sense that

$$y \in C^2\left([0, +\infty); L^2_{\frac{1}{a}}(0,1)\right) \cap C^1\left([0, +\infty); H^2_{\frac{1}{a},0}(0,1)\right) \cap C([0, +\infty); D(A))$$

and the equation of (1) holds for all $t \geq 0$.

Remark 1. *Due to the reversibility in time of the equation, solutions exist with the same regularity for $t < 0$. We will use this fact in the proof of the controllability result by considering a backward problem whose final time data will be transformed in initial data: this is the reason for the notation of the initial data in problem (1).*

The last important result of this section is given by the next proposition. Let us start with

Hypothesis 4. *Assume a (WD) or (SD), d (WD) with $K_a + 2K_d \leq 2$, $\lambda \neq 0$ with $\lambda < \frac{1}{C_{HP}}$ and $\beta, \gamma \geq 0$.*

Proposition 3. *Assume Hypothesis 4 and define*

$$|||z|||^2 := \int_0^1 (z'')^2 dx - \lambda \int_0^1 \frac{z^2}{ad} dx + \beta z^2(1) + \gamma(z'(1))^2$$

for all $z \in H^2_{\frac{1}{a},0}(0,1)$. Then, the norms $||| \cdot |||$ and $|| \cdot ||_{2,\circ}$ are equivalent in $H^2_{\frac{1}{a},0}(0,1)$. Moreover, for every $\rho, \mu \in \mathbb{R}$, the variational problem

$$\int_0^1 z''\varphi'' dx - \lambda \int_0^1 \frac{z\varphi}{ad} + \beta z(1)\varphi(1) + \gamma z'(1)\varphi'(1) = \rho\varphi(1) + \mu\varphi'(1), \quad \forall \varphi \in H^2_{\frac{1}{a},0}(0,1),$$

admits a unique solution $z \in H^2_{\frac{1}{a},0}(0,1)$, which satisfies the estimates

$$\|z\|^2_{\frac{1}{a}} \leq \frac{4C_{HP}}{C_\epsilon}(|\rho| + |\mu|)^2, \quad \text{and} \quad |||z|||^2 \leq (|\rho| + |\mu|)^2, \tag{21}$$

where

$$C_\epsilon := \begin{cases} 1, & \lambda < 0, \\ \epsilon, & \lambda > 0. \end{cases} \tag{22}$$

In addition, $z \in D(A_\lambda)$ and solves

$$\begin{cases} A_\lambda z = 0, \\ \beta z(1) - z'''(1) = \rho, \\ \gamma z'(1) + z''(1) = \mu. \end{cases} \tag{23}$$

Proof. As a first step, observe that for all $z \in H^2_{\frac{1}{a},0}(0,1)$, one has

$$|z'(x)| = \left| \int_0^x z''(t) dt \right| \leq \|z''\|_{L^2(0,1)} = \|z\|_{2,\circ}, \tag{24}$$

and

$$|z(x)| = \left| \int_0^x z'(t) dt \right| = \left| \int_0^x \int_0^t z''(\tau) d\tau \, dt \right| \leq \|z''\|_{L^2(0,1)} = \|z\|_{2,\circ} \tag{25}$$

for all $x \in [0,1]$. Thus, $\||\cdot\||$ and $\|\cdot\|_{2,\circ}$ are equivalent. Indeed, for all $z \in H^2_{\frac{1}{a},0}(0,1)$, if $\lambda < 0$, one proves immediately that

$$\|z\|^2_{2,\circ} = \|z''\|^2_{L^2(0,1)} \leq \||z\||^2. \tag{26}$$

If $\lambda \in \left(0, \frac{1}{\tilde{C}_{HP}}\right)$, by Proposition 2, one has

$$\int_0^1 (z''(x))^2 dx - \lambda \int_0^1 \frac{z^2(x)}{a(x)d(x)} dx \geq \epsilon \int_0^1 (z''(x))^2 dx. \tag{27}$$

for all $z \in H^2_{\frac{1}{a},0}(0,1)$, and so

$$\|z\|^2_{2,\circ} \leq \frac{1}{\epsilon} \||z\||^2, \tag{28}$$

for all $z \in H^2_{\frac{1}{a},0}(0,1)$. In conclusion, we have

$$\|z\|^2_{2,\circ} \leq \frac{1}{C_\epsilon} \||z\||^2. \tag{29}$$

Now, we prove that there is $C > 0$ such that

$$\||z\||^2 \leq C \|z\|^2_{2,\circ},$$

for all $z \in H^2_{\frac{1}{a},0}(0,1)$. Clearly, (25) and (24) imply $\beta z^2(1) \leq \beta \|z\|^2_{2,\circ}$ and $\gamma(z'(1))^2 \leq \gamma \|z\|^2_{2,\circ}$, respectively; hence, if $\lambda > 0$, one proves immediately that $\||z\||^2 \leq (1 + \beta + \gamma)\|z\|^2_{2,\circ}$; if $\lambda < 0$, by (15), then

$$\||z\||^2 \leq (1 - \lambda \tilde{C}_{HP} + \beta + \gamma)\|z\|^2_{2,\circ}.$$

In any case, the claim holds.

Now, consider the bilinear and symmetric form $\Lambda : H^2_{\frac{1}{a},0}(0,1) \times H^2_{\frac{1}{a},0}(0,1) \to \mathbb{R}$ such that

$$\Lambda(z, \varphi) := \int_0^1 z'' \varphi'' dx - \lambda \int_0^1 \frac{z\varphi}{ad} dx + \beta z(1)\varphi(1) + \gamma z'(1)\varphi'(1).$$

As in [22] or in [17], one can easily prove that Λ is coercive and continuous. Now, consider the linear functional

$$\mathcal{L}(\varphi) := \rho\varphi(1) + \mu\varphi'(1),$$

with $\varphi \in H^2_{\frac{1}{a},0}(0,1)$ and $\rho, \mu \in \mathbb{R}$. Clearly, $\mathcal{L}$ is continuous and linear. Thus, by the Lax-Milgram Theorem, there is a unique solution $z \in H^2_{\frac{1}{a},0}(0,1)$ of

$$\Lambda(z,\varphi) = \mathcal{L}(\varphi) \tag{30}$$

for all $\varphi \in H^2_{\frac{1}{a},0}(0,1)$. In particular,

$$|||z|||^2 = \Lambda(z,z) = \int_0^1 (z'')^2 dx - \lambda \int_0^1 \frac{z^2}{ad}dx + \beta z^2(1) + \gamma(z'(1))^2 = \rho z(1) + \mu z'(1). \tag{31}$$

Concerning the other estimates, by (24)–(26) and (31), we have $|||z|||^2 = \rho z(1) + \mu z'(1) \leq (|\rho| + |\mu|)|||z|||$; thus,

$$|||z||| \leq |\rho| + |\mu|. \tag{32}$$

Moreover, by the equivalence of the norms in $H^2_{\frac{1}{a},0}(0,1)$, Proposition 2, and (13), one has

$$|||z|||^2 = \|z\|^2_{2,\circ} - \lambda \int_0^1 \frac{z^2}{ad}dx + \beta z^2(1) + \gamma(z'(1))^2 \geq C_\epsilon \|z\|^2_{2,\circ} \geq \frac{C_\epsilon}{4C_{HP}} \|z\|^2_{\frac{1}{a}},$$

where C_ϵ is as in (22). Thus, by (32), $\|z\|^2_{\frac{1}{a}} \leq \frac{4C_{HP}}{C_\epsilon}|||z|||^2 \leq \frac{4C_{HP}}{C_\epsilon}(|\rho| + |\mu|)^2$.

Now, we will prove that z belongs to $D(A)$ and solves (23). To this end, consider (30) again; clearly, it holds for every $\varphi \in C_c^\infty(0,1)$, so that $\int_0^1 z''\varphi'' dx - \lambda \int_0^1 \frac{z\varphi}{ad}dx = 0$ for all $\varphi \in C_c^\infty(0,1)$. Thus, $z'''' = \lambda\frac{z\varphi}{ad}$ a.e. in $(0,1)$ (see, e.g., ([23], Lemma 1.2.1)) and so $az'''' - \lambda\frac{z\varphi}{d} = 0$ a.e. in $(0,1)$, in particular $A_\lambda z = 0 \in L^2_{\frac{1}{a}}(0,1)$; this implies that $z \in D(A)$.

Now, coming back to (30) and using (19) and the fact that $A_\lambda z = 0$, we have

$$\int_0^1 z''\varphi'' dx - \lambda \int_0^1 \frac{z\varphi}{ad}dx + \beta z(1)\varphi(1) + \gamma z'(1)\varphi'(1) = \rho\varphi(1) + \mu\varphi'(1)$$
$$\iff -z'''(1)\varphi(1) + (z''\varphi')(1) + \beta z(1)\varphi(1) + \gamma(z'\varphi')(1) = \rho\varphi(1) + \mu\varphi'(1)$$

for all $\varphi \in H^2_{\frac{1}{a},0}(0,1)$. Thus, $-z'''(1) + \beta z(1) = \rho$ and $\gamma z'(1) + z''(1) = \mu$, that is, z solves (23). □

3. Energy Estimates and Exponential Stability

In this section, we prove the main result of this paper. In particular, proving some estimates of the energy associated with (1), we obtain the exponential stability.

To begin with, we give the next definition:

Definition 3. *For a mild solution y of (1), we define its energy as the continuous function*

$$E_y(t) := \frac{1}{2}\int_0^1 \left(\frac{y_t^2(t,x)}{a(x)} + y_{xx}^2(t,x) - \frac{\lambda}{ad}y^2(t,x)\right)dx + \frac{\beta}{2}y^2(t,1) + \frac{\gamma}{2}y_x^2(t,1), \quad \forall\, t \geq 0. \tag{33}$$

Recalling that $\beta, \gamma \geq 0$, one proves that if y is a mild solution and if $\beta, \gamma \neq 0$, then

$$y^2(t,1) \leq \frac{2}{\beta}E_y(t) \quad \text{and} \quad y_x^2(t,1) \leq \frac{2}{\gamma}E_y(t);$$

on the other hand, thanks to Equations (24)–(26), for all $\beta \geq 0$ and $\gamma \geq 0$,

$$y^2(t,1) \leq \frac{2}{C_\epsilon} E_y(t) \quad \text{and} \quad y_x^2(t,1) \leq \frac{2}{C_\epsilon} E_y(t),$$

where C_ϵ is as in (22). Thus, we have

$$y^2(t,1) \leq C_\beta E_y(t) \quad \text{and} \quad y_x^2(t,1) \leq C_\gamma E_y(t), \tag{34}$$

where $C_\beta := \begin{cases} 2\min\left\{\frac{1}{C_\epsilon}, \frac{1}{\beta}\right\}, & \beta \neq 0, \\ \frac{2}{C_\epsilon}, & \beta = 0 \end{cases}$ and $C_\gamma := \begin{cases} 2\min\left\{\frac{1}{C_\epsilon}, \frac{1}{\gamma}\right\}, & \gamma \neq 0, \\ \frac{2}{C_\epsilon}, & \gamma = 0. \end{cases}$

Observe that if $\beta > 1$, being $\frac{1}{\beta} < 1$ and $\frac{1}{C_\epsilon} \geq 1$ (recall that $\epsilon \in (0,1)$), $\min\left\{\frac{1}{C_\epsilon}, \frac{1}{\beta}\right\} = \frac{1}{\beta}$. Analogously for γ.

As in ([21], Thoerem 3.1), it is possible to prove that the energy is a non-increasing function.

Theorem 1. *Assume Hypothesis 4 and let y be a classical solution of (1). Then, the energy is non-increasing. In particular,*

$$\frac{dE_y(t)}{dt} = -y_t^2(t,1) - y_{tx}^2(t,1), \quad \forall\, t \geq 0.$$

Actually, one can prove that the previous monotonicity result also holds under weaker assumptions on the functions a and d.

Proposition 4. *Assume Hypothesis 4. For the fixed $T > 0$, if y is a classical solution of (1), then*

$$\begin{aligned}
0 = {} & 2\int_0^1 \left[y_t \frac{x}{a} y_x\right]_{t=s}^{t=T} dx - \frac{1}{a(1)} \int_s^T y_t^2(t,1)\,dt + \int_{Q_s} \frac{y_t^2}{a}\left(1 - \frac{xa'}{a}\right) dx\,dt \\
& - \frac{\lambda}{a(1)d(1)} \int_0^T y^2(t,1)\,dt + 3 \int_{Q_s} y_{xx}^2 dx\,dt + 2\beta \int_s^T y_x(t,1)y(t,1)\,dt \\
& + 2\int_s^T y_x(t,1)y_t(t,1)\,dt + 2\gamma \int_s^T y_x^2(t,1)\,dt + 2\int_s^T y_x(t,1)y_{tx}(t,1)\,dt \\
& - \int_s^T y_{xx}^2(t,1)\,dt + \lambda \int_{Q_s}\left(1 - \frac{xa'}{a} - \frac{xd'}{d}\right)\frac{y^2}{ad} dx\,dt,
\end{aligned} \tag{35}$$

for every $0 < s < T$. Here, $Q_s := (s,T) \times (0,1)$.

Proof. Since some computations are similar to the ones of ([21], Proposition 4.7), we sketch them. Fix $s \in (0,T)$. Multiplying the equation in (1) by $\frac{xy_x}{a}$ and integrating over Q_s, we have

$$0 = \int_{Q_s} y_{tt} \frac{xy_x}{a} dx\,dt + \int_{Q_s} ay_{xxxx} \frac{xy_x}{a} dx\,dt - \lambda \int_{Q_s} \frac{xyy_x}{ad} dx\,dt. \tag{36}$$

As in [21], one proves that

$$\begin{aligned}
& \int_{Q_s} y_{tt} \frac{xy_x}{a} dx\,dt + \int_{Q_s} ay_{xxxx} \frac{xy_x}{a} dx\,dt \\
= {} & \int_0^1 \left[y_t \frac{xy_x}{a}\right]_{t=s}^{t=T} dx - \frac{1}{2a(1)} \int_s^T y_t^2(t,1)\,dt + \frac{1}{2}\int_{Q_s} \frac{y_t^2}{a}\left(1 - \frac{xa'}{a}\right) dx\,dt \\
& + \frac{3}{2} \int_{Q_s} y_{xx}^2 dx\,dt + \beta \int_s^T y_x(t,1)y(t,1)\,dt + \int_s^T y_x(t,1)y_t(t,1)\,dt \\
& + \gamma \int_s^T y_x^2(t,1)\,dt + \int_s^T y_x(t,1)y_{tx}(t,1)\,dt - \frac{1}{2}\int_s^T y_{xx}^2(t,1)\,dt.
\end{aligned}$$

Hence, it remains to compute $-\lambda \int_{Q_s} \frac{xyy_x}{ad} dxdt$. As in [17], one proves

$$-\lambda \int_{Q_s} \frac{xyy_x}{ad} dxdt = -\frac{\lambda}{2} \int_s^T \left[\frac{xy^2}{ad}\right]_{x=0}^{x=1} dt + \frac{\lambda}{2} \int_{Q_s} \left(\frac{ad - x(a'd + ad')}{(ad)^2}\right) y^2 dxdt$$

$$= -\frac{\lambda}{2} \int_s^T \left[\frac{xy^2}{ad}\right]_{x=0}^{x=1} dt + \frac{\lambda}{2} \int_{Q_s} \left(1 - \frac{xa'}{a} - \frac{xd'}{d}\right) \frac{y^2}{ad} dxdt.$$

By ([17], Lemma 1)

$$\lambda \int_0^T \left[y^2 \frac{x}{ad}\right]_{x=0}^{x=1} = \frac{\lambda}{a(1)d(1)} \int_0^T y^2(t,1)dt$$

and the thesis follows. □

As a consequence of the previous equality, we have the next relation:

Proposition 5. *Assume Hypothesis 4 and fix $T > 0$. If y is a classical solution of (1), then for every $0 < s < T$, we have*

$$\int_{Q_s} \frac{y_t^2}{a}\left(\frac{K_a}{2} + 1 - \frac{xa'}{a}\right) dx\, dt + \int_{Q_s} y_{xx}^2 \left(3 - \frac{K_a}{2}\right) dx\, dt$$

$$+ \lambda \int_{Q_s} \left(1 - \frac{xa'}{a} - \frac{xd'}{d} + \frac{K_a}{2}\right) \frac{y^2}{ad} dxdt = (B.T.),$$
(37)

where

$$(B.T.) = \frac{K_a}{2} \int_0^1 \left[\frac{yy_t}{a}\right]_{t=s}^{t=T} dx - 2 \int_0^1 \left[y_t \frac{x}{a} y_x\right]_{t=s}^{t=T} dx + \frac{K_a \beta}{2} \int_s^T y^2(t,1)dt$$

$$+ \frac{K_a}{2} \int_s^T y(t,1)y_t(t,1)dt + \gamma\left(\frac{K_a}{2} - 2\right) \int_s^T y_x^2(t,1)dt$$

$$+ \left(\frac{K_a}{2} - 2\right) \int_s^T y_x(t,1)y_{tx}(t,1)dt + \int_s^T \frac{y_t^2(t,1)}{a(1)} dt - 2\beta \int_s^T y_x(t,1)y(t,1)dt$$

$$- 2\int_s^T y_x(t,1)y_t(t,1)dt + \int_s^T y_{xx}^2(t,1)dt + \frac{\lambda}{a(1)d(1)} \int_s^T y^2(t,1)dt.$$

Proof. Let y be a classical solution of (1) and fix $s \in (0,T)$. Multiplying the equation in (1) by $\frac{y}{a}$, integrating by parts over Q_s, and using (19), we obtain

$$0 = \int_0^1 \left[y_t \frac{y}{a}\right]_{t=s}^{t=T} dx - \int_{Q_s} \frac{y_t^2}{a} dx\, dt + \int_s^T (yy_{xxx})(t,1)dt$$

$$- \int_s^T (y_x y_{xx})(t,1)dt + \int_{Q_s} y_{xx}^2 dx\, dt - \lambda \int_{Q_s} \frac{y^2}{ad} dxdt.$$
(38)

Obviously, all the previous integrals make sense, and by multiplying (38) by $\frac{K_a}{2}$, one has

$$0 = \frac{K_a}{2} \int_{Q_s} \left(-\frac{y_t^2}{a} + y_{xx}^2 - \lambda \frac{y^2}{ad}\right) dx\, dt + \frac{K_a}{2} \int_0^1 \left[y_t \frac{y}{a}\right]_{t=s}^{t=T} dx$$

$$+ \frac{K_a}{2} \int_s^T y(t,1)y_{xxx}(t,1)dt - \frac{K_a}{2} \int_s^T y_x(t,1)y_{xx}(t,1)dt.$$
(39)

By summing (35) and (39) and using the boundary conditions at 1, we obtain the thesis. □

An immediate consequence of (37) is the next result. However, to prove it, we assume an additional hypothesis on functions a and d.

Hypothesis 5. *Assume a (WD) or (SD), d (WD) with $K_a + 2K_d < 2$, $\lambda \neq 0$ with $\lambda < \frac{1}{\tilde{C}_{HP}}$ and $\beta, \gamma \geq 0$.*

Observe that this hypothesis is more restrictive than Hypothesis 4; indeed, in Hypothesis 5, we exclude the case $K_a + 2K_d = 2$. In fact, as we can see already from the next result, the condition $K_a + 2K_d < 2$ is important for the technique used in the following proposition:

Proposition 6. *Assume Hypothesis 5, fix $T > 0$ and let y be a classical solution of (1). Then, for every $0 < s < T$ and for all $\varepsilon_0 \in (0, 2 - K_a - 2K_d)$, one proves*

$$\frac{\varepsilon_0}{2} \int_{Q_s} \left(\frac{y_t^2}{a} + y_{xx}^2 - \lambda \frac{y^2}{ad} \right) dx\, dt \leq \left(4\vartheta + \varrho + \frac{C_\gamma}{2}\left(2 - \frac{K_a}{2}\right) \right) E_y(s)$$

$$+ \left(\frac{K_a}{4} + \beta + \frac{K_a \beta}{2} + \frac{\lambda}{a(1)d(1)} \right) \int_s^T y^2(t, 1)\, dt + (\beta + 1 + 2\gamma^2) \int_s^T y_x^2(t, 1)\, dt,$$

if $\lambda > 0$, and

$$\frac{\varepsilon_0}{2} \int_{Q_s} \left(\frac{y_t^2}{a} + y_{xx}^2 - \lambda \frac{y^2}{ad} \right) dx\, dt \leq \left(4\vartheta + \varrho + \frac{C_\gamma}{2}\left(2 - \frac{K_a}{2}\right) \right) E_y(s)$$

$$+ \left(\frac{K_a}{4} + \beta + \frac{K_a \beta}{2} \right) \int_s^T y^2(t, 1)\, dt + (\beta + 1 + 2\gamma^2) \int_s^T y_x^2(t, 1)\, dt$$

$$- 4\lambda \tilde{C}_{HP}\left(1 + \frac{3}{2}K_a + K_d \right) \int_s^T E_y(t)\, dt,$$

if $\lambda < 0$.

Here, $\vartheta := \max\left\{ \frac{1}{\varepsilon}\left(\frac{4}{a(1)} + K_a C_{HP} \right), 1 + \frac{K_a}{4} \right\}$ and $\varrho := \max\left\{ 2, \frac{K_a}{4} + 1 + \frac{1}{a(1)} \right\}$.

Proof. By assumption, we can take $\varepsilon_0 \in (0, 2 - K_a - 2K_d)$; thus,

$$\begin{aligned} 1 - \frac{xa'}{a} + \frac{K_a}{2} &> \frac{\varepsilon_0}{2}, \\ 3 - \frac{K_a}{2} &> \frac{\varepsilon_0}{2}, \\ 1 - \frac{xa'}{a} - \frac{xd'}{d} + \frac{K_a}{2} &\geq \frac{\varepsilon_0}{2}. \end{aligned} \quad (40)$$

Now, we distinguish between the cases $\lambda > 0$ and $\lambda < 0$.
Case $\lambda > 0$.

In this case, the distributed terms in (37) can be estimated from below in the following way:

$$\int_{Q_s} \frac{y_t^2}{a}\left(\frac{K_a}{2} + 1 - \frac{xa'}{a} \right) dx\, dt + \int_{Q_s} y_{xx}^2 \left(3 - \frac{K_a}{2} \right) dx\, dt + \lambda \int_{Q_s} \left(1 - \frac{xa'}{a} - \frac{xd'}{d} + \frac{K_a}{2} \right) \frac{y^2}{ad} dx\, dt \quad (4?)$$

$$\geq \frac{\varepsilon_0}{2} \int_{Q_s} \left(\frac{y_t^2}{a} + y_{xx}^2 + \lambda \frac{y^2}{ad} \right) dx\, dt \geq \frac{\varepsilon_0}{2} \int_{Q_s} \left(\frac{y_t^2}{a} + y_{xx}^2 - \lambda \frac{y^2}{ad} \right) dx\, dt.$$

Now, we estimate the boundary terms in (37) from above. First of all, consider the integral $\int_0^1 \left(-2 y_t \frac{x}{a} y_x + \frac{K_a}{2} \frac{y y_t}{a} \right)(\tau, x)\, dx$ for all $\tau \in [s, T]$. Using the fact that $\frac{x^2}{a(x)} \leq \frac{1}{a(1)}$, together with the classical Hardy inequality (12) and proceeding as in ([12], Proposition 3.3), one proves

$$\int_0^1 \left(-2y_t \frac{x}{a} y_x + \frac{K_a}{2} \frac{yy_t}{a}\right)(\tau, x) dx \le$$
$$\le \frac{4}{a(1)} \int_0^1 y_{xx}^2(\tau, x) dx + \left(1 + \frac{K_a}{4}\right) \int_0^1 \frac{y_t^2}{a}(\tau, x) dx + K_a C_{HP} \int_0^1 y_{xx}^2(\tau, x) dx.$$

Hence, by Proposition 2,

$$\int_0^1 \left(-2y_t \frac{x}{a} y_x + \frac{K_a}{2} \frac{yy_t}{a}\right)(\tau, x) dx$$
$$\le \left(\frac{4}{a(1)} + K_a C_{HP}\right) \int_0^1 y_{xx}^2(\tau, x) dx + \left(1 + \frac{K_a}{4}\right) \int_0^1 \frac{y_t^2}{a}(\tau, x) dx$$
$$\le \frac{1}{\epsilon} \left(\frac{4}{a(1)} + K_a C_{HP}\right) \left(\int_0^1 y_{xx}^2(\tau, x) dx - \lambda \int_0^1 \frac{y^2}{ad}(\tau, x) dx\right) + \left(1 + \frac{K_a}{4}\right) \int_0^1 \frac{y_t^2}{a}(\tau, x) dx$$
$$\le 2 \max\left\{\frac{1}{\epsilon}\left(\frac{4}{a(1)} + K_a C_{HP}\right), 1 + \frac{K_a}{4}\right\} E_y(\tau),$$

for all $\tau \in [s, T]$. Hence, since the energy is non-increasing,

$$\int_0^1 \left[-2y_t \frac{x}{a} y_x + \frac{K_a}{2} \frac{yy_t}{a}\right]_{t=s}^{t=T} dx \le 4 \max\left\{\frac{1}{\epsilon}\left(\frac{4}{a(1)} + K_a C_{HP}\right), 1 + \frac{K_a}{4}\right\} E_y(s). \quad (42)$$

Now, based on (34) and the fact that $K_a < 2$, we have

$$\gamma\left(\frac{K_a}{2} - 2\right) \int_s^T y_x^2(t, 1) dt + \left(\frac{K_a}{2} - 2\right) \int_s^T y_x(t, 1) y_{tx}(t, 1) dt$$
$$\le \left(\frac{K_a}{2} - 2\right) \frac{1}{2} \int_s^T (y_x(t, 1)^2)_t dt = \left(\frac{K_a}{2} - 2\right) \frac{1}{2} (y_x^2(T, 1) - y_x^2(s, 1)) \quad (43)$$
$$\le \left(2 - \frac{K_a}{2}\right) \frac{1}{2} y_x^2(s, 1) \le \left(2 - \frac{K_a}{2}\right) \frac{C_\gamma}{2} E_y(s).$$

Obviously,

$$\frac{K_a}{2} \int_s^T y(t, 1) y_t(t, 1) dt \le \frac{K_a}{4} \int_s^T y^2(t, 1) dt + \frac{K_a}{4} \int_s^T y_t^2(t, 1) dt, \quad (44)$$

$$-\beta \int_s^T 2y_x(t, 1) y(t, 1) dt \le \beta \int_s^T 2|y_x(t, 1) y(t, 1)| dt \le \beta \int_s^T y_x^2(t, 1) dt + \beta \int_s^T y^2(t, 1) dt \quad (45)$$

and

$$-\int_s^T 2y_x(t, 1) y_t(t, 1) dt \le \int_s^T 2|y_x(t, 1) y_t(t, 1)| dt \le \int_s^T y_x^2(t, 1) dt + \int_s^T y_t^2(t, 1) dt. \quad (46)$$

Furthermore, recalling that $\gamma y_x(t, 1) + y_{xx}(t, 1) + y_{tx}(t, 1) = 0$,

$$\int_s^T y_{xx}^2(t, 1) dt \le 2\gamma^2 \int_s^T y_x^2(t, 1) dt + 2 \int_s^T y_{tx}^2(t, 1) dt. \quad (47)$$

Hence, by (37), (41)–(47) and Theorem 1, we have

$$\frac{\varepsilon_0}{2}\int_{Q_s}\left(\frac{y_t^2}{a}+y_{xx}^2-\lambda\frac{y^2}{ad}\right)dx\,dt \le 4\max\left\{\frac{1}{\epsilon}\left(\frac{4}{a(1)}+K_aC_{HP}\right),1+\frac{K_a}{4}\right\}E_y(s)$$

$$+\left(2-\frac{K_a}{2}\right)\frac{C_\gamma}{2}E_y(s)+\left(\frac{K_a}{4}+1+\frac{1}{a(1)}\right)\int_s^T y_t^2(t,1)dt+2\int_s^T y_{tx}^2(t,1)dt$$

$$+\left(\frac{K_a}{4}+\beta+\frac{K_a\beta}{2}+\frac{\lambda}{a(1)d(1)}\right)\int_s^T y^2(t,1)dt+(\beta+1+2\gamma^2)\int_s^T y_x^2(t,1)dt$$

$$\le 4\max\left\{\frac{1}{\epsilon}\left(\frac{4}{a(1)}+K_aC_{HP}\right),1+\frac{K_a}{4}\right\}E_y(s)+\left(2-\frac{K_a}{2}\right)\frac{C_\gamma}{2}E_y(s)$$

$$+\max\left\{2,\frac{K_a}{4}+1+\frac{1}{a(1)}\right\}\int_s^T -\frac{d}{dt}E_y(t)dt$$

$$+\left(\frac{K_a}{4}+\beta+\frac{K_a\beta}{2}+\frac{\lambda}{a(1)d(1)}\right)\int_s^T y^2(t,1)dt+(\beta+1+2\gamma^2)\int_s^T y_x^2(t,1)dt$$

$$\le 4\max\left\{\frac{1}{\epsilon}\left(\frac{4}{a(1)}+K_aC_{HP}\right),1+\frac{K_a}{4}\right\}E_y(s)+\left(2-\frac{K_a}{2}\right)\frac{C_\gamma}{2}E_y(s)$$

$$+\max\left\{2,\frac{K_a}{4}+1+\frac{1}{a(1)}\right\}E_y(s)$$

$$+\left(\frac{K_a}{4}+\beta+\frac{K_a\beta}{2}+\frac{\lambda}{a(1)d(1)}\right)\int_s^T y^2(t,1)dt+(\beta+1+2\gamma^2)\int_s^T y_x^2(t,1)dt.$$

Hence,

$$\frac{\varepsilon_0}{2}\int_{Q_s}\left(\frac{y_t^2}{a}+y_{xx}^2-\lambda\frac{y^2}{ad}\right)dx\,dt \le \left(4\vartheta+\varrho+\left(2-\frac{K_a}{2}\right)\frac{C_\gamma}{2}\right)E_y(s)$$

$$+\left(\frac{K_a}{4}+\beta+\frac{K_a\beta}{2}+\frac{\lambda}{a(1)d(1)}\right)\int_s^T y^2(t,1)dt+(\beta+1+2\gamma^2)\int_s^T y_x^2(t,1)dt$$

and the thesis follows.

Case $\lambda < 0$. In this case, based on the definition of energy and (15), one proves

$$\int_{Q_s}\frac{y^2}{ad}dxdt \le \tilde{C}_{HP}\int_{Q_s} y_{xx}^2(t,x)dxdt \le 2\tilde{C}_{HP}\int_s^T E_y(t)dt;$$

hence,

$$-\lambda\int_{Q_s}\frac{y^2}{ad}dxdt \le -2\lambda\tilde{C}_{HP}\int_s^T E_y(t)dt. \tag{48}$$

Moreover, by (37) and (40), one has

$$\frac{\varepsilon_0}{2}\int_{Q_s}\left(\frac{y_t^2}{a}+y_{xx}^2-\lambda\frac{y^2}{ad}\right)dx\,dt \le \int_{Q_s}\frac{y_t^2}{a}\left(\frac{K_a}{2}+1-\frac{xa'}{a}\right)dx\,dt+\int_{Q_s} y_{xx}^2\left(3-\frac{K_a}{2}\right)dx\,dt$$

$$-\lambda\int_{Q_s}\left(1-\frac{xa'}{a}-\frac{xd'}{d}+\frac{K_a}{2}\right)\frac{y^2}{ad}dxdt \tag{49}$$

$$= (B.T.) - 2\lambda\int_{Q_s}\left(1-\frac{xa'}{a}-\frac{xd'}{d}+\frac{K_a}{2}\right)\frac{y^2}{ad}dxdt,$$

where (B.T.) is the boundary terms in (37). Now, by (48),

$$-2\lambda\int_{Q_s}\left(1-\frac{xa'}{a}-\frac{xd'}{d}+\frac{K_a}{2}\right)\frac{y^2}{ad}dxdt \le -4\lambda\tilde{C}_{HP}\left(1+\frac{3}{2}K_a+K_d+M\right)\int_s^T E_y(t)dt.$$

Proceeding as for the case $\lambda > 0$ and using the fact that $\frac{\lambda}{a(1)d(1)} < 0$, one can estimate the boundary terms in the following way:

$$(B.T.) \leq 4\max\left\{\frac{1}{\epsilon}\left(\frac{4}{a(1)} + K_a C_{HP}\right), 1 + \frac{K_a}{4}\right\} E_y(s)$$

$$+ \left\{\max\left\{2, \frac{K_a}{4} + 1 + \frac{1}{a(1)}\right\} + \left(2 - \frac{K_a}{2}\right)\frac{C_\gamma}{2}\right\} E_y(s)$$

$$+ \left(\frac{K_a}{4} + \beta + \frac{K_a \beta}{2}\right) \int_s^T y^2(t,1)dt + (\beta + 1 + 2\gamma^2) \int_s^T y_x^2(t,1)dt.$$

Hence,

$$\frac{\epsilon_0}{2} \int_{Q_s} \left(\frac{y_t^2}{a} + y_{xx}^2 - \lambda \frac{y^2}{ad}\right) dx\, dt \leq \left(4\vartheta + \varrho\left(2 - \frac{K_a}{2}\right)\frac{C_\gamma}{2}\right) E_y(s)$$

$$+ \left(\frac{K_a}{4} + \beta + \frac{K_a \beta}{2}\right) \int_s^T y^2(t,1)dt + (\beta + 1 + 2\gamma^2) \int_s^T y_x^2(t,1)dt$$

$$- 4\lambda \tilde{C}_{HP}\left(1 + \frac{3}{2}K_a + K_d\right) \int_s^T E_y(t)dt$$

and the thesis follows. □

In the next proposition, we will find an estimate from above for $\int_s^T y^2(t,1)dt + \int_s^T y_x^2(t,1)dt$. To this end, set

$$\tilde{C}_\beta := \begin{cases} \frac{1}{\beta}, & \beta \neq 0, \text{ for all considered } \lambda, \\ \frac{1}{C_\epsilon}, & \beta = 0, \text{ for all considered } \lambda, \end{cases}$$

$$\tilde{C}_\gamma := \begin{cases} \frac{1}{\gamma}, & \gamma \neq 0, \text{ for all considered } \lambda, \\ \frac{1}{C_\epsilon}, & \gamma = 0, \text{ for all considered } \lambda, \end{cases}$$

and

$$\nu := \frac{1}{\tilde{C}_\beta + \tilde{C}_\gamma}. \tag{50}$$

Proposition 7. *Assume Hypothesis 5 and fix $T > 0$. If y is a classical solution of (1), then for every $0 < s < T$ and for every $\delta \in (0, \nu)$, we have*

$$\int_s^T y^2(t,1)dt + \int_s^T y_x^2(t,1)dt \leq \frac{\delta}{C_\delta} \int_s^T E_y(t)dt$$

$$+ \frac{1}{C_\delta}\left[\frac{2}{C_\epsilon}(1 + 2C_{HP}(C_\beta + C_\gamma)) + \frac{1}{\delta}\left(\frac{4C_{HP}}{C_\epsilon} + \frac{1}{2}\right)\right] E_y(s),$$

where

$$C_\delta := 1 - \delta(\tilde{C}_\beta + \tilde{C}_\gamma).$$

Proof. Set $\rho = y(t,1)$, $\mu = y_x(t,1)$, where $t \in [s, T]$, and let $z = z(t, \cdot) \in H^2_{\frac{1}{a},0}(0,1)$ be the unique solution of

$$\int_0^1 z_{xx}\varphi'' dx - \lambda \int_0^1 \frac{z\varphi}{ad} dx + \beta z(t,1)\varphi(1) + \gamma z'(t,1)\varphi'(1) = \rho\varphi(1) + \mu\varphi'(1),$$

for all $\varphi \in H^2_{\frac{1}{a},0}(0,1)$. By Proposition 3, $z(t, \cdot) \in D(A_\lambda)$ for all t and solves

$$\begin{cases} A_\lambda z = 0, \\ \beta z(t,1) - z_{xxx}(t,1) = \rho, \\ \gamma z_x(t,1) + z_{xx}(t,1) = \mu. \end{cases} \tag{51}$$

By (21), we also have

$$\|z(t)\|^2_{L^2_{\frac{1}{a}}(0,1)} \leq \frac{8C_{HP}}{C_\epsilon}(y^2(t,1) + y_x^2(t,1)) \quad \text{and} \quad |||z(t)|||^2 \leq 2(y^2(t,1) + y_x^2(t,1)), \tag{52}$$

where C_ϵ is defined in (22). Moreover, if $\beta \neq 0$ and $\gamma \neq 0$, then by Proposition 2 if $\lambda > 0$, one proves

$$z^2(t,1) \leq \frac{1}{\beta}|||z|||^2 \leq \frac{2}{\beta}(y^2(t,1) + y_x^2(t,1))$$

and

$$z_x^2(t,1) \leq \frac{1}{\gamma}|||z|||^2 \leq \frac{2}{\gamma}(y^2(t,1) + y_x^2(t,1)).$$

On the other hand, if $\beta = 0$ and $\gamma = 0$, then by (24), (25) and (29), it results in $z^2(t,1), z_x^2(t,1) \leq \|z\|^2_{2,\circ} \leq \frac{1}{C_\epsilon}|||z|||^2 \leq \frac{1}{C_\epsilon}(|\rho| + |\mu|)^2 \leq \frac{2}{C_\epsilon}(y^2(t,1) + y_x^2(t,1))$. In every case, for all considered λ, we have

$$z^2(t,1) \leq 2\tilde{C}_\beta(y^2(t,1) + y_x^2(t,1)), \tag{53}$$

and

$$z_x^2(t,1) \leq 2\tilde{C}_\gamma(y^2(t,1) + y_x^2(t,1)). \tag{54}$$

Finally, observe that for all considered λ and all $t > 0$, we have

$$\frac{1}{2}\int_0^1 \left(\frac{1}{a}y_t^2(t,x) + y_{xx}^2(t,x)\right)dx \leq \frac{1}{C_\epsilon}E_y(t). \tag{55}$$

Indeed, consider, first of all, $\lambda < 0$, then

$$\frac{1}{2}\int_0^1 \left(\frac{1}{a}y_t^2(t,x) + y_{xx}^2(t,x)\right)dx \leq E_y(t).$$

If $\lambda \in \left(0, \frac{1}{\tilde{C}_{HP}}\right)$ and $\epsilon \in (0,1)$ is as in (18), we obtain (27), which implies that

$$2E_y(t) \geq \epsilon \int_0^1 y_{xx}^2(t,x)dx + \int_0^1 \frac{y_t^2(t,x)}{a(x)}dx + \beta y^2(t,1) + \gamma y_x^2(t,1)$$

$$\geq \epsilon\left(\int_0^1 y_{xx}^2(t,x)dx + \int_0^1 \frac{y_t^2(t,x)}{a(x)}dx\right) + \beta y^2(t,1) + \gamma y_x^2(t,1);$$

in particular,

$$\frac{1}{2}\int_0^1 \left(\frac{1}{a}y_t^2(t,x) + y_{xx}^2(t,x)\right)dx \leq \frac{1}{\epsilon}E_y(t),$$

for all $t \geq 0$.

Now, multiplying the equation in (1) by $\frac{z}{a}$ and integrating over Q_s, we have

$$0 = \int_{Q_s} y_{tt}\frac{z}{a}dx\,dt + \int_{Q_s} zy_{xxxx}dx\,dt - \lambda \int_{Q_s} \frac{y}{ad}zdxdt$$

$$= \int_0^1 \left[y_t\frac{z}{a}\right]_{t=s}^{t=T}dx - \int_{Q_s} \frac{y_t z_t}{a}dx\,dt + \int_s^T z(t,1)y_{xxx}(t,1)dt - \int_s^T z_x(t,1)y_{xx}(t,1)dt \tag{56}$$

$$+ \int_{Q_s} z_{xx}y_{xx}dx\,dt - \lambda \int_{Q_s} \frac{y}{ad}zdxdt.$$

Hence, (56) reads

$$\int_0^1 \left[y_t \frac{z}{a}\right]_{t=s}^{t=T} dx - \int_{Q_s} \frac{y_t z_t}{a} dx\,dt - \lambda \int_{Q_s} \frac{y}{ad} z\,dx\,dt$$
$$= -\int_s^T z(t,1)y_{xxx}(t,1)dt + \int_s^T z_x(t,1)y_{xx}(t,1)dt - \int_{Q_s} z_{xx}y_{xx}dx\,dt. \tag{57}$$

On the other hand, multiplying the equation in (51) by $\frac{y}{a}$ and integrating over Q_s, we have $\int_{Q_s} z_{xxxx} y\, dx\, dt = 0$. By (19), we obtain $\int_{Q_s} z_{xx} y_{xx} dx\, dt = -\int_s^T z_{xxx}(t,1)y(t,1)dt + \int_s^T y_x(t,1)z_{xx}(t,1)dt$. Substituting in (57), using the fact that $z_{xxx}(t,1) = \beta z(t,1) - \rho$, $z_{xx}(t,1) = -\gamma z_x(t,1) + \mu$, $\rho = y(t,1)$, $\mu = y_x(t,1)$ and proceeding as in [12], we have

$$\int_0^1 \left[y_t \frac{z}{a}\right]_{t=s}^{t=T} dx - \int_{Q_s} \frac{y_t z_t}{a} dx\,dt - \lambda \int_{Q_s} \frac{y}{ad} z\,dx\,dt$$
$$= -\int_s^T z(t,1)y_{xxx}(t,1)dt + \int_s^T z_x(t,1)y_{xx}(t,1)dt + \int_s^T y(t,1)[\beta z(t,1) - \rho]dt$$
$$- \int_s^T y_x(t,1)[-\gamma z_x(t,1) + \mu]dt$$
$$= \int_s^T z(t,1)[\beta y(t,1) - y_{xxx}(t,1)]dt$$
$$+ \int_s^T z_x(t,1)[y_{xx}(t,1) + \gamma y_x(t,1)]dt - \int_s^T y^2(t,1)dt - \int_s^T y_x^2(t,1)dt.$$

Then,

$$\int_s^T y^2(t,1)dt + \int_s^T y_x^2(t,1)dt = -\int_s^T (y_t z)(t,1)dt - \int_s^T (z_x y_{tx})(t,1)dt$$
$$- \int_0^1 \left[y_t \frac{z}{a}\right]_{t=s}^{t=T} dx + \int_{Q_s} \frac{y_t z_t}{a} dx\,dt + \lambda \int_{Q_s} \frac{y}{ad} z\,dx\,dt. \tag{58}$$

Thus, in order to estimate $\int_s^T y^2(t,1)dt + \int_s^T y_x^2(t,1)dt$, we have to consider the four terms in the previous equality.

So, by (21), (34), and Theorem 1, we have, for all $\tau \in [s,T]$,

$$\int_0^1 \left|\frac{y_t z}{a}(\tau,x)\right|dx \leq \frac{1}{2}\int_0^1 \frac{y_t^2(\tau,x)}{a(x)}dx + \frac{1}{2}\int_0^1 \frac{z^2(\tau,x)}{a(x)}dx$$
$$\leq \frac{1}{2}\int_0^1 \frac{y_t^2(\tau,x)}{a(x)}dx + \frac{2C_{HP}}{C_\epsilon}\left(y^2(\tau,1) + y_x^2(\tau,1)\right)$$
$$\leq \frac{1}{C_\epsilon} E_y(\tau) + \frac{2C_{HP}}{C_\epsilon}(C_\beta + C_\gamma)E_y(\tau)$$
$$\leq (1 + 2C_{HP}(C_\beta + C_\gamma))\frac{1}{C_\epsilon}E_y(s).$$

By Theorem 1, we have

$$\left|\int_0^1 \left[\frac{y_t z}{a}\right]_{t=s}^{t=T} dx\right| \leq 2(1 + 2C_{HP}(C_\beta + C_\gamma))\frac{1}{C_\epsilon}E_y(s). \tag{59}$$

Moreover, for any $\delta > 0$, we have

$$\int_s^T |(y_t z)(t,1)|dt \leq \frac{1}{2\delta}\int_s^T y_t^2(t,1)dt + \frac{\delta}{2}\int_s^T z^2(t,1)dt$$
$$\leq \frac{1}{2\delta}\int_s^T y_t^2(t,1)dt + \delta \tilde{C}_\beta \int_s^T (y^2 + y_x^2)(t,1)dt, \tag{60}$$

by (53). In a similar way, using (54), it is possible to find the next estimate

$$\int_s^T |(z_x y_{tx})(t,1)| dt \leq \frac{1}{2\delta} \int_s^T y_{tx}^2(t,1) dt + \delta \tilde{C}_\gamma \int_s^T (y^2 + y_x^2)(t,1) dt. \tag{61}$$

Therefore, by summing (60) and (61) and applying Theorem 1, we obtain

$$\int_s^T |(y_t z)(t,1)| dt + \int_s^T |(z_x y_{tx})(t,1)| dt$$

$$\leq \frac{1}{2\delta} \int_s^T -\frac{d}{dt} E_y(t) dt + \delta \left(\tilde{C}_\beta + \tilde{C}_\gamma\right) \int_s^T (y^2 + y_x^2)(t,1) dt \tag{62}$$

$$\leq \frac{E_y(s)}{2\delta} + \delta \left(\tilde{C}_\beta + \tilde{C}_\gamma\right) \int_s^T (y^2 + y_x^2)(t,1) dt.$$

Finally, we estimate the integral $\int_{Q_s} \left|\frac{y_t z_t}{a}\right| dx\, dt$. To this end, consider again the problem (23) and differentiate with respect to t. Thus,

$$\begin{cases} a(z_t)_{xxxx} - \lambda \frac{z_t}{d} = 0, \\ \beta z_t(t,1) - (z_t)_{xxx}(t,1) = y_t(t,1), \\ \gamma(z_t)_x(t,1) + (z_t)_{xx}(t,1) = (y_x)_t(t,1). \end{cases}$$

Clearly, z_t satisfies (52), in particular

$$\|z_t(t)\|_{L^2_{\frac{1}{a}}(0,1)}^2 \leq \frac{8 C_{HP}}{C_\epsilon}(y_t^2(t,1) + y_{tx}^2(t,1))$$

and

$$|||z_t(t)|||^2 \leq 2(y_t(^2t,1)| + y_{tx}^2(t,1)).$$

Thus, by (55) and the previous estiamte, for $\delta > 0$, we find

$$\int_{Q_s} \left|\frac{y_t z_t}{a}\right| dx\, dt \leq \frac{\delta}{2} \int_{Q_s} \frac{y_t^2}{a} dx\, dt + \frac{1}{2\delta} \int_{Q_s} \frac{z_t^2}{a} dx\, dt$$

$$\leq \delta \int_s^T E_y(t) dt + \frac{4 C_{HP}}{\delta C_\epsilon} \int_s^T (y_t^2(t,1) + y_{tx}^2(t,1)) dt$$

$$= \delta \int_s^T E_y(t) dt + \frac{4 C_{HP}}{\delta C_\epsilon} \int_s^T -\frac{d}{dt} E_y(t) dt \tag{63}$$

$$\leq \delta \int_s^T E_y(t) dt + \frac{4 C_{HP}}{\delta C_\epsilon} E_y(s).$$

Coming back to (58) and using (59), (62), and (63), we find

$$\int_s^T (y^2 + y_x^2)(t,1) dt \leq 2 \left(\frac{1}{C_\epsilon} + \frac{2 C_{HP}}{C_\epsilon}(C_\beta + C_\gamma)\right) E_y(s) + \frac{E_y(s)}{2\delta}$$

$$+ \delta \left(\tilde{C}_\beta + \tilde{C}_\gamma\right) \int_s^T (y^2 + y_x^2)(t,1) dt$$

$$+ \delta \int_s^T E_y(t) dt + \frac{4 C_{HP}}{\delta C_\epsilon} E_y(s).$$

Hence, for every $\delta \in (0, \nu)$,

$$C_\delta \int_s^T (y^2(t,1) + y_x^2(t,1)) dt \leq 2 \left(\frac{1}{C_\epsilon} + \frac{2 \tilde{C}_{HP}}{C_\epsilon}(C_\beta + C_\gamma)\right) E_y(s)$$

$$+ \delta \int_s^T E_y(t) dt + \frac{1}{\delta}\left(\frac{4 C_{HP}}{C_\epsilon} + \frac{1}{2}\right) E_y(s),$$

and the thesis follows. □

As a consequence of Propositions 6 and 7, we can formulate the main result of the paper, whose proof is based on ([18], Theorem 8.1).
Set
$$C_1 := \frac{1}{C_\delta}\left[\frac{2}{C_\epsilon}(1+2C_{HP}(C_\beta+C_\gamma)) + \frac{1}{\delta}\left(\frac{4C_{HP}}{C_\epsilon}+\frac{1}{2}\right)\right],$$

$$C_2 := \left(4\vartheta + \varrho + \frac{C_\gamma}{2}\left(2 - \frac{K_a}{2}\right)\right),$$

$$C_3 := \begin{cases} \left(\frac{K_a\beta}{2} + \frac{K_a}{4} + \beta + \varepsilon_0\frac{\beta}{2} + \frac{\lambda}{a(1)d(1)}\right), & \lambda > 0, \\ \left(\frac{K_a}{4} + \beta + \frac{K_a\beta}{2} + \varepsilon_0\frac{\beta}{2}\right), & \lambda < 0, \end{cases}$$

and
$$C_4 := \left(\beta + 1 + 2\gamma^2 + \varepsilon_0\frac{\gamma}{2}\right).$$

Theorem 2. *Assume Hypothesis 5, fix $T > 0$ and if $\lambda < 0$, then $\lambda \in \left(\frac{-\varepsilon_0}{4\tilde{C}_{HP}(1+\frac{3}{2}K_a+K_d)}, 0\right)$. Let y be a mild solution for (1). Then, for all $t > 0$ and for all $\delta \in (0, \min\{\nu, \mu\})$*

$$E_y(t) \leq E_y(0)e^{1-\frac{t}{M}}, \tag{64}$$

where
$$\mu := \begin{cases} \frac{\varepsilon_0 C_\delta}{\max\{C_3,C_4\}}, & \lambda > 0, \\ \frac{\varepsilon_0+4\lambda\tilde{C}_{HP}(1+\frac{3}{2}K_a+K_d)}{\max\{C_3,C_4\}+(\varepsilon_0+4\lambda\tilde{C}_{HP}(1+\frac{3}{2}K_a+K_d))(\tilde{C}_\beta+\tilde{C}_\gamma)}, & \lambda < 0 \end{cases}$$

and
$$M := \begin{cases} \frac{C_\delta(C_2+\max\{C_3,C_4\}C_1)}{\varepsilon_0 C_\delta - \delta\max\{C_3,C_4\}}, & \lambda > 0, \\ \frac{C_\delta(C_2+\max\{C_3,C_4\}C_1)}{C_\delta(\varepsilon_0+4\lambda C_{HP}(1+\frac{3}{2}K_a+K_d)) - \delta\max\{C_3,C_4\}}, & \lambda < 0. \end{cases}$$

Here, ν is defined as in (50).

Proof. As a first step, consider y a classical solution of (1) and $\lambda > 0$. Take $\delta \in \left(0, \min\left\{\nu, \frac{\varepsilon_0 C_\delta}{\max\{C_3,C_4\}}\right\}\right)$. Then, based on the definition of E_y and Propositions 6 and 7, we have

$$\varepsilon_0 \int_s^T E_y(t)dt = \frac{\varepsilon_0}{2}\int_{Q_s}\left(\frac{y_t^2(t,x)}{a(x)} + y_{xx}^2(t,x) - \frac{\lambda}{ad}y^2(t,x)\right)dxdt$$
$$+ \varepsilon_0\frac{\beta}{2}\int_s^T y^2(t,1)dt + \varepsilon_0\frac{\gamma}{2}\int_s^T y_x^2(t,1)dt$$
$$\leq C_2 E_y(s) + C_3\int_s^T y^2(t,1)dt + C_4\int_s^T y_x^2(t,1)dt$$
$$\leq C_2 E_y(s) + \max\{C_3,C_4\}\left(\int_s^T y^2(t,1) + y_x^2(t,1)\right)dt$$
$$\leq C_2 E_y(s) + \max\{C_3,C_4\}\frac{\delta}{C_\delta}\int_s^T E_y(t)dt + \max\{C_3,C_4\}C_1 E_y(s).$$

This implies $\left[\varepsilon_0 - \max\{C_3, C_4\}\frac{\delta}{C_\delta}\right]\int_s^T E_y(t)dt \leq (C_2 + \max\{C_3, C_4\}C_1)E_y(s)$. Hence, we can apply ([18], Theorem 8.1) with $M := \frac{C_\delta(C_2+\max\{C_3,C_4\}C_1)}{\varepsilon_0 C_\delta - \delta \max\{C_3,C_4\}}$ and (64) holds.

Now, consider $\lambda < 0$. By Propositions 6 and 7, we have

$$\varepsilon_0 \int_s^T E_y(t)dt = \frac{\varepsilon_0}{2}\int_{Q_s}\left(\frac{y_t^2(t,x)}{a(x)} + y_{xx}^2(t,x) - \frac{\lambda}{ad}y^2(t,x)\right)dxdt$$

$$+ \varepsilon_0\frac{\beta}{2}\int_s^T y^2(t,1)dt + \varepsilon_0\frac{\gamma}{2}\int_s^T y_x^2(t,1)dt$$

$$\leq C_2 E_y(s) + \max\{C_3, C_4\}\left(\int_s^T y^2(t,1)dt + \int_s^T y_x^2(t,1)dt\right)$$

$$- 4\lambda\tilde{C}_{HP}\left(1 + \frac{3}{2}K_a + K_d\right)\int_s^T E_y(t)dt$$

$$\leq (C_2 + \max\{C_3, C_4\}C_1)E_y(s) + \max\{C_3, C_4\}\frac{\delta}{C_\delta}\int_s^T E_y(t)dt$$

$$- 4\lambda\tilde{C}_{HP}\left(1 + \frac{3}{2}K_a + K_d\right)\int_s^T E_y(t)dt.$$

Hence,

$$\left(\varepsilon_0 + 4\lambda\tilde{C}_{HP}\left(1 + \frac{3}{2}K_a + K_d\right) - \max\{C_3, C_4\}\frac{\delta}{C_\delta}\right)\int_s^T E_y(t)dt$$
$$\leq (C_2 + \max\{C_3, C_4\}C_1)E_y(s).$$

Recalling that $C_\delta := 1 - \delta(\tilde{C}_\beta + \tilde{C}_\gamma)$, where $\delta < \mu$, one proves that

$$\varepsilon_0 + 4\lambda\tilde{C}_{HP}\left(1 + \frac{3}{2}K_a + K_d\right) - \max\{C_3, C_4\}\frac{\delta}{C_\delta} > 0.$$

Hence, again by ([18], Theorem 8.1) with $M := \frac{C_\delta(C_2+\max\{C_3,C_4\}C_1)}{C_\delta(\varepsilon_0+4\lambda\tilde{C}_{HP}(1+\frac{3}{2}K_a+K_d))-\delta\max\{C_3,C_4\}}$, (64) holds.

If y is the mild solution for the problem, we can proceed as in [22], obtaining the thesis. □

4. Conclusions and a Open Problems

In this paper, we study the exponential stability of the energy related to (1). In particular, in Theorem 2, we show that

If λ is small and a, d are not too degenerate, then
the energy of the solution to (1) converges exponentially to 0 as time diverges.

This result leads to some open problems. The first one is to prove the stability if $K_a + 2K_d \geq 2$. As we have seen, the condition $K_a + 2K_d < 2$ is crucial in Proposition 6 and the condition $K_a + 2K_d \leq 2$ is important for finding that the two domains $D(A)$ and $D(A_\lambda)$ coincide. On the other hand, $K_a + K_d \leq 2$ is crucial to obtain the estimate given in Proposition 1.

Another important open problem is to prove the stability of (1), when $\lambda \leq \frac{-\varepsilon_0}{4\tilde{C}_{HP}(1+\frac{3}{2}K_a+K_d)}$.

Author Contributions: Investigation, validation: M.A., G.F. and A.S.; conceptualization, methodology, formal analysis, G.F. All authors have read and agreed to the published version of the manuscript.

Funding: This research received no external funding.

Data Availability Statement: The data presented in this study are available on request from the corresponding author.

Acknowledgments: G. Fragnelli is a member of *Gruppo Nazionale per l'Analisi Matematica, la Probabilità e le loro Applicazioni (GNAMPA)* of the Istituto Nazionale di Alta Matematica (INdAM), *UMI "Modellistica Socio-Epidemiologica (MSE)"*, and *UMI "CliMath"*. She is partially supported by INdAM GNAMPA Project *Mathematical Methods for Climate Impacts: Control, Game Theory, and Inverse Problems for EBCM* (CUP E5324001950001) and by the FFABR Fondo per il finanziamento delle attività base di ricerca 2017.

Conflicts of Interest: The authors have no competing interests to declare that are relevant to the content of this article.

References

1. Behn, C.; Steigenberger, J.; Will, C. Effects of Boundary Damping on Natural Frequencies in Bending Vibrations of Intelligent Vibrissa Tactile Systems. *Int. J. Adv. Intell. Syst.* **2015**, *8*, 245–254.
2. Biselli, A.; Coleman, M.P. The Exact Frequency Equations for the Euler-Bernoulli Beam Subject to Boundary Damping. *Int. J. Acoust. Vib.* **2020**, *25*, 183–189. [CrossRef]
3. Chen, G.; Krantz, S.G.; Ma, D.W.; Wayne, C.E.; West, H.H. *The Euler-Bernoulli Beam Equation with Boundary Energy Dissipation*; Operator Methods for Optimal Control Problems (New Orleans, LA, 1986), Lecture Notes in Pure and Applied Mathematics; Dekker: New York, NY, USA, 1987; Volume 108, pp. 67–96.
4. Chen, G.; Delfour, M.C.; Krall, A.M.; Payre, G. Modeling, stabilization and control of serially connected beams. *SIAM J. Control Optim.* **1987**, *25*, 526–546. [CrossRef]
5. Chen, G.; Zhou, J. The wave propagation method for the analysis of boundary stabilization in vibrating structures. *SIAM J. Appl. Math.* **1990**, *50*, 1254–1283. [CrossRef]
6. Coleman, M.P.; McSweeney, L.A. The Exact Frequency Equations for the Rayleigh and Shear Beams with Boundary Damping. *Int. J. Acoust. Vib.* **2020**, *25*, 3–8. [CrossRef]
7. Sandilo, S.H.; Horssen, W.T.V. On Boundary Damping for an Axially Moving Tensioned Beam. *J. Vib. Acoust.* **2012**, *134*, 8. [CrossRef]
8. Cavalcanti, M.M.; Cavalcanti, V.N.D.; Silva, M.A.J.; Narciso, V. Stability for extensible beams with a single degenerate nonlocal damping of Balakrishnan-Taylor type. *J. Differ. Equ.* **2021**, *290*, 197–222. [CrossRef]
9. Cong, Z.; Chunyou, S. Stability for a Class of Extensible Beams with Degenerate Nonlocal Damping. *J. Geom. Anal.* **2023**, *33*, 295. [CrossRef]
10. Narciso, V.; Ekinci, D.; Piskin, E. On a beam model with degenerate nonlocal nonlinear damping. *Evol. Equ. Control Theory* **2023**, *12*, 732–751. [CrossRef]
11. Camasta, A.; Fragnelli, G. Fourth-order differential operators with interior degeneracy and generalized Wentzell boundary conditions. *Electron. J. Differ. Equ.* **2022**, *2022*, 87. [CrossRef]
12. Camasta, A.; Fragnelli, G. A stability result for a degenerate beam equation. *SIAM J. Control Optim.* **2024**, *62*, 630–649. [CrossRef]
13. Alabau-Boussouira, F.; Cannarsa, P.; Leugering, G. Control and stabilization of degenerate wave equations. *SIAM J. Control Optim.* **2017**, *55*, 2052–2087. [CrossRef]
14. Fragnelli, G.; Mugnai, D. Carleman estimates for singular parabolic equations with interior degeneracy and non smooth coefficients. *Adv. Nonlinear Anal.* **2017**, *6*, 61–84. [CrossRef]
15. Dias, N.; Jorge, C.; Prata, J. Vibration modes of the Euler–Bernoulli beam equation with singularities. *J. Differ. Equ.* **2024**, *381*, 185–208. [CrossRef]
16. Akil, M.; Fragnelli, G.; Sbai, A. Degenerate/Singular Beam-Type Equations: A Controllability Result. *submitted for publication*. Available online: https://hal.science/hal-04901715 (accessed on 18 January 2025).
17. Fragnelli, G.; Mugnai, D.; Sbai, A. Stabilization for degenerate equations with drift and small singular term. *Math. Meth. Appl. Sci.* **2025**, *48*, 5086–5109. [CrossRef]
18. Komornik, V. *Exact Controllability and Stabilization: The Multiplier Method*, RAM: Research in Applied Mathematics Volume 36; Masson: Paris, France; John Wiley: Chichester, UK, 1994.
19. Cannarsa, P.; Fragnelli, G.; Rocchetti, D. Controllability results for a class of one-dimensional degenerate parabolic problems in nondivergence form. *J. Evol. Equ.* **2008**, *8*, 583–616. [CrossRef]
20. Fragnelli, G.; Mugnai, F. *Control of Degenerate and Singular Parabolic Equations. Carleman Estimates and Observability*; SpringerBriefs in Mathematics; Springer International Publishing: Cham, Switzerland, 2021.

21. Camasta, A.; Fragnelli, G. Boundary controllability for a degenerate beam equation. *Math. Meth. Appl. Sci.* **2024**, *47*, 907–92 [CrossRef]
22. Fragnelli, G.; Mugnai, D. Linear Stabilization for a Degenerate Wave Equation in Non Divergence Form with Drift. Bulletin Mathematical Sciences. Available online: https://www.worldscientific.com/doi/10.1142/S1664360725500018 (accessed on February 2025).
23. Jost, J.; Li-Jost, X. *Calculus of Variations*; Cambridge University: Cambridge, UK, 1998.

Disclaimer/Publisher's Note: The statements, opinions and data contained in all publications are solely those of the individual author(s) and contributor(s) and not of MDPI and/or the editor(s). MDPI and/or the editor(s) disclaim responsibility for any injury to people or property resulting from any ideas, methods, instructions or products referred to in the content.

MDPI AG
Grosspeteranlage 5
4052 Basel
Switzerland
Tel.: +41 61 683 77 34

Axioms Editorial Office
E-mail: axioms@mdpi.com
www.mdpi.com/journal/axioms

Disclaimer/Publisher's Note: The title and front matter of this reprint are at the discretion of the Guest Editors. The publisher is not responsible for their content or any associated concerns. The statements, opinions and data contained in all individual articles are solely those of the individual Editors and contributors and not of MDPI. MDPI disclaims responsibility for any injury to people or property resulting from any ideas, methods, instructions or products referred to in the content.

www.ingramcontent.com/pod-product-compliance
Lightning Source LLC
LaVergne TN
LVHW072347090526
838202LV00019B/2495